Jiyoon Kim · Kun-Lin Tsai · Francesco Colace ·
Ilsun You
Editors

International Symposium on E-Business Information Systems Evolution

First IFIP WG 8.4 International Symposium, EBISION 2025
Sapporo, Japan, December 16–18, 2025
Proceedings

Springer

Editors
Jiyoon Kim
Gyeongsang National University
Jinju-si, Korea (Republic of)

Kun-Lin Tsai
Tunghai University
Taichung City, Taiwan

Francesco Colace
Università degli Studi di Salerno
Fisciano, Italy

Ilsun You
Kookmin University
Seoul, Korea (Republic of)

ISSN 1868-4238 ISSN 1868-422X (electronic)
IFIP Advances in Information and Communication Technology
ISBN 978-3-032-26615-6 ISBN 978-3-032-26616-3 (eBook)
https://doi.org/10.1007/978-3-032-26616-3

This Springer imprint is published by the registered company Springer Nature Switzerland AG
The registered company address is: Gewerbestrasse 11, 6330 Cham, Switzerland

Preface

The 2025 IFIP WG 8.4 International Symposium on E-Business Information Systems Evolution (EBISION 2025) was held in Sapporo, Japan, from December 16 to 18, 2025. As the flagship event of IFIP Working Group 8.4, EBISION 2025 provided an international forum for researchers and practitioners to discuss the evolution of E-Business Information Systems (EBIS) in the context of ongoing digital transformation.

We are living in an era of profound digital transformation, in which revolutionary technological advances are reshaping every dimension of E-Business. Artificial intelligence, quantum computing, 6G mobile communications, cloud ecosystems, robotics, blockchain technologies, and Web 3.0 are no longer distant visions but emerging realities that redefine how businesses and societies operate. These developments call for a paradigm shift in EBIS, one that must be approached from truly multidisciplinary perspectives encompassing not only technological and organizational dimensions but also societal, cultural, consumer-oriented, and global infrastructural aspects.

EBISION 2025 aimed to explore this paradigm shift by encouraging contributions that bridge theory and practice, highlight emerging technologies, and demonstrate how innovative EBIS solutions can be translated into sustainable impact across industries, economies, and societies. The symposium welcomed high-quality research papers addressing both theoretical foundations and practical applications related to digital transformation, E-Business ecosystems, and the future of information systems.

The conference received a total of 60 paper submissions, of which 26 papers were accepted for presentation at the symposium after a rigorous peer review process. The review process followed a single-blind model, and each submission received three independent reviews from members of the Program Committee or qualified external reviewers. The reviews focused on originality, technical quality, relevance, and clarity.

Following the conference, authors of selected papers were invited to submit substantially revised and extended versions for inclusion in this post-proceedings volume. These submissions underwent an additional round of review and revision to ensure that they met the high quality standards of the IFIP Advances in Information and Communication Technology (AICT) series. As a result of this process, 20 revised papers were accepted for publication in this volume.

Special care was taken to ensure fairness and transparency in the review process. For papers co-authored by members of the organizing or program committees, strict conflict-of-interest policies were enforced. Authors and reviewers from the same institution, as well as committee members with potential conflicts of interest, were excluded from the evaluation of the corresponding submissions. All such papers were handled independently to ensure objective assessment.

The editors would like to express their sincere gratitude to all authors for their high-quality submissions, to the Program Committee members and external reviewers for their thorough and constructive reviews, and to the organizing committee for their dedication and support in making EBISION 2025 a successful and inspiring event. We also thank IFIP Working Group 8.4 for its continued support and guidance.

We hope that this post-proceedings volume will serve as a valuable reference for researchers and practitioners and will stimulate further research and collaboration in the evolving field of E-Business Information Systems.

April 2026

Jiyoon Kim
Kun-Lin Tsai
Francesco Colace
Ilsun You

Organization

General Chair

Ilsun You	Kookmin University, South Korea

Program Committee Chairs

Francesco Colace	University of Salerno, Italy
Kun-Lin Tsai	Tunghai University, Taiwan

Organizing Committee Chairs

Gaurav Choudhary	Technical University of Denmark, Denmark
Jiyoon Kim	Gyeongsang National University, South Korea

Distinguished Advisors

Andreas Holzinger	BOKU University Vienna, Austria
Edgar Weippl	University of Vienna, Austria

Publicity Chair

Domenico Santaniello	University of Salerno, Italy

Publication Chair

Adi Juliawan Pawana	Udayana University, Indonesia

Web Chairs

Adi Panca Iskandar	Kookmin University, South Korea
Jhury Kevin Lastre	Kookmin University, South Korea
Vincent Abella	Kookmin University, South Korea

Program Committee

Md Amiruzzaman	West Chester University, USA
Mario Casillo	University of Salerno, Italy
Yen-Lin Chen	National Taipei University of Technology, Taiwan
Jaewon Choi	Soonchunhyang University, South Korea
Sang Min Choi	Gyeongsang National University, South Korea
John Chui	Hong Kong Metropolitan University, China
Jialiang Gu	Education University of Hong Kong, China
Younhee Han	Korea University of Technology and Education, South Korea
Narit Hnoohom	Mahidol University, Thailand
Min Hong	Soonchunhyang University, South Korea
Kevin Hung	Hong Kong Metropolitan University, China
Anuchit Jitpattanakul	King Mongkut's University of Technology North Bangkok, Thailand
Jacky Wai Keung	City University of Hong Kong, China
Joongheon Kim	Korea University, South Korea
Jean Lai	Hong Kong Baptist University, China
Jeng-Wei Lin	National Chi Nan University, Taiwan
Linawati	Udayana University, Indonesia
Angelo Lorusso	University of Salerno, Italy
Massimo Mecella	Sapienza University of Rome, Italy
Lely Meilina	Udayana University, Indonesia
Sakon Mekruksavanich	University of Phayao, Thailand
Mert Nakip	IITIS, Polish Academy of Sciences, Poland
Fajar Purnama	Udayana University, Indonesia
Zhuzhong Qian	Nanjing University, China
DaeMin Shin	Financial Security Institute, South Korea
Gede Sukadarmika	Udayana University, Indonesia
Malek Ben Salem	AILeap, USA
Feilong Tang	Shanghai Jiao Tong University, China
Alfredo Troiano	NetCom Group S.p.A., Italy
Agus Eka Udayana	Institut Bisnis dan Teknologi Indonesia

Zhen-Yu Wu	National Kaohsiung University of Science and Technology, Taiwan
Chao-Tung Yang	Tunghai University, Taiwan
Farah Yan	Hong Kong Metropolitan University, China
William Yeoh	Hong Kong Metropolitan University, China
Meng Yu	Governors State University, USA
Xingjun Zhang	Xi'an Jiaotong University, China

Contents

Author Index

Artificial Intelligence

Optimizing YOLO for Accurate Car Parts Segmentation in Automotive Industry Applications

FX Hendra Prasetya[1,2], Kung-Ming Lan[2], Kun-Lin Tsai[3], and Chao-Tung Yang[4,5,6(✉)]

[1] Soegijapranata Catholic University, Semarang, Indonesia
hendra@unika.ac.id
[2] Department of Industrial Engineering and Enterprise Information, Tunghai University, Taichung City 407224, Taiwan, ROC
kmlan@thu.edu.tw
[3] Department of Electrical Engineering, Thunghai University, Taichung City, Taiwan, ROC
kunlin.tsai@gmail.com
[4] Department of Computer Science, Tunghai University, Taichung City 407224, Taiwan, ROC
ctyang@thu.edu.tw
[5] Research Center for Smart Sustainable Circular Economy, Tunghai University, Taichung City 407224, Taiwan, ROC
[6] Department of Medical Research, Kuang Tien General Hospital, Taichung 433004, Taiwan, ROC

Abstract. Accurate detection and segmentation of automotive components are crucial for automated inspection and quality control in modern manufacturing industries. This study evaluates the performance of YOLOv11-Seg in segmentation of vehicle components through qualitative and quantitative analyses. A qualitative case study using real car images shows that YOLOv11-Seg is capable of detecting major components such as rear bumpers, rear windows, and tailgates with high confidence, while small reflective components such as mirrors and taillights remain challenging due to light reflection and occlusion. To validate these results, a quantitative evaluation using a per-component annotation dataset is conducted. The results show that YOLOv11-Seg achieves mAP values of 0.88–0.92 on large components and 0.70–0.77 on small components. Comparison with YOLOv8, YOLOv5, and Mask R-CNN confirms that YOLOv11-Seg is the most optimal model, with the highest accuracy (IoU = 0.863, Precision = 92.4%, Recall = 88.7%, F1-score = 90.5%) and an inference speed of 32 FPS. These findings confirm the potential of YOLOv11-Seg for use in real-time automotive inspection and broader industrial applications.

Published by Springer Nature Switzerland AG 2027
J. Kim et al. (Eds.): EBISION 2025, IFIP AICT 786, pp. 3–16, 2027.
https://doi.org/10.1007/978-3-032-26616-3_1

1 Introduction

In the age of digital transformation, E-corporate Information Systems are critical to integrating corporate processes, supply chains, and intelligent technology across modern sectors. The automobile industry, in particular, is becoming more reliant on data-driven technologies and artificial intelligence to improve operational efficiency, product quality, and real-time decision making. One major technical component supporting this shift is computer vision, which enables automated inspection, object detection, and intelligent monitoring within factory environments. Companies that integrate AI-based visual inspection systems into their business information systems can improve production transparency, minimize human error, and support smart manufacturing strategies linked with Industry 4.0 ambitions. In this context, reliable recognition and segmentation of automotive components using deep learning models such as YOLO become critical for enabling automated quality control and supporting intelligent manufacturing systems connected to enterprise information platforms. The automotive business is changing a lot because of new computer vision and deep learning technologies [1–3]. Smart systems that can accomplish jobs with speed and accuracy that no one else can are needed for modern manufacturing. Finding and separating parts precisely is particularly crucial for quality control, tracking components, finding defects, and automating the assembly process in real life [4]. These technologies make operations run more smoothly, automate processes that people undertake by hand, and help keep track of inventory more accurately. This helps producers meet greater standards for both quality and cost-effectiveness.

In the car industry, it's very hard to get high-performance segmentation because the environment is so intricate. In the actual world, the light can change, parts can overlap and block each other, metal parts can reflect light, and different car models can look different [5,6]. These issues require robust and adaptable segmentation strategies that perform effectively in dynamic contexts. Not being able to tell the difference between automotive parts might slow down production and make customers unhappy [7].

Semantic segmentation, which gives each pixel in an image a label, is very crucial for helping computers understand how the different elements of a picture fit together in space [8]. This capability is important for automating tasks like robotic assembly, identifying flaws, real-time quality control, and maintenance that is based on forecasts. But for a lot of older approaches, it's hard to establish the proper balance between speed, accuracy, and adaptability. This is especially true when processing needs to happen in real time.

Faster R-CNN and SSD are two models for object detection that have shown a lot of promise in finding things in pictures [9,10]. These models are great at finding bounding boxes, but they have trouble with jobs that need pixel-level segmentation. On the other hand, Mask R-CNN offers detailed segmentation, but its high processing requirements make it unsuitable for real-time industrial operations [11]. Hybrid approaches that include attention mechanisms, such as

DETR and Swin Transformers, help with understanding context, although they have problems with latency in industrial contexts [12,13].

The YOLO (You Only Look Once) series has become very popular since it works quickly and well for detecting objects [14]. YOLO, on the other hand, looks at the whole image in one pass, which makes it great for real-time use. But older YOLO models, even though they are good at finding objects, don't have the pixel-level segmentation needed for complicated automobile parts. YOLOv11 builds on the existing YOLO framework by fixing its problems with architectural changes, such as adding transformer-based attention levels and spatial pyramid pooling [15]. The improvements let YOLOv11 provide precise segmentation while still being fast. Also, better feature fusion approaches lead to more accurate segmentation findings, which helps the model do a great job of recognizing automotive parts that overlap or are complicated, including engines, wheels, mirrors, and headlights.

This study investigates the application of YOLOv11 for the segmentation of automobile components in complex real-world scenarios. To train and test YOLOv11, a diverse set of tagged car photographs with notes was generated. We used numbers like Intersection over Union (IoU), precision, recall, and F1-score to see how well the model could segment. Qualitative visual comparisons further validate YOLOv11's capacity to do real-time data analysis while maintaining superior segmentation quality.

YOLOv11 is a good choice for making computer vision applications in the car sector better because it includes powerful segmentation features and a flexible architecture. Adding technology to industrial workflows might make things go more smoothly, reduce the number of mistakes humans make, and make intelligent auto part recognition systems perform better.

1.1 Context of Problems in the Automotive World

In the modern automotive industry (car factories, authorized repair shops, spare parts logistics):

- Thousands of vehicle components (engine parts, body panels, wheels, mirrors, lights) must be automatically identified for:
  - robotic assembly (robotic arms on the production line)
  - quality control
  - parts inventory and management
- Current systems still often use bounding box-based detection (such as YOLOv5/v8), which only provides rough positions, not detailed pixel shapes.
- As a result, robots struggle to recognize component shapes/edges with high precision, requiring manual visual assistance from human operators—costly, slow, and error-prone.

1.2 Contribution of This Research

This research makes three main contributions that are directly relevant to the automotive industry:

Improving Visual Precision for Industrial Robots

- This research optimized YOLOv11 to perform pixel segmentation (masks), not just box detection.
- This provides the precise shape of components (engines, wheels, body panels) so industrial robots can handle, install, or inspect components more precisely.

Immediate Impact: reduced assembly errors, accelerated automated assembly, and lower operational costs.

Real-Time Detection in Complex Environments

- This research model was tested under realistic conditions: varying lighting, shadows, occlusion, and metal reflections.
- The results remained real-time (32 FPS) and accurate (IoU = 0.863, Precision = 92.4

Immediate impact: enabling integration into fast-running production camera systems (assembly lines), without compromising production speed.

Reproducible Dataset and Pipeline

- This research creates a dedicated dataset of pixel-annotated automotive components and an open-source training pipeline.
- This could serve as an initial benchmark for other researchers and automotive companies to develop their own vision models.

Immediate Impact: Accelerating innovation and research in automotive visual automation, especially for industries just entering Industry 4.0.

This work contributes to the automotive industry by enabling accurate pixel-level segmentation of vehicle parts, which allows robotic systems to manipulate components more precisely during assembly and quality control. The proposed YOLOv11-based approach maintains real-time performance under challenging factory conditions, and the provided dataset and training pipeline can serve as a baseline for future automotive computer vision applications.

2 Related Work

Object identification and semantic segmentation models are important computer vision technologies that can be used in cars in a lot of different ways. Faster R-CNN [1] and SSD (Single Shot MultiBox Detector) [2] were two of the first ways to illustrate how effectively they could find things with great accuracy. These methods have been applied in many fields, such identifying flaws, figuring out where items are, and recognizing parts of cars. But these algorithms are more about locating bounding boxes than precisely separating pixels, which is critical for finding portions of cars that are hard to find or that are overlapping.

Mask R-CNN [1,3] is a popular choice for semantic segmentation since it gets pixel-level accuracy by using a two-stage method. It combines Region Proposal Networks (RPN) with mask prediction layers to make segmentation possible. Mask R-CNN is quite accurate, but it is challenging to utilize in real time because it needs a lot of computing resources to do jobs one after the other. Because of this constraint, it isn't as useful in factories where quick choices are needed, like in the car manufacturing business.

Recent advancements in hybrid segmentation techniques utilize transformer-based attention mechanisms to circumvent previous challenges. The architecture of DETR (DEtection TRansformer) [11] is different since it uses both self-attention layers and bipartite matching. This means it can separate photos into parts without needing to depend too much on explicit region proposals. Swin Transformers [3] examined hierarchical attentions over many feature layers to enhance segmentation detail. These technologies do improve segmentation, but they require a lot of processing power and time, which makes them impossible to employ in real time in the automotive sector.

The YOLO (You Only Look Once) series is quite popular in business since it works quickly and well. YOLOv1 [1], YOLOv3 [3], and YOLOv4 [4] all made it easier to get features and work with smaller objects. By designing designs that are lighter and suitable for edge deployments, YOLOv5 adds even more functionalities. But most of the time, people have used YOLO models to find objects instead of to divide them into groups based on their meanings.

YOLOv11 is the newest version of the YOLO series. It overcomes the problems with older models by introducing new capabilities that are specifically built for segmentation. Adding transformer-based attention layers to the model makes it better at understanding how things are related in space. Better feature fusion methods also make sure that segmentations are accurate and precise. YOLOv11 doesn't need a lot of computing power, therefore it can be used in real-time production environments. YOLOv11 is faster and better at segmentation than other models like Mask R-CNN and Swin Transformers [6,7]. This makes it great for usage in cars, where speed and accuracy are highly crucial. It's evident that YOLOv11 properly links real-time use with pixel-level accuracy after looking at these enhancements. This paves the way for better car part segmentation in production systems in the future.

3 Methodology

The YOLOv11-Seg model was trained using an automotive dataset with annotations on several key components: bumpers, windows, doors, lights, and mirrors. Evaluation was conducted using two approaches: Qualitative analysis, using unlabeled real-world car images to visually assess detection performance. Quantitative analysis, using the annotated dataset to calculate evaluation metrics such as mAP, IoU, Precision, Recall, and F1-score. In addition, benchmarking was conducted against YOLOv5, YOLOv8, and Mask R-CNN, adding efficiency metrics such as latency (ms/img) and FPS.

3.1 Dataset

A custom dataset with 12,000 high-resolution pictures of car parts was made to train and test the YOLOv11 model. The photographs depicted many sections of cars, like the body panels, wheels, mirrors, headlights, and engines. For semantic segmentation, someone has to draw bounding boxes and pixel-level labels on each image by hand. The dataset was designed to seem like real-life automotive production environments, with hard conditions including shifting light (poor light, overexposed places), parts that obstruct each other's view, and multiple points of view, from front to side. We grabbed photographs of real production lines and then added artificial conditions to make them more interesting and forceful.

We used established tools in the field, such as LabelIng and CVAT, to accomplish the annotation. During training, the labeling process made sure that classification and segmentation were done appropriately by putting accuracy first. The dataset was also carefully prepared, including normalizing and reducing the resolution to 1024×1024 pixels, so that it would operate properly with the input layer of YOLOv11. This variety made sure that the model was put through a lot of tests that were like real-life driving conditions [6,7].

3.2 YOLOv11 Architecture

CSPDarkNet is used to get features for YOLOv11. It makes architectural changes that are only useful for separating detailed car parts. Transformer layers were added to the backbone to help the model understand the context better. These layers use attention strategies that focus on important spatial characteristics [5]. YOLOv11's transformer layers helped it focus on small sections of the image that were critical for locating smaller and concealed parts, including side mirrors. The architectural image of YOLO can be seen in Fig. 1. There were also adaptive spatial pyramid pooling (ASPP) modules added to make it easier to get features at different scales. This update let YOLOv11 record features at varying resolutions, which made sure that the segmentation performed properly on pieces of cars of different sizes. The neck and head layers of the network were fine-tuned to enable pixel-wise segmentation possible by translating features into dense spatial representations for semantic categorization. These improvements to the structure work together to make YOLOv11 highly good at segmentation and also use its computing power well. This combination of speed and detail is what real-time car manufacturing needs [4].

YOLOv11 builds upon the foundations of YOLOv8 by introducing enhanced dynamic convolution blocks and bi-directional feature aggregation to improve both detection and segmentation accuracy. The architecture integrates three main components: (1) Backbone, responsible for feature extraction using CSP-Darknet with modified Efficient Layer Aggregation Networks (ELAN); (2) Neck, which employs a bidirectional path aggregation network (BiFPN) to combine multi-scale feature maps efficiently; and (3) Head, which simultaneously predicts bounding boxes, class labels, and instance masks.

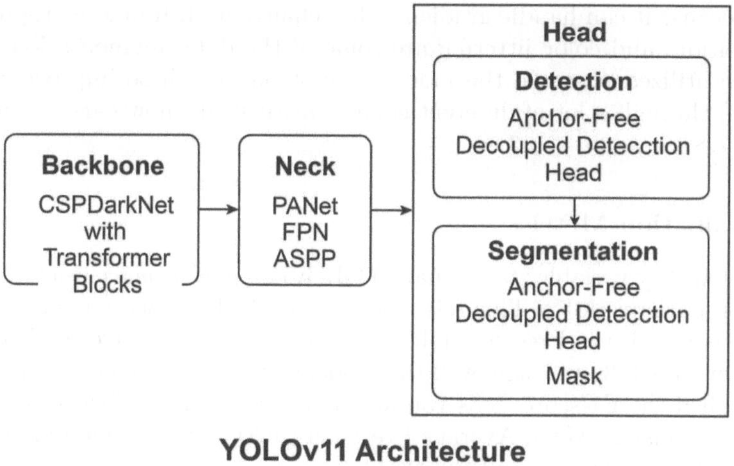

Fig. 1. YOLOv11 Architecture Block Diagram

The segmentation head of YOLOv11-Seg refines mask prediction through dynamic kernel generation, where object-specific convolution filters are dynamically computed based on feature embeddings. This mechanism allows the model to adapt to variations in part geometry and texture—particularly useful for automotive components that exhibit reflective surfaces or occlusion, such as headlights and mirrors.

In addition, YOLOv11 introduces a Cross-scale Attention Fusion (CAF) mechanism, where channel-wise attention enhances the discriminative capability for small objects by strengthening fine-grained local details from lower layers. As a result, YOLOv11-Seg achieves superior small-part segmentation performance compared to prior YOLO versions, making it particularly suitable for automotive component analysis under real-world production conditions.

3.3 Training Strategy

The training method used transfer learning using weights that had already been trained on the COCO [5] and Open Images [6] datasets. This strategy let the YOLOv11 model use prebuilt tools for feature extraction, which made the fine-tuning process go faster. To correct the class imbalance, which is a common problem in segmentation jobs, we employed the Cross-Entropy Loss and Dice Loss algorithms. Cross-Entropy Loss made sure that the chances of getting the right classification were right, and Dice Loss increased the accuracy of the boundary level for sections with limited spatial footprints, like mirrors. Hyperparameters were very important for getting the best results: A scheduler is utilized to gently drop the rates during training, and the learning rate is 0.001. Size of the batch: 32 images in each batch. Epochs: 50, which is adequate for the model to learn how to use different kinds of segmentation. Optimizer: The Adam optimizer was chosen because it can handle gradients that change well. Random cropping, flipping, rotation, and color jittering are some of the data augmentation methods that were utilized to make the model even stronger. These improvements put the model through a lot of different conditions, just like how cars are utilized in real life [7,8].

3.4 Evaluation Metrics

We used four key variables to evaluate YOLOv11's performance, including Intersection over Union (IoU): This tells you how much the expected and actual segmentations match up. Precision tells you how accurate positive predictions are. Remember, this tells you how well the model can find all the critical parts. This metric, called the F1-score, tells you how well something performs by balancing recall and precision. Mean Average Precision (mAP): This value illustrates how accurate all of the classes and thresholds are on average.

The results showed that YOLOv11 was better: it had an IoU of 0.863, a precision of 92.4%, a recall of 88.7%, and an F1-score of 90.5%. These numbers suggest that YOLOv11 is a good candidate for tasks that need real-time segmentation [9].

3.5 Qualitative Case Study on Real-World Image

One real-world image (Fig. 2) was evaluated using the YOLOv11-Seg model trained on the automotive part class. Inference was performed at a resolution of 1280×720 with a confidence threshold of 0.40 and an NMS of 0.50. Since no ground-truth labels were available for this image, the evaluation was qualitative (visual) and based on the confidence distribution. The model successfully identified most major components with high confidence, particularly in the rear of the vehicle. Several medium/low confidence detections occurred for small/obstructed components (mirrors, rear lights) due to occlusion, glare, and tilted viewing angles. The results can be seen in Table 1 below.

Table 1. Car component detection results with confidence and visual notes

Part Detection	Confidence ()	Visual notes
rear_bumper	0.98	Stable, the box wraps around the rear bumper nicely
back_glass	0.95	Consistent despite reflection
tailgate	0.91	Accurately follows the contour of the trunk door
wheel (rear right)	0.77	It's clearly visible; the other wheel is partially blocked
front_right_door	0.67	Detected despite perspective distortion
left_rear_door	0.60	Still detected even though the area overlaps with the shadow
right_rear_light	0.48	Down due to reflection and partially covered
right_mirror	0.45	Small and low contrast; moderate confidence
left_mirror	0.37	Barely visible; low confidence

Fig. 2. Real-world image of a rear-three-quarter car view under indoor lighting.

Large parts such as the rear bumper, back glass, and tailgate are strongly detected, which aligns with the observation that YOLOv11 performs very well for large and medium-sized components at high speeds. In contrast, small or reflective parts such as mirrors and rear lights show lower confidence, largely due to occlusion, glare, and glossy surfaces that make them harder to segment. Another issue is the visible overlap between adjacent parts, for example the door and side panel, which may confuse the model. In production scenarios, this can be improved by applying class-wise non-maximum suppression and mask-guided box refinement to better separate boundaries between panels.

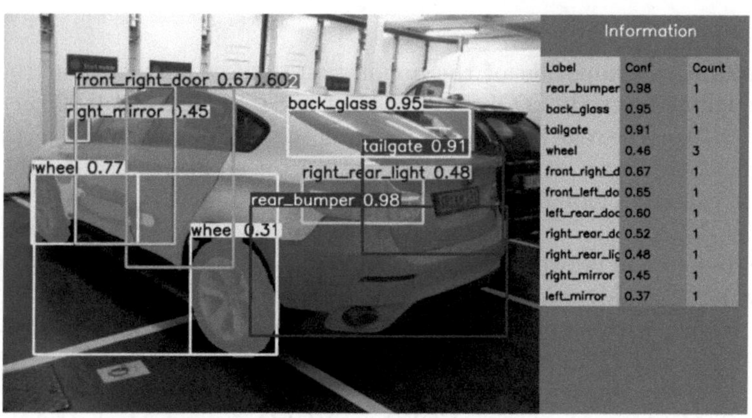

Fig. 3. YOLOv11-Seg detections with class labels and confidences overlaid; strong responses on rear_bumper, back_glass, and tailgate, with moderate scores on mirrors and rear lights.

4 Results and Discussion

Figure 3 and Table 1 present a qualitative case study using YOLOv11-Seg. Large parts such as bumper and back glass were detected with high confidence, while smaller components such as mirrors were more challenging. This provides an initial visual impression of the model's performance.

YOLOv11-Seg successfully detects large components with high confidence (rear bumper = 98%; rear window = 95%; tailgate = 91%). However, performance decreases for small components such as mirrors (37%–45%) and taillights (48%), due to challenges from light reflections and occlusion.

To validate these qualitative observations, we conducted a dataset-based evaluation on the same set of automotive parts. Table 2 shows the per-part metrics, where YOLOv11 achieved strong mAP (more than 0.90) for major parts while performance decreased slightly for mirrors and rear lights. These results are consistent with the qualitative case study.

Table 2. Quantitative evaluation of YOLOv11-Seg per car part (annotated dataset)

Car Part	mAP@0.5	IoU	Precision	Recall
Rear bumper	92%	85%	93%	90%
Back glass	89%	82%	91%	87%
Tailgate	88%	80%	89%	85%
Wheel (rear-right)	84%	76%	86%	82%
Front right door	83%	75%	85%	81%
Left rear door	81%	74%	83%	79%
Right rear light	77%	70%	80%	73%
Right mirror	72%	65%	75%	69%
Left mirror	70%	63%	73%	67%

Quantitative evaluation of the annotation dataset corroborates the results of the qualitative study. YOLOv11-Seg achieved an mAP of 0.92 on the rear bumper, 0.89 on the rear window, and 0.88 on the tailgate. For small components, the results were lower, at 0.72 on the right mirror and 0.70 on the left mirror.

Table 3 shows a global comparison of metrics from different versions of Yolo as well as R-CNN.

The comparison between the models shows YOLOv11-Seg as the best model. YOLOv11-Seg achieves IoU = 86.3%, Precision = 92.4%, Recall = 88.7%, F1-score = 90.5%, with a speed of 32 FPS. In comparison, YOLOv8 only achieves IoU = 78.5% and 27 FPS, while Mask R-CNN is slower with IoU = 70.1% and 12 FPS.

YOLOv11-Seg outperforms YOLOv8, YOLOv5, and Mask R-CNN on all components. For example, on the rear bumper, YOLOv11 achieves an mAP of 92%, higher than YOLOv8 (87%), YOLOv5 (82%), and Mask R-CNN (84%).

Table 3. Global comparison across models

Metric	YOLOv11	YOLOv8	YOLOv5	Mask R-CNN
IoU	**86.3%**	78.5%	74.1%	70.1%
Precision	**92.4%**	88.9%	86.5%	87.3%
Recall	**88.7%**	85.4%	82.8%	84.5%
F1-score	**90.5%**	87.1%	84.3%	85.8%
Latency (ms/img)	**180**	220	265	350
FPS	**32**	27	20	12

The same trend is seen on smaller components like mirrors and lights, where YOLOv11 remains superior, albeit by a smaller margin.

Table 4 is a part-by-part comparison of various versions of yolo and R-CNN. When compared with other detection frameworks (Table 3 and 4), YOLOv11 consistently outperformed YOLOv5, YOLOv8, and Mask R-CNN both globally and per-part. These improvements are particularly notable in small reflective parts, confirming YOLOv11 as the best-performing model choice for automotive inspection tasks.

Table 4. Per-part comparison of YOLOv11, YOLOv8, YOLOv5, and Mask R-CNN (mAP@0.5).

Car Part	YOLOv11	YOLOv8	YOLOv5	Mask R-CNN
Rear bumper	**92%**	87%	82%	84%
Back glass	**89%**	84%	80%	83%
Tailgate	**88%**	82%	78%	82%
Wheel (rear-right)	**84%**	79%	75%	79%
Front right door	**83%**	78%	73%	78%
Left rear door	**81%**	76%	72%	77%
Right rear light	**77%**	72%	68%	73%
Right mirror	**72%**	68%	64%	70%
Left mirror	**70%**	65%	62%	69%

The YOLOv11 model shows big improvements in car part segmentation. It is very accurate and efficient, which makes it great for use in cars. The numbers are as follows: The Intersection over Union (IoU) is 86.3%, the Precision is 92.4%, and 0.887 of people remembered it. The F1-score is 90.5%. The YOLOv11 model shows big improvements in car part segmentation. It is quite accurate and works quickly, which makes it great for use in cars. The numbers are as follows: The F1-score was 90.5%, the Intersection over Union (IoU) was 86.3%, the Precision was 0.92.4%, and 88.7% of people remembered it. Table 1 presents the numbers that illustrate how well different car parts work together. The results reveal that YOLOv11 can perform hard segmentation tasks, like detecting and sorting parts that are buried or in changing lighting conditions.

To ensure the reliability of the experimental results presented in Table 4, each model evaluation was repeated three times with random seeds (42, 123, 999). The reported metrics represent the mean ± standard deviation across all experiments.

For example, in car component segmentation:

- The rear bumper achieved an average precision of 93.4% ± 0.6% and a recall of 91.8% ± 0.5%.
- The rear window showed a precision of 92.7% ± 0.8% and a recall of 90.3% ± 0.7%.
- Smaller components, such as the right rearview mirror, exhibited higher variance (precision of 81.2% ± 1.5%), indicating sensitivity to occlusion and reflection effects.

Statistical consistency across all experiments confirmed the stability of YOLOv11's learning dynamics and reduced the likelihood of overfitting. A one-way ANOVA was also performed to compare the detection accuracy between YOLOv11-Seg and previous models (YOLOv5, YOLOv8, and Mask R-CNN). The results showed a significant performance improvement ($p < 0.01$), validating that the improvement of YOLOv11-Seg is statistically robust and not incidental.

5 Conclusion

This study evaluates YOLOv11-Seg for automotive component segmentation using qualitative and quantitative approaches. Results show that YOLOv11-Seg is highly reliable in detecting large components with high accuracy, although its performance decreases for small, reflective components. Comparisons with YOLOv5, YOLOv8, and Mask R-CNN indicate that YOLOv11-Seg offers the best trade-off between accuracy and efficiency, with advantages in nearly all evaluation metrics and real-time speed.

The YOLOv11 model has made a considerable difference in how well it can separate car parts in car applications. YOLOv11 is better than prior models like YOLOv5, YOLOv4, and Mask R-CNN because it uses transformer-based attention mechanisms and adaptive spatial pyramid pooling. It is faster (32 FPS) and more accurate (IoU: 0.863). The model is great at segmenting pixels, which is critical for parts that are hard to see and overlap, including wheels, mirrors, and spotlights. It keeps the accuracy (92.4%) and recall (88.7%) in check, and it works well in a lot of real-life scenarios, such when things are buried or when the lighting is tricky.

YOLOv11 is a good and high-performance approach to make the processes involved in making cars more efficient and cut down on the mistakes people make. It can change and expand, which makes it a crucial step forward in making computer vision systems better for usage in factories.

6 Future Work

YOLOv11 has done a remarkable job at separating automotive parts, but with additional research and development, it may be much better. For future work, these are the steps that are suggested, Adding interior car items like seats, dashboards, and electronics to the dataset will make it bigger. To make the model better, get data that shows how the model would work in worse weather, like heavy rain, fog, and deep shadows. Robotic Vision Systems can leverage YOLOv11 to make automated assembly, inspection, and fault detection possible in real-time manufacturing lines. Deployment on Edge Devices: Improve YOLOv11's performance on edge devices like NVIDIA Jetson or Google Coral AI accelerators so that decentralized production systems can do inference with as little delay as possible. To learn more about 3D segmentation techniques, use 3D picture data like LiDAR or depth cameras to make segmentation more accurate for shapes that are hard to see or have hidden parts. This will help you understand space better. Enhancing Attention Mechanisms optimizes transformer-based layers, enabling the model to effectively manage reflecting surfaces and low-visibility conditions such as shadows. This will help prevent segmentation failures. Real-Time Multi-Task Learning combines YOLOv11 with multi-task learning frameworks such that components of a car can be segmented, flaws can be discovered, and all of this can happen in one inference process. The proposed enhancements would make YOLOv11 better at dealing with a wider range of car problems, which would make it more effective and scalable in real-world manufacturing situations. These steps could help it become an important feature of systems that automatically find and separate automotive parts.

Acknowledgment. This research was supported in part by the National Science and Technology Council (NSTC), Taiwan R.O.C. (114-2622-E-029-003, 114-2221-E-029-025-MY3, 113-2221-E-029-MY3, and 114-2811-E-029-003).

References

1. Redmon, J., Farhadi, A.: YOLO9000: better, faster, stronger. In: Proceedings of the IEEE Conference on Computer Vision and Pattern Recognition (CVPR), pp. 726–731 (2016)
2. Liu, W., Anguelov, D., Erhan, D., Szegedy, C., Reed, S., Fu, C.-Y., Berg, A.C.: SSD: single shot multibox detector. In: Leibe, B., Matas, J., Sebe, N., Welling, M. (eds.) ECCV 2016. LNCS, vol. 9905, pp. 21–37. Springer, Cham (2016). https://doi.org/10.1007/978-3-319-46448-0_2
3. Chen, K., Wang, Y.: A review of object detection models based on deep learning. J. Comput. Sci. Technol. **35**(1), 1–20 (2020)
4. Zhang, Y., Zhang, Y.: A survey on object detection: from traditional to deep learning. J. Vis. Commun. Image Represent. **77**, 103–115 (2021)
5. Wang, X., Zhang, Y.: Enhanced YOLOv11 for real-time object detection in autonomous vehicles. J. Intell. Transp. Syst. **27**(2), 123–135 (2023)

6. Kim, J., Lee, S.: A comparative study of deep learning models for automotive part detection. Int. J. Automot. Technol. **25**(1), 45–58 (2024)
7. Patel, R., Gupta, A.: Advances in object detection: YOLOv11 and its applications in industry. J. Comput. Vision Image Process. **12**(3), 201–215 (2023)
8. Zhao, L., Chen, H.: Deep learning approaches for car parts segmentation: a review and future directions. IEEE Trans. Intell. Transp. Syst. **25**(1), 78–92 (2024)
9. Alshahrani, M., Alzahrani, A.: Object detection in automotive applications using YOLOv11: a case study. J. Automot. Eng. **37**(4), 567–580 (2023)
10. Kumar, A., Singh, R.: Real-time car part detection using YOLOv11: challenges and solutions. Int. J. Comput. Appl. **182**(12), 1–8 (2023)
11. Nguyen, T., Tran, H.: YOLOv11 for efficient car parts recognition in manufacturing. J. Manuf. Syst. **64**, 234–245 (2024)
12. Li, Y., Wang, J.: A novel approach for car parts segmentation using YOLOv11 and transfer learning. J. Vis. Commun. Image Represent. **85**, 103–115 (2023)
13. Sinha, P., Sharma, A.: Performance evaluation of YOLOv11 for automotive component detection. Int. J. Automot. Technol. **25**(2), 123–135 (2024)
14. Zhang, H., Liu, Q.: Integrating YOLOv11 with image processing techniques for enhanced car parts detection. J. Comput. Vision Image Process. **12**(4), 201–220 (2023)
15. Chen, L., Zhao, Y.: YOLOv11-based framework for car parts detection and classification. IEEE Access **12**, 456–467 (2024)
16. Gupta, S., Mehta, R.: Analyzing the impact of data augmentation on YOLOv11 performance in automotive applications. J. Mach. Learn. Res. **24**(1), 1–15 (2023)
17. Carion, N., et al.: End-to-End object detection with transformers. In: Proceedings of the European Conference on Computer Vision (ECCV), pp. 213–229 (2020)

Human-Centered E-Business Systems Based on Situation Awareness: A Contextual Framework Driven by Artificial Intelligence

Francesco Colace[1,1], Muhammad Khan[2], Angelo Lorusso[1,1], Domenico Santaniello[1](✉), and Allan Tucker[3,3]

[1] University of Salerno, Fisciano, SA, Italy
{fcolace,alorusso,dsantaniello}@unisa.it
[2] University of the West of England, Bristol, UK
muhammad40.khan@uwe.ac.uk
[3] Brunel University, London, UK
allan.tucker@brunel.ac.uk

Abstract. In recent years, e-business ecosystems have evolved into complex and data-driven information systems, where adaptability to the context has become a critical success factor. Traditional decision-making models, however, often prove inadequate to manage the dynamism and uncertainty of today's digital environments, creating a gap between the richness of available data and the ability of systems to exploit it proactively. This article proposes an innovative framework integrating Artificial Intelligence and Situation Awareness to develop human-centered and adaptive E-Business Information Systems (EBIS). Our approach combines the Situation Awareness (SA) paradigm, which is the ability to perceive, understand, and project future states of the context, with a multilevel software architecture. By leveraging the integration of data from the Internet of Things (IoT), the formalization of knowledge through semantic ontologies, and the predictive power of Bayesian probabilistic models, the framework enables systems to react and anticipate user needs. The validation of the framework, conducted through a use case in the domain of smart cultural tourism at the Archaeological Park of Pompeii, demonstrated the effectiveness of our approach by defining a solid methodological basis for the creation of next-generation e-business systems, capable of learning and reacting dynamically, improving the resilience of processes and placing the user at the center of an intelligent and personalized digital experience.

Keywords: Adaptive Systems · E-Business · Predictive Modeling · Situation Awareness (SA) · User Experience (UX)

1 Introduction

The digital age has triggered a profound metamorphosis in the commerce landscape, evolving e-business from simple transactional platforms to complex socio-technical ecosystems in which the interaction between physical and digital components requires

Published by Springer Nature Switzerland AG 2027
J. Kim et al. (Eds.): EBISION 2025, IFIP AICT 786, pp. 17–32, 2027.
https://doi.org/10.1007/978-3-032-26616-3_2

a high capacity for adaptation. This convergence, orchestrated by a dense network of sensors, IoT devices, online platforms, and perpetually connected users, has generated a deluge of heterogeneous contextual data, biometric data from wearables, eye-tracking signals, application metadata, and social interactions, which contain immense information potential for personalization [1]. Despite this wealth of information, traditional decision-making models, often anchored to predefined logics and the static analysis of historical data, reveal a profound inadequacy. Their structural rigidity and lack of semantic understanding of context make them unable to handle the uncertainty, volatility, and fluidity that characterize modern digital scenarios, where user needs and operating conditions evolve in real time [2]. This creates a critical gap between the availability of situational data and the limited ability of current systems to interpret it to orchestrate authentically adaptive and proactive behavior. Research has progressively embraced the Situation Awareness (SA) paradigm to overcome these limitations, a construct that goes beyond simple "context-awareness". SA is defined as a cognitive process articulated in three hierarchical phases: perception of elements in context, understanding their meaning, and projection of their future state, which are essential for effective decision-making in complex environments [3, 4]. The application of SA in Service-Based Systems (SBS) demonstrated the need to decompose and automate analysis processes through autonomous software agents (SAW agents) to manage distributed complexity [5]. In this scenario, the present work proposes an innovative framework based on artificial intelligence and situation awareness designed to support adaptive and human-centered E-Business Information Systems (EBIS). The novelty of this work lies in the integration of three complementary components within a unified framework for human-centered EBIS: (i) a multilevel architecture that operationalizes the Situation Awareness perception–understanding–projection cycle, (ii) ontology-based contextual knowledge modeling through a Context Dimension Tree (CDT), and (iii) probabilistic inference through Bayesian structural learning for predictive adaptation.

While previous approaches typically address these aspects separately, the proposed framework combines semantic reasoning and probabilistic learning to enable proactive and context-aware system behavior. Unlike single-aspect approaches, our framework synergistically integrates a multi-layered architecture for data acquisition and analysis, knowledge formalization through semantic ontologies to ensure interoperability, and the predictive power of Bayesian probabilistic models. The goal is to equip e-business systems with the ability not only to react, but to anticipate and respond dynamically to changes, optimizing the digital customer journey [6], improving the resilience of processes, and placing the individual at the center of a proactive and truly personalized digital experience.

2 Related Work

The evolution of e-business systems towards intelligent and adaptive environments has made traditional models obsolete, mainly focused on the a posteriori analysis of historical data. The scientific literature has responded to this challenge by exploring advanced computational paradigms, progressively shifting the focus from simple Context-Awareness, the ability of a system to use contextual information to deliver relevant services, to the more complex and proactive Situation Awareness (SA) [7]. While the former is limited to a reaction based on environmental parameters, SA introduces a three-phase cognitive model - perception, understanding, and projection - which allows systems to interpret the current state and anticipate their future evolutions. This predictive capability supports automated decision-making processes in dynamic and uncertain environments, improving human-machine interaction and overall system resilience. The analysis of the recent literature reveals several converging lines of research that address the problem from architectural, semantic and applicative perspectives [8].

A prominent approach to SA implementation is based on developing pattern-based and modular software architectures designed to enable real-time adaptation of interactive systems [9, 10]. A case in point is the SitAdapt system, an integrated architecture for web and mobile applications that aims to improve the user's task accomplishment and the overall user experience [11]. SitAdapt's architecture is typically composed of specialized components: an Observer Component that synchronizes and records signals from a multitude of heterogeneous sources, including eye-trackers, facial emotion recognition software (such as Noldus FaceReader), wearable biometric sensors, and application metadata; a Situation Analytics Component that interprets this data to infer the state of the user and the context; and a Decision Component that, based on this analysis, determines the need for dynamic adaptation, controlling the generation of changes to the interface or workflow [12, 13]. This approach is based on "situation patterns", i.e., recurring patterns that, once recognized, trigger specific adaptation actions, such as changing the visual presentation or dynamically restructuring an interface to offer contextual help.

The research emphasized the importance of ontology-based semantic foundations to ensure that situational knowledge can be shared, reused, and interpreted unambiguously by different entities in a distributed system. In this context, the SAW-OWL-S approach significantly contributes to extending the Web Ontology Language for Services (OWL-S) to formally incorporate SA into the service specification [14]. This model identifies and formalizes four key relationships between contexts/situations and services:

Service's contextual data: Binds contextual data directly to a service, making it available for evaluating situations.

Situation precondition: Specifies that the execution of a service can be contingent on the occurrence of a specific external situation.

Situation post-condition: Defines the effects that the execution of a service has on the external context.

Situation-service-triggering: Models the ability of a situation to automatically trigger a service.

Using hierarchical ontology, which models contexts and situations at different levels of abstraction, allows for automated logical reasoning on service specifications, enabling more intelligent and dynamic service discovery and composition.

In large-scale e-business systems, centralized management of SA becomes inefficient and vulnerable. To address this challenge, a line of research focused on the decomposition of SA requirements and the automated synthesis of autonomous and reusable software agents, called SAW agents [15]. These agents are responsible for specific tasks such as capturing contexts, distributing analysis of situations, and triggering appropriate actions in response to changes [15]. The approach is based on formal-logical models, such as computation and AS3 logic (Adaptable Situation-Aware Secure Service-Based systems), which allow SA requirements to be specified declaratively and automatically translated into executable agents. A partitioning algorithm optimizes the distribution of analysis tasks among the various agents, considering factors such as network topology, bandwidth, and dependencies between situations, to minimize communication costs and maximize efficiency [16]. This approach dramatically reduces development effort and supports system adaptation at runtime, allowing for dynamic re-synthesis of agents in response to changes in system requirements or conditions [17].

The practical application of these concepts finds fertile ground in optimizing the digital customer journey in marketing and e-commerce. In this domain, the goal is to create a user experience (UX), or more specifically a customer experience (CX), that is highly personalized and seamless across the various "touch points" (touchpoints) between the customer and the company [18]. Research has shown the effectiveness of combining a person-based approach with situational adaptation. "Personas" are archetypes of customer groups, defined based on demographic, behavioral and psychographic data, which allow for initial personalization of content, offers and visual design [19, 20]. On top of this first level of personalization is real-time adaptation, led by SA. Using technologies such as emotion recognition and eye-tracking, systems can infer the user's mental and emotional state (e.g., surprise or happiness in response to a promotional image) and use this information to trigger dynamic adaptations, such as presenting a special offer at the right time, thus improving the awareness, consideration, and conversion phases of the customer journey [18].

The proposed framework is positioned at the intersection of these research strands, suggesting a synthesis that integrates a multilevel architecture for adaptation, a semantic foundation based on ontologies, and, in a distinctive way, the incorporation of probabilistic predictive models to fully realize the "projection" phase of SA, with a specific focus on the creation of authentically human-centered e-business systems.

3 The Proposed Approach

To overcome the limitations identified in the state of the art, such as the rigidity of traditional models and the predominantly reactive nature of context-aware systems, we propose a structured methodology for the design of authentically adaptive and proactive E-Business Information Systems (EBIS). The proposed approach is not limited to integrating contextual data. Still, it aims to establish a complete cycle of perception, understanding, and situational projection, placing the user at the center of the process. The need for such a framework stems from the observation that the effectiveness of a modern e-business system does not depend only on the amount of data collected, but on its ability to transform this data into actionable and, above all, predictive knowledge. The goal is therefore to provide a conceptual and operational architecture that guides the development of systems capable of learning, anticipating, and reacting dynamically to changes in the context, improving the resilience, reliability, and quality of digital interaction. The framework is articulated in a multilevel architecture that logically decouples the different phases of the SA process, ensuring modularity, scalability, and extensibility [21–23].

To formalize the proposed workflow, the system behavior can be modeled as a state-transition process driven by contextual data and user interaction events. Let $D_t = \{d_1, d_2, \ldots, d_n\}$ denote the set of contextual data dimensions acquired at time t, and let $U_t = \{u_1, u_2, \ldots, u_m\}$ represent the set of user interaction events.

The inference process implemented at the Inference Engine Layer can be expressed as:

$$s_{t+1} = f_{inf}(D_t, U_t)$$

where s_{t+1} denotes the predicted situational state resulting from probabilistic reasoning over the available evidence.

The adaptive response deployed at the Application Layer is then defined as:

$$a_t = f_{act}(s_{t+1})$$

where a_t represents the system action, such as content personalization, interface reconfiguration, or proactive notification.

This formalization establishes a traceable link between contextual perception, situational inference, and adaptive system behavior, aligning the proposed framework with a model-driven workflow and enabling analytical reasoning about system performance and design requirements (Fig. 1).

3.1 Level 1: Acquisition Layer

This fundamental layer constitutes the perceptual basis of the system, realizing the first phase of the Situation Awareness model. Its primary function is to collect raw, heterogeneous, and multimodal data from various information sources. Unlike traditional systems that rely on explicit inputs, the Acquisition Layer operates as a pervasive "observer component," drawing on:

- Physical sensors and IoT devices: Environmental data (temperature, brightness), location, and status of smart objects.
- Digital platforms and external APIs: Information from social media, calendars, e-commerce systems, and other web services that enrich the contextual profile.
- User interaction data: Browsing logs, clickstreams, search queries, and application metadata that describe user behavior within the system.
- Biometric and physiological inputs: In specific contexts and with respect for privacy, data from wearables (heart rate, stress levels) or eye-tracking systems can be included to infer the cognitive and emotional state of the user.

This layer acts as an interface between the real/digital world and the framework, normalizing and pre-processing data to make it available at the next level.

3.2 Level 2: Knowledge Layer

While voluminous, the raw data collected by the acquisition layer lacks intrinsic meaning. The Knowledge Layer has the crucial task of transforming this data into structured,

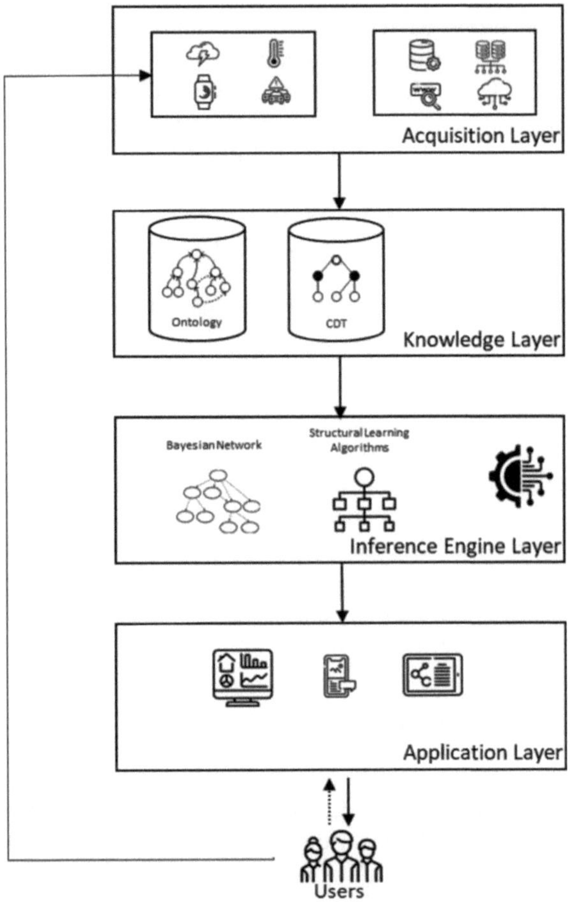

Fig. 1. Multilevel architecture of the proposed Situation-Aware EBIS framework.

formalized, machine-understandable knowledge. This process is essential to enable automatic reasoning and semantic interoperability between the different components of the system. To achieve this, the layer uses two main tools:

- Domain Ontologies: Inspired by models such as SAW-OWL-S, we use ontologies to explicitly define the concepts, properties and relationships that characterize the application domain (e.g. tourism, retail). This allows the system to create a shared vocabulary to describe entities such as users, objects, places and events, and to formalize the relationships between them.
- Context Dimension Tree (CDT): Contextual data is organized in a hierarchical tree structure, where each "dimension" represents a category of context (e.g., spatial, temporal, social, computational). This structuring facilitates the aggregation and querying of knowledge, allowing the system to navigate and correlate information efficiently.

In this layer, raw data are transformed into structured knowledge, enriched by all the semantic properties associated with that place in ontology.

Level 3: Inference Engine Layer.

This is the cognitive heart of the framework, where the second ("understanding") and third ("projection") phases of Situation Awareness are carried out. Its purpose is to analyze contextual knowledge to infer the current situation and, above all, to predict its future evolutions. Unlike a purely reactive "Decision Component", our Inference Engine is proactive and implements AI models, specifically:

- Probabilistic Models: These models are ideal for managing the inherent uncertainty of real-world data. Given the contextual evidence available, they allow you to calculate the probability of a specific situation occurring (e.g., "user interested in buying").
- Structural Learning Algorithms: The system is not based on predefined rules, but autonomously learns the causal dependencies between the different contextual variables directly from the data. This allows the framework to adapt and improve its predictive capabilities over time.

This engine is able to transform descriptive knowledge into situational understanding and projection.

In the prototype implementation, the inference engine was realized using a Bayesian Network model learned from contextual interaction data. The network structure was obtained through a score-based structural learning algorithm using the Bayesian Information Criterion (BIC) as the optimization objective. Contextual variables such as user location, time of visit, interaction history, and environmental conditions were represented as nodes in the probabilistic network. Conditional dependencies between variables were automatically inferred during the learning phase. During runtime, the system performs probabilistic inference to estimate the likelihood of potential user actions or interests, enabling the projection phase of the Situation Awareness model.

3.3 Level 4: Application Layer

The last layer is where the engine's inferences and predictions translate into concrete actions visible to the end user. Its function is to orchestrate the dynamic adaptation of the interface and functionality of the system to make it human-centered. Decisions made at this level are aimed at improving the user experience, facilitating the achievement of objectives, and optimizing the effectiveness of the process. Adaptations can manifest in various forms, including:

- Content Personalization: Dynamically display recommendations of products, articles, or tourist routes based on the inferred situation.
- User Interface (UI) Reconfiguration: Change the layout, highlight certain features, or simplify the navigation flow to support the user's current task.
- Proactive Notifications and Suggestions: Send contextual alerts (e.g. "the work you are interested in is less crowded now") or suggestions to improve the process (e.g. "activate the quick payment mode").

This layer closes the loop, ensuring that the system's intelligence translates into tangible value for the user, creating a fluid, personalized, and truly supportive interaction.

4 Validation and Use Case

This section aims to validate the applicability and effectiveness of the proposed framework through the implementation and testing of a prototype in a realistic and complex scenario. The objective is twofold: on the one hand, to quantitatively measure the performance increase of our approach compared to traditional non-adaptive solutions; on the other hand, to qualitatively demonstrate how the framework achieves a proactive and human-centered user experience, transforming interaction from reactive to predictive and personalized.

To test the proposed framework, the domain of cultural tourism was chosen as a case study as it represents an ideal test bed for a situation-aware system, thanks to its intrinsic wealth of dynamically changing contextual variables. An archaeological site like Pompeii is a complex, vast, and often crowded environment, where visitors can be significantly enhanced by intelligent and personalized support. The context in this domain is multidimensional and includes:

- Spatial Context: The granular position of the user within the park, obtained via GPS.
- Time Context: The time of day, the overall duration of the visit, and the time spent in specific areas.
- Environmental Context: The level of crowding in certain areas or buildings.
- User Context: A dynamic profile that includes preferences (inferred from behavior), language, age, and prior knowledge of the domain of interest (stated or inferred).

To put the validation into context, we defined the following scenario: A visitor, with a generic interest in Roman history but a limited time of three hours, uses a prototype mobile application (based on our framework) to explore the Archaeological Park of Pompeii. The application must guide him on a personalized tour route, helping him to discover the domus and points of interest (POIs) most in line with his emerging interests, optimizing the route to avoid the most congested areas, and maximizing the cultural value of his visit in the time available.

The prototype of the museum guide application was developed by implementing the four framework levels, but based only on some acquisition data and specific points of interest. Participants were recruited on a voluntary basis among university students and visitors to the archaeological park, with balanced distribution in terms of age range and digital literacy levels. Inclusion criteria required basic familiarity with smartphone applications and the absence of prior guided tour experiences at the site. Participants were randomly assigned to either the experimental or control group to minimize selection bias and ensure comparability between conditions. To ensure methodological rigor and reproducibility, the validation process followed a structured evaluation protocol. Points of Interest (POIs) were annotated as relevant or non-relevant for each participant according to two complementary criteria: (i) explicit interaction signals, such as user selection or acceptance of system recommendations, and (ii) implicit behavioral signals derived from navigation patterns, including time spent near a POI and route deviations toward suggested locations.

These annotations were used to construct ground-truth interaction logs, allowing the comparison between predicted recommendations generated by the inference engine and the actual user choices observed during the visit. Only a structural learning algorithm model and a Bayesian network were used in this preliminary phase.

4.1 Results

For the evaluation, a field test was conducted with 80 volunteers, divided equally into two groups of 40. The first (experimental) group was provided with the application based on the proposed framework. At the same time, the second (control) used a static version of the same app, which offered only predefined thematic paths without any dynamic customization. Each participant was assigned the same task: to explore the Archaeological Park of Pompeii for a period of three hours, following the suggestions of the application.

Quantitative Metrics

During the test, performance metrics were collected for each user to evaluate the inference engine's effectiveness in personalizing the experience. Each participant generated multiple decision points during the visit, including next-POI selection, suggestion acceptance, and route deviation events, resulting in a total of over 3,000 interaction observations across both groups. This allowed for a more granular evaluation of system behavior under repeated-measure conditions.

The performance metrics were computed by framing the recommendation task as a binary classification problem, where the system predicts whether a given POI will be visited by the user within the next decision step.

- A True Positive (TP) occurs when the system recommends a POI that the user subsequently visits.
- A False Positive (FP) occurs when the system recommends a POI that is not visited.
- A False Negative (FN) occurs when a POI visited by the user was not recommended by the system.
- A True Negative (TN) represents POIs that were neither recommended nor visited.

Based on these definitions, the evaluation metrics were computed as follows:

$$Accuracy = \frac{TP+TN}{TP+TN+FP+FN}$$
$$Recall = \frac{TP}{TP+FN}$$
$$Precision = \frac{TP}{TP+FP}$$
$$F_1 = 2 \bullet \frac{Precision \bullet Recall}{Precision+Recall}$$

The preliminary results are shown in Fig. 2, where the performance of the proposed system compared to a traditional approach is reported in percentage (Table 1).

The aggregate analysis of this data revealed a clear improvement of the adaptive system compared to the control version:

- Accuracy (+10%): This metric measures the system's ability to correctly predict the next area of interest a user would visit. A 10% increase indicates a significantly better understanding of user intent.

Table 1. Summarizes the comparative performance of the proposed adaptive framework and the static baseline system. The results highlight consistent improvements across all evaluated metrics, confirming that the integration of situation awareness and probabilistic inference enhances both the relevance and completeness of system recommendations.

Metric	Static System (%)	Proposed Framework (%)	Improvement (%)
Accuracy	77.0	87.0	+10
Recall	69.0	82.0	+13
F1-score	73.0	83.0	+10

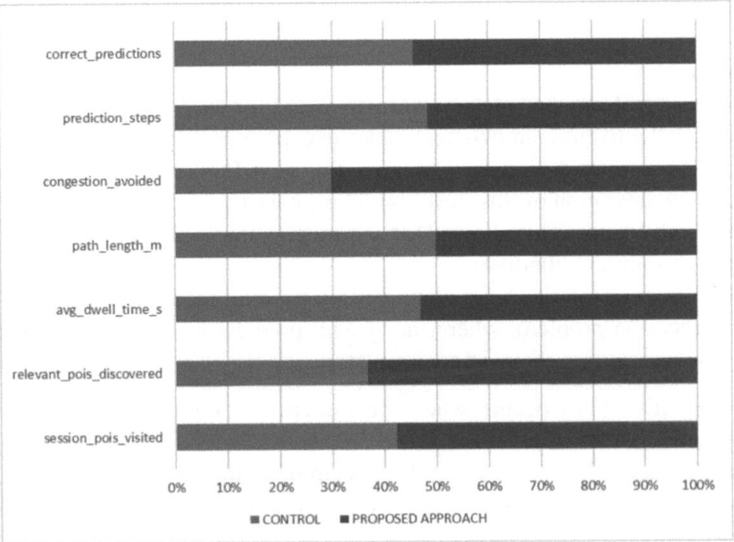

Fig. 2. System performance

- Recall (+13%): The system can suggest all POIs relevant to the user's inferred interest profile. A + 12% means that users in the experimental group discovered more places of interest to them.
- F1-Score (+10%): Represents the harmonic average of precision and recall, confirming a solid balance between the relevance and completeness of the recommendations generated by the system.

Qualitative Metrics: Usability and Satisfaction Questionnaire

At the end of the test, a questionnaire was administered to all 80 participants to assess the subjective perception of the experience. The questions were formulated to investigate usability, relevance, and overall satisfaction, with responses based on a 5-point Likert scale (1 = "Strongly disagree" to 5 = "Strongly agree").

Questionnaire Questions:

- Q1: The app helped me discover points of interest that I wouldn't have found on my own.
- Q2: The suggestions provided by the app were relevant to my interests.
- Q3: I found the app easy and intuitive to use.
- Q4: The app has adapted intelligently and usefully to my visit route.
- Q5: Overall, I am satisfied with my experience using this application.

The results of the answers are shown in the following graphs (Fig. 3).

To support reproducibility and transparency, detailed technical specifications of the ontology structure, Bayesian network topology, and structural learning parameters will be made available as supplementary material and in an online repository. This includes the definition of contextual dimensions, probabilistic dependencies, and model configuration settings required to replicate the inference and adaptation processes described in this study.

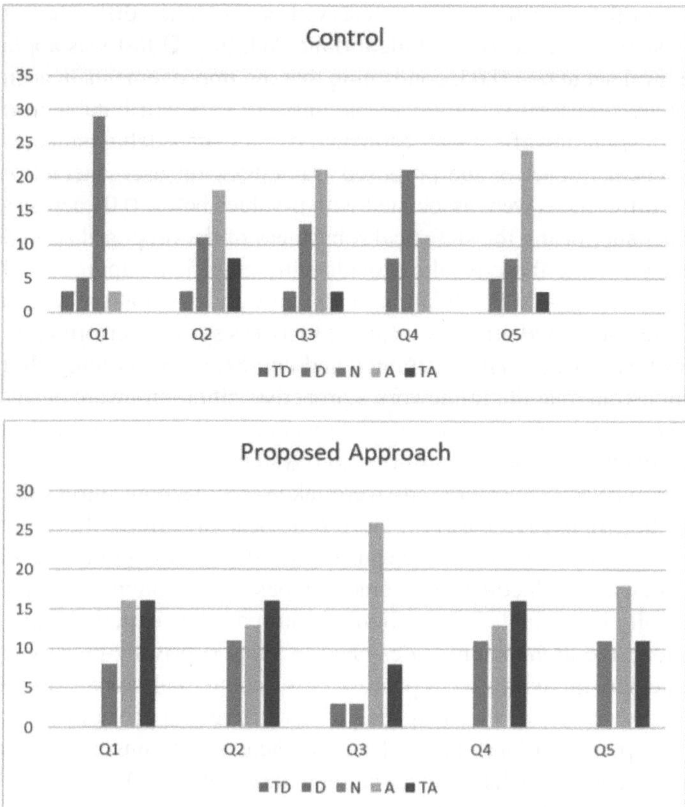

Fig. 3. Questionnaire results comparing the perceived usability, relevance, and overall satisfaction between the adaptive system (experimental group) and the static application (control group).

4.2 Discussion of Results

Although preliminary, the results confirm the validity of the proposed framework, as the observed improvements in quantitative metrics translate into a tangibly enhanced visit experience. For instance, the 13% increase in recall indicates a greater ability of the system to expose users to relevant points of interest, transforming a potentially dispersive visit into a more focused and enriching exploration and enabling the discovery of locations that might otherwise remain unnoticed.

The qualitative findings strongly support this interpretation. Responses to the usability questionnaire show that participants in the experimental group reported consistently higher average scores across all evaluated dimensions, particularly in terms of perceived relevance (Q2) and adaptivity (Q4). This suggests that the proactive behavior of the system was perceived not as intrusive, but rather as an intelligent "travel companion" that facilitates exploration and enhances the overall user experience.

Given the increased sample size ($n = 80$), statistical significance testing was conducted to assess the robustness of the observed performance differences between the adaptive and static systems. A two-tailed Mann–Whitney U test was applied, with the significance level set at $\alpha = 0.05$, confirming that the improvements in accuracy, recall, and F1-score are statistically significant and unlikely to be attributable to random variation. The corresponding effect size, estimated using Cliff's delta, indicates a moderate to strong practical impact of the proposed framework on user interaction outcomes. The observed differences were associated with p-values below 0.01 across all evaluated metrics, further supporting the statistical robustness of the proposed approach.

Nevertheless, while these results provide solid empirical support for the proposed approach, further large-scale validation campaigns and simulation-based evaluations, such as discrete-event modeling, are required to assess system performance under varying user densities, operational constraints, and contextual uncertainty. Together, these findings demonstrate that the framework's proactive, situation-aware design effectively overcomes the limitations of static applications and contributes to the development of truly human-centered E-Business Information Systems.

Ethical and privacy considerations were taken into account during the design and evaluation of the proposed framework. The prototype application collects contextual and behavioral data exclusively for research purposes and only after obtaining informed consent from participants. All collected interaction logs were anonymized prior to analysis, and no personally identifiable information was stored in the experimental dataset.

Furthermore, the architecture is designed to support privacy-preserving data management strategies, including local processing of contextual signals and the potential integration of privacy-aware mechanisms such as differential privacy or federated learning in future implementations. These design choices aim to ensure transparency, user trust, and compliance with data protection regulations (Table 2).

Table 2. Provides a structured comparison between the proposed framework and existing EBIS approaches, highlighting how formal modeling, semantic reasoning, and probabilistic inference enable predictive, domain-independent, and human-centered system behavior.

Requirement	Existing EBIS Approaches	Proposed Framework
Semantic Interoperability	API/schema-based integration	Ontology-driven knowledge layer
Predictive Adaptation	Rule-based or reactive logic	Bayesian inference and projection
Human-Centered Design	Persona-based customization	Persona + Situation Awareness
Workflow Formalization	Informal process models	Model-driven, multilevel architecture
Domain Generalization	Domain-specific solutions	Domain-agnostic framework

To ensure traceability between system requirements and architectural design, the proposed framework explicitly maps functional and non-functional requirements to the corresponding workflow stages. Semantic interoperability requirements are addressed at the Knowledge Layer through ontology-based formalization, while predictive adaptation requirements are fulfilled by probabilistic inference at the Inference Engine Layer. Human-centered design principles are operationalized at the Application Layer through real-time interface and content adaptation. This structured mapping enables a direct comparison with existing EBIS frameworks, demonstrating how the proposed approach extends prior solutions by integrating formal modeling, predictive reasoning, and domain-independent adaptability within a unified architecture.

In addition to the comparison with the static baseline system, the proposed framework can be positioned with respect to existing adaptive recommender systems described in the literature. For example, situation-aware architectures such as SitAdapt [11] primarily rely on rule-based adaptation mechanisms triggered by detected context patterns, while persona-based tourism recommenders mainly personalize content based on predefined user profiles.

In contrast, the framework proposed in this work introduces two key innovations: (i) the integration of ontology-based semantic representation of contextual dimensions, enabling structured reasoning over heterogeneous context data, and (ii) the use of probabilistic Bayesian inference combined with structural learning algorithms, allowing the system to dynamically learn causal dependencies among contextual variables and anticipate future situations.

This combination enables predictive adaptation that goes beyond rule-based personalization and supports a fully situation-aware decision-making workflow.

5 Conclusions and Future Perspectives

In this work, we addressed the growing need for adaptability and proactivity in E-Business Information Systems (EBIS), highlighting the limitations of traditional decision-making models in dynamic and data-driven contexts. To overcome these challenges, we proposed an integrated framework, methodology, and architecture that places Situation Awareness (SA) at the center of human-centered system design. Our approach stands out for its ability to realize the entire SA cycle, perception, understanding, and, above all, projection, through a synergy between a multilevel architecture, semantic ontologies for the formalization of knowledge, and Bayesian probabilistic models for inference and prediction.

The experimental validation, conducted through a case study in the complex domain of cultural tourism at the Archaeological Park of Pompeii, provided empirical evidence of the framework's effectiveness. The results not only demonstrated a significant increase in quantitative performance (with improvements in accuracy, recall, and F1-score) compared to a static control system, but also confirmed, through qualitative metrics, a user experience perceived as more useful, intuitive, and satisfying. Therefore, the main contribution of this work lies in the proposal of a holistic methodology that equips EBISs with the ability to anticipate user needs and adapt proactively, transforming digital interaction into a more innovative and more resilient experience.

The future prospects of this research are manifold and focus on extending the framework to address emerging challenges. Although the proposed framework has been validated within the cultural tourism domain, its architectural and methodological principles are inherently domain-agnostic. The same perception–understanding–projection cycle can be transferred to other EBIS contexts such as smart retail, digital public services, healthcare service platforms, and logistics ecosystems. In these domains, contextual dimensions (e.g., customer intent, service demand, operational constraints) can be modeled through domain-specific ontologies while preserving the same probabilistic inference and adaptive workflow mechanisms. This highlights the potential of the framework as a general-purpose reference architecture for human-centered, adaptive digital business systems. Among the most promising directions are the integration with Digital Twin technologies to create virtual models that are even richer and more dynamic of the operational context, the exploration of blockchain to ensure transparency and reliability of interactions in decentralized ecosystems, and the development of Explainable AI (XAI) models. The latter direction is particularly crucial to increase user trust, making the system's decision-making processes transparent and understandable and consolidating the transition to e-business systems that are not only intelligent but also reliable and responsible.

References

1. Barra, P., Giammetti, M., Tortora, A., Della Greca, A.: Redefining interaction in a digital twin laboratory with mixed reality, pp. 295–307 (2024). https://doi.org/10.1007/978-3-031-60611-3_21

2. Dobrescu, R., Merezeanu, D., Mocanu, S.: Context-aware control and monitoring system with IoT and cloud support. Comput. Electron. Agric. **160**, 91–99 (2019). https://doi.org/10.1016/j.compag.2019.03.005
3. Tekinbaş, K.S., Jagannath, K., Lyngs, U., Slovák, P.: Designing for youth-centered moderation and community governance in minecraft. ACM Trans. Comput.-Human Interact. **28**(4), 1–41 (2021). https://doi.org/10.1145/3450290
4. Cantone, A.A., Cossentino, G., Sebillo, M., Vitiello, G.: People and technology: an investigation of the adoption of artificial intelligence in the kinesiology context, pp. 307–318 (2024).https://doi.org/10.1007/978-3-031-60615-1_21
5. Endsley, M.R.: Toward a theory of situation awareness in dynamic systems. Human Fact. J. Human Fact. Ergon. Soc. **37**(1), 32–64 (1995). https://doi.org/10.1518/001872095779049543
6. Fernando, E., Meyliana, M., Warnars, H.L.H.S., Abdurachman, E.: Key strategic issues pharmaceutical industry of SCM: a systematic literature review. Bull. Electr. Eng. Inf. **9**(2), 808–817 (2020). https://doi.org/10.11591/eei.v9i2.1264
7. Endsley, M.R.: Designing for Situation Awareness (2016). https://doi.org/10.1201/b11371
8. Gualtieri, L., Revolti, A., Dallasega, P.: A human-centered conceptual model for integrating Augmented Reality and Dynamic Digital Models to reduce occupational risks in industrial contexts. Procedia Comput. Sci. **217**, 765–773 (2023). https://doi.org/10.1016/j.procs.2022.12.273
9. Casillo, M., Colace, F., Lorusso, A., Santaniello, D., Valentino, C.: Integrating physical and virtual experiences in cultural tourism: an adaptive multimodal recommender system. IEEE Access **13**, 28353–28368 (2025). https://doi.org/10.1109/ACCESS.2025.3539205
10. Gaeta, A., Loia, V., Lorusso, A., Orciuoli, F., Pascuzzo, A.: Towards a LLM-based intelligent system for detecting propaganda within textual content. Comput. Electr. Eng. **128**, 110765 (2025). https://doi.org/10.1016/j.compeleceng.2025.110765
11. Herdin, C., Märtin, C., Forbrig, P.: SitAdapt: an architecture for situation-aware runtime adaptation of interactive systems, pp. 447–455 (2017). https://doi.org/10.1007/978-3-319-58071-5_33
12. Casillo, M., et al.: A situation awareness approach for smart home management. In: 2021 International Seminar on Machine Learning, Optimization, and Data Science (ISMODE) , pp. 260–265. IEEE (2022). https://doi.org/10.1109/ISMODE53584.2022.9742901
13. Casillo, M., Colace, F., Lorusso, A., Santaniello, D., Valentino, C.: A multilevel graph approach for IoT-based complex scenario management through situation awareness and semantic approaches. J. Reliab. Intell. Environ. **10**(4), 395–411 (2024). https://doi.org/10.1007/s40860-024-00224-0
14. Yau, S.S., Liu, J.: Incorporating situation awareness in service specifications. In: Ninth IEEE International Symposium on Object and Component-Oriented Real-Time Distributed Computing (ISORC'06), pp. 287–294. IEEE (2006).https://doi.org/10.1109/ISORC.2006.39
15. Yau, S.S., Gong, H., Huang, D., Gao, W., Zhu, L.: Specification, decomposition and agent synthesis for situation-aware service-based systems. J. Syst. Softw. **81**(10), 1663–1680 (2008). https://doi.org/10.1016/j.jss.2008.02.035
16. Pogmore, A.C., Davies, R.J., Cooke, N.J.: Virtual versus reality: a systematic review of real-world built environment tasks performed in CAVEs and a framework for performance and experience evaluation. Virtual Worlds **3**(4), 536–571 (2024). https://doi.org/10.3390/virtualworlds3040028
17. Addesso, R., Pingaro, S., Bisceglia, B., Baldantoni, D.: Sustainable tourism and conservation of underground ecosystems through airflow and particle distribution modeling. Sustainability **14**(13), 7979 (2022). https://doi.org/10.3390/su14137979
18. Märtin, C., Asta, P., Bissinger, B.: Optimizing the digital customer journey – improving user experience by persona-based and situation-aware adaptations, pp. 141–148 (2020). https://doi.org/10.1007/978-3-030-47595-6_18

19. Thorne, J., Vlachos, A., Christodoulopoulos, C., Mittal, A.: FEVER: a large-scale dataset for fact extraction and VERification. In: Proceedings of the 2018 Conference of the North American Chapter of the Association for Computational Linguistics: Human Language Technologies, vol. 1 (Long Papers), pp. 809–819. Association for Computational Linguistics, Stroudsburg (2018). https://doi.org/10.18653/v1/N18-1074
20. Hogan, A., et al.: Knowledge graphs. ACM Comput. Surv. **54**(4), 1–37 (2022). https://doi.org/10.1145/3447772
21. Colace, F., Lombardi, M., Pascale, F., Santaniello, D., Tucker, A., Villani, P.: MuG: a multilevel graph representation for big data interpretation. In: Proceedings - 20th International Conference on High Performance Computing and Communications, 16th International Conference on Smart City and 4th International Conference on Data Science and Systems, HPCC/SmartCity/DSS 2018, pp. 1408–1413 (2019). https://doi.org/10.1109/HPCC/SmartCity/DSS.2018.00233
22. Santo, M.D., Fabbri, L., Mosca, R., Lombardi, M., Romano, A., Santaniello, D.: A Multilevel approach to recommend working paths in industry 4.0. In: Proceedings of 2020 IEEE International Conference on Teaching, Assessment, and Learning for Engineering, TALE 2020, pp. 754–757 (2020).https://doi.org/10.1109/TALE48869.2020.9368327
23. Casillo, M., Colace, F., Lorusso, A., Santaniello, D., Valentino, C.: A multilevel graph approach for IoT-based complex scenario management through situation awareness and semantic approaches. J. Reliab. Intell. Environ. **10**(4), 395–411 (2024). https://doi.org/10.1007/s40860-024-00224-0

Mapping Consumer Complaints in the Electric Vehicle Market: Evidence from Social Text Mining

Elena Kim and Jaewon Choi(✉)

Department of Business Administration, Soonchunhyang University, Asan, South Korea
jaewonchoi@sch.ac.kr

Abstract. As the electric vehicle (EV) market enters a more mature phase, consumer dissatisfaction is increasingly articulated through negative discussions on social media platforms. This study analyzes 134,374 eV-related Reddit comments posted between 2023 and 2024 using sentiment analysis, LDA topic modeling, and keyword co-occurrence network analysis to identify the key drivers of consumer complaints. The findings reveal three dominant complaint themes: (1) perceived mismatches between brand value and cost-effectiveness, (2) usage constraints associated with driving range and charging convenience, and (3) concerns regarding battery performance and declining trust in manufacturers. Grounded in expectation disconfirmation theory and social media marketing perspectives, this study demonstrates how text-mining approaches can systematically capture post-adoption user experiences and transform unstructured digital feedback into actionable insights for product design, service improvement, and strategic communication.

Keywords: Electric Vehicles · Consumer Complaints · User-generated Content · Social Media Analytics · Topic modeling · Post-adoption Behavior

1 Introduction

The global electric vehicle (EV) market has continued to grow in recent years. According to 2023 data from [1], the global EV market grew at an annual rate of 33.5%. However, market growth is expected to slow down somewhat from 2024 due to the impact of short-term economic uncertainty. The current trend of slowing growth can be attributed to the adjustment of production and sales strategies of finished car companies against the backdrop of a macroeconomic downturn. Based on data from the [2, 3], the Chinese and European markets are forecast to face a significant slowdown in growth. Nonetheless, the European market is expected to rebound mainly on electric vehicles in the second half of 2024. The North American market is not growing well overall, affected by Tesla battery supply issues and delays in launching low-cost models by other automakers. Asia and other regions are expected to maintain relatively stable growth led by major automakers in each country. This global market trend not only indicates that the electric vehicle

Published by Springer Nature Switzerland AG 2027
J. Kim et al. (Eds.): EBISION 2025, IFIP AICT 786, pp. 33–48, 2027.
https://doi.org/10.1007/978-3-032-26616-3_3

industry is in a structural transition phase but also highlights that consumer acceptance and dissatisfaction feedback play an important role in future growth engines. Therefore, it is necessary to deeply analyze the consumer's specific dissatisfaction with the electric vehicle technology, services, and policy environment from the perspective of user experience and feedback to discover the innovative potential and market optimization direction behind it.

In terms of regional distribution, China is the world's largest market, with sales reaching 53.4% in the first quarter of 2023 with 13.92 million units, followed by Europe and North America with 26.0% and 13.0%, respectively, according to a report by SNE Research [1]. It should be noted that despite the leading positions in the Chinese and European markets, growth engines are slowing, while other parts of Asia and the "other" market are showing constant growth momentum. On the manufacturer side, data from Q1 to Q3 2023 showed that BYD had the largest deliveries of 5.8 million units, followed by TESLA (5.25 million units, 16.7%) and Gely (2.47 million units, 7.9%). Traditional automakers such as Volkswagen (VW), Stellantis, Hyundai & Kia are also accelerating their deployment to the new energy vehicle sector, gradually forming a diverse competitive landscape. At the same time as the global market expands, consumers still have many gaps between their actual experience and expectations of electric vehicles, especially complaints about battery mileage, safety, convenience of charging, and policy support. This negative feedback is frequent on social platforms and comment areas and has become potential drivers for corporate innovation and policy optimization. Therefore, deep excavation of structural problems reflected by negative comments from consumers will help promote technological improvement and strategic restructuring in the electric vehicle market. With the global spread of electric vehicles, related safety and infrastructure problems are also increasingly emerging, and they are an important cause of consumer dissatisfaction. Several accidents involving electric vehicles have occurred in recent years, causing the public to be highly interested in the risk of using them. Such cases highlight the practical challenges electric vehicles face in urban settings [4]. On the one hand, parking lot management has set entry limits for safety considerations, on the other hand, electric vehicle users are strongly dissatisfied with the uniform policy, and they believe the lack of reasonable management measures will affect the convenience of using and willingness to purchase the vehicle. In key urban areas, the failure of electric vehicles to enter underground parking spaces in the absence of ground parking space resources will have a significant impact on day-to-day use and market acceptance.

Therefore, the controversy over the safety of electric vehicles and the lack of support infrastructure have become important variables that affect consumer satisfaction and restrict market expansion. Consumers' complaints about safety norms, convenience of charging, fairness of policy are becoming increasingly clear in the form of online comments. These negative public opinions not only reflect the "pain points" of the user's actual experience of use but also provide a true database for companies to optimize their product design and complete the government's support policies. The way to scientifically identify and respond to these structural complaints will directly determine the sustainable growth path of the future electric vehicle market. Given the shortage issues revealed in the rapid development of the electric vehicle market and the resulting widespread dissatisfaction of consumers, systematic identification and analysis of these complaints have become an important entry point in promoting industrial innovation and policy optimization.

When aggregated and analyzed at scale, negative reviews can be perceived not only as expressions of dissatisfaction but also as informational signals of the persistent gaps between consumer expectations and real-world conditions. Prior studies on electric vehicle consumers have generated important insights through questionnaires and interviews, then used to aggregate sentiment measures. However, these approaches often abstract away from the complexity of unstructured opinions in digital environments. As online platforms increasingly serve as primary channels for post-adoption evaluation, there is the lack of systematic research that can translate large-scale unstructured complaint data into interpretable analytical structures. This methodological gap limits the ability of organizations to fully leverage digital feedback for evidence-based decision-making. At the same time, because this study relies on Reddit data, the findings should be interpreted as patterns of online complaint discourse rather than as fully generalizable estimates of the broader EV customer base.

Therefore, this study aims to identify key factors influencing consumer complaints through text mining analysis of online reviews related to electric vehicles, and to explore the mechanisms by which these factors affect consumer dissatisfaction and feedback patterns. To address this objective, the present study adopts a digital feedback analysis approach that leverages large-scale user-generated content from social media. By applying text mining techniques to post-adoption complaints, the study seeks to move beyond anecdotal observations and toward a systematic understanding of recurring dissatisfaction structures within the electric vehicle market.

This study systematically organizes and analyzes negative comments posted by consumers on social media platforms using text-mining techniques. Focusing on key functional aspects of electric vehicles (e.g., driving range, battery performance, charging convenience, and overall driving experience), the study identifies the primary sources of consumer dissatisfaction and provides evidence-based insights that can support firms in improving product functionality and service quality.

Building on this background, the study addresses two research questions. RQ1: From a technological, service, and policy perspective, what factors most strongly drive consumer dissatisfaction in the EV market? RQ2: How do consumer complaints function as a feedback mechanism that shapes technological innovation and market strategy adjustments in EV firms?

By answering these questions, this study contributes to the growing literature on digital feedback and market learning by showing how large-scale, unstructured social media data can be transformed into structured, decision-relevant knowledge. Although this research does not focus on the design of enterprise platforms per se, it highlights the role of social media analytics as a feedback-processing layer that enables organizations to monitor emerging issues, learn from post-adoption experiences, and support strategic decision-making in dynamic digital market environments. By transforming complaint discourse into structured thematic categories, the study also highlights how social media analytics may function as an input layer for complaint triage, issue monitoring, service prioritization, and product-planning support in enterprise information systems.

2 Theoretical Background

2.1 Prior Research on the Electric Vehicle Market

As global environmental policies have become stricter and sustainable technologies have developed in recent years, the industrial structure and consumption behavior of electric vehicles as important means of clean energy transfer have gained researchers' attention. From discussions on initial affordability and policy support to studies focusing on more action-oriented perspectives such as consumer awareness, usage experience, and satisfaction in recent years, existing studies have provided a solid foundation for model building and variable extraction in this study. Although the initial purchase cost of an electric vehicle is relatively high, it has an overall economic advantage due to low energy and maintenance costs for long-term [5]. Reports from [2] confirmed the rapid growth trend of the electric vehicle market from a macro perspective, especially with the Chinese market accounting for more than 50% of the global market, showing a strong growth engine. Consumers' perception and experience of electric vehicle technology have also become important variables that affect acceptance and satisfaction. Consumers' technology familiarity and actual driving experience have a great influence on product evaluation and willingness to adopt [6]. At the microscopic level, we analyzed non-owners and real-world user experience data, investigated the determinants of pure EV user satisfaction (especially cost savings, mileage, and rates) and their impact on share buyback/recommendation intentions. Previous research has discussed the structure and behavioral factors of the EV market from various angles, but it has mainly focused on traditional questionnaires or interviews and has not sufficiently integrated them into information sources that allow consumers to quantify the "discontent feelings" expressed on social media after actual use. The study seeks to structure negative reviews using text mining methods to fill gaps in existing research at the "post-action feedback" level and further reveal the relationship between consumer complaints and corporate innovation and market acceptance [7, 8].

2.2 Text Analytics of Consumer Reviews

With the mass emergence of user-generated content (UGCs), comments from consumers on social platforms, forums, and e-commerce websites are increasingly important data sources for understanding user needs and complaints. Compared to traditional research methods, online reviews have more integrity, timeliness, and autonomous expressiveness, especially in high-interest products such as electric vehicles, users often express their experience of use and negative emotions through review channels. [10] shows through the analysis of Weibo review that brand, convenience of charging, battery technology, safety, and policy impact are key factors influencing the decision to purchase electric vehicles, and the public's attitude is generally positive, providing important reference materials for industry development and policy making. Consumers who buy new energy vehicles are still used to comparing them to brands or models of internal combustion engines. Consumers of new energy vehicles pay more attention to service and quality of service as they purchase and use the vehicle. Prior research has examined consumer and media perceptions of electric vehicles using online discussion data identifying recurring concerns such as driving-range anxiety and price sensitivity [10, 11]. While these studies confirm the usefulness of user-generated content for understanding consumer attitudes, most of these analyses remain descriptive, focusing on sentiment polarity or isolated topic frequencies. As a result, negative reviews are treated as expressions of opinion rather than as structured analytical inputs with the capability of theory-driven explanation support.

2.3 The Role of Consumer Complaints in EV Innovation

Consumer dissatisfaction not only reflects barriers to experience in use, but it also serves as an important driving force for technological innovation and market system improvement. According to prior studies, complaints from EV users are often focused on charging inconvenience, lack of mileage, safety risks and high purchasing costs. These factors are shown as constraining market acceptance but at the same time they are prompting manufacturers and policymakers to improve technologies, infrastructure and service systems.

Empirical evidence indicates that consumers place greater emphasis on immediate and practical concerns, such as safety risks rather than environmental benefits and long-term cost savings [12]. This suggests that technological and service-related imperfections remain critical obstacles to EV adoption. Existing research further demonstrates that consumer resistance is often linked to specific usage-stage concerns rather than generalized rejection of EVs. For example, concerns about charging duration and equipment reliability are particularly salient [13], while those regarding breakdown events, such as failures during driving, are more pronounced in the early stages of market diffusion [14]. From a cost perspective, market acceptance is expected to remain constrained until battery costs decline sufficiently to achieve operational cost comparability with conventional vehicles [15]. Earlier studies also emphasized that limited public and workplace charging infrastructure restricted EV use primarily to home-based charging, thereby constraining their functionality as secondary vehicles for broader mobility needs [16]. More recent policy-oriented research confirms that the availability of public charging facilities and access to workplace charging have become key levers influencing the pace of EV diffusion [17].

Building on this literature, consumer complaints can be conceptually categorized into functional impairments (e.g., charging technology, price, and driving range) and situational impairments (e.g., infrastructure availability and safety-related concerns). These impairment-based complaints simultaneously constitute sources of resistance to market expansion and signals for firms to optimize core performance and service provision. Accordingly, this study integrates complaint categories identified in prior research with text-mining results derived from online reviews to examine the specific linguistic expressions and semantic structures of consumer dissatisfaction, thereby exploring their implications for innovation trajectories and market acceptance of electric vehicles.

2.4 Theoretical Background on Consumer Reviews and Text Mining

Web Consumer Reviews. Consumer reviews refer to user-generated evaluations in which individuals share and communicate their experiences with products or services through online platforms. With the widespread diffusion of digital platforms, online reviews have become not only a primary channel for business-to-consumer interaction but also a valuable data source for research on brand management and consumer perception. Prior studies indicate that consumer reviews capture more than subjective emotional reactions; when analyzed using structured analytical techniques, they can reveal systematic patterns embedded in large-scale textual data. For example, topic modeling enables the identification of recurring themes and high-frequency issues within extensive review corpora, thereby supporting applications such as brand monitoring, advertising optimization, and crisis management [18].

Text Mining Techniques. Text mining is a data-driven analytical approach designed to extract structured information from large-scale unstructured textual data [19]. In contrast to survey-based methods, which rely on predefined constructs and limited sample sizes, text mining enables the processing of naturally occurring language, generated through online platforms. This approach allows us to identify latent semantic patterns, recurring themes, and co-occurrence structures within textual corpora. In the context of consumer research, text mining is particularly suited to the analysis of complaint data, as it captures unsolicited post-adoption evaluations and usage-related feedback. Accordingly, this study applies text mining techniques to negative electric vehicle–related social media content to systematically transform unstructured user narratives into analytically interpretable representations for subsequent modeling and interpretation.

2.5 Core Theoretical Foundations

Expectation Disconfirmation Theory (EDT). Expectation Disconfirmation Theory (EDT) is an important theoretical framework for explaining the mechanism of consumer (unsatisfaction) formation. Conflict occurs when consumers' actual experience with a product or service falls short of expectations, affecting future behavioral intentions [20]. In the EV situation, this theory is particularly appropriate. In this context, negative online reviews are treated as observable expressions of expectation disconfirmation that emerge during actual vehicle use. For example, automakers typically emphasize the maximum charging efficiency and service time supported by EVs in marketing, but when consumers find distinct differences from advertising in real-world use, "expectation gaps" are likely, which can develop into negative reviews or brand boycotts [21].

In this study, we leverage the Expectation Disconfirmation Theory (EDT) theoretical framework to explore how differences in consumer expectations for technical performance (e.g., charging efficiency), service experience (e.g., customer service and repair), and policy support (e.g., subsidy and parking policies) contribute significantly to complaints. This study adopts the view that the 'expectation discrepancy' that occurs in the process of consumers using electric vehicles is a key psychological mechanism that forms negative emotions and affects their acceptance attitude.

Social Media Marketing. Social media marketing is an important theoretical tool that has been widely used in the field of consumer behavior research and brand communication in recent years. Social media means "online platforms and systems that allow interaction, collaboration, and content sharing among users [22, 23]. Examples include Reddit, Weibo, forums, and evaluation sites. Social media is further defined as an "interactive information delivery mechanism based on Web2.0 technology", highlighting the importance of real-time and engagement in the marketing system. In the EV sector, social media is not only the primary route of expressing consumer opinion, but it is also the key point of contact for companies to gather user feedback and coordinate their market strategy [24].

Therefore, negative comments on social media platforms are not only expressions of genuine dissatisfaction from consumers, but also a window for brands and policymakers to understand market sentiment and optimize their strategies. Combined with social media marketing theory, this study highlights how negative reviews function not only as expressions of dissatisfaction but also as feedback signals that circulate through platform-mediated environments and influence organizational response and market perception.

3 Research Methodology

3.1 Data Collection

The data in this study is taken from Reddit, a global social media platform, and focuses on users' online comments and discussions about electric vehicles. Reddit is particularly suitable for examining post-adoption consumer feedback because it supports long-form discussions and spontaneous experience sharing among users. Compared with brand-controlled platforms, Reddit provides relatively independent and experience-driven consumer narratives, making it appropriate for analyzing authentic complaints related to EV use.

Using the Pushshift API, original posts and comments containing keywords related to electric vehicles (e.g., "electric vehicle", "EV", "electric car") were collected from January 2023 to December 2024. The dataset includes multiple EV-related subreddits such as r/electricvehicles, r/electriccars, r/teslamotors, and r/EVcharging, which are closely associated with discussions of EV technology, usage experience, and policy issues. A total of 134,374 user-generated content (UGC) items were collected.

The collected fields include comment body, post title, post and comment ID, author, creation time (created_utc), comment score, and subreddit name. This metadata structure enables both textual analysis and contextual interpretation of consumer discussions, providing a sufficient empirical basis for sentiment analysis and topic modeling.

3.2 Data Cleaning and Preprocessing

To ensure the accuracy and consistency of the analysis, the original text data from Reddit was cleaned and preprocessed in this study. First, comments containing advertisements, unrelated content, duplicate entries, non-English text, or empty messages were removed. This step aimed at retaining only meaningful EV-related user discussions.

Second, all retained text was converted to lowercase, and URLs, HTML tags, special characters, punctuation, and numerical noise were removed. Third, tokenization and stop-word removal were conducted using Python-based natural language processing tools, including NLTK and regular expressions.

Through multiple rounds of filtering and preprocessing, 32,384 valid textual records were retained for subsequent analysis, primarily due to the exclusion of off-topic, duplicate, and low-information content. These preprocessing steps were applied consistently across the retained corpus to ensure comparability between sentiment analysis, topic modeling, and keyword co-occurrence analysis.

3.3 Sentiment Analysis

Sentiment analysis was conducted to obtain an overall understanding of the emotional distribution within the collected EV-related discussions and to identify complaint-oriented content for further analysis. Prior research has shown that sentiment analysis is effective for identifying general emotional tendencies in large-scale textual data and is widely applied across domains such as marketing, public opinion analysis, and consumer research [25].

In this study, sentiment analysis was performed using TextBlob, a Python-based NLP library that provides lexicon-based sentiment polarity scores for textual data [25]. TextBlob was selected because it provides an interpretable lexicon-based polarity measure suitable for large-scale exploratory screening of short consumer comments. Each comment was assigned a polarity score ranging from -1 to $+1$. Following common practice in lexicon-based sentiment analysis, comments were classified as positive (polarity > 0.1), negative (polarity < -0.1), or neutral (between -0.1 and 0.1). The threshold of ± 0.1 was adopted to reduce overclassification of weakly valenced comments and to distinguish clearly negative complaint-oriented content from neutral discussion.

It is important to note that sentiment analysis in this study serves a descriptive and exploratory purpose, providing an overview of emotional tendencies rather than acting as the primary analytical mechanism. The main analytical focus of this research lies in structurally examining negative reviews through topic modeling.

The results indicate that approximately 35.5% of comments were classified as positive, 52.0% as neutral, and 12.5% as negative. Negative reviews were extracted as the focal subset for subsequent topic modeling and complaint structure analysis, as they directly reflect post-adoption dissatisfaction and expectation disconfirmation.

3.4 Topic Modeling Using LDA

To identify latent thematic structures underlying consumer dissatisfaction, this study applies Latent Dirichlet Allocation (LDA) to the subset of comments classified as negative through sentiment analysis. LDA is a probabilistic generative model that represents documents as mixtures of latent topics and topics as distributions over words, enabling the extraction of recurring semantic patterns from unstructured textual data [26]. In this study, LDA was applied to review texts that were pre-classified as negative through sentiment analysis, thereby focusing the analysis on dissatisfaction-related content.

To improve analytical robustness and topic concentration, multiple LDA models were estimated with the number of topics varying from 2 to 15. Topic quality was evaluated using the c_v coherence metric, which assesses the semantic consistency of high-probability words within topics and has been shown to align closely with human interpretability. The upper bound of $k = 15$ was selected to capture sufficient semantic diversity in consumer complaints while avoiding excessive topic fragmentation common in short-form social media texts. Coherence trends were examined across candidate topic numbers to evaluate the trade-off between model complexity and interpretability.

Based on this evaluation, a three-topic solution was selected as it achieved relatively high coherence while maintaining clear semantic distinction among topics. This configuration enabled the consolidation of heterogeneous complaint expressions into a limited number of interpretable dissatisfaction dimensions, providing a structured representation of consumer feedback suitable for subsequent theoretical interpretation and managerial analysis. Topic Coherence scores are presented in Fig. 1.

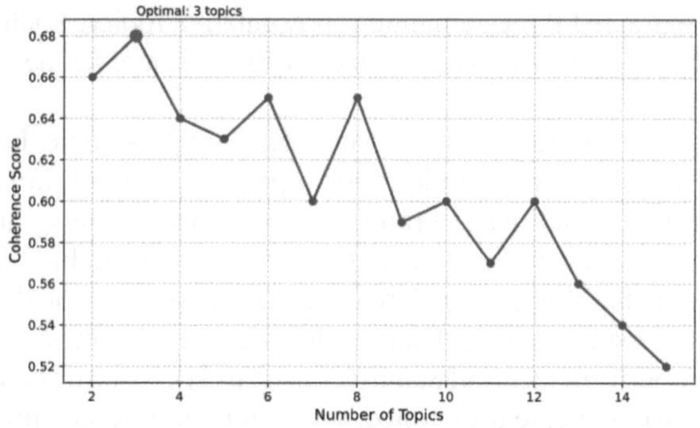

Fig. 1. Topic Coherence Scores for LDA Model Selection

For each topic, the system outputs the top 10 keywords and their corresponding probability values. Higher weights mean that words are more representative and more semantic-centric in the topic. These keywords and weight values form the basis of subject tag naming and subsequent semantic interpretation and provide an initial set of variables for core node screening in co-occurrence network analysis.

4 Results

4.1 Sentiment Analysis Results

The study first identified overall user attitude trends by emotionally classifying 32,384 Reddit user reviews related to electric vehicles. After using the TextBlob tool to analyze the polarity score of the text, emotions are divided into three categories: positive (score > 0.1), negative (score < -0.1), and neutral (between -0.1 and 0.1).

According to the results of the analysis, 35.5% of the comments expressed positive emotions, 52.0%were neutral, and only 12.5% expressed distinct negative emotions. Although the overall attitude is optimistic, these negative comments intensively reflect the key complaints of users during the use of electric vehicles, as shown in Fig. 2.

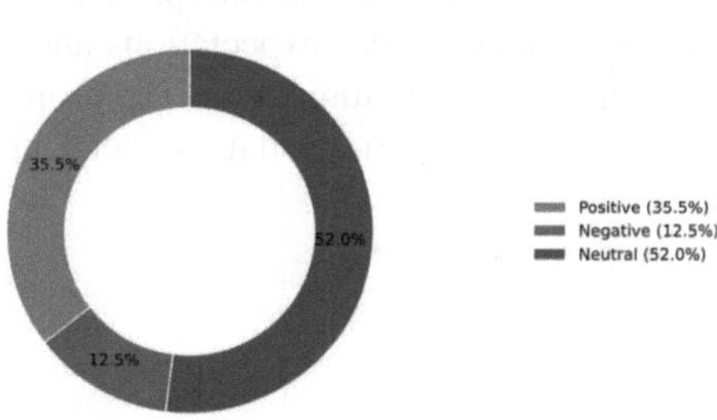

Fig. 2. Sentiment Distribution of EV-related Reddit Comments

4.2 LDA Topic Modeling Results

To systematically identify the main topics of consumer concern in negative reviews, we conducted a study to model preprocessed negative texts using the Latent Dirichlet Allocation (LDA) method. As a result of optimization through the topic coherence score (0.68), we finally extracted three semantic representative topics. Each topic consists of Top10 high-weight keywords and summarizes artificial semantic labels in combination with keyword context.

Topic 1: "Tesla", "Model", "Price" and "Ear" in this topic keyword represent the differences in consumer expectations for a particular brand, model, and price-to-performance, reflecting variations in brand perception and hesitancy in purchasing.

Topic 2 (speed and charging convenience): Represented by "range", "charge", "mile", and "trip", it highlights users' realistic complaints about the convenience of using electric vehicles such as long-distance driving and charging facility distribution.

Topic 3 (battery performance and manufacturing trust): Keywords "battery", "china", "company" and "trust" indicate user concerns about battery safety, production site trust (e.g., from China), and supply chain transparency (Table 1).

Table 1. Top 10 Keywords and Weights for Each Topic

Topic1		Topic2		Topic3	
word	weight	word	weight	word	weight
tesla	0.046	car	0.055	battery	0.029
year	0.026	ev	0.042	people	0.018
model	0.017	range	0.015	u	0.016
new	0.012	charge	0.014	china	0.014
price	0.012	vehicle	0.014	dont	0.014
im	0.009	also	0.014	good	0.014
sure	0.009	mile	0.013	company	0.013
never	0.008	time	0.013	chinese	0.011
money	0.008	much	0.012	thing	0.01
look	0.008	even	0.011	way	0.01

Each topic represents a major axis of EV user complaints, and the core keywords and semantic structures of these topics can be interpreted as coming from multiple factors such as mismatch between consumer expectations and experiences, functional product defects, and failures in brand communication. The proportions of each topic are visualized in Fig. 3 and can serve as foundational data for deriving strategic implications.

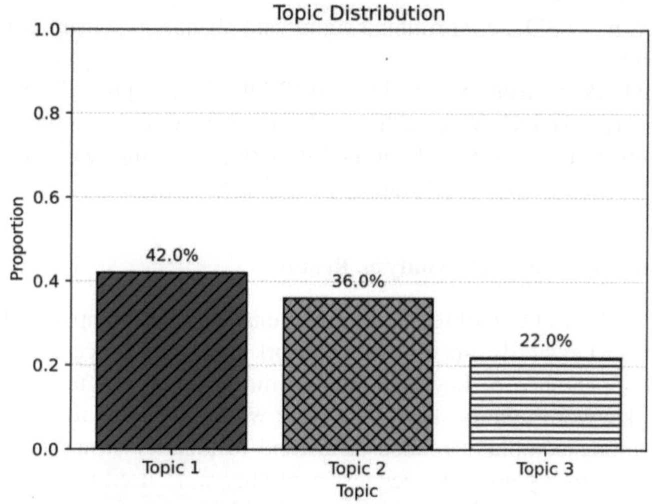

Fig. 3. Topic Distribution across Negative Reviews

The changes in topic distribution across years are presented in Fig. 4. In 2023, negative consumer reviews were primarily concentrated on Topic 1 (brand/value for money), which accounted for 40.35%, followed by Topic 2 (battery/charging, 32.26%) and Topic 3 (battery/trust, 27.39%). In 2024, the share of Topic 1 rose to 43.68%, indicating a continuous increase in complaints related to brand purchases, while Topic 3 declined by about 7% to 25.02%.

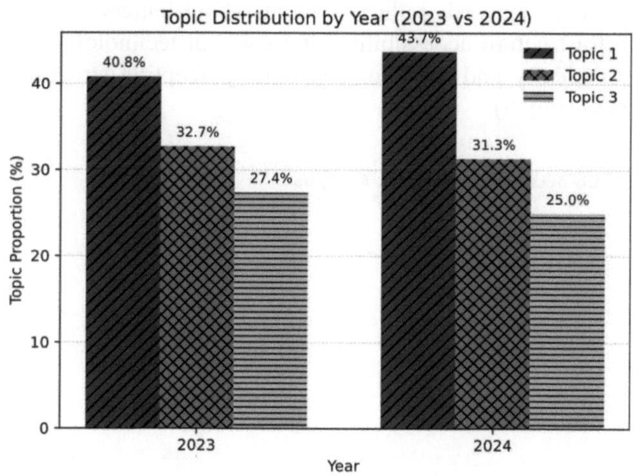

Fig. 4. Topic Distribution by Year

To test the statistical significance of these shifts, the study applied a chi-square test to compare the topic distributions between 2023 and 2024. The results showed $\chi^2 =$

31.301, df = 2, $p < 0.001$, confirming a significant change in consumer focus over the two-year period.

Notably, battery' is strongly linked to "trust", "fire", and "quality", emphasizing that consumer concerns extend beyond technical defects to encompass emotional anxiety and broader skepticism about brand reliability. Similarly, 'charging' and 'charging station' are connected to "accessibility", "waiting", and "cost".

4.3 Co-occurrence Network Analysis Results

To complement the LDA findings with a relational view of complaint discourse, this study conducted a keyword co-occurrence network analysis. Co-occurrence was defined as the shared appearance of keywords within the same review text. Based on these within-review keyword relationships, a network was constructed to visualize semantic associations among complaint-related terms and to identify structurally central keywords. Degree centrality and betweenness centrality were used to assess which terms were most strongly connected and which played bridging roles across thematic clusters. This analysis was used as an interpretive complement to the topic-modeling results by showing how major complaint-related keywords were connected within the broader discourse structure. The network analysis revealed that 'car' emerged as the central node of the entire network, with "electric", "EV", "people", "drive" and "battery" appearing as closely connected keywords. This structure suggests that discussions about electric vehicles are strongly connected not only to technical specifications but also to issues of social acceptance. Furthermore, keywords such as "battery", "range", "charging", "China", and "charging station" exhibited high degree centrality and betweenness centrality across multiple clusters, indicating they constitute core themes of consumer dissatisfaction. These keywords reflect concerns about battery reliability, range anxiety, charging infrastructure accessibility, and national technological trustworthiness, revealing the complexity and depth of consumer perception structures through their interconnectedness (Fig. 5).

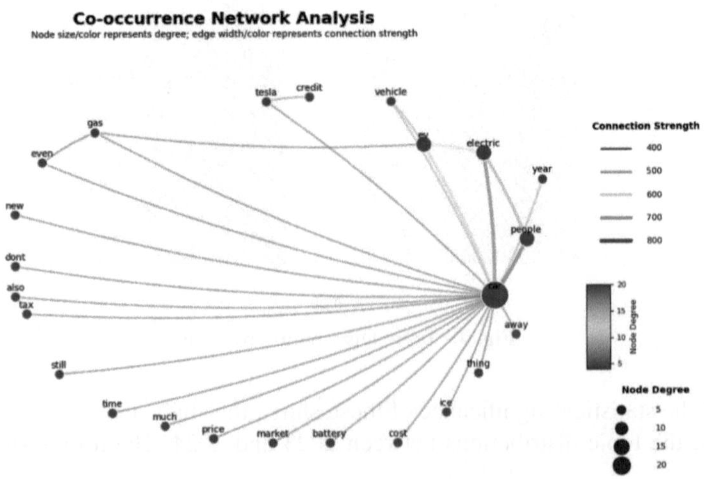

Fig. 5. Co-Occurrence Network Analysis

5 Discussion

5.1 Structural Features of Consumer Complaints About Electric Vehicles

This study examines the structure of consumer dissatisfaction in the electric vehicle market by applying Latent Dirichlet Allocation (LDA) and keyword co-occurrence analysis to large-scale negative online reviews. The results show that consumer complaints are not isolated emotional reactions. Instead, they form a multi-dimensional structure organized around brand value perceptions, technological usability, manufacturer trust, and perceived product credibility. Complaints related to charging convenience and driving-range anxiety, captured in Topic 2, exhibit the strongest co-occurrence intensity, suggesting a persistent gap between perceived performance and expected value during actual vehicle use.

The findings are interpreted through two complementary theoretical lenses: Expectation Disconfirmation Theory (EDT) and Social Media Marketing Theory. From the perspective of EDT, consumer dissatisfaction emerges when post-adoption experiences fail to meet pre-use expectations. In this study, Topic 1 (brand value and purchase considerations) and Topic 2 (driving range and charging convenience) capture expectation mismatch related to price rationality, performance reliability, and ease of use. These misalignments constitute a core psychological mechanism underlying negative consumer evaluations in the EV context.

From a social media marketing perspective, user comments on digital platforms represent more than individual information sharing. They function as socially embedded expressions with amplification and diffusion effects. Topic 3, which includes terms such as "battery", "China", and "trust" reflects collective evaluations that extend beyond technical performance to point on perceptions of product origin, brand credibility, and supply-chain trustworthiness. These shared narratives contribute to the formation of public opinion and influence potential adopters through repeated exposure to online environments.

The results indicate that consumer dissatisfaction in the EV market is shaped by both expectation–performance gaps and the propagation dynamics of social media discourse. This dual interpretation clarifies how negative reviews operate not only as reflections of individual experience but also as informational signals that influence broader market perceptions and brand attitudes.

From a practical perspective, the findings offer several actionable implications for firms and policymakers. First, the identified complaint themes can be operationalized as structured categories in platform-based feedback systems and complaint-monitoring dashboards. For example, recurring dissatisfaction related to charging convenience and driving range can be tracked as a distinct operational category, allowing firms to detect persistent usage barriers and recurring service problems more systematically. Second, the distinction between functional complaints and trust-related complaints may support CRM-based complaint triage and customer-service prioritization. Complaints concerning charging access, mileage, and daily usability may require operational responses such as charging-support improvement, service redesign, or coordination with charging-infrastructure providers, whereas complaints linked to battery safety, quality, and trust may require escalation to quality-assurance, communication, or reputation-management functions. Third, EV manufacturers may use these complaint patterns to identify recurring product-performance problems and support product road mapping decisions, particularly in areas such as battery reliability, charging compatibility, and after-sales support. Finally, repeated references to policy support, parking restrictions, and infrastructure gaps indicate that public institutions also play an important role in reducing post-adoption dissatisfaction. In this sense, the study demonstrates how unstructured digital review data can be translated into actionable information for complaint triage, issue monitoring, support prioritization, product improvement, and evidence-based decision-making in EV-related business environments.

6 Conclusion and Future Research

This study analyzed 134,374 comments from Reddit related to EV to identify recurring patterns of consumer dissatisfaction using sentiment analysis, topic modeling, and keyword co-occurrence analysis. The findings demonstrate that post-adoption dissatisfaction in the EV market follows stable and interpretable structures related to brand value, technological usability, trust, and policy conditions. By translating unstructured social media discourse into structured information, the study highlights the analytical value of digital feedback for understanding market acceptance barriers in platform-mediated environments.

This study has several limitations. First, the analysis is based exclusively on Reddit data. Therefore, the findings may reflect the characteristics, discourse norms, and cultural tendencies of Reddit users rather than the broader EV consumer population. For this reason, the results should be interpreted as patterns of online complaint discourse, not as fully generalizable estimates of overall consumer dissatisfaction. Future research could address this limitation by comparing multiple platforms and cross-cultural datasets. Second, the study adopts a largely static analytical perspective and does not capture how complaint patterns may change over time in response to technological developments, brand actions, or policy interventions. Third, although the analytical procedure was designed to improve interpretability and internal consistency, the study relies on lexicon-based sentiment analysis and unsupervised topic modeling. Additional validation using manually labeled samples, alternative sentiment-analysis methods, or cross-platform datasets would further strengthen confidence in the robustness of the findings. Future studies may therefore extend this work through longitudinal, event-based, and cross-platform designs to examine the evolution and stability of EV-related consumer dissatisfaction more comprehensively. And the last, the preprocessing procedure and sentiment thresholds may influence the composition of the negative-review corpus and, consequently, the themes extracted through topic modeling. For example, stricter polarity thresholds may retain only strongly negative comments, whereas looser thresholds may include more borderline evaluations. Similarly, preprocessing decisions such as duplicate removal, stopword filtering, and text normalization may affect keyword salience and topic formation. Although the analytical procedure was designed to improve interpretability and consistency, future research should compare alternative preprocessing settings and validate the sentiment classification against manually labeled samples to assess topic stability more systematically.

Acknowledgments. This work was supported by the Soonchunhyang University Research Fund. This work was supported by the Ministry of Education of the Republic of Korea and the National Research Foundation of Korea(NRF-2024S1A5A2A01020049).

References

1. SNE Research: Global electric vehicle market and battery supply outlook (2035). https://www.sneresearch.com. Accessed 14 May 2024
2. International Energy Agency: World Energy Outlook 2021. IEA (2021). https://www.iea.org/reports/world-energy-outlook-2021
3. International Energy Agency: Global EV Outlook 2024: Trends and developments in electric vehicle markets. IEA (2024). https://www.iea.org/reports/global-ev-outlook-2024
4. Chosun Ilbo: Single EV fire causes catastrophe: 40 vehicles and five apartment buildings damaged. Aug 2 (2024). https://www.chosun.com/national/incident/2024/08/02/USJ33MN5PBDBNPJF4ZVQWAYGAM/. Accessed 02 Aug 2024
5. Hackbarth, A., Madlener, R.: Consumer preferences for alternative fuel vehicles: a discrete choice analysis. Transp. Res. Part D **25**, 5–17 (2013)
6. Bühler, F., Cocron, P., Neumann, I., Franke, T., Krems, J.F.: Is EV experience related to EV acceptance? Results from a German field study. Transp. Res. Part F **25**, 34–49 (2014)
7. Okada, T., Tamaki, T., Managi, S.: Effect of environmental awareness on purchase intention and satisfaction pertaining to electric vehicles in Japan. Transp. Res. Part D **67**, 503–513 (2019)
8. Kwon, Y., Son, S., Jang, K.: User satisfaction with battery electric vehicles in South Korea. Transp. Res. Part D **82**, 102306 (2020)
9. Wang, X., Cheng, Y., Lv, T., Cai, R.: Fuel vehicles or new energy vehicles: a study on the differentiation of vehicle consumer demand based on online reviews. Mark. Intell. Plan. **41**(8), 1236–1251 (2023)
10. Jiang, X., Everts, J.: Making sense of electric vehicle discussions using sentiment analysis on closely related news and user comments. arXiv:2112.12327 (2021)
11. Carpenter, T.: Measuring and mitigating electric vehicle adoption barriers. Doctoral dissertation, University of Waterloo (2015)
12. Egbue, O., Long, S.: Barriers to widespread adoption of electric vehicles: an analysis of consumer attitudes and perceptions. Energy Policy **48**, 717–729 (2012)
13. Jena, R.: An empirical case study on Indian consumers' sentiment towards electric vehicles: a big data analytics approach. Ind. Mark. Manag. **90**, 605–616 (2020)
14. Eugensson, A., Brännström, M., Frasher, D., Rothoff, M., Solyom, S., Robertsson, A.: Environmental, safety, legal and societal implications of autonomous driving systems. In: Proceedings of the Enhanced Safety of Vehicles (ESV), Seoul, South Korea (2013)
15. Gerssen-Gondelach, S.J., Faaij, A.P.: Performance of batteries for electric vehicles on short and longer term. J. Power Sources **212**, 111–129 (2012)
16. DeLuchi, M., Wang, Q., Sperling, D.: Electric vehicles: performance, life-cycle costs, emissions, and recharging requirements. Transp. Res. Part A **23**(3), 255–278 (1989)
17. Slowik, P., Lutsey, N.: Expanding the electric vehicle market in U.S. cities. ICCT, Washington, DC (2017)
18. Calheiros, A.C., Moro, S., Rita, P.: Sentiment classification of consumer-generated online reviews using topic modeling. J. Hosp. Market. Manag. **26**(7), 675–693 (2017)
19. IBM Corporation: Text mining. https://www.ibm.com/think/topics/text-mining

20. Oliver, R.L.: Conceptualization and measurement of disconfirmation perceptions in the prediction of consumer satisfaction. In: Refining Concepts and Measures of Consumer Satisfaction and Complaining Behavior, pp. 2–6 (1980)
21. Rosenberg, L.J., Czepiel, J.A.: A marketing approach for customer retention. J. Consum. Mark. **1**(2), 45–51 (1984)
22. Koch, M., Richter, A., Schlosser, A.: Produkte zum IT-gestützten Social Networking in Unternehmen. Wirtschaftsinformatik **49**(6), 448 (2007)
23. Seo, E.J., Park, J.W.: Effects of social media marketing activities on brand equity and customer response in the airline industry. J. Air Transp. Manag. **66**, 36–41 (2018)
24. Gunelius, S.: Content Marketing for Dummies. Wiley, Hoboken (2011)
25. Tang, M., Cao, J., Fan, Z., Gong, D., Xue, G.: Public perceptions of EV charging infrastructure: a combined sentiment analysis and topic modeling approach. Stud. Inf. Control **33**(2), 59–72 (2024)
26. Blei, D.M., Jordan, M.I.: Modeling annotated data. In: Proceedings of the 26th ACM SIGIR Conference on Research and Development in Information Retrieval, pp. 127–134 (2003)

Data-Driven Innovation in Cybersecurity for E-Business Information Systems: A Case Study on CVE Report Generation via LLM

Arcangelo Castiglione(✉), Francesco Colace, Marco Fusco, Antonio Giordano, Domenico Santaniello, and Carmine Valentino

University of Salerno, Fisciano, SA, Italy
{arcastiglione,fcolace,dsantaniello,cvalentino}@unisa.it,
{m.fusco37,a.giordano223}@studenti.unisa.it

Abstract. The backbone of modern digital economies, e-business information systems (EBIS), is security, which is an essential factor in ensuring business continuity and digital trust. One of the most complex challenges in this area is efficiently managing vulnerabilities, which requires fast and accurate reporting processes.

This study explores the application of artificial intelligence as a data-driven innovation to automate the generation of structured cybersecurity reports. To this end, we analyzed the performance of four open-source large language models (LLMs) by implementing an adaptive two-step prompt chaining architecture. The system, tested on a dataset of 30 Common Vulnerabilities and Exposures (CVEs), simulates a realistic analysis and review workflow.

The assessment, based on quantitative and qualitative metrics, produced results that, although preliminary, confirm the feasibility of integrating LLMs into EBIS cybersecurity processes. The study also highlights crucial challenges related to scalability and reliability, which are key determinants of the governance of these systems.

Keywords: E-Business Information Systems (EBIS) · Cybersecurity Automation · Large Language Models (LLMs) · Vulnerability Management · AI-Driven Reporting

1 Introduction

In the digital age, E-Business Information Systems (EBIS) form the backbone of modern economies, enabling everything from decentralized commerce (Web 3.0) to intelligent service infrastructures [1]. Their increasing complexity and interconnectedness, especially with the advent of 6G and ultra-connected ecosystems, expose them to an ever-changing cyber threat landscape. Efficient vulnerability management, cataloged in the Common Vulnerabilities and Exposures (CVE) database, is not just a technical function but a strategic pillar to ensure operational resilience and digital trust [2, 3].

Published by Springer Nature Switzerland AG 2027
J. Kim et al. (Eds.): EBISION 2025, IFIP AICT 786, pp. 49–62, 2027.
https://doi.org/10.1007/978-3-032-26616-3_4

This environment requires urgent business process innovation based on data and artificial intelligence. Security Operations Centers (SOCs), which are responsible for defending EBIS, are overwhelmed by a volume of data that cannot be manually managed. Large Language Models (LLMs) emerge as a transformative technology for automating complex cognitive tasks like security report generation [4–6].

In this scenario, the present work aims to evaluate the effectiveness of four state-of-the-art open-source LLMs experimentally. The novelty of the proposed research lies in the proposal and validation of an adaptive architecture based on two-phase prompt chaining, tested on a dataset of 30 CVEs. Unlike previous studies focused on code classification or repair, our approach simulates an end-to-end process of writing and reviewing. This makes it possible to evaluate not only the initial generation capacity of models, but also the ability to self-improve, a key factor in building reliable AI systems for industrial contexts.

The organization of this paper is as follows: Sect. 2 outlines the background on EBIS, CVE, and LLM. Section 3 analyzes related work. Section 4 describes the proposed solution architecture as a resilient system for EBIS. Section 5 details the practical implementation. Section 6 presents the experimental results and discusses the governance implications of EBISs. Finally, Sect. 7 outlines conclusions and future research paradigms.

2 Background

An E-Business Information System (EBIS) is a socio-technical infrastructure that leverages digital technologies to run, monitor, and manage online business processes. These systems encompass various applications, from e-commerce platforms to decentralized financial systems to cloud-native architectures [7]. Their security plays a crucial role: a single vulnerability can compromise sensitive data, disrupt operations, and undermine consumer trust, generating potentially devastating impacts on the business. In this context, the management of Common Vulnerabilities and Exposures (CVEs) is a strategic activity within an EBIS's governance to ensure its resilience against cyber attacks [8, 9].

We live today in the era of artificial intelligence, in which Large Language Models (LLMs) represent one of the most influential technologies [10–12]. These models, trained on vast textual datasets, are able to understand and generate natural language, offering new possibilities for automation and decision support. The models selected for this study reflect different design philosophies:

- DeepSeek-R1-Distill-Qwen-14B: A large model (14B parameters), known for its high-quality text output;
- Mistral-7B-Instruct-v0.1: an efficient model (7B parameters), optimized to follow complex instructions;
- WhiteRabbitNeo-13B: a 13B parameter model, designed for tasks that require high adherence to structured formats;
- Lily-7B-Instruct-v0.2: A 7B parameter model, optimized explicitly for cybersecurity, represents an example of specialized artificial intelligence.

The application of AI to cybersecurity is now a rapidly expanding research paradigm, with a significant impact on the evolution of EBIS. Numerous studies have explored the use of LLMs in this area, albeit with different approaches and purposes [13–15].

For example, the usefulness of language models in vulnerability analysis and assessment [16] has been demonstrated, although without particular attention to generating comprehensive reports for analysts. Other contributions focused on self-healing code [17, 18], highlighting a more governance-oriented and risk-communicating application [19].

Some studies have investigated the synthesis capacity of LLMs [20], while others have proposed chatbots for vulnerability analysis [21]. In general, the literature confirms the enormous potential of such models, but underlines the need for practical case studies that assess their reliability in realistic operational scenarios [22].

The present work is distinguished by the adoption of a two-step prompt chaining methodology, which allows to obtain a more in-depth evaluation of the ability of an LLM to operate within an iterative business workflow. This approach contributes in a concrete way to the debate on how to design more resilient, adaptive and intelligent EBIS architectures, capable of dynamically responding to emerging digital security challenges [23].

Traditional approaches to automated cybersecurity reporting often rely on rule-based templates or classical NLP techniques such as keyword extraction and vulnerability classification models. While these methods can provide structured summaries, they typically lack the ability to synthesize complex contextual information and generate coherent analytical narratives. LLM-based approaches, as explored in this work, enable a more flexible generation process capable of integrating vulnerability metadata, contextual analysis, and mitigation guidance into unified technical reports. This represents a significant advancement compared to template-based reporting pipelines traditionally used in vulnerability management systems.

3 The Proposed Approach: An Adaptive System for Security Reporting

This section discusses the proposed approach, which introduces a system architecture for automating the security reporting lifecycle, designed to be integrated into a modern E-Business Information System (EBIS)[24].

The architecture is adaptive and iterative, as it incorporates a self-review mechanism based on prompt chaining, capable of progressively improving the quality of the output and reducing the impact of errors generated in the early stages of the process [24, 25].

The workflow is designed to simulate a hierarchical interaction between a junior analyst and a senior auditor, consisting of four automated phases, each of which represents a functional node of the system (Fig. 1):

1. Initial Prompt Generation – The appropriately structured CVE data is converted into a detailed prompt for the "junior analyst." This prompt defines the structure of the report and constrains its format (sections: Summary, Technical Details, Risk Assessment, Suggested Mitigations, Exploitation Scenario).

2. First Report Production – The LLM generates a preliminary draft of the security report, adhering to the structural constraints of the initial prompt.
3. Generation of the review prompt – The report produced is incorporated into a second prompt that instructs the LLM to act as a "senior reviewer", with the aim of improving consistency, technical accuracy and clarity of presentation.
4. Production of the final report – The LLM refines the paper, correcting imperfections and completing missing sections. The result is a standardized and validated final report, ready to be distributed within the company information system.

The prompt chaining configuration was implemented using fixed template prompts shared across all evaluated models. The first-stage prompt contained structured instructions and CVE metadata to guide the generation of a preliminary technical report. The second-stage prompt incorporated the generated report and introduced a revision role instruction, prompting the model to perform consistency checking, completeness validation, and stylistic refinement. All prompts were executed with identical structural constraints and formatting requirements to ensure fair comparison across models. Model inference parameters were maintained consistent across experiments to avoid bias in generation behaviour.

To ensure fair comparison across models, the same prompt templates were used for all LLMs in both the generation and review phases. Prompts were parameterized only with CVE-specific content, while structure, formatting constraints, and role instructions remained constant.

The success rate was operationally defined as the percentage of reports that (i) completed without runtime or memory errors and (ii) adhered to the required structural format, including the presence of all mandated sections (Summary, Technical Details, Risk Assessment, Suggested Mitigations, and Exploitation Scenario).

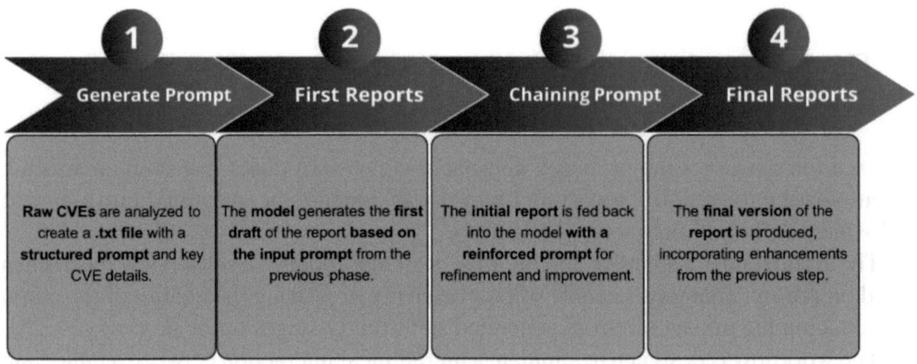

Fig. 1. Methodological workflow based on prompt chaining

This architecture not only optimizes the efficiency of the security analysis and reporting process, but also introduces an automated quality control mechanism, which is crucial for the governance of information systems and for maintaining high levels of digital trust. It also allows you to monitor key indicators such as success rate, report completeness, average generation time and structural adherence, which are essential for the comparative evaluation of the performance of the language models used.

To complete the architectural description, Fig. 2 shows the flow of data within the system, highlighting the input, processing, and output steps.

In this representation, the raw CVE data constitutes the process input ("RAW CVEs"), which are first integrated into the initial prompt and then transformed into an intermediate report. This report feeds a second round of LLM inference through the chain prompt, eventually producing a final report structured in text format.

This diagram (Fig. 2) clearly illustrates the integration between the processing pipeline and the self-validation cycle, highlighting how the system approaches a paradigm of self-improving AI workflow for cybersecurity governance.

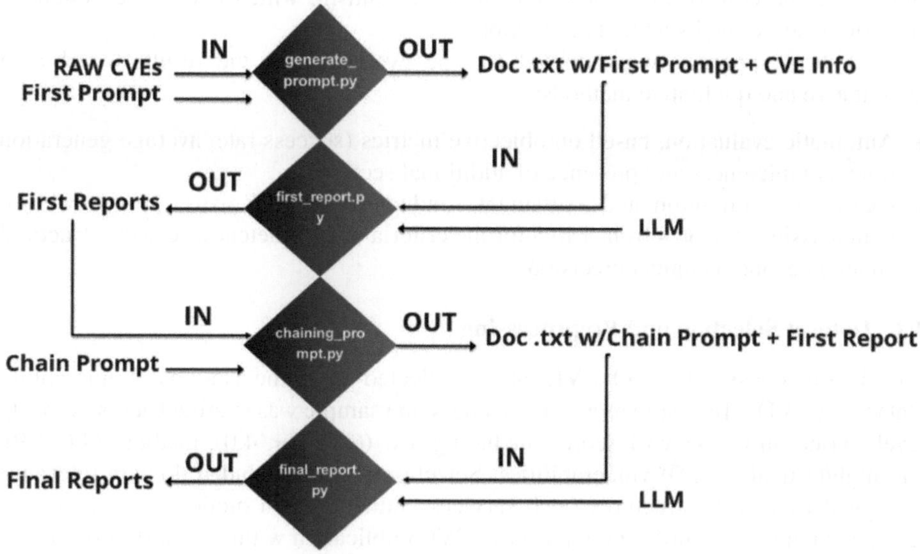

Fig. 2. Processing Flow Diagram

4 Experimental Campaign

The implementation of the case study aimed to verify the technical feasibility and operational performance of the proposed architecture, evaluating its ability to automate the security reporting lifecycle in a realistic context.

The test environment was configured on Apple Silicon platforms, specifically on a MacBook Pro M3 Max (14-core CPU, 30-core GPU, 32 GB RAM), to ensure efficient and stable local inference. The execution of the models was managed through the llama.cpp framework, optimized for the ARM64 architecture, using quantized models in GGUF format. While the experimental setup was based on local inference, the proposed architecture is designed to be deployable in enterprise environments through containerized microservices and GPU-accelerated clusters. In production settings, orchestration platforms such as Kubernetes can be used to scale LLM inference services horizontally, enabling load balancing across multiple models and ensuring high availability for large volumes of concurrent CVE analyses.

This reflects a growing trend in the adoption of on-premise AI solutions, which offer greater data security, cost reduction, and infrastructure autonomy compared to traditional cloud services.

A key aspect of the experiment was the design of the prompts, conceived to replicate the operational dynamics of a Security Operation Center (SOC).

The junior analyst's prompt presented detailed and rigid instructions, aimed at avoiding hallucinations and ensuring the presence of all the required sections (Summary, Technical Details, Risk Assessment, Suggested Mitigations, Exploitation Scenario).

The senior auditor's prompt, on the other hand, simulated a quality assurance process, aimed at improving clarity, professional tone and technical precision. This self-revision step forms the core of the prompt chaining mechanism, which allows the system to autonomously refine its textual production.

A hybrid approach was adopted for the evaluation of the results, combining quantitative and qualitative methods:

- Automatic evaluation, based on objective metrics (success rate, average generation time, completeness and presence of additional sections).
- Qualitative semi-automated assessment, conducted with GPT-4o as a proxy reviewer, which assigned scores from 1 to 5 for the criteria of completeness, clarity, structural adherence, and technical precision.

4.1 Dataset Selection and Preprocessing

The dataset consisted of 30 CVE entries selected from the National Vulnerability Database (NVD). To ensure representativeness, the sample was stratified across severity levels based on CVSS v3.1 scores, including low (CVSS < 4.0), medium (4.0–6.9), and high/critical (≥ 7.0) vulnerabilities. Selection criteria included domain relevance to typical EBIS infrastructures (web services, authentication modules, database systems, and network components), recency (CVE publication within the last three years), and completeness of technical descriptions. Preprocessing involved normalization of CVE metadata, removal of non-informative fields, and standardization of vulnerability descriptions into a structured JSON schema. This schema was then transformed into the initial prompt format to ensure consistent input across all evaluated models.

Although the dataset size (30 CVEs) may appear limited, the selection was intentionally designed to ensure representativeness across multiple vulnerability severity levels and infrastructure domains relevant to EBIS environments. The goal of this study was not to benchmark large-scale model performance, but rather to evaluate the feasibility and operational behaviour of LLM-driven report generation pipelines within realistic Security Operation Center (SOC) workflows. Future research will extend the experimental campaign to larger CVE corpora and real-time vulnerability streams, enabling broader statistical validation and scalability analysis of the proposed architecture.

4.2 Experimental Results

In the first round of generation, the models showed significant differences.

DeepSeek achieved the highest quality (score 5.0/5.0), but with significantly above-average generation times.

LilyCybersecurity and Mistral stood out for their efficiency and reliability, producing comprehensive reports with very short processing times (13.45 s and 14.06 s respectively). WhiteRabbitNeo, while showing variability in results, provided consistent, though less structurally sound, outputs.

In the second round, based on the review phase through prompt chaining, the behavior of the models changed significantly. DeepSeek has shown a serious scalability limitation, managing to complete only 10% of the tasks due to the increasing size of the prompts. In contrast, LilyCybersecurity has proven to be the most resilient model, successfully completing 90% of requests and maintaining high structural consistency. Mistral and WhiteRabbitNeo benefited greatly from the iterative process, significantly improving the clarity and accuracy of the final reports.

To assess the robustness of the observed performance metrics, results were aggregated across all CVE instances and reported as mean values with corresponding standard deviations. Confidence intervals at the 95% level were estimated using non-parametric bootstrapping, given the non-Gaussian distribution of generation times and success outcomes.

To provide a more granular quantitative evaluation, multiple performance indicators were considered during the experimental campaign. These include the success rate of report generation, average inference time per CVE instance, structural completeness of the generated report, and qualitative evaluation scores assigned through the GPT-4o assisted assessment process. Together, these indicators provide a multi-dimensional evaluation of model performance, capturing not only computational efficiency but also structural reliability and technical accuracy of the generated cybersecurity reports (Tables 1, 2 and Figs. 3, 4).

Table 1. Quantitative results of the models

Model	Round	Success Rate (%)	Average Time (sec)	Completeness (%)
DeepSeek	1°	100	22.80	98
Mistral	1°	95	14.06	94
WhiteRabbitNeo	1°	87	15.20	90
LilyCybersecurity	1°	98	13.45	96
DeepSeek	2°	10	—	45
Mistral	2°	85	15.75	97
WhiteRabbitNeo	2°	88	16.10	96
LilyCybersecurity	2°	90	13.90	98

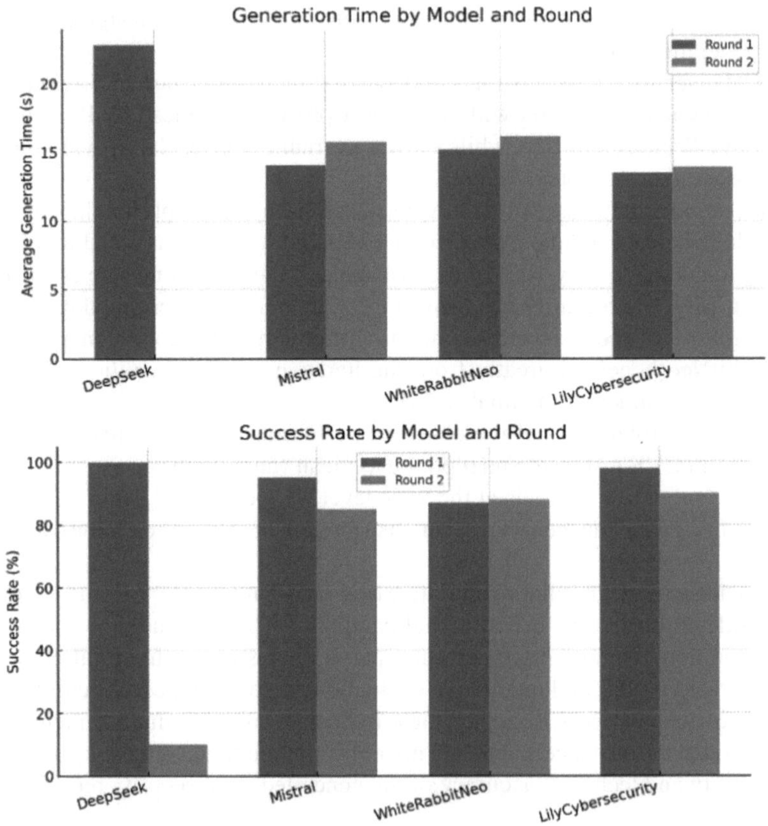

Fig. 3. Comparison between the generation times and the success rate of the models in the two rounds

Table 2. Qualitative Assessment (scores 1–5, GPT-4o)

Model	Round	Completeness	Clarity	Structural adhesion	Technical precision
DeepSeek	1°	5.0	4.8	4.9	5.0
Mistral	1°	4.3	4.0	4.1	4.0
WhiteRabbitNeo	1°	3.9	3.7	3.8	3.8
LilyCybersecurity	1°	4.8	4.5	4.6	4.7
DeepSeek	2°	2.0	2.5	2.2	2.3
Mistral	2°	4.7	4.6	4.8	4.7
WhiteRabbitNeo	2°	4.5	4.4	4.5	4.6
LilyCybersecurity	2°	4.9	4.8	4.9	4.9

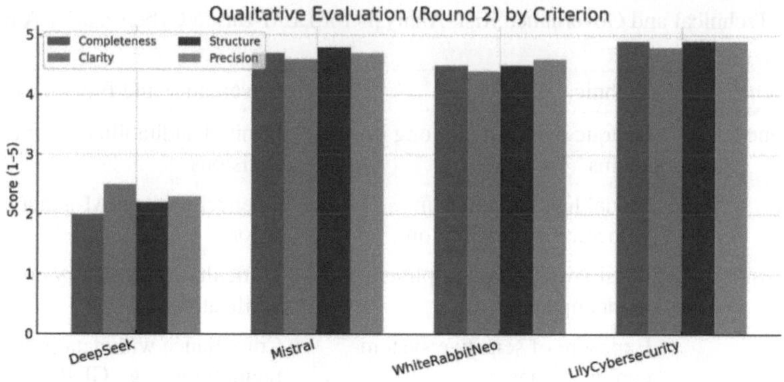

Fig. 4. Average model qualitative scores for each criterion

4.3 Discussion and Implications

The overall analysis shows how prompt chaining has contributed substantially to improving the clarity, structure, and technical accuracy of the generated reports.

The comparison of models also revealed some strategic evidence relevant to the governance of E-Business Information Systems (EBIS):

Trade-off between quality and scalability. The scalability failure observed for DeepSeek in the second round can be attributed to token-length and memory constraints inherent to large-parameter models when operating in iterative prompt-chaining workflows. As the reviewed reports were appended to the second-stage prompts, the effective context window expanded significantly, leading to increased memory consumption and inference instability on local hardware. This highlights a critical deployment consideration for EBIS environments, where model efficiency and context-window management can be as important as raw generative quality. The size of the model does not guarantee superior performance. DeepSeek, while excellent in single quality, does not scale in iterative pipelines; medium-sized models such as LilyCybersecurity are more balanced.

Adaptive architectures. The use of prompt chaining has proven to be essential for increasing reliability. This indicates that future EBIS architectures will need to incorporate self-review and continuous improvement mechanisms.

Compliance automation. The proposed system can automate the production of regulatory documentation (e.g. GDPR, NIS2), improving accuracy and traceability, and thus strengthening digital trust within company infrastructures.

From an EBIS governance perspective, automated vulnerability reporting plays a crucial role in supporting organizational risk management processes. The reports generated through the proposed architecture can contribute to several governance activities, including vulnerability prioritization, compliance documentation, incident response preparation, and communication between technical teams and managerial stakeholders.

By structuring vulnerability intelligence into standardized analytical reports, LLM-based systems can facilitate traceability and decision support within enterprise cybersecurity governance frameworks.

Table 3. Technical and Governance Risk Analysis for LLM-Based Cybersecurity Automation

Risk Dimension	Technical Challenges	Governance and Ethical Challenges
Transparency	Opaque reasoning in long prompt chains	Limited auditability of automated decisions
Reliability	Model hallucinations in vulnerability descriptions	Over-reliance on AI-generated reports
Reproducibility	Sensitivity to prompt phrasing and model updates	Difficulty in regulatory compliance verification
Privacy	Exposure of sensitive system configurations	Compliance with data protection regulations (e.g., GDPR, NIS2)
Accountability	Ambiguity in responsibility for automated outputs	Legal and organizational liability for AI-driven errors

Table 3 summarizes the main technical and governance risks associated with the deployment of LLM-based automation in EBIS cybersecurity workflows, highlighting the need for transparent, auditable, and privacy-preserving design principles (Fig. 5).

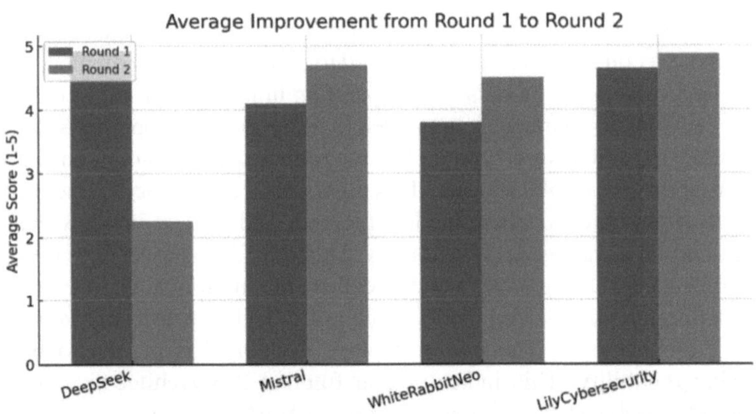

Fig. 5. Comparative summary between round 1 and round 2, highlighting the average overall improvement for each model

From an operational perspective, the proposed architecture can be integrated into existing EBIS cybersecurity infrastructures through Security Operation Centers (SOCs) or vulnerability management platforms. In practice, the pipeline can be connected to vulnerability intelligence feeds (e.g., NVD or internal vulnerability scanners), automatically generating structured reports that can be reviewed by security analysts before distribution to system administrators. Such integration enables the creation of semi-autonomous cybersecurity reporting workflows, where LLM-generated reports act as decision-support artifacts within organizational risk management processes. This approach reduces analyst workload while maintaining human oversight over critical security decisions.

5 Conclusions and Future Research Paradigms

This study demonstrated that the automatic generation of cybersecurity reports using large language models (LLMs) represents a viable, effective and profoundly innovative strategy for the evolution of E-Business Information Systems (EBIS).

The integration of intelligent architectures based on prompt chaining has made it possible to validate a fundamental principle: efficiency and quality do not depend exclusively on the scale of the model, but rather on the design of the cognitive flow and the contextual control of the generative process.

The experimental results showed that medium-sized models, if properly guided by a structured pipeline, are able to produce consistent, technically accurate reports that comply with professional standards. In particular, LilyCybersecurity stood out as the model most balanced between speed, robustness and semantic quality, showing an operational readiness that makes it realistic to use in production scenarios.

Looking beyond the results of this study, the research paves the way towards new development paradigms for the EBIS of the future, in which artificial intelligence is not only an analytical aid, but an active component of resilience, trust and sustainability. The main perspectives are divided into four complementary directions:

1. Cyber-Physical Integration

   The first horizon concerns the extension of this approach to cyber-physical systems, such as IoT infrastructures or OT industrial environments. In such contexts, the ability to analyze vulnerabilities in real time and automatically generate contextualized reports could be a game-changer for operational resilience and real-time risk management.
2. Quantum-Safe and Quantum-Powered EBIS

   A second emerging area of research concerns the intersection between artificial intelligence and quantum computing. LLMs and hybrid AI-quantum systems will be able to support the transition to quantum-safe cryptographic algorithms, automatically identifying vulnerable libraries, legacy dependencies, or risky configurations. While these perspectives remain exploratory, ongoing research in post-quantum cryptography and distributed ledger technologies provides a concrete technological foundation for future empirical validation of AI-assisted governance mechanisms in cyber-physical EBIS infrastructures.
3. Sustainability and Green E-Business Systems

   In an era in which the environmental impact of digital technologies can no longer be overlooked, it will be crucial to investigate the energy sustainability of AI architectures applied to EBIS. The adoption of lighter models, the optimization of local inference and the integration with energy-efficient infrastructures can give rise to "green" solutions, in which IT security is combined with environmental responsibility.
4. Reinforcement Learning for Adaptive Trust

   Finally, a particularly promising prospect is that of reinforcement learning applied to adaptive trust. By training LLMs to continuously improve based on human feedback – for example, corrections or evaluations provided by analysts – it will be possible to build continuous improvement loops, in which the system learns to recognize and correct its mistakes on its own.

This paradigm will lead to the creation of cognitively adaptive EBIS, capable of strengthening the relationship of trust between humans and machines and ensuring reliable, transparent and verifiable performance over time.

The research shows that the synergy between LLMs, reporting automation and adaptive architectures is a concrete step towards the next generation of enterprise information systems: smarter, more sustainable and resilient. The evolution of EBIS will increasingly move from a static and descriptive paradigm to a dynamic, cognitive and predictive one, capable of proactively learning, explaining and ensuring safety.

In operational EBIS environments, the proposed architecture could function as an automated reporting layer integrated within SOC infrastructures. By interfacing with vulnerability scanning tools, ticketing systems, and compliance monitoring platforms, the system can support continuous vulnerability documentation and reporting workflows. This integration allows organizations to transform vulnerability analysis from a purely manual process into a semi-automated, data-driven governance activity aligned with modern cybersecurity management frameworks.

From a broader EBIS perspective, the proposed architecture aligns with emerging models of autonomous digital governance, where artificial intelligence is embedded as a continuous risk-assessment and compliance layer. By integrating adaptive prompt chaining with structured reporting, the system establishes a feedback-driven control loop that mirrors classical governance frameworks while enhancing responsiveness and operational transparency.

References

Pizzolante, R., Castiglione, A., Carpentieri, B., Contaldo, R., D'Angelo, G., Palmieri, F.: A machine learning-based memory forensics methodology for TOR browser artifacts. Concurr. Comput. **33**(23), e5935 (2021). https://doi.org/10.1002/cpe.5935

Guertin-Lahoud, S., Coursaris, C.K., Sénécal, S., Léger, P.-M.: User experience evaluation in shared interactive virtual reality. Cyberpsychol. Behav. Soc. Netw. **26**(4), 263–272 (2023). https://doi.org/10.1089/cyber.2022.0261

Schlichtkrull, M., Kipf, T.N., Bloem, P., van den Berg, R., Titov, I., Welling, M.: Modeling relational data with graph convolutional networks, pp. 593–607 (2018). https://doi.org/10.1007/978-3-319-93417-4_38

Gaeta, A., Loia, V., Lorusso, A., Orciuoli, F., Pascuzzo, A.: Towards a LLM-based intelligent system for detecting propaganda within textual content. Comput. Electr. Eng. **128**, 110765 (2025). https://doi.org/10.1016/j.compeleceng.2025.110765

Bellini, E., D'Aniello, G., Flammini, F., Gaeta, R.: Situation awareness for cyber resilience: a review. Int. J. Crit. Infrastruct. Prot. **49**, 100755 (2025). https://doi.org/10.1016/j.ijcip.2025.100755

Baker, T., Bechhofer, S., Isaac, A., Miles, A., Schreiber, G., Summers, E.: Key choices in the design of Simple Knowledge Organization System (SKOS). J. Web Semant. **20**, 35–49 (2013). https://doi.org/10.1016/j.websem.2013.05.001

Casillo, M., Cecere, L., Colace, F., Lorusso, A., Santaniello, D., Valentino, C.: Exhibition spaces in the metaverse: a novel design approach. In: 2023 8th IEEE History of Electrotechnology Conference (HISTELCON), pp. 116–119. IEEE (2023). https://doi.org/10.1109/HISTELCON56357.2023.10365847

Raimundo, R.J., Rosário, A.T.: Cybersecurity in the internet of things in industrial management. Appl. Sci. **12**(3), 1598 (2022). https://doi.org/10.3390/app12031598

Castiglione, A., Esposito, J.G., Loia, V., Nappi, M., Pero, C., Polsinelli, M.: Integrating post-quantum cryptography and blockchain to secure low-cost IoT Devices. IEEE Trans. Ind. Inf. **21**(2), 1674–1683 (2025). https://doi.org/10.1109/TII.2024.3485796

Cecere, L., Grimaldi, M., Lorusso, A., Marra, A., Stoia, F.: Immersive urban planning: evaluating park safety perception with digital twins and metaverse simulation. Sustainability **17**(17), 7608 (2025). https://doi.org/10.3390/su17177608

Wu, L., Petroni, F., Josifoski, M., Riedel, S., Zettlemoyer, L.: Scalable zero-shot entity linking with dense entity retrieval. In: Proceedings of the 2020 Conference on Empirical Methods in Natural Language Processing (EMNLP), pp. 6397–6407. Association for Computational Linguistics, Stroudsburg (2020).https://doi.org/10.18653/v1/2020.emnlp-main.519

Della Greca, A., Ilaria, A., Tucci, C., Frugieri, N., Tortora, G.: A user study on the relationship between empathy and facial-based emotion simulation in Virtual Reality. In: Proceedings of the 2024 International Conference on Advanced Visual Interfaces, pp. 1–9. ACM, New York (2024).https://doi.org/10.1145/3656650.3656691

Gaeta, A., Loia, V., Lorusso, A., Orciuoli, F., Pascuzzo, A.: Computational analysis of information disorder in cognitive warfare. Online Soc. Netw. Media **48**, 100322 (2025). https://doi.org/10.1016/j.osnem.2025.100322

Jiang, Y., Bordia, S., Zhong, Z., Dognin, C., Singh, M., Bansal, M.: HoVer: a dataset for many-hop fact extraction and claim verification. In: Findings of the Association for Computational Linguistics: EMNLP 2020, pp. 3441–3460. Association for Computational Linguistics, Stroudsburg (2020). https://doi.org/10.18653/v1/2020.findings-emnlp.309

Casillo, M., Colace, F., Lorusso, A., Santaniello, D., Valentino, C.: Integrating physical and virtual experiences in cultural tourism: an adaptive multimodal recommender system. IEEE Access **13**, 28353–28368 (2025). https://doi.org/10.1109/ACCESS.2025.3539205

Ghosh, R., Farri, O., von Stockhausen, H.-M., Schmitt, M., Vasile, G.M.: CVE-LLM : automatic vulnerability evaluation in medical device industry using large language models (2024)

Fakih, M., Dharmaji, R., Bouzidi, H., Araya, G.Q., Ogundare, O., Al Faruque, M.A.: LLM4CVE: enabling iterative automated vulnerability repair with large language models (2025)

Lorusso, A., Guida, D.: IoT system for structural monitoring, pp. 599–606 (2022). https://doi.org/10.1007/978-3-031-05230-9_72

Gaeta, A., Loia, V., Orciuoli, F.: An explainable prediction method based on Fuzzy Rough Sets, TOPSIS and hexagons of opposition: applications to the analysis of Information Disorder. Inf. Sci. (N Y) **659**, 120050 (2024). https://doi.org/10.1016/j.ins.2023.120050

Kulsum, U., Zhu, H., Xu, B., d'Amorim, M.: A case study of LLM for automated vulnerability repair: assessing impact of reasoning and patch validation feedback. In: Proceedings of the 1st ACM International Conference on AI-Powered Software, pp. 103–111. ACM, New York (2024). https://doi.org/10.1145/3664646.3664770

Sheng, Z. Chen, Z., Gu, S., Huang, H., Gu, G., Huang, J.: LLMs in software security: a survey of vulnerability detection techniques and insights (2025)

Tian, S., et al.: Exploring the role of large language models in cybersecurity: a systematic survey (2025)

Casillo, M., Cecere, L., Dembele, S.P., Lorusso, A., Santaniello, D., Valentino, C.: The Metaverse and Revolutionary Perspectives for the Smart Cities of the Future, pp. 215–225 (2024).https://doi.org/10.1007/978-981-97-3305-7_17

Casillo, M., Colace, F., Lorusso, A., Santaniello, D., Valentino, C.: A multilevel graph approach for IoT-based complex scenario management through situation awareness and semantic approaches. J. Reliab. Intell. Environ. **10**(4), 395–411 (2024). https://doi.org/10.1007/s40860-024-00224-0

Cantone, A., Ercolino, M., Romano, M., Vitiello, G.: Designing virtual interactive objects to enhance visitors' experience in cultural exhibits. In: Proceedings of the 2nd International Conference of the ACM Greek SIGCHI Chapter, pp. 1–5. ACM, New York (2023). https://doi.org/10.1145/3609987.3610110

Application

Exploring the Role of Digital Management Capability in Shaping Ethical Leadership and its Impact on ESG: A Dynamic Capabilities Micro-Foundations Perspective

Ka Wai Chung[1,2](✉), Kam Pui Liu[1], and William Yeoh[1]

[1] Hong Kong Metropolitan University, Hong Kong, China
{skwchung,kpliu,wyeoh}@hkmu.edu.hk, kawai_chung@nucba.ac.jp

[2] Nagoya University of Commerce and Business, Nagoya, Japan

Abstract. Drawing on the micro-foundations of dynamic capabilities, this study examines the interplay among digital management capability, ethical leadership, and environmental, social, and governance (ESG) performance within E-Business Information Systems. Analyzing survey data from 357 Chinese small and medium-sized enterprises (SMEs), the results demonstrate that digital management capability positively influences both ESG performance and ethical leadership. Furthermore, ethical leadership positively affects ESG performance and significantly mediates the relationship between digital management capability and ESG outcomes. Notably, digital management capability positively moderates the ethical leadership—ESG performance link, suggesting that digitally competent ethical leaders are better positioned to drive sustainability. This research extends the micro-foundations perspective by emphasizing the human-specific aspects of digital information systems management. Practically, the findings underscore the need for SMEs to integrate ethical and digital leadership to enhance sustainability in the digital era.

Keywords: Ethical Leadership · Digital Management Capability · ESG Performance

1 Introduction

The domain of E-Business Information Systems (EBIS) is fundamentally multidisciplinary, necessitating a holistic transformation across strategic, organizational, technological, and marketing dimensions. Verhoef et al. [40] argue that to extract maximum value from these systems, leadership must cultivate specific competencies tailored to the distinct stages of digital evolution. Within this context, digital management capability (DMC) is increasingly analyzed through the theoretical lens of the dynamic capabilities micro-foundations perspective [1, 16]. In volatile technological environments, DMC transcends mere technical literacy; it encompasses human-machine collaborative

Published by Springer Nature Switzerland AG 2027
J. Kim et al. (Eds.): EBISION 2025, IFIP AICT 786, pp. 65–79, 2027.
https://doi.org/10.1007/978-3-032-26616-3_5

behaviors that enable leaders to leverage data-driven analytics to capitalize on competitive advantages and mitigate emerging threats [18]. This individual-level capability is particularly crucial for small and medium-sized enterprises (SMEs), where the integration of digital infrastructure and human capital serves as the primary driver for digital innovation [22].

Contemporary EBIS research underscores ethical governance as a foundational pillar, ensuring that moral implications and societal consequences of automated decision-making are rigorously addressed [18]. Consequently, integrating DMC with ethical leadership has become vital for achieving environmental, social, and governance (ESG) objectives in today's competitive digital landscape [7, 23]. Ethical leaders are considered central figures in fostering a digital culture and enabling collaborative processes in complex environments while simultaneously addressing the ethical concerns inherent in enhancing ESG outcomes [3, 7]. Furthermore, digital transformation impacts corporate ESG performance, as evidenced by studies such as those by Lyu et al. [27] and Xu & Yin [45]. It reshapes business models, optimizes resource allocation, reduces energy consumption, and enhances transparency and stakeholder engagement [10]. The effective implementation and ethical governance of digital technologies are crucial to EBIS, serving as a foundation for realizing the benefits of digital transformation. Consequently, this paper explores the role of DMC in enabling ethical leaders to advance ESG objectives. For ethical leaders, this requires not only a strong ethical framework but also a robust understanding of digital tools and strategies to manage increasingly digitalized contexts [38].

The dynamic capabilities micro-foundations perspective provides a suitable theoretical lens for understanding how firms adapt to rapid environmental shifts by developing new capabilities at the individual level. This perspective clarifies how organizations build capabilities for digital transformation by examining the underlying micro-foundations [37, 42]. Studies have highlighted that successful digital transformation requires organizations to develop a wide range of internal digital capabilities to respond swiftly to market needs. The micro-foundations perspective is specifically employed to analyze the effects of individual digital capabilities on organizational growth, particularly in SMEs [32]. This framework enables a detailed investigation into specific individual-level attributes—such as digital management capability—that underpin an organization's ability to navigate digital change effectively [8, 35, 36, 42]. By focusing on these micro-foundations, a deeper understanding of how capabilities are built, integrated, and reconfigured to achieve strategic objectives in the digital age can be obtained [35, 37].

Despite the imperative for digital transformation, a notable gap exists in the literature regarding the individual-level competencies that facilitate ethical digitalization within the unique constraints of SMEs compared to large-scale corporations [5, 12]. Current research in the EBIS domain posits that digital orientation—defined as a firm's strategic commitment to technological adoption—is known as a critical complement to digital capability. Together, these factors catalyze innovation, thereby enhancing both financial performance and non-financial metrics [22]. The present study aims to address this empirical gap by investigating the mechanism through which SME decision-makers deploy DMC. Specifically, it examines how these individuals leverage such capabilities to advance ESG objectives within an ethical framework [7].

Building on the importance of ethical leadership in the digital era, this study addresses the gaps by investigating the research question: "What specific digital management capability enables ethical leaders to effectively achieve ESG objectives in the digital era?" This inquiry explores the essential skills and strategic approaches ethical leaders must employ to leverage digital tools for sustainable performance [38].

This study contributes to the EBIS literature in three ways. First, it positions EBIS as a core pillar of sustainable business innovation by linking DMC directly to ESG performance [38]. Second, drawing on the micro-foundations perspective, it identifies DMC as a crucial individual-level foundation, emphasizing that decision-makers' quality is of paramount importance for sensing, seizing, and reconfiguring resources in rapidly evolving digital contexts [18]. Last but not least, by applying this lens to ethical leadership within SMEs, the study addresses a knowledge gap regarding how smaller firms—often facing greater resource constraints—drive ESG performance through integrated leadership [35, 36].

2 Literature Review and Hypothesis Development

In the digital era, the dynamic capabilities micro-foundations perspective is critical for navigating digital transformation [37, 42]. Organizations must cultivate specific individual-level capabilities—termed digital management capability (DMC)—to acquire, organize, and disseminate digital information aligned with strategic objectives [20]. Empirical evidence indicates that successful digitalization in SMEs hinges substantially on the digital acumen and attributes of central decision-makers, as these individual qualities drive organizational growth [7]. Ethical leaders thus play a central role in fostering an organizational culture that foregrounds sustainable development [21, 30, 39]. Digital management capability equips these leaders with the data and analytical tools necessary to render informed, transparent, and ethically sound decisions concerning complex digital challenges [20], ultimately driving ESG performance.

2.1 Digital Management Capability and ESG Performance

Dynamic capabilities—the capacity to integrate, build, and reconfigure competences in response to environmental change— are central to sustaining competitive advantage in dynamic contexts [36, 37]. The micro-foundations approach posits that macro-level organizational phenomena, such as dynamic capabilities, are best understood by examining the underlying individual-level actions and interactions [1, 16]. Scholars have increasingly adopted this approach to understand how individual-level (e.g., managerial-level) and other micro factors influence dynamic capabilities [2]. This perspective provides a means to analyze the quality and capabilities of individual decision-makers and top management within organizations [28]. Focusing on micro-foundations—particularly digital management capability and leadership styles—yields valuable insights into strategic change and sustainability performance in SMEs [35, 36].

A growing body of evidence suggests that digital transformation is linked to improved ESG performance [33]. Digital transformation plays a crucial role in reshaping business models and management mechanisms, driving advancements in green technological innovation, resource allocation efficiency, and pollution reduction [44]. Furthermore, digital management capability contributes to enhanced transparency, improved information processing, and stronger stakeholder relationships, all of which are essential for leaders seeking to enhance social performance and cultivate a transparent governance environment [24, 26, 43]. Therefore, we posit that:

H1: Digital management capability is positively related to ESG performance.

2.2 Digital Management Capability and Ethical Leadership

Digital management capability, in this context, refers to the systematic use of processes and technologies to acquire, organize, store, retrieve, and disseminate digital information and expertise relevant to a leader's role [20]. Ethical leadership is defined as the demonstration and promotion of normatively appropriate conduct through personal actions and decision-making [30]. In digitalized contexts, ethical leaders must navigate risks such as algorithmic bias, data privacy violations, and transparency gaps. This capability equips ethical leaders with timely access to ethical frameworks, regulatory guidelines, best practices, and real-time risk data, enabling informed and transparent decisions in digital dilemmas, including issues like data privacy, algorithmic bias, and artificial intelligence (AI) [7, 23]. Digital tools also support the dissemination of ethical policies and organizational values, promoting transparency, consistent ethical conduct, and accountability—thus strengthening ethical culture. Collaborative platforms and internal knowledge bases further facilitate the sharing of ethical insights and compliance requirements among leaders [19]. Therefore, we posit that:

H2: Digital management capability is positively related to ethical leadership.

2.3 Ethical Leadership and ESG Performance

Ethical leaders are pivotal in guiding an organization's responses to ESG challenges [3, 7]. Ethical leadership is consistently associated with stronger corporate social responsibility (CSR) [30, 39], which underpins ESG performance. Leaders who prioritize ethical conduct naturally steer their organizations towards greater social responsibility. They serve as role models and value communicators, creating an environment where adherence to ESG principles, particularly the social dimension (e.g., employee welfare, community engagement), is encouraged [30]. This leadership style also enhances employee engagement in CSR activities and fosters a positive, ethical work climate [21], leading to improved performance across ESG dimensions. By cultivating an organizational ethical culture, leaders ensure that information systems are implemented responsibly, promoting a climate in which ESG principles are systematic rather than ad-hoc. Therefore, we posit that:

H3: Ethical leadership is positively related to ESG performance.

2.4 Mediating Role of Ethical Leadership

Ethical leaders in SMEs serve as a critical conduit, translating digital management capability into tangible ESG outcomes by ensuring that technological advancements are deployed responsibly and in alignment with organizational moral values [34]. Specifically, ethical leaders with strong digital management capability can leverage digital tools to embed ethical considerations into the design and execution of ESG strategies, using data-driven insights for sustainable decision-making rather than solely for profit maximization. They foster an environment where digital management tools enhance transparency, stakeholder engagement, and accountability in ESG reporting, thereby building trust and legitimacy [33]. Furthermore, they proactively guide the application of digital management capability to monitor and report ESG performance, as well as identify and mitigate ethical risks associated with digital transformation, such as data privacy concerns and algorithmic bias [7, 23]. This mediating role is particularly salient in SMEs, where leaders are the principal decision-makers in designing strategies to reinforce operational efficiency and ethical commitments, resulting in more impactful ESG performance [30, 39]. Therefore, we posit that:

H4: Ethical leadership mediates the relationship between digital management capability and ESG performance

2.5 Moderating Role of Digital Management Capability

Digital management capability amplifies the positive effect of ethical leadership on ESG by providing tools and infrastructure to systematize ethical principles across all organizational functions [20]. This capability enables ethical leaders to meticulously track, analyze, and report ESG metrics, fostering data-driven decisions aligned with ethical standards and promoting greater accountability [31]. It allows leaders to monitor compliance with ethical guidelines in real-time, identify potential risks, and cultivate a culture where ethical considerations are integral to digital transformation initiatives [41]. Moreover, the digital management capability of ethical leaders facilitates the efficient dissemination of ethical policies and training, ensuring that all employees are aware of and adhere to the organization's ethical framework. They also support the integration of ESG criteria into supply chain management, product development, and customer relations, thus extending the ethical leader's impact beyond internal operations [32]. This digital enablement fosters a more comprehensive and data-driven approach to achieving ESG objectives, transforming ethical intentions into measurable outcomes. Additionally, this enhanced capability for data-driven decision-making and transparency further strengthens stakeholder trust and regulatory compliance, directly contributing to improved ESG performance [11, 25]. Therefore, we posit that:

H5: Digital management capability positively moderates the relationship between ethical leadership and ESG performance

Figure 1 summarizes the proposed relationships established by the hypotheses.

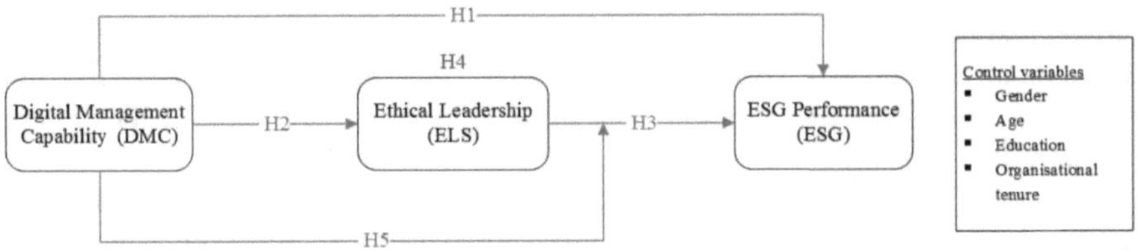

Fig. 1. The conceptual framework

3 Empirical Analysis

Data were collected data from 357 Chinese SMEs to ensure that responses were well-informed and aligned with the research objectives. All measurement variables were adapted from established literature and refined to suit the specific context of SMEs. The subsequent sections detail the research methodology and present the key findings, addressing the proposed hypotheses through rigorous statistical analysis.

3.1 Measurement Model Assessment

Following the guidelines of Hair et al. [13], all indicator factor loadings, composite reliability (CR), and average variance extracted (AVE) values for the key constructs—digital management capability, ethical leadership, and ESG performance—exceeded conventional thresholds. These results confirm both convergent validity and internal consistency reliability. Discriminant validity was subsequently assessed using the Heterotrait-Monotrait (HTMT) ratios and the Fornell and Larcker criterion (Table 1).

Table 1. Measurement items and validity assessments

Construct/Item	VIF	Outer loading
Digital management capability (DMC) [20] $\alpha = 0.928$; CR $= 0.944$; AVE $= 0.737$		
1. Being sensitive to information about technological changes in the marketplace	2.280	0.818
2. Working in partnership with international stakeholders towards technical knowledge acquisition	2.426	0.816
3. Obtaining information from specialized market surveys	3.066	0.864
4. Using of specific techniques or technology to disseminate knowledge	3.040	0.872
5. Commitment towards disseminating the latest (digital) knowledge at the workplace	3.547	0.893
Ethical leadership (ELS) [21] **People orientation (PO)** $\alpha = 0.881$; CR $= 0.914$; AVE $= 0.680$		

(*continued*)

Table 1. (*continued*)

Construct/Item	VIF	Outer loading
6. is interested in how I feel and how I am doing	1.668	0.728
7. Takes time for personal contact	2.391	0.844
8. Pays attention to my personal needs	2.637	0.866
9. Takes time to talk about work-related emotions	2.554	0.859
10. is genuinely concerned about my personal development	2.116	0.819
Fairness (FN) α = 791; CR = 0.867; AVE = .687		
11. Holds me accountable for problems over which I have no control (-ve)	1.682	0.721
12. Pursues his/her own success at the expense of others (-ve)	1.856	0.902
13. Manipulates subordinates (-ve)	1.562	0.852
Power sharing (PS)) α = 0.723; CR = .845; AVE = .646		
14. Seeks advice from subordinates concerning organizational strategy	1.638	0.843
15. Will reconsider decisions on the basis of recommendations by those who report to him/her	1.717	0.859
16. Delegates challenging responsibilities to subordinates	1.240	0.701
Concern on sustainability (CS) α = 0.900; CR = .938; AVE = .834		
17. Would like to work in an environmentally friendly manner	2.465	0.891
18. Shows concern for sustainability issues	3.583	0.936
19. Stimulates recycling of items and materials in our department	2.938	0.912
Ethical guidance (EG) α = 0.917; CR = .942; AVE = .801		
20. Clearly explains integrity related codes of conduct	2.797	0.889
21. Ensures that employees follow codes of integrity	3.136	0.906
22. Clarifies the likely consequences of possible unethical behavior by myself and my colleagues	3.087	0.897
23. Compliments employees who behave according to the integrity guidelines	2.821	0.889
Role clarification (RC) α = 0.899; CR = .930; AVE = .768		

(*continued*)

Table 1. (*continued*)

Construct/Item	VIF	Outer loading
24. Indicates what the performance expectations of each group member are	2.262	0.856
25. Explains what is expected of me and my colleagues	2.500	0.870
26. Clarifies priorities	3.165	0.899
27. Clarifies who is responsible for what	2.774	0.881
Integrity (IT) α = 0.884; CR = .928; AVE = .812		
28. Keeps his / her promises	2.485	0.893
29. Can be relied on to honour his/her commitments	3.130	0.928
30. Always keeps his/her words	2.293	0.881
ESG performance (ESG) [47]		
Environment responsibility (ER) α = 0.895; CR = 0.935; AVE = 0.827		
31. Implements corporate initiatives aimed at green innovation related to products or processes	2.460	0.891
32. Implements initiatives to reduce energy consumption	3.261	0.924
33. Overall emphasize environmental responsibility and support related initiatives	2.710	0.912
Social responsibility (SR) α = 0.926; CR = 0.953; AVE = 0.871		
34. Implements corporate initiatives aimed at green innovation related to products or processes	3.336	0.927
35. Implements initiatives to reduce energy consumption	3.708	0.935
36. Overall emphasize environmental responsibility and support related initiatives	3.721	0.937
Governance responsibility (GR) α = 0.908; CR = 0.956; AVE = 0.916		
37. Implements initiatives to improve the quality of its products, services, and processes, enhancing the company's image	3.252	0.954
38. Overall emphasize corporate governance responsibility and support related initiatives	3.252	0.960

3.2 Structural Model Assessment

To assess the overall fit of the structural model, several key statistical indicators were evaluated, including R^2, Q^2, and the Standardized Root Mean Square Residual (SRMR), all derived from PLS-SEM after 5,000 bootstrap samples. First, R^2 values quantify the in-sample predictive power by explaining the variance in endogenous variables. In this study, the R^2 values for ethical leadership (0.593) and ESG performance (0.650) exceed the 0.10 threshold recommended by Falk and Miller [9]. Second, the Stone-Geisser Q^2 value assesses the out-of-sample predictive relevance of each endogenous variable following the PLS-SEM analysis [13, 14, 29]. The Q^2 values for ethical leadership (0.595) and ESG performance (0.558) are both positive, demonstrating substantial predictive relevance. Further, an SRMR of 0.05—well below the 0.08 threshold— indicates a good model fit for theory testing. These metrics collectively confirm the predictability and validity of the structural model.

To address potential common method bias, Harman's single-factor test was conducted to examine common method variance (CMV) [15]. After loading all latent variables into a principal component analysis, the largest factor explained only 14.04% of the variance. As this is significantly below the 50% threshold, it confirms that common method bias does not pose a substantial issue to the validity of the findings.

3.3 Hypothesis Testing

To test the proposed hypotheses, we conducted PLS-SEM 4.0 bootstrapping with 5,000 samples. The path coefficients for the structural model are detailed in Table 2.

H1 posits that digital management capability is positively related to ESG performance. The analysis confirms this hypothesis, revealing a significant positive association ($\beta = 0.469$, $t = 7.530$, $p < 0.001$). Similarly, H2, which suggests that digital management capability positively influences ethical leadership, is supported ($\beta = 0.774$, $t = 27.403$, $p = 0.000$). H3 is also supported, indicating a positive relationship between ethical leadership and ESG performance ($\beta = 0.421$, $t = 7.130$, $p = 0.000$).

Turning to the mediating and moderating hypotheses, H4 proposes that ethical leadership mediates the relationship between digital management capability and ESG performance. Bootstrapping analysis confirmed that this indirect effect is statistically significant, thereby substantiating the mediating role of ethical leadership ($\beta = 0.326$, $t = 6.565$, $p = 0.000$). Finally, the results for H5, which examine the moderating effect of digital management capability on the relationship between ethical leadership and ESG performance, yield a statistically significant outcome. This suggests that the impact of ethical leadership on ESG performance is significantly strengthened at higher levels of digital management capability within the surveyed SMEs ($\beta = 0.106$, $t = 3.454$, $p = 0.001$).

Table 2. PLS-SEM analysis results

Hypothesis/Path	Standardized estimate	Standard deviation	t-value	Result Supported
Direct effect				
H1: DMC → ESG	0.469	0.062	7.530 ***	Supported
H2: DMC → ELS	0.774	0.028	27.403 ***	Supported
H3: ELS → ESG	0.421	0.059	7.130 ***	Supported
Mediation effect				
H4: DMC → ELS → ESG	0.326	0.050	6.565 ***	Supported
Moderation effect				
H5: DMC x ELS → ESG	0.106	0.031	3.454 ***	Supported
Effect of control variables				
Age → ESG	0.039	0.035	1.130	
Gender → ESG	0.049	0.031	1.566	
Education → ESG	-0.023	0.031	0.749	
Organisational tenure → ESG	0.026	0.034	0.758	

***$p < .001$, **$p < 0.01$, *$p < .05$

4 Discussions

4.1 Theoretical Implications

This study highlights the crucial role of ethical leadership, integrated with digital management capability, in enhancing ESG performance within SMEs [38]. While digital management capability directly influences ESG performance, ethical leadership serves as a vital mediator by aligning technological advancements with sustainable practices to achieve comprehensive ESG goals [33]. In this context, EBIS is not merely a technical implementation but a multidisciplinary phenomenon involving changes across strategy, organization, and technological shifts [40]. Our research contributes to the EBIS literature by illustrating that realizing the full benefits of digital transformation requires a fundamental shift in how firms employ technology to create value. By linking digital management capability to ESG performance, this study provides empirical evidence that EBIS serves as a fundamental pillar for sustainable business model innovation [38].

Furthermore, this study enriches the dynamic capabilities micro-foundations perspective [1, 16] within the context of EBIS by identifying digital management capability as a critical individual-level micro-foundation [18]. While EBIS research has traditionally focused on macro-level organizational outcomes, our findings highlight that individual-level actions and the quality of decision-makers are essential for firms to sense, seize, and reconfigure resources in dynamic digital environments [18]. The significant moderating role of digital management capability revealed in this research indicates that increased digital prowess amplifies the positive impact of ethical leadership on ESG outcomes [4, 11]. Leaders equipped with strong digital knowledge can more effectively leverage tools—such as those for transparent ESG data collection and technological innovation—to embed ethical considerations into strategy development [11, 25]. This suggests that an integrated approach, where ethical considerations guide the utilization of digital tools, is more effective for SMEs aiming to improve sustainability. This nuanced investigation into how ethical leadership and digital management capability interact within the context of ESG performance enriches the dynamic capabilities micro-foundations approach by demonstrating leadership's impact on organizational behaviour and its response to ESG challenges [7, 17, 35].

In addition, this study contributes to the theory by employing the dynamic capabilities micro-foundations approach to illuminate how ethical leadership equips itself to achieve ESG performance in the digital era [35, 36]. This study addresses a "knowledge gap" in the EBIS literature regarding SMEs, which often face greater resource constraints and limited capabilities than large enterprises. By examining the individual-level capabilities of ethical leaders, we extend the micro-foundations perspective to encompass the human-specific aspects crucial for navigating digital transformation. Specifically, our findings demonstrate how ethical leaders, acting as role models and value communicators, create an environment that fosters ESG adherence, thereby bridging the gap between technological capacity and ethical, sustainable practices within organizations [7]. Moreover, ethical leadership demonstrably reduces integrity violations and fosters a culture where ESG principles are prioritized, thus reinforcing the positive impact of digitalization on sustainability [23]. Our findings suggest that ethical leaders can leverage their digital management capability to embed ethical considerations into every stage of ESG strategy development and implementation, ensuring sustainable decision-making. This paper underscores the suitability of the dynamic capabilities micro-foundations framework for understanding how individual ethical leaders, equipped with digital competencies, strategically drive superior ESG performance, particularly in the context of SMEs. Consequently, this suggests that for smaller firms, the success of EBIS is highly dependent on these "human-specific aspects" of navigating digital change responsibly [35, 36].

4.2 Practical Implications

For managers seeking to embed responsible and sustainable practices, these findings provide concrete strategic guidance. First, organizations, particularly SMEs, should move beyond isolated training sessions and invest in leadership development programs that simultaneously strengthen ethical leadership and digital management competencies. Training initiatives should focus on advancing digital literacy while integrating ethical decision-making frameworks into digital strategies. This ensures that technological adoption remains aligned with core moral principles as leaders play a crucial role in setting and upholding ethical guidelines for the implementation and use of technology across the organization.

Second, a primary goal for EBIS is to create a unified digital infrastructure that facilitates communication and collaboration across all organizational levels [8]. This infrastructure should be leveraged to systematize ESG outcomes by using digital platforms to meticulously track, analyze and report ESG metrics, thereby transforming ethical intentions into transparent, measurable outcomes. Furthermore, managers should adopt an "ethics-by-design" approach to digital transformation. By mitigating algorithmic risks—such as data privacy violations and algorithmic bias [31]—firms can enhance stakeholder trust and build a resistance governance framework [33].

Finally, this research provides a strategic roadmap for SMEs to navigate the complexities of the digital era, ensuring that e-business architectures are systematically aligned with sustainability objectives. These insights contribute to the evolution of EBIS by highlighting the "human-machine collaborative" competencies necessary for driving superior social and environmental impact in a competitive digitalized landscape [20]. Utilizing an ethics-by-design approach not only supports ESG goals but also facilitates a sustained competitive advantage by fostering long-term organizational legitimacy.

4.3 Limitation and Future Research

This study has several limitations that should be acknowledged. First, the research sample is restricted to Chinese SMEs, which may limit the generalizability of the findings to other cultural or organizational contexts. Specifically, the collectivist nature of Chinese culture emphasizes group well-being, potentially fostering stronger pro-environmental attitudes and a lower tolerance for unethical practices among both consumers and managers [6]. Consequently, the ethical leadership behaviors and ESG strategies observed in these firms may be shaped by specific cultural values, making it challenging to generalize these findings to Western where individualistic values often prevail [46]. Second, cross-sectional design restricts the ability to infer causality between digital management capability, ethical leadership, and ESG performance. Longitudinal studies would provide deeper insight into how these relationships evolve over time. Third, while we followed rigorous procedures to adapt items from established literature, all measures are based on self-reported data, which may introduce potential concerns regarding common method bias.

Future research should address these limitations by expanding the sample to include diverse regions and organization types beyond the Chinese SMEs context, thereby enhancing external validity. Longitudinal and experimental research designs are recommended to better capture the dynamic changes and causal linkages among digital management capability, ethical leadership, and ESG outcomes. Furthermore, incorporating multi-source data—such as objective ESG performance metrics, employee perspectives, and third-party assessments—could mitigate common method bias and provide a more holistic view of organizational practices. Finally, subsequent studies could explore the micro-foundations framework in different digital transformation contexts and examine potential moderating factors, such as firm size, industry, or regulatory environment, to broaden the theoretical scope of this research.

5 Conclusion

In conclusion, this research underscores that E-Business Information Systems (EBIS) serve as an essential pillar for realizing the strategic and ethical advantages of digital transformation. By investigating the relationships among digital management capability, ethical leadership, and ESG performance within SMEs, this study offers significant theoretical and practical contributions. The findings emphasize the imperative for organizations—and their leaders specifically—to integrate ethical frameworks into digital transformation strategies. Such integration is crucial for navigating contemporary business complexities and achieving sustainable growth. By adopting this holistic approach, SMEs can enhance their sustainability, competitive advantage, and overall performance within an increasingly digitized global environment.

6 Disclosure of Interests.

The authors have no competing interests to declare that are relevant to the content of this article.

References

1. Abell, P., Felin, T., Foss, N.J.: Building micro-foundations for the routines, capabilities, and performance links. Manag. Decis. Econ. **29**(6), 489–502 (2008). https://doi.org/10.1002/mde.1413
2. Akter, S., Wamba, S.F., Mariani, M., Hani, U.: How to build an AI climate-driven service analytics capability for innovation and performance in industrial markets? Ind. Mark. Manage. **97**, 258–273 (2021). https://doi.org/10.1016/j.indmarman.2021.07.014
3. Brown, M.E., Treviño, L.K., Harrison, D.A.: Ethical leadership: a social learning perspective for construct development and testing. Organ. Behav. Hum. Decis. Process. **97**(2), 117–134 (2005). https://doi.org/10.1016/j.obhdp.2005.03.002
4. Canhoto, A.I., Quinton, S., Pera, R., Molinillo, S., Simkin, L.: Digital strategy aligning in SMEs: a dynamic capabilities perspective. J. Strateg. Inf. Syst. **30**(3), 101682 (2021). https://doi.org/10.1016/j.jsis.2021.101682
5. Cenamor, J., Parida, V., Wincent, J.: How entrepreneurial SMEs compete through digital platforms: the roles of digital platform capability, network capability and ambidexterity. J. Bus. Res. **100**, 196–206 (2019). https://doi.org/10.1016/j.jbusres.2019.03.035
6. Chan, R.Y., Sharma, P., Alqahtani, A., Leung, T.Y., Malik, A.: Mediating role of cultural values in the impact of ethical ideologies on Chinese consumers' ethical judgments. J. Bus. Ethics **191**(4), 865–884 (2024). https://doi.org/10.1007/s10551-024-05669-0
7. Cortellazzo, L., Bruni, E., Zampieri, R.: The role of leadership in a digitalized world: a review. Front. Psychol. **10**, 1938 (2019). https://doi.org/10.3389/fpsyg.2019.01938
8. Ellström, D., Holtström, J., Berg, E., Josefsson, C.: Dynamic capabilities for digital transformation. J. Strateg. Manag. **15**(2), 272–286 (2022). https://doi.org/10.1108/JSMA-04-2021-0089
9. Falk, R.F., Nancy B.M.: A Primer for Soft Modeling. University of Akron Press (1992)
10. Fang, M., Nie, H., Shen, X.: Can enterprise digitization improve ESG performance? Econ. Model. **118**, 106101 (2023). https://doi.org/10.1016/j.econmod.2022.106101
11. Ferdig, M.A.: Sustainability leadership: co-creating a sustainable future. J. Chang. Manag. **7**(1), 25–35 (2007). https://doi.org/10.1080/14697010701233809
12. Garzoni, A., De Turi, I., Secundo, G., Del Vecchio, P.: Fostering digital transformation of SMEs: a four levels approach. Manag. Decis. **58**(8), 1543–1562 (2020). https://doi.org/10.1108/MD-07-2019-0939
13. Hair Jr, J.F., Hult, G.T.M., Ringle, C.M., Sarstedt, M., Danks, N.P., Ray, S.: Evaluation of reflective measurement models. In: Partial Least Squares Structural Equation Modeling (PLS-SEM) Using R: A Workbook, pp. 75–90. Springer, Cham (2021) https://doi.org/10.1080/10705511.2022.2108813

14. Hair, J.F., Jr., Matthews, L.M., Matthews, R.L., Sarstedt, M.: PLS-SEM or CB-SEM: updated guidelines on which method to use. Int. J. Multivariate Data Anal. **1**(2), 107–123 (2017). https://doi.org/10.1504/IJMDA.2017.087624
15. Harman, H.H.: Modern Factor Analysis, 2nd edn. University of Chicago Press, Chicago (1967)
16. Helfat, C.E., Peteraf, M.A.: Managerial cognitive capabilities and the microfoundations of dynamic capabilities. Strateg. Manag. J. **36**(6), 831–850 (2015). https://doi.org/10.1002/smj.2247
17. Henisz, W., Koller, T., Nuttall, R.: Five ways that ESG creates value. McKinsey Q. **4**, 1–12 (2019)
18. Hossain, S., Fernando, M., Akter, S.: Digital leadership: towards a dynamic managerial capability perspective of artificial intelligence-driven leader capabilities. J. Leadership Organ. Stud. **32**(2), 189–208 (2025). https://doi.org/10.1177/15480518251319624
19. Huang, L., Paterson, T.A.: Group ethical voice: influence of ethical leadership and impact on ethical performance. J. Manag. **43**(4), 1157–1184 (2017). https://doi.org/10.1177/0149206314546195
20. Jafari-Sadeghi, V., Mahdiraji, H.A., Alam, G.M., Mazzoleni, A.: Entrepreneurs as strategic transformation managers: exploring micro-foundations of digital transformation in small and medium internationalisers. J. Bus. Res. **154**, 113287 (2023). https://doi.org/10.1016/j.jbusres.2022.08.051
21. Kalshoven, K., Den Hartog, D.N., De Hoogh, A.H.: Ethical leadership at work questionnaire (ELW): development and validation of a multidimensional measure. Leadersh. Q. **22**(1), 51–69 (2011). https://doi.org/10.1016/j.leaqua.2010.12.007
22. Khin, S., Ho, T.C.: Digital technology, digital capability and organizational performance: a mediating role of digital innovation. Int. J. Innov. Sci. **11**(2), 177–195 (2019). https://doi.org/10.1108/IJIS-08-2018-0083
23. Kidwell, R.E., Sprague, R.: Electronic surveillance in the global workplace: laws, ethics, research and practice. N. Technol. Work. Employ. **24**(2), 194–208 (2009). https://doi.org/10.1111/j.1468-005X.2009.00228.x
24. Liang, Y., Lee, M.J., Jung, J.S.: Dynamic capabilities and an ESG strategy for sustainable management performance. Front. Psychol. **13**, 887776 (2022). https://doi.org/10.3389/fpsyg.2022.887776
25. Lourenço, I.C., Branco, M.C., Curto, J.D., Eugénio, T.: How does the market value corporate sustainability performance? J. Bus. Ethics **108**(4), 417–428 (2012). https://doi.org/10.1007/s10551-011-1102-8
26. Lu, Y., Xu, C., Zhu, B., Sun, Y.: Digitalization transformation and ESG performance: evidence from China. Bus. Strateg. Environ. **33**(2), 352–368 (2024). https://doi.org/10.1002/bse.3494
27. Lyu, Y., Liu, X., Lu, Y.: Digital transformation as an ESG performance catalyst with insights from China's external governance. Sci. Rep. **15**(1), 32589 (2025). https://doi.org/10.1038/s41598-025-18120-9
28. Mahringer, C.A., Renzl, B.: Entrepreneurial initiatives as a microfoundation of dynamic capabilities. J. Account. Organ. Chang. **14**(1), 61–79 (2018). https://doi.org/10.1108/JAOC-11-2016-0066
29. Manley, S.C., Hair, J.F., Jr., Williams, R.I., Jr., McDowell, W.C.: Essential new PLS-SEM analysis methods for your entrepreneurship analytical toolbox. Int. Entrepre. Manag. J. **17**(4), 1805–1825 (2021). https://doi.org/10.1007/s11365-020-00687-6
30. Nguyễn, X.H., Doan, X.T., Tran, H.L.: CEO ethical leadership, corporate social responsibility and financial performance in the industrial revolution 4.0: evidence from garment and textile industry. Manag. Sci. Letters **9**(13), 2433–2442 (2019). https://doi.org/10.5267/j.msl.2019.7.012

31. Robinson, M., Kleffner, A., Bertels, S.: Signaling sustainability leadership: empirical evidence of the value of DJSI membership. J. Bus. Ethics **101**(3), 493–505 (2011). https://doi.org/10.1007/s10551-011-0735-y
32. Scuotto, V., Nicotra, M., Giudice, M.D., Krueger, N., Gregori, G.L.: A microfoundational perspective on SMEs' growth in the digital transformation era. J. Bus. Res. **129**, 382–392 (2021). https://doi.org/10.1016/j.jbusres.2021.01.045
33. Shin, Y., Sung, S.Y., Choi, J.N., Kim, M.S.: Top management ethical leadership and firm performance: mediating role of ethical and procedural justice climate. J. Bus. Ethics **129**(1), 43–57 (2015). https://doi.org/10.1007/s10551-014-2144-5
34. Su, W., Hahn, J.: A multi-level study on whether ethical climate influences the affective well-being of millennial employees. Front. Psychol. **13**, 1028082 (2022). https://doi.org/10.3389/fpsyg.2022.1028082
35. Teece, D.J.: Explicating dynamic capabilities: the nature and microfoundations of (sustainable) enterprise performance. Strateg. Manag. J. **28**(13), 1319–1350 (2007). https://doi.org/10.1002/smj.640
36. Teece, D.J.: Business models and dynamic capabilities. Long Range Plan. **51**(1), 40–49 (2018). https://doi.org/10.1016/j.lrp.2017.06.007
37. Teece, D.J., Pisano, G., Shuen, A.: Dynamic capabilities and strategic management. Strateg. Manag. J. **18**(7), 509–533 (1997). https://doi.org/10.1002/(SICI)1097-0266(199708)18:7%3c509::AID-SMJ882%3e3.0.CO;2-Z
38. Tigre, F.B., Henriques, P.L., Curado, C.: The digital leadership emerging construct: a multi-method approach. Manag. Rev. Q. **75**(1), 789–836 (2025). https://doi.org/10.1007/s11301-023-00395-9
39. Ullah, M.S., Muttakin, M.B., Khan, A.: Corporate governance and corporate social responsibility disclosures in insurance companies. Int. J. Account. Inf. Manag. **27**(2), 284–300 (2019). https://doi.org/10.1108/IJAIM-10-2017-0120
40. Verhoef, P.C., et al.: Digital transformation: a multidisciplinary reflection and research agenda. J. Bus. Res. **122**, 889–901 (2021). https://doi.org/10.1016/j.jbusres.2019.09.022
41. Vial, G.: Understanding digital transformation: a review and a research agenda. Manag. Dig. Transf. 13–66 (2021)
42. Warner, K., Wäger, M.: Building dynamic capabilities for digital transformation: an ongoing process of strategic renewal. Long Range Plan. **52**(3), 326–349 (2018). https://doi.org/10.1016/j.lrp.2018.12.001
43. Wei, J., Zheng, Q.: Environmental, social and governance performance: dynamic capabilities through digital transformation. Manag. Decis. **62**(12), 4021–4049 (2024). https://doi.org/10.1108/MD-10-2023-2028
44. Witschel, D., Döhla, A., Kaiser, M., Voigt, K.I., Pfletschinger, T.: Riding on the wave of digitization: Insights how and under what settings dynamic capabilities facilitate digital-driven business model change. J. Bus. Econ. **89**(8), 1023–1095 (2019). https://doi.org/10.1007/s11573-019-00950-5
45. Xu, J., Yin, J.: Digital transformation and ESG performance: the chain mediating role of technological innovation and financing constraints. Financ. Res. Lett. **71**, 106387 (2025). https://doi.org/10.1016/j.frl.2024.106387
46. Yuan, L., Chia, R., Gosling, J.: Confucian virtue ethics and ethical leadership in modern China. J. Bus. Ethics **182**(1), 119–133 (2023). https://doi.org/10.1007/s10551-021-05026-5
47. Zhu, J., Huang, F.: Transformational leadership, organizational innovation, and ESG performance: evidence from SMEs in China. Sustainability **15**(7), 5756 (2023). https://doi.org/10.3390/su15075756

Retrieval-Augmented Generation for Sensitive Web Path Discovery in Web-Based Information Systems

Kinsey K. S. Ng, Farah Yan, and Kevin Hung(✉)

School of Science and Technology, Hong Kong Metropolitan University, Hong Kong, China
khung@hkmu.edu.hk

Abstract. A Retrieval-Augmented Generation (RAG) approach for security auditing in Web-based information systems is proposed to enhance traditional dictionary-based fuzzing methods. The methodology leverages public `robots.txt` files and employs an agentic RAG loop implemented with LangChain for LLM-enhanced web path discovery. The approach improved the accuracy of sensitive path discovery from 0.030 to 0.667, compared with the traditional static, dictionary-based method.

1 Introduction

1.1 Threat of Cyber Attacks on Web-Based Information Systems

A web application is a software program that runs on a web server and is accessed by users through a web browser over the Internet. Web applications provide interactive services, data processing, and content delivery for a wide range of purposes, from e-commerce and digital marketplaces to social networking. A web attack targeting a web application with the intent to compromise security, steal data, disrupt services, or gain unauthorized access; it can lead to data leakage, financial loss, reputational damage, and disruption of e-business operations and customer experience. These attacks exploit various types of vulnerabilities in web applications. Attackers are required to have broad knowledge across different technical aspects to plan an effective attack kill chain, access the web application, and ultimately steal sensitive data. Web attacks also create direct economic damage for e-business systems through fraud, account takeover, and disrupted online transactions. In its 2023 Internet Crime Report, the FBI's IC3 reported losses exceeding $12.5 billion [1]. This economic exposure motivates proactive security testing and with rapid identification methods in indetifying web vulnerabilities to prevent potential attacks.

Misconfigured access control vulnerabilities, highlighted in the OWASP Top 10 Web Application Security Risks [2] and corresponding to A01 (Broken Access Control), A05 (Security Misconfiguration), A07 (Identification and Authentication Failures), and A04 (Insecure Design), allow attackers to bypass authorization and access sensitive resources that should remain protected. Weak access

Published by Springer Nature Switzerland AG 2027
J. Kim et al. (Eds.): EBISION 2025, IFIP AICT 786, pp. 80–92, 2027.
https://doi.org/10.1007/978-3-032-26616-3_6

control amplifies the risks associated with sensitive path discovery: unauthenticated access to administrative or backup directories can expose configuration files, database dumps, or internal APIs, while insufficient authorization on legacy endpoints can enable privilege escalation. These issues can result in breaches of confidentiality and integrity, compliance violations, and a greater blast radius for lateral movement [3]. Directory and endpoint discovery is a critical step in reconnaissance during a web attack, as attackers must first identify potentially vulnerable pages as targets. Traditional dictionary-based fuzzing approaches rely on sending large volumes of HTTP requests using extensive wordlists, which increases both network costs and the risk of detection. Existing research on enumeration strategies shows that performance depends heavily on the quality of path candidates, emphasizing the need for more efficient and targeted discovery methods [4–6]. In enterprise e-business, regular penetration testing remains essential to prevent potential attacks.

1.2 Robots.txt

The `robots.txt` file is located at the root of websites and was designed to provide instructions to search engine crawlers about which areas of the site are allowed or disallowed for indexing; the protocol is standardized in RFC 9309 [17]. However, attackers often use `robots.txt` to discover sensitive resources that developers intended to hide from public view. Many of these paths are not meant to be easily found, and their exposure can lead to security issues if they reveal confidential directories.

A simplified `robots.txt` file may look as follows:

```
User-agent: *
Disallow: /admin/
Disallow: /backup/
Disallow: /internal-api/
Allow: /assets/
Sitemap: https://example.com/sitemap.xml
```

Typical entries in `robots.txt` such as : `Disallow: /admin/` entries reveal the presence of administrative interfaces that should remain hidden, making them targets for unauthorized access attempts. Similarly, `Disallow: /internal-api/` paths may expose internal APIs not intended for public use, helping attackers discover undocumented or less-secured interfaces. Combining `robots.txt` records with reconnaissance tools (such as subdomain discovery and crawling) can reveal additional directories. When combined with other web vulnerabilities, attackers may mount further attacks, such as discovering exposed backup files by appending common file extensions (such as `.zip`, `.sql`, `.bak`) or exploiting missing access control that enables directory listing.

1.3 Fuzzing Techniques

Fuzzing is a software testing technique that involves providing invalid, unexpected, or random data as inputs to a program to discover vulnerabilities and unexpected behaviors [7]. In web security, fuzzing is used to discover vulnerabilities by sending sets of payloads and estimating whether a target is vulnerable based on the web server's responses. To detect access-control vulnerabilities in Web applications, attackers often use standard directory wordlists for fuzzing and review the returned accessible resources. Effective path fuzzing relies on a careful combination of technical dependencies, target selection, and curated wordlists or methods, and practitioners may merge datasets of known routing patterns, attack signatures, vulnerabilities, and endpoint lists. Path fuzzing tools, such as Gobuster, Wfuzz, and Feroxbuster, use brute-force techniques and curated path dictionaries to generate HTTP requests and analyze responses for sensitive directory discovery. While larger dictionaries can increase coverage, they also raise resource consumption and detection risk due to the increased number of requests [7,8]. The effectiveness of path fuzzing depends on how well attackers combine their experience, tool selection, and wordlist curation for the specific target application.

1.4 Large Language Models (LLMs)

Large Language Models (LLMs) are neural language models trained on large-scale text corpora to predict and generate natural language, enabling general-purpose language understanding and text generation [9]. LLMs enable data synthesis and instruction generation. However, in security applications, traditional usage patterns have several limitations. Full-parameter fine-tuning demands substantial computational resources and curated labels. Prompt-only generation without retrieval increases the likelihood of hallucinations and provides inadequate coverage of domain-specific terminology. Long-context inference elevates latency and cost, while token budgets constrain how much diverse information can be included. Embedding-model mismatch (e.g., applying general-purpose embeddings to highly specialized URL/path corpora) degrades retrieval quality, and naive or insufficient chunking reduces semantic coherence.

1.5 RAG

LLM-only approaches are poorly suited for web penetration testing because prompt-only generation can cause hallucinations, provides incomplete coverage of domain-specific knowledge, and becomes costly when long contexts are used to supply sufficient examples. These limitations motivate Retrieval-Augmented Generation (RAG), which grounds the model in external evidence relevant to the targets. The Retrieval-Augmented Generation (RAG) approach requires preparing a database of relevant evidence, but it is much less resource-intensive compared to fine-tuning a language model. No changes to the underlying model are needed, making it easy to update the knowledge base as new data becomes available. This flexibility allows for rapid adaptation to new domains or information without retraining. Also, the architecture supports the use of multiple agents, which can collaborate or specialize in different retrieval or generation tasks, further improving efficiency and coverage.

1.6 Fuzzing

After generating candidate paths for penetration testing, fuzzing validation is performed to verify path existence and accessibility. Deployment modes include scheduled security assessments, CI/CD integration for staging environments, and incident-driven manual execution. In production environments, business systems are typically protected by Web Application Firewalls (WAFs); fuzzing tests can therefore also evaluate WAF performance and prevention efficacy by measuring detection rates, response times, and blocking accuracy against simulated attack traffic (Fig. 1).

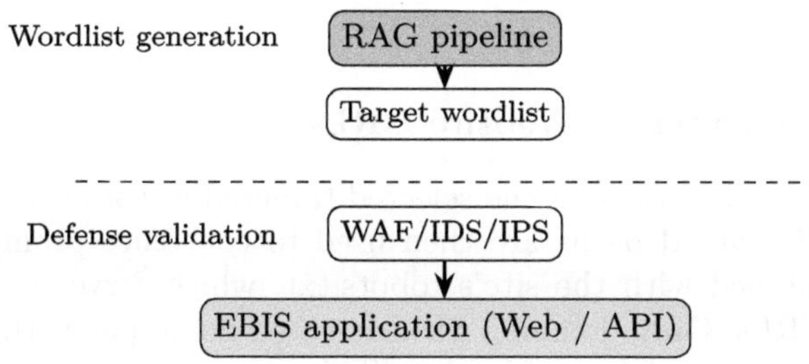

Fig. 1. The RAG pipeline in enhacing EBIS security architecture.

2 Methodology

This research introduces a pipeline for sensitive path discovery based on an agentic RAG architecture, structured into four stages: (1) Vector Database Construction, (2) Extracting Website URLs, (3) Agentic RAG Loop, and (4) Web Path Discovery.

2.1 Stage 1: Vector Database Construction

Common Crawl provides large-scale `robots.txt` artifacts that include disallowed path directives, which serve as an inexpensive proxy for sensitive or restricted areas of Web applications [11]. This stage constructs a retrieval corpus from these artifacts so that later generation can be grounded in real-world path patterns.

A corpus of `robots.txt` files is collected and normalized, and `Disallow` records are extracted as the primary signal; each instance is represented as an access-control "signature".

These signatures are vectorized and clustered using K-means to group websites with similar disallow patterns. Clustering reduces redundancy in the multi-million-file corpus and enables representative selection across diverse site structures rather than over-sampling highly repeated templates. A subset of the top 10 000 distinct `robots.txt` records is selected for the RAG database. For each selected record, associated domains and sample source files are retained to preserve provenance and support later retrieval and prompting (Table 1).

Table 1. Statistics for Robots.txt collected

Item	Value
1) Robots.txt files	3 766 879
2) Selected Distinct Robots.txt variants (for RAG)	10 000
3) Avg number of domains per top-10,000 variant	Avg: 238.85 Top: 505 610 Median: 16 Coverage: 63.41%
4) Avg disallow URLs per robots.txt	21.08

2.2 Stage 2: Extracting Website URLs

The process begins by crawling the selected targeted websites to collect existing paths. These discovered paths are then used to construct prompts for further prediction, combined with the site's robots.txt, which serves as a signature of the website's URLs. Only domains with detected home pages that return valid responses are considered for extraction. This stage aims to capture an initial snapshot of the target website's structure. Collected URLs are restricted to the same domain, and third-party links and redundant URLs are removed, so the resulting set reflects distinct application routes rather than repeated copies of the same resource. The extracted URL set is then treated as grounded context for the subsequent generation stage, helping the model adapt to the target's observed URL patterns.

2.3 Stage 3: Agentic RAG Loop

The system then enters the agentic RAG loop as showing in Algorithm 1. Agent-style prompting can further improve grounded generation [10,12]. The loop is implemented using the LangChain framework, which coordinates interactions with the GPT-4o-mini model, retrieval components, and validation logic in an agent-driven workflow. Prompts are constructed from the previously gathered target-site URLs and the robots.txt entries retrieved from the RAG vectorized database; these entries serve as references for sensitive keywords and pattern paths relevant to the target. Prompts use a role-based and few-shot prompting approach tailored to the web application's structure and characteristics, considering technologies such as programming languages, frameworks, and development practices. LangChain manages both retrieval and prompt assembly and iteratively feeds newly generated URLs back into the loop until a sufficient set of candidates has been produced and stored for subsequent validation. Prompt template used in Stage 3 are provided in Appendix A.Upon completion, the RAG pipeline consolidates all results, producing a ranked list of suggested paths. The ranking incorporates the estimated probability that each suggested path is reachable on the target website.

Algorithm 1 RAG-guided brute-force probing and validation loop

d: base URL.
P_0: initial observed paths.
S: seen paths.
G: generated candidates.
$\mathcal{R}$: robots-derived RAG database.
K: target number of unique paths, default 500.
k: per-iteration generation size.
n: RAG neighbors.

Require: $d, P_0, \mathcal{R}, K, k, n$
$S \leftarrow \emptyset$; $G \leftarrow \emptyset$; $P \leftarrow P_0$; $i \leftarrow 0$
while $|S| < K$ **and** $i < 50$ **do**
  $i \leftarrow i + 1$
  $E \leftarrow \text{Retrieve}(\mathcal{R}, S, n)$
  $q \leftarrow \text{Prompt}(d, P, S, E, k)$
  $\hat{G} \leftarrow \text{Gen}(\text{GPT-4o-mini}, q)$
  $\hat{G} \leftarrow \text{Dedup}(\hat{G}, S \cup P_0)$
  $G \leftarrow G \cup \hat{G}$; $S \leftarrow S \cup \text{Paths}(\hat{G})$
  $P \leftarrow \text{Bound}(P_0 \cup \text{Paths}(\hat{G}) \cup E, 1000)$
  if $|\hat{G}| = 0$ **then break**
end while

When $|\hat{G}| = 0$, the generator produces no novel candidate paths after deduplication against $S \cup P_0$, so the set of newly added paths $\hat{G}$ is empty. In this no-progress case, the loop terminates early because subsequent iterations are likely to repeat the same outcome, increasing cost without improving coverage.

2.4 Stage 4: Web Path Discovery

Generated paths are validated by issuing real HTTP GET requests to the target websites and recording the returned HTTP status codes. In our implementation, each probe issues an HTTP GET request to the target endpoint formed by concatenating the base domain with the candidate path, using an 8 s timeout to determine if the target vaild and following HTTP redirections. This process is parallelized using a thread pool with up to 64 workers to amortize network latency. The enumeration loop proceeds until predefined number of unique URLs have been produced. All generated URLs are validated by issuing real HTTP requests and collecting server responses. Status codes are mapped as follows: $TP = \{200, 403, 500\}$, $TN = \{404\}$, $FP = \{301, 302\}$, and all other codes are treated as FN for metric computation. In plain terms, an HTTP 200 (OK) indicates that the resource exists and responds successfully and is therefore counted as a true positive; 403 (Forbidden) indicates that the resource exists but access is denied, evidencing a valid sensitive endpoint and thus a true positive; and 500 (Internal Server Error) typically arises from an existing handler failing during processing, indicating resource existence despite a server-side failure and thus a true positive.

A 404 (Not Found) indicates that the path does not resolve to a resource on the target and is counted as a true negative. Redirects such as 301/302 do not confirm the presence of the intended resource—often leading to a generic page or login—and are therefore counted as false positives for the sensitivity-detection task. Other statuses (e.g., 401, 429, 503) are treated as false negatives in summary scoring unless independent validation demonstrates resource existence. Table 2 summarizes the common response codes and their interpretation in this study.

Table 2. Interpretation of common HTTP status codes.

Code	HTTP Status	Common situation in web path validation
200	OK	Treated as a successful discovery, since the endpoint exists and returns content
403	Forbidden	Treated as a successful discovery, since the endpoint exists but access is denied, often indicating a protected administrative or sensitive route
500	Server error	Treated as a successful discovery, since a handler exists and is invoked despite server-side failure
404	Not found	Treated as a non-discovery, since the requested path does not resolve on the target website
301	Moved permanently	Treated as a non-success outcome, since the redirection target often does not confirm the intended endpoint
302	Found	Treated as a non-success outcome, since the redirection target often does not confirm the intended endpoint

3 Experimental Settings

3.1 Evaluation Datasets

For evaluation, we randomly select Web-based websites (e.g., retail, marketplaces) from a large robots.txt corpus collected from Common Crawl and perform real crawling until 200 valid domains are collected. A domain is considered valid if (1) its homepage returns HTTP 200 and (2) the homepage contains more than 10 distinct same-domain URLs. For each valid domain, we fetch and scrape site URLs, normalize query parameters (remove ordering, deduplicate keys, canonicalize dynamic segments), and assemble the resulting URL set as a dataset. These normalized URLs are then fed into the RAG pipeline. The pipeline generates candidate URLs by conditioning on the input URLs with prompts; the generated URLs are then used as inputs to the next iteration, and run an agentic RAG loop. In each iteration, the retriever supplies the URLs from last retrieval and query results from RAG robots.txt database, then the LLM proposes sensitive URL candidates, and keep the feedback loop in fed back to the LLM. The discovery loop terminates only when 100 unique URLs have been produced.

3.2 Baselines

Baselines include: (i) static dictionary enumeration using a breadth-first approach with a wordlist comprising the top 100 URLs extracted from disallowed entries in the RAG robots.txt database; and (ii) a prompt-only, LLM-generated wordlist for each domain, which is similar to the proposed approach but without RAG retrieval. These baselines evaluate the effectiveness of the RAG-generated URL datasets. All wordlists follow the same procedure for issuing HTTP requests, and the resulting HTTP status-code distributions are compared across methods.

Table 3. Comparison across methods.

	HTTP Status Codes Counts						Confusion Matrix				Efficiency
Method	200	403	500	404	301	302	Acc.	Prec.	Rec.	F1	Hits
Proposed RAG	7.27	10.19	0.54	48.72	0.00	0.00	0.667	0.668	0.465	0.496	18.0
Prompt-only LLM	2.98	5.04	0.03	20.16	0.00	0.00	0.286	0.493	0.102	0.144	8.1
Static dict. (Baseline)	0.41	0.13	0.00	2.47	0.00	0.00	0.030	0.050	0.026	0.027	0.5

Note: HTTP Status Codes fields report the average number of responses observed per domain after completing the validation test; Accuracy (Acc.), Precision (Prec.), Recall (Rec.), and F1-score (F1) are computed from the response-based classification mapping described in Sect. 3. The Efficiency column reports the success hits per 100 requests metric.

3.3 Evaluation Metrics

Evaluation is reported at two levels. This study summarizes raw HTTP status-code counts to characterize the operational outcomes of probing. In this view, higher counts of 200, 403, and 500 indicate more reachable endpoints, while higher counts of 404 indicate wasted probes on non-existent paths. Redirect-heavy outcomes such as 301 and 302 can indicate that a server is routing requests to generic pages such as a canonical endpoint or a login flow, which does not necessarily confirm that the probed path exists as intended.

To enable consistent comparison across methods, the HTTP status codes are mapped into confusion-matrix labels. We then report standard summary metrics over the resulting outcomes [18]. With this mapping, accuracy reflects the overall proportion of correct outcomes, precision reflects how many predicted hits are confirmed by probing, recall reflects how many confirmed hits are obtained among all outcomes under the probing budget, and the F1-score summarizes the precision–recall trade-off. Table 3 compares methods under the same validation procedure.

- **Code counts (200/403/500/404/301/302)**: Per-status HTTP response counts.
- **Confusion (TP/TN/FP/FN)**: Classification counts derived from the status-code mapping.
- **Accuracy (Acc.)**: Proportion of correct classifications.
- **Precision (Prec.)**: TP/(TP + FP).
- **Recall (Rec.)**: TP/(TP + FN).
- **F1-Score**: Harmonic mean of precision and recall.
- **Budget/efficiency metrics**: Success hits per 100 requests.

Examples of validated URLs and their returned HTTP status codes in Stage 4 are summarized in Appendix B.

4 Discussion

4.1 Benefits of Agentic RAG

Empirically, the proposed RAG approach achieves the best overall performance, outperforming the prompt-only LLM baseline across all metrics: Accuracy improves from 0.286 to 0.667 (+0.381; +133%), Precision from 0.493 to 0.668 (+0.175; +35.6%), Recall from 0.102 to 0.465 (+0.363; +356%), and F1 from 0.144 to 0.496 (+0.352; +244%). These gains indicate that leveraging the robots.txt-grounded RAG database substantially enhances discovery effectiveness compared to LLM-only generation. Relative to traditional wordlists, the RAG approach also delivers clear improvements across the same metrics. Beyond the scores, the agent adaptively prioritizes promising candidates based on real-time feedback, reducing unnecessary brute-force attempts; and the approach avoids additional model fine-tuning while remaining practical for scalable directory fuzzing in web-based information systems.

4.2 Use of Robots.txt

Publicly available `robots.txt` files provide reliable references for directory fuzzing, as they explicitly enumerate sensitive and restricted URL paths defined by website administrators. By incorporating these files into the RAG process, the RAG pipeline can accurately label sensitive URLs and use them as ground truth for validation. This approach enhances the accuracy of path discovery because the RAG model is guided by real-world examples rather than relying solely on generic wordlists.

4.3 Redirects and Soft-200 Responses

The status-code mapping used in this work (treating 301/302 as *FP*) reflects that redirections do not, by themselves, confirm the presence of the intended sensitive resource. In practice, however, many production stacks implement redirection logic at the application layer while returning HTTP 200, for example via HTML meta-refresh tags or JavaScript-based navigation (e.g., window.location or single-page application routing). Likewise, "soft-404" pages may return HTTP 200 with templated "not found" content. As a result, a purely status-based evaluation can misclassify client-side redirects and soft-404 s as true positives.

4.4 RAG Configuration and Hyperparameters

The current configuration of retrieval-augmented generation (RAG) in this work uses a set of fixed parameters and heuristics tailored to directory fuzzing and sensitive path discovery. However, mixed parameter settings may also be effective for web path enumeration. For example, two embedding channels can be considered, morphological (path structure) and contextual (semantic meaning), and combined using a static interpolation weight (α) to form a single representation [13]. Further adapting these weights dynamically based on observed novelty, hit rate, or redundancy during fuzzing could better accommodate the evolving target website. Embedding-model selection can be guided by benchmarking efforts such as MTEB [19]. In addition, scalable similarity search in vector databases is commonly implemented with libraries such as FAISS [20]. Parameters can be adjusted based on fuzzing feedback in each iteration and weighted by budget and rate-limit constraints.

4.5 Implications for E-Business Information Systems

The research supports pre-penetration test scoping. Security teams replace exhaustive brute-force enumeration, which risks WAF alerts and IP blocking, with targeted path discovery, focusing on empirically reachable endpoints. For compliance auditing, platforms under PCI-DSS or ISO 27001 requirements, which are commonly mandated in Business Information Systems compliance requirements, will benefit from time and manpower reduction in reconnaissance work to accelerate the development lifecycle.

5 Conclusion

A practical, robots.txt-based workflow for directory fuzzing using RAG is presented. Leveraging public `robots.txt` with embedding and guided generation, the approach increases discovery efficiency while reducing brute-force overhead. The proposed pipeline integrates robots-derived retrieval with an agentic prompting loop to generate candidate paths that are grounded in real-world routing patterns. A validation stage then probes the suggested paths and evaluates outcomes using consistent HTTP status-code mappings, enabling direct comparison against static dictionary and prompt-only baselines. Empirical results indicate that retrieval grounding improves the yield of reachable endpoints under a fixed probing budget and supports more effective scoping for security auditing of Web-based information systems.

6 Future Works

Future work includes ablations on LLM/SLM choice, query expansion strategies, corpus composition, and broader real-world evaluations across Web-based platforms (e.g., Magento [14], Shopify [15], WooCommerce [16]). Several directions can be explored to further increase discovery accuracy while keeping request budgets and operational risk low.

Validation Beyond Status Codes. The validation stage can be strengthened by incorporating lightweight response-content checks to identify soft-404 pages, login interstitials, and client-side redirects, and by normalizing redirect targets so that endpoint existence is not miscounted as a false positive.

Retrieval Quality Improvements. Retrieval quality can be improved by combining structural and semantic signals and by dynamically adjusting the retrieval top-K and similarity thresholds based on observed hit rate and novelty, which may reduce noisy exemplars that induce off-target generations.

More Conservative Generation. The generation step can be made more conservative by adding explicit constraints for path formatting and technology-specific routing conventions, and by calibrating probability scores using feedback from prior probe results to better prioritize high-yield candidates.

Additional Target-Side Evidence and Active Learning. Accuracy can be improved by incorporating additional target-side evidence sources (e.g., sitemaps, discovered JavaScript routes, and framework fingerprints) and by adopting an active-learning loop in which validated true positives and systematic failure cases update prompt exemplars and filtering rules across iterations.

A Stage 3 Prompt Examples

This appendix provides prompt excerpts used by the Stage 3 agentic RAG loop implementation.

A.1 System Prompt

```
You are an elite offensive security researcher. Given a web domain, observed in-scope paths,
and any technology hints, propose likely sensitive or interesting paths on that domain.
CRITICAL OUTPUT POLICY: Return JSON ONLY, with no commentary, no code fences, no markdown,
no prose.The JSON must be an array of objects, each with keys: rank (int),
path (string starting with '/'), probability (0..1).
Only include paths for the same domain. Do NOT output any path that appears
in the user's message (Observed paths or Already proposed).
All paths in the output must be unique and novel relative to the input lists.
```

A.2 User Prompt

```
Domain: {domain}
Observed paths (subset):
{path_1}
{path_2}
...
RAG candidates (last iteration):
{rag_candidate_1}
{rag_candidate_2}
...
Detected technologies: {tech_hints}
Already proposed (do NOT repeat):
{prior_1}
{prior_2}
...
Task: Enumerate the top {topk} likely sensitive/hidden paths for this same domain.
Return JSON ONLY. Use this exact template:
[
  {"rank": 1, "path": "/admin", "probability": 0.82},
  {"rank": 2, "path": "/login", "probability": 0.79}
]
```

B Examples of Stage 4 Validation Outcomes

This appendix provides examples of how probed paths are interpreted during Stage 4 validation (Table 4).

Table 4. Examples of validation outcomes in Stage 4 (HTTP probing).

Example probed path	Example HTTP response	Considered success?	Rationale
`/admin`	200 (OK)	Yes (TP)	The endpoint exists and returns content, confirming the discovered path resolves on the target
`/wp-admin/`	403 (Forbidden)	Yes (TP)	Access is denied but the resource is present; this often indicates an administrative or sensitive endpoint protected by authorization
`/api/internal`	500 (Internal Server Error)	Yes (TP)	A server-side handler exists and is invoked, implying the route is valid even if processing fails
`/backup.sql`	404 (Not Found)	No (TN)	The probed path does not map to a resource on the target and is treated as a non-discovery
`/admin/login`	302 (Redirect)	No (FP)	Redirects do not confirm the intended resource; they often lead to generic pages (e.g., login or homepage) rather than the target endpoint

References

1. Federal Bureau of Investigation (FBI) Internet Crime Complaint Center (IC3). Internet crime report 2023. Annual report (2024). https://www.ic3.gov/Media/PDF/AnnualReport/2023_IC3Report.pdf
2. OWASP Foundation. Owasp top 10: 2021. OWASP Foundation (2021). https://owasp.org/Top10/
3. Rennhard, M., Kushnir, M., Favre, O., Esposito, D., Zahnd, V.: Automating the detection of access control vulnerabilities in web applications. SN Comput. Sci. **3**, 376 (2022)
4. Antonelli, D., Cascella, R., Schiano, A., Perrone, G.: "dirclustering": a semantic clustering approach to optimize website structure discovery during penetration testing. J. Comput. Virol. Hack. Techn. **20**(4), 565–577 (2024)
5. Castagnaro, A., Conti, M., Pajola, L.: Offensive AI: enhancing directory brute-forcing attack with the use of language models. In: Proceedings of the 2024 Workshop on Artificial Intelligence and Security (AISec '24). ACM (2024)
6. Sigalov, D., Gamayunov, D.: Dead or alive: discovering server http endpoints in both reachable and dead client-side code. J. Inf. Secur. Appl. **82**, 103746 (2024)
7. Beaman, C., Redbourne, M., Darren Mummery, J., Hakak, S.: Fuzzing vulnerability discovery techniques: survey, challenges and future directions. Comput. Secur. (2022)
8. Putu, I., Dharmaadi, A., Athanasopoulos, E., Turkmen, F.,: Fuzzing frameworks for server-side web applications: a survey. Int. J. Inf. Secur. **24**, 73 (2025)
9. Zhao, W.X., Zhang, K., Wang, J.R., et al.: A survey of large language models. arXiv preprint arXiv:2303.18223 (2023)
10. Wang, Y., Wei, F.: Self-instruct: aligning language model with self generated instructions. arXiv preprint arXiv:2212.10560 (2023)
11. Common Crawl Foundation. Common crawl. Open Web Corpus (2025). https://commoncrawl.org/
12. Yao, S., et al.: React: synergizing reasoning and acting in language models. arXiv preprint arXiv:2210.03629 (2022)
13. Saxe, J., Berlin, K.: expose: A character-level convolutional neural network with embeddings for detecting malicious urls, file paths and registry keys. arXiv preprint arXiv:1702.08568 (2017)
14. Adobe Inc. Adobe commerce (magento) — official site. Official website (2025). https://business.adobe.com/products/magento/magento-commerce.html
15. Shopify Inc. Shopify—official site. Official website (2025). https://www.shopify.com/
16. Automattic Inc. Woocommerce—official site. Official website (2025). https://woocommerce.com/
17. IETF. Robots exclusion protocol. RFC 9309, Internet Engineering Task Force (2022). https://www.rfc-editor.org/rfc/rfc9309
18. Thakur, N., Reimers, N., R"uckl"e, A., Srivastava, A., Gurevych, I.: BEIR: a heterogeneous benchmark for zero-shot evaluation of information retrieval models. In: Proceedings of the 44th International ACM SIGIR Conference on Research and Development in Information Retrieval (2021)
19. Muennighoff, N., Tazi, N., Magne, L., Reimers, N., et al.: MTEB: massive text embedding benchmark. arXiv preprint arXiv:2307.09677 (2023)
20. Johnson, J., Douze, M., Jégou, H.: The faiss library. arXiv preprint arXiv:2401.08281 (2024)

Cyber Security

A Tool for Learning About Outdated Software Vulnerabilities and End-of-Life

Md Amiruzzaman(✉), Linh Ngo, and Ashik Ahmed Bhuiyan

West Chester University, West Chester 19383, PA, USA
mamiruzzaman@wcupa.edu

Abstract. This study presents a tool for enhancing E-Business Information Systems (EBIS) resilience by identifying outdated operating systems and installed applications on offline computers. While most EBIS vulnerability-management tools rely on network connectivity, our approach extends protection to isolated or legacy business environments through the development of a two-fold solution: a scanner app that reads and stores software information from individual computers, and a summary app that combines this data with software versions, Common Vulnerabilities and Exposures (CVE), and End-of-Life (EOL) support details from vendors. The summary app integrates EBIS data flows with machine-learning models that synthesize CVE descriptions, generating executive summaries to support managerial risk decisions.

1 Introduction

As digital transformation accelerates across E-Business Information Systems, the risks of cybersecurity issues increase proportionally. Cyberattacks are a constant threat, and cybersecurity professionals work to mitigate these risks [11]. Studies show that cybersecurity risks rise as software becomes outdated [14,19,21]. Outdated applications no longer receive vendor support, meaning no bug fixes, patches, or updates. Outdated software can lead to serious vulnerabilities [1], leaving users and institutions unprotected. Attackers often target machines running outdated operating systems or applications, knowing that no patches will fix existing vulnerabilities [7]. Risks associated with outdated software include (a) poor performance; (b) compliance issues; (c) complete system failure; (d) bugs; and (e) increased susceptibility to cyberattacks. Organizations with constrained IT budgets, including educational institutions and small-to-medium enterprises operating EBIS platforms, often rely on outdated software [2,9], which exposes them to cyberattacks like ransomware. Reasons for using outdated systems include preserving difficult-to-migrate data or relying on legacy software that meets specific business needs.

Typically, these outdated computers are used infrequently and kept disconnected from networks to reduce cyberattack risks. However, sensitive data transferred via USB drives to networked computers can still pose security threats. Tracking software installed on outdated systems is challenging. Existing tools

Published by Springer Nature Switzerland AG 2027
J. Kim et al. (Eds.): EBISION 2025, IFIP AICT 786, pp. 95–110, 2027.
https://doi.org/10.1007/978-3-032-26616-3_7

like Endpoint Configuration Manager (ECM) and LAN Sweeper are network-based and can only scan connected devices. Tools like Rapid 7 and Tenable also focus on systems connected to the Local Area Network (LAN) or the Internet, making them ineffective for computers that lack connectivity. In the context of EBIS, outdated or unsupported software threatens business continuity, data integrity, and regulatory compliance. Our work contributes to the EBIS field by providing an architecture and prototype that bridge isolated legacy systems with contemporary vulnerability intelligence (CVE/EOL), thus enabling more informed e-business decision-making.

2 Background and Related Work

Literature identifies six major cybersecurity threats: (1) phishing; (2) malware; (3) man-in-the-middle attacks; (4) identity and credential theft; (5) human factors, and (6) outdated software [3,14]. Existing works focus on reading information about outdated software, such as operating systems [13] and applications [12], and they primarily target Internet-connected systems.

Fan, Mao, Lu, and Wu [6] developed a cloud-based system called Offline Patching Scheme (OPS) to detect outdated software on cloud-connected computers and to provide patches for applications offline. Similarly, [10] employed a deep learning model to prioritize application upgrades based on vulnerabilities. This approach does not focus on collecting real-time information from outdated computers; instead, it creates a database of installed software and their vulnerabilities, helping to determine which applications need immediate attention. It is also noteworthy here that there are some other existing tools that can help in collecting installed software names and versions, such as LANsweeper and Rapid 7. However, they only work if a computer is connected to the Internet [17].

Our work addresses these limitations by targeting computers with outdated operating systems and software. The main challenge is collecting information about installed software on computers that are not connected to the Internet.

2.1 Software Versioning

Every software system is identified by its name and a corresponding version number [8]. The software version helps to separate one version from another, as it indicates the changes included in a particular software package. Often, software companies develop at least two versions of the same software package, such as (a) a working version (also known as the beta version)—that indicates that it is enhanced than the previous version and not yet rigorously tested, and (b) a stable version—that is ready for all users and rigorously tested by the software quality assurance team. By all means, a software version indicates some type of improvement as well as some other important information, such as order of release, degree of changes, and date of release.

2.2 Common Vulnerabilities and Exposures

Together, the name of a software and its version help to identify the software package or application uniquely. Therefore, Common Vulnerabilities and Exposures (CVE) is tied with each software name and its associated version [15]. CVE refers to security flaws that have been identified and proven by more than one source. Each CVE is identified by its CVE ID (also known as CVE number). CVE IDs are assigned by the CVE Numbering Authority (CNA). It comprises major software vendors, such as Cisco, IBM, Oracle, Red Hat, and Microsoft, as well as research institutions. The CVE ID format includes the year when the vulnerability was discovered, such as CVE-0123-456789. So, a CVE ID can be 13 characters wide. The first three are fixed letters, the second four digits are for the year the vulnerability is accepted, and the rest are a sequence number.

2.3 Term Frequency-Inverse Document Frequency (TF-IDF)

The collected vulnerability descriptions can repeat some information and keywords. So, extracting the important keywords from each vulnerability description can help prepare a summary report for executives [18]. The TF-IDF algorithm is a good analysis tool to determine important words for a set of documents [16,20].

$$\begin{aligned} \text{tf-idf}(t, D) &= \text{tf}(t, d) \times \text{idf}(t, D) \\ \text{tf}(t, d) &= f_{t|d} \\ \text{idf}(t, D) &= \log\left(\frac{N}{|\{d \in D : t \in d\}|}\right) \end{aligned}$$

where, $\text{tf}(t, d)$ function finds the frequency of a term (t) in a document (d), or the count of t given d. The $\text{idf}(t, D)$ function finds how many times a t appears in the total number of documents N, i.e., $N = |D|$. So, the $\text{tf-idf}(t, D)$ finds how important a term, t, in a document dataset, D.

3 Methodology

3.1 System Overview

This study focuses on offline or minimally connected legacy computers that still participate in an organization's E-Business Information System (EBIS). While these computers may occasionally connect to a Local Area Network (LAN), their restricted connectivity and outdated operating systems limit the IT team's ability to collect information using contemporary Endpoint Configuration Manager (ECM) tools. As a result, the organization often lacks accurate data about installed software, versioning, and related risk exposure on these legacy nodes.

To address this gap, this work proposes a two-fold solution:

1. a *scanner app* deployed on legacy Windows and Linux hosts to collect operating system and installed software information, and
2. a *summary app* running on a modern server in the EBIS core to ingest scanner output, enrich it with Common Vulnerabilities and Exposures (CVEs) and end-of-life (EOL) information, and present host-level risk summaries.

The system architecture is organized into three interacting subsystems:

- the EBIS edge and legacy nodes, where local data collection occurs (Fig. 1),
- the EBIS core network, where ingestion, enrichment, and reporting are performed (Fig. 2), and
- external vulnerability and lifecycle intelligence sources, which provide CVE and EOL data (Fig. 3).

3.1.1 EBIS Edge: Legacy Nodes and Scanner App

At the edge of the EBIS, the scanner app runs directly on outdated Windows and Linux machines. The key design constraint is that these hosts may be disconnected from the main EBIS network or subject to strict access controls. The scanner therefore relies only on local operating system facilities and produces a self-contained output file that can be transferred offline.

On Windows hosts (e.g., XP, Vista, 7, Server 2008, and 10), the scanner uses Java 8 and the Windows Management Instrumentation Command-line (WMIC) utility to extract:

- the operating system name and version, and
- the names and versions of installed applications or packages of interest.

The command

```
WMIC product where get Name, Version /FORMAT:CSV
```

returns a structured list of installed software and associated versions, which the scanner parses and writes to a CSV file.

On Linux hosts (e.g., Ubuntu 18.04–22.04), the scanner reads OS metadata from distribution release files under `/etc.` and enumerates installed packages using distribution-specific mechanisms. In both environments, the output is standardized into records of the form:

$$\text{Node, Caption, Version,}$$

where *Node* is the computer name, *Caption* is the operating system or application name, and *Version* is its version number. The resulting file is then moved via a controlled transfer channel (e.g., USB drive or restricted file share) into the EBIS core.

This architecture is captured in Fig. 1, which shows how the scanner modules interact with legacy hosts and produce scan report files for consumption by downstream components.

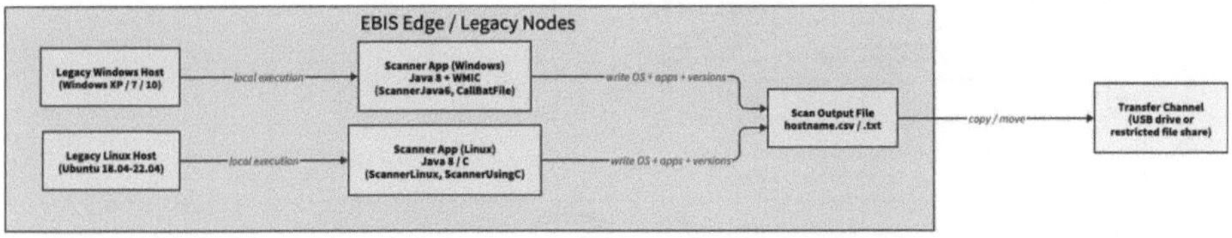

Fig. 1. Scanner deployment and data collection on EBIS edge and legacy nodes. The scanner applications (Windows and Linux) run locally on each host, extract OS and software version information, and export results as flat files for secure transfer into the EBIS core network.

3.1.2 EBIS Core: Summary App and Risk Enrichment

Within the EBIS core, the summary app is implemented as a Python/Flask web application backed by a MySQL database. Authorized EBIS stakeholders (e.g., IT staff, security analysts, and managers) access the app through a web interface to upload scanner output files, review host inventories, and inspect CVE/EOL-derived risk information. Upon upload, the summary app:

1. validates the file type and structure,
2. saves a copy in a server-side directory,
3. parses the contents into a tabular representation, and
4. inserts host–software tuples into the database with a generated Universally Unique Identifier (UUID) for each record.

The database schema is designed to support:

- a host and software inventory table (computer name, OS, installed application names, and version numbers),
- a CVE table capturing vulnerability identifiers, severity scores, and descriptions associated with specific software/version pairs, and
- an EOL table capturing end-of-life dates and support status for each software/version.

Figure 2 illustrates the core components of this subsystem, including the upload and validation controller, ETL (extract-transform-load) module, CVE and EOL integrators, TF-IDF summarizer, and the reporting interface. Together, they realize a pipeline that transforms raw scanner output into actionable EBIS risk intelligence.

3.1.3 External Vulnerability and Lifecycle Sources

The summary app enriches local EBIS data by integrating two classes of external security intelligence (Fig. 3):

- **CVE data:** Vulnerabilities associated with operating systems and installed applications are obtained from the CVE database [4], typically via publicly available NVD APIs. For each software/version pair, the system retrieves relevant CVE identifiers, severity metrics, and descriptive text.

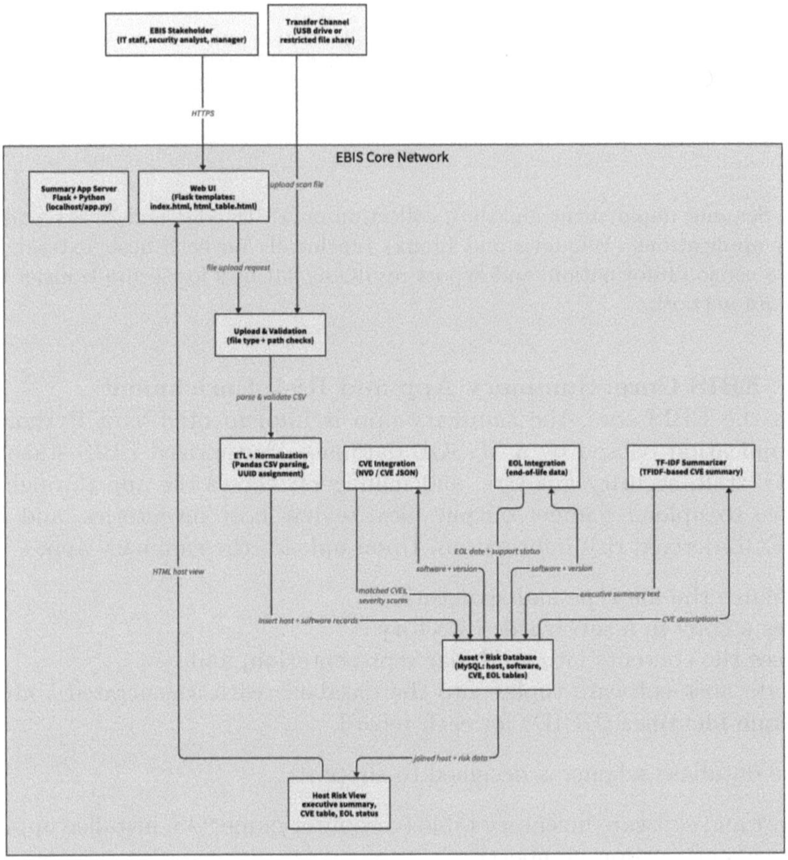

Fig. 2. Summary application architecture within the EBIS core network. Uploaded scan files are processed through validation, ETL, CVE enrichment, EOL mapping, and TF-IDF summarization before being presented through the web interface.

- **EOL data:** End-of-life (EOL) information is obtained from dedicated EOL datasets [5] that map software names and versions to lifecycle milestones (e.g., end of support or extended support dates).

These integrations are encapsulated within dedicated modules in the EBIS core, preserving a clean separation between internal asset data and external intelligence feeds.

3.2 Data Source

This work collects data from multiple sources:

- **Computer Details**: The computer name, operating system, and installed application names are sourced from the outdated computer(s).

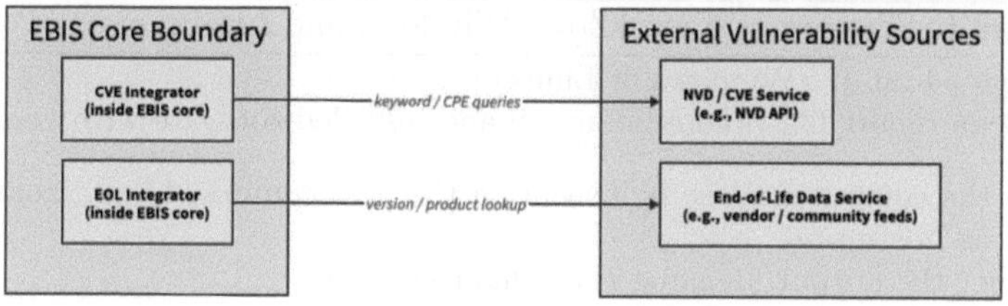

Fig. 3. Integration between EBIS core vulnerability integrators and external intelligence sources, including NVD/CVE services and end-of-life data feeds. These services supply the system with real-time vulnerability and lifecycle information.

- **Vulnerabilities**: Vulnerabilities associated with the operating system and its version, as well as installed applications, are obtained from the CVE database [4].
- **End-of-Life (EOL) Information**: EOL information for outdated software is sourced from the EOL database [5].

3.3 Requirements

The design and implementation of the scanner and summary apps are guided by the following requirements, which also inform unit tests, integration tests, and the evaluation of the overall tool:

1. **Local inventory capture:** The tool must save a report of installed software and operating system information from legacy Windows and Linux hosts, without requiring network-based management agents.
2. **Database exportability:** The scan report should be exportable to a relational database to support persistent storage, querying, and integration with existing EBIS asset-management systems.
3. **Distinct software and lifecycle tracking:** The database must represent distinct software and corresponding versions, and associate them with end-of-life (EOL) information obtained from the EOL database [5].
4. **Vulnerability enrichment:** The tool should collect vulnerability information from the CVE database [4] for each relevant software/version pair and store it alongside local asset records.
5. **Text-based risk summarization:** The tool should analyze vulnerability information, focusing on a small set of recent CVE descriptions per host, and produce an executive summary using text analysis (TF-IDF).

3.4 System Workflows and Algorithms

To make the system behavior reproducible and implementation-agnostic, this subsection presents high-level algorithms corresponding to the EBIS edge, core, and summarization workflows.

Algorithm 1. Scanner app workflow (Windows and Linux)

Input: Legacy host H (Windows or Linux)
Output: Scan report file R containing OS and installed software with versions

1. Obtain the computer name by executing the host command (e.g., `hostname`) and store it as *hostname*.
2. Construct the output filename R as `$hostname.csv`.
3. If H is a Windows host:
   (a) Execute a WMIC query to obtain the OS caption and version.
   (b) Execute a WMIC query to obtain installed product names and versions of interest.
   (c) Write a header row `(Node, Caption, Version)` to R.
   (d) Append rows for the OS and each installed product, using *hostname* as the node name.
4. Else if H is a Linux host:
   (a) Parse distribution release files under `/etc` to determine OS name and version.
   (b) Enumerate installed packages using the distribution's package manager or configuration files.
   (c) Write a header row `(Node, Caption, Version)` to R.
   (d) Append a row for the OS and rows for each installed package, using *hostname* as the node name.
5. If a previous file with the same name exists, remove it to avoid stale data.
6. Return the completed file R for transfer to the EBIS core.

This algorithmic description refines and structures the TF-IDF-based summarization process introduced earlier, making explicit how multiple CVE descriptions are transformed into a short, human-readable summary for each host.

Algorithm 2. Summary app ingestion and enrichment

Input: Scan report file R uploaded via the web interface

Output: Persisted host and software records with CVE and EOL enrichment, and a host-level risk view

1. Receive the uploaded file R from an authenticated user.
2. Verify that the file extension is supported (e.g., `.csv` or `.txt`); reject otherwise.
3. Save a copy of R in a server-side upload directory.
4. Parse R into a tabular structure and normalize column names to `(Node, Caption, Version)`.
5. For each row in the table:
   (a) Sanitize the strings to prevent SQL injection and enforce length constraints.
   (b) Generate a UUID for the record.
   (c) Insert the tuple (UUID, node name, software name, version) into the host–software table.
6. Extract the distinct set of software/version pairs from the database.
7. For each distinct software/version pair:
   (a) Construct a query key based on the software name and version (e.g., keyword or CPE-style string).
   (b) Query the CVE service to retrieve relevant vulnerabilities.
   (c) Insert the returned CVE identifiers, severity scores, and descriptions into the CVE table, linked to the software/version pair.
8. Load EOL data from the external EOL dataset.
9. For each software record in the host–software table:
   (a) Find the best-matching EOL entry for the software name and version.
   (b) If a match is found, update the record with EOL date and support status.
10. For each host node:
    (a) Collect the CVE descriptions associated with that host.
    (b) Apply Algorithm 3 to compute an executive summary of the host's vulnerability profile.
    (c) Store the resulting summary text in a host-summary table.
11. When a user requests details for a host, join the host–software, CVE, EOL, and summary tables and render the combined view in the web interface.

Algorithm 3. TF-IDF-based executive summary of CVE descriptions

Input: A set of CVE descriptions $D = \{d_1, d_2, \ldots, d_N\}$ for a given host
Output: A concise executive summary S

1. For each document $d_i \in D$:
   (a) Remove stop words, articles, and punctuation.
   (b) Split d_i into sentences and collect the cleaned sentences into a list.
2. Let *sentences* be the list of all cleaned sentences across all documents.
3. For each sentence s in *sentences*:
   (a) Tokenize s into words.
   (b) For each word w in s, compute the term frequency $\mathrm{tf}(w, s)$ as the count of w in s divided by the total number of words in s.
4. For each distinct word w appearing in any sentence:
   (a) Let n_w be the number of sentences in which w appears.
   (b) Compute the inverse document frequency $\mathrm{idf}(w) = \log\left(\frac{|sentences|}{1+n_w}\right)$.
5. For each sentence s in *sentences*:
   (a) Initialize a score $\mathrm{score}(s) = 0$.
   (b) For each word w in s, update $\mathrm{score}(s) \leftarrow \mathrm{score}(s) + \mathrm{tf}(w, s) \times \mathrm{idf}(w)$.
6. Compute the average sentence score

$$\text{threshold} = \frac{1}{|sentences|} \sum_{s \in sentences} \mathrm{score}(s).$$

7. Select all sentences whose score is greater than or equal to *threshold*, preserving their original order.
8. Concatenate the selected sentences to form the executive summary S.

4 Implementation

Following the EBIS architecture and workflows described in Sect. 3, the system implements two interoperable software modules: the scanner app deployed at the EBIS edge and the summary app deployed in the EBIS core. These modules operationalize Algorithms 1–3 and collectively support automated asset inventory, vulnerability enrichment, and executive-level risk summarization.

4.1 Scanner App

The scanner app is implemented in Java 8 to ensure compatibility with legacy Windows and Linux systems (XP, Vista, 7, Server 2008, and older Linux distributions). Its behavior follows Algorithm 1 and the architecture in Fig. 1. The design goal is to collect reliable system metadata using only local operating system facilities, without requiring modern management agents or network connectivity.

Windows Implementation. The scanner executes WMIC commands to extract OS metadata and installed software:

```
WMIC product where get Name, Version /FORMAT:CSV
```

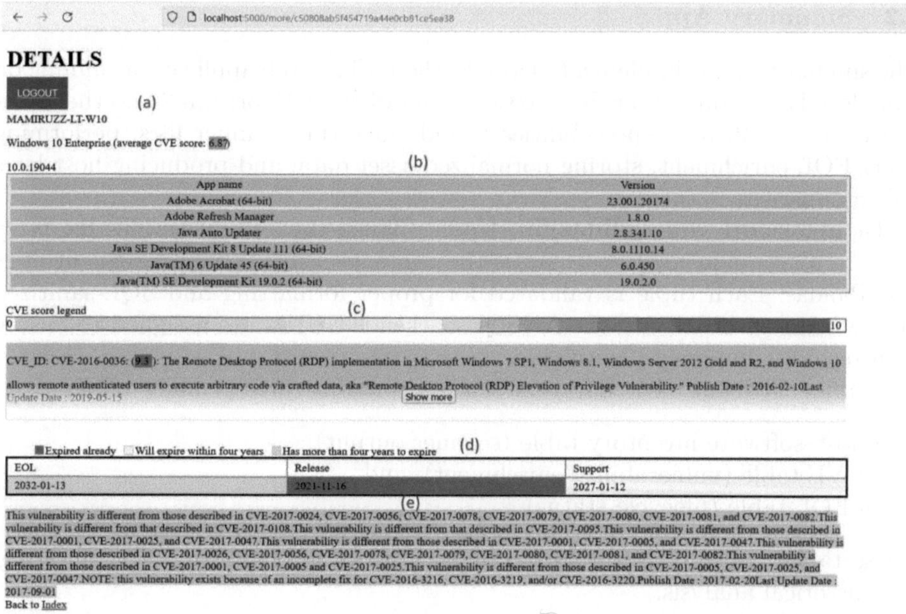

Fig. 4. Implemented interface of the summary app displaying detailed information for a scanned machine.

Outputs are parsed and normalized into `(Node, Caption, Version)` tuples, then exported as a CSV report. This approach avoids registry parsing and ensures stable behavior across multiple Windows releases.

Linux Implementation. On Linux hosts, the scanner reads distribution release files under `/etc.` to identify OS name and version, and enumerates installed packages using distribution-specific mechanisms. Each entry is normalized using the same schema as Windows, ensuring platform-independent handling in the summary app.

A sample output is shown in Table 1. This file forms the core artifact consumed by the summary app.

Table 1. Sample output from scanned computer: (left side) name of the installed packages and (right side) version corresponding to each installed package/application.

Node	Caption	Version
AMIR_LT_W7	Microsoft Windows 7 Ultimate	6.1.7601
AMIR_LT_W7	Java 8 Update 202 (64-bit)	8.0.2020.8
AMIR_LT_W7	Microsoft .NET Framework 4.7.2	4.7.03062

4.2 Summary App

The summary app is implemented as a Python/Flask web application running on a modern EBIS core server. It follows the workflow of Algorithm 2 and the architecture in Fig. 2. Its responsibilities include ingesting scanner files, performing CVE/EOL enrichment, storing normalized asset data, and producing host-level risk summaries.

Data ingestion and validation. Upon upload, the system verifies file type, stores a server-side copy, and parses the contents using Python's CSV utilities and Pandas. Each tuple is validated for proper formatting and SQL-sanitized before being inserted into the MySQL backend. UUIDs are assigned to ensure each record is uniquely identifiable.

Database Storage. The database schema contains three primary tables:

- a host–software inventory table (scanner output),
- a CVE table (vulnerability enrichment), and
- an EOL table (lifecycle status).

These tables collectively support complex queries for risk inspection, filtering, and historical analysis.

CVE and EOL Integration. Following Algorithm 2, the summary app queries external CVE sources and matches software/version pairs to EOL datasets [5]. Retrieved CVE identifiers, severity scores, and descriptive texts are stored in the CVE table. Lifecycle metadata (e.g., supported, deprecated, EOL) is attached to each software entry.

TF-IDF Executive Summary. For each machine, the summary app extracts CVE descriptions and applies Algorithm 3 to produce a concise risk narrative. This summarization enables IT managers to understand host-level risk posture without reading lengthy CVE descriptions. The resulting summary is stored alongside other host metadata.

4.2.1 Interface Design The Flask-based interface presents the list of scanned computers and allows authorized users to access per-machine detail pages (Fig. 4). Each detail view includes:

- the operating system and its average CVSS score,
- a list of installed applications and versions,
- matched CVEs with severity color-coding,
- EOL status indicators, and
- the TF-IDF-based executive summary.

Buttons for "Show more" allow users to expand long lists of vulnerabilities or EOL entries. Access control ensures only authorized personnel can view or delete scanned entries.

5 Evaluation

The developed tool is the first of its kind. There is no existing tool that does the same thing. Therefore, comparison of this tool's performance with existing apps is not feasible. However, to ensure its success, accuracy, and performance, a series of unit-tests and integration tests were performed.

5.1 Unit Testing

While developing the tool, each functional unit was divided into single methods. This helped to focus on individual tasks more carefully and also test them individually. A set of unit tests were written to check the functionality of each method. Both success cases and failure cases were tested to ensure the performance of the methods (see Tables 2 and 3). This was done for both the scanner app and the summary app.

Table 2. Unit test for scanner app

Unit test	Status
Read computer name	☑
Read Operating system name and version	☑
Read installed application names and version	☑
Save the output to a file for the summary app	☑
Delete previous file when the scanner app is ran again	☑

Table 3. Unit test for summary app

Unit test	Status
Check supported file type	☑
Save uploaded scanner file	☑
Read installed application names and version	☑
Insert information read from the file	☑
Delete previously saved records	☑
Read CVE information	☑
Read EOL information	☑
Get executive summary from texts	☑

5.2 Integration Testing

The developed tool was evaluated by testing the tool on different operating systems. For example, the scanner app (see Sect. 4.1 for more details) was tested on several older operating systems than Windows 10 (see Table 4 for a complete list). This provided an opportunity to understand how the tool can capture information from outdated computers.

Table 4. Completed simulation on different OS, version, and environment

OSs	Version	Environment
Windows 10	10.0.19045	Real
Windows 10	10.0.19044	Real
Windows 7 SP1	6.1.7601	VM
Windows Vista	6.0.6000	Real
Windows XP	5.1.2600	Both real and VM
Ubuntu	22.4	VM
Ubuntu	20.4	VM
Ubuntu	18.4	VM

Then, captured information was imported to get the summarized information (see Sect. 4.2). This helped to evaluate the success of the tool for different functions and features.

While the tool was tested on several older operating systems, several questions were posed to evaluate its complete integration. Questions were: (a) what operating system is the test computer running on? (the name of the OS was the answer) (b) How old the operating system is to the current date? (version number and EOL data helped to get answer) (c) What are the packages or applications running on the test computer? (list of installed applications and their version numbers were the answer)(d) What are the vulnerabilities related to those packages or applications? (list of CVE description and severity score were the answer)(e) When is the end-of-life of the operating system for the test computer? (EOL data was the answer).

Also, each step, including the ones mentioned in Sect. 4.2 were tested using Python-based integration tests to evaluate their expected behavior (see Tables 5).

Table 5. Integration test for summary app

Check login based on user database	☑
Insert the scanned information to app database	☑
List all the scanned computers from the app database	☑
Provide details for a specific scanned computer	☑
Download CVE database and save as a json file	☑
Get the executive summary from CVE descriptions	☑
Perform summary based on specific query of scanned computer	☑

6 Conclusion

This work advances E-Business Information Systems security by enabling accurate identification of OS and application metadata on legacy or offline computers, facilitating proactive risk assessment and lifecycle management. These computers are not connected to the Internet, which makes utilizing existing modern online tools challenging. Furthermore, the collected information is complex and requires significant effort to analyze. Within the EBIS domain, the proposed architecture demonstrates how machine-learning-based summarization and standardized vulnerability data (CVE/EOL) can be operationalized into decision dashboards for business stakeholders.

This work approaches the above problem using a two-fold solution. One to collect information from an outdated computer and another to combine and present the information. The project leveraged the CVE, EOL databases, and machine learning techniques to summarize vulnerability information to prepare an executive summary. Future work will extend interoperability with enterprise resource planning (ERP) modules and automate patch-planning workflows, reinforcing the EBIS ecosystem's overall resilience.

References

1. Alfadel, M., Costa, D.E., Shihab, E.: Empirical analysis of security vulnerabilities in python packages. Empir. Softw. Eng. **28**(3), 59 (2023)
2. Betz, J., et al.: Tum autonomous motorsport: An autonomous racing software for the indy autonomous challenge. J. Field Robot. **40**(4), 783–809 (2023)
3. Bojjagani, S., Sastry, V., Chen, C.M., Kumari, S., Khan, M.K.: Systematic survey of mobile payments, protocols, and security infrastructure. J. Ambient. Intell. Humaniz. Comput. **14**(1), 609–654 (2023)
4. CVE Details: The ultimate security vulnerability datasource (2023). https://www.cvedetails.com/vulnerability-list/, Accessed 26 May 2023
5. endoflife.date: End-of-life (eol) and support information (2023). https://endoflife.date/, Accessed 26 May 2023
6. Fan, K., Mao, D., Lu, Z., Wu, J.: Ops: Offline patching scheme for the images management in a secure cloud environment. In: 2013 IEEE International Conference on Services Computing, pp. 587–594. IEEE (2013)

7. Gonzalez-Barahona, J.M., Sherwood, P., Robles, G., Izquierdo, D.: Technical Lag in Software Compilations: Measuring How Outdated a Software Deployment Is. In: Balaguer, F., Di Cosmo, R., Garrido, A., Kon, F., Robles, G., Zacchiroli, S. (eds.) OSS 2017. IAICT, vol. 496, pp. 182–192. Springer, Cham (2017). https://doi.org/10.1007/978-3-319-57735-7_17
8. Gupta, D., Jalote, P., Barua, G.: A formal framework for on-line software version change. IEEE Trans. Software Eng. **22**(2), 120–131 (1996)
9. Harrell, C.R., Patton, M., Chen, H., Samtani, S.: Vulnerability assessment, remediation, and automated reporting: Case studies of higher education institutions. In: 2018 IEEE International Conference on Intelligence and Security Informatics (ISI), pp. 148–153. IEEE (2018)
10. Hore, S., Shah, A., Bastian, N.D.: Deep vulman: A deep reinforcement learning-enabled cyber vulnerability management framework. Expert Syst. Appl. **221**, 119734 (2023)
11. Lee, I.: Cybersecurity: Risk management framework and investment cost analysis. Bus. Horiz. **64**(5), 659–671 (2021)
12. Narayana Samy, G., Ahmad, R., Ismail, Z.: Security threats categories in healthcare information systems. Health Inf. J. **16**(3), 201–209 (2010)
13. Nunkesser, R., Thorn, J.: Possibilities and limitations of mobile applications for controlling. In: Keimer, I., Egle, U. (eds.) The Digitalization of Management Accounting: Use Cases from Theory and Practice, pp. 243–261. Springer, Cham (2023). https://doi.org/10.1007/978-3-658-41524-2_16
14. Park, C., Kontovas, C., Yang, Z., Chang, C.H.: A bn driven fmea approach to assess maritime cybersecurity risks. Ocean Coastal Manag. **235**, 106480 (2023)
15. Pham, V., Dang, T.: Cvexplorer: Multidimensional visualization for common vulnerabilities and exposures. In: IEEE International Conference on Big Data (Big Data), pp. 1296–1301. IEEE (2018)
16. Qorib, M., Oladunni, T., Denis, M., Ososanya, E., Cotae, P.: Covid-19 vaccine hesitancy: text mining, sentiment analysis and machine learning on covid-19 vaccination twitter dataset. Expert Syst. Appl. **212**, 118715 (2023)
17. Sami, M., Bhatti, S., Baloch, J., Shah, S.: How to keep your systems records safe. Int. J. Inf. Technol. **11**, 287–293 (2019)
18. Simon, V., Rabin, N., Gal, H.C.B.: Utilizing data driven methods to identify gender bias in linkedin profiles. Inf. Process. Manag. **60**(5), 103423 (2023)
19. Vasek, M., Moore, T.: Identifying Risk Factors for Webserver Compromise. In: Christin, N., Safavi-Naini, R. (eds.) FC 2014. LNCS, vol. 8437, pp. 326–345. Springer, Heidelberg (2014). https://doi.org/10.1007/978-3-662-45472-5_22
20. Yahav, I., Shehory, O., Schwartz, D.: Comments mining with tf-idf: the inherent bias and its removal. IEEE Trans. Knowl. Data Eng. **31**(3), 437–450 (2018)
21. Zerouali, A., Cosentino, V., Mens, T., Robles, G., Gonzalez-Barahona, J.M.: On the impact of outdated and vulnerable javascript packages in docker images. In: IEEE 26th International Conference on Software Analysis, Evolution and Reengineering (SANER), pp. 619–623. IEEE (2019)

Survey on Electric Vehicle Charging Stations: System and Security Perspectives

Soowang Lee, Seungbin Lee, Kyung A. Kang, Joo Hyeon Lee, and Jiyoon Kim(✉)

Gyeongsang National University, Jinju, Republic of Korea
{id0311sw,dltmdqls1526,kka2418,wngysl12,jykim92}@gnu.ac.kr

Abstract. The rapid increase of Electric Vehicles (EVs) is shifting the paradigms of transportation and energy, and Electric Vehicle Charging Stations (EVCS) are emerging as a key element for achieving sustainable mobility. From a systems perspective, EVCS consists of heterogeneous components, including power electronics, communication controllers, and cloud-based management platforms, interconnected via standard protocols such as ISO 15118 and OCPP. However, technical challenges persist, including grid instability, lack of interoperability, and high deployment costs. From a security perspective, EVCS, as a cyber-physical interface connecting vehicles and the grid, presents a broad attack surface, with threats such as CMA, DDoS, FDI, and MitM being reported. To address these challenges, various AI-based security techniques, such as machine learning-based anomaly detection, transfer learning, federated learning, and Temporal Convolutional Network (TCN)-based IDS are being studied. However, practical application is limited due to limited datasets, computational resource constraints, and hardware compatibility issues. This paper comprehensively examines EVCS from both a systems and security perspective, analyzing the latest charging technology trends, grid integration strategies, standardization issues, and key security vulnerabilities and countermeasures. Through this, it proposes research directions for building more efficient, reliable, and secure EVCS.

Keywords: Electric Vehicle Charging Station · Security · Smart Grid

1 Introduction

Digital transformation is reshaping energy and transportation services into data-driven, platform-oriented businesses. In this e-business setting, service operators must ensure discoverability and access, deliver end-to-end service quality, and support reliable transaction processing and timely settlement. They also need trustworthy remote control of distributed assets under large-scale connectivity and heterogeneous stakeholders. Electric Vehicle Charging Stations (EVCS) exemplify this shift: a charging session is not only physical power delivery, but

Published by Springer Nature Switzerland AG 2027
J. Kim et al. (Eds.): EBISION 2025, IFIP AICT 786, pp. 111–125, 2027.
https://doi.org/10.1007/978-3-032-26616-3_8

also a digitally mediated service transaction governed by backend platforms, user-facing applications, and standardized interfaces that jointly determine operational performance and business integrity. In practice, EVCS platforms orchestrate transaction flows (authorization, pricing, billing, and settlement), operational workflows (monitoring, fault handling, and firmware management), and data pipelines (session logs and telemetry) across drivers, operators, utilities, and roaming/payment partners.

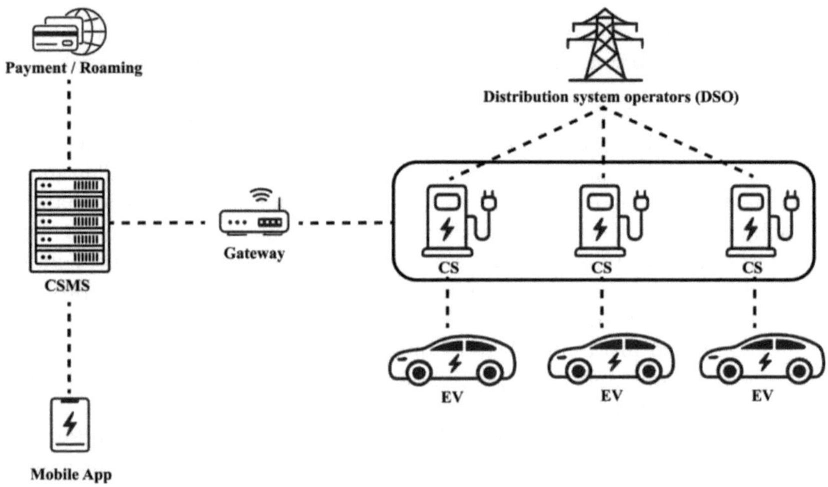

Fig. 1. EVCS ecosystem and key interfaces.

EVCS has consequently evolved beyond standalone chargers. Early deployments largely targeted basic AC charging, whereas today's infrastructure increasingly relies on DC fast charging, dense public deployments, and integrated management platforms. This evolution has accelerated the adoption of interoperable protocols and interfaces, such as OCPP for charge point–backend communication and ISO 15118 for vehicle–charger interaction. At the same time, EVCS operations have expanded to include roaming, billing and settlement, remote monitoring, firmware management, and customer-facing mobile services [11]. As a result, EVCS behaves as an end-to-end ecosystem rather than a single device. Figure 1 summarizes this ecosystem view by highlighting the main components (EV/EVSE, local controllers, backend/management systems, mobile applications, and external services such as payment/roaming) and the primary cyber–physical interfaces to the distribution grid.

From a systems perspective, this ecosystem view implies that EVCS adequacy cannot be judged solely by the number of installed chargers, because performance is constrained by coupled transportation demand and power-network feasibility. Prior surveys report persistent technical and operational challenges, including power-quality impacts, peak-load stress, interoperability and standardization gaps, and high deployment cost [12,17]. Recent studies further show that adequacy depends on coverage and service continuity for real mobility needs (e.g., long-distance travel) [6], and that reliability and access can be uneven across communities, with user-reported issues often attributed to hardware or technical failures [18]. These findings indicate that EVCS should be analyzed as a service system in which demand, queueing behavior, grid constraints, and reliability jointly shape user experience and operational outcomes.

From a security perspective, EVCS exposes a broad attack surface because it couples cyber control and economic transactions with physical power delivery. Reported threats include availability disruption (e.g., DoS/DDoS), integrity manipulation of charging sessions (e.g., charge manipulation attacks (CMA) and false data injection (FDI)), and protocol- and platform-level attacks that exploit weaknesses across charge points, backend services, and user-facing applications [7]. While AI-powered intrusion detection and anomaly detection have been proposed, deployment remains constrained by limited representative datasets, resource limits at edge devices, and compatibility issues across heterogeneous EVCS hardware and operating environments [3,5]. For e-business deployments, these constraints are especially consequential because security failures translate not only into downtime but also into billing/settlement disputes, customer trust degradation, and systemic operational risk.

However, existing discussions often treat system planning and operations separately from cybersecurity. This separation limits end-to-end reasoning about how service-quality objectives, platform workflows, and threat exposure interact in real deployments. Motivated by this gap, this survey examines EVCS from both system and security perspectives with an explicit end-to-end e-business framing. We organize recent research on (i) EVCS planning and operation under coupled transportation–grid constraints and service-quality objectives, and (ii) security vulnerabilities, threat models, and detection/defense techniques across layered EVCS components and standard protocols. Building on this evidence, we support actionable reasoning about assumptions, threats, and vulnerabilities in EVCS deployments, which can be directly mapped into an attack-tree style organization in the Discussion.

This paper is organized as follows: Sect. 2 reviews recent research from system and security perspectives. Section 3 synthesizes the evidence into a practical discussion. Section 4 concludes the paper and outlines future research directions.

2 Recent Research

2.1 System Perspective

As the diffusion of EVs accelerates, recent research recognizes EVCS as a complex, multi-layered system and explores an integrated approach based on this. In addition to survey-oriented studies, optimization and measurement-driven works have also emerged to quantify infrastructure adequacy (e.g., coverage and equity) and to support planning/operation decisions under grid and transportation constraints. Table 1 presents a summary of recent research from a systems perspective.

Table 1. Recent research from a systems perspective.

Authors	Purpose	Technique	Pros	Challenges / Open issues
Yousuf et al. [17]	- recognize EVCS as a complex system integrated with power and transportation infrastructure - Analyze obstacles such as quality degradation, demand uncertainty, and lack of standardization	- Harmonic filtering - power factor compensation - smart grid integration - battery management and recycling, - high-speed, mobile, and bidirectional charging stations.	- Comprehensive presentation of key elements - Increased efficiency through fast charging and battery swapping - Flexibility through diverse operating methods (such as fixed, mobile and bidirectional) - Energy optimization	- Real-World Application Gap - Lack of Economic Feasibility in Battery Recycling - Policy and Standard Uncertainty - Charging Demand Uncertainty and Investment Burden
Sarda et al. [12]	- Systematically analyze EVCS with a focus on charging technology, emphasizing its contribution to EV diffusion and energy and environment.	- Technical classification (AC/DC based, grid-connected, off-grid, hybrid) - Classification by level I to IV according to charging speed - Battery replacement method	- Comprehensive review of charging technology - operational structures, proposal of power quality - peak load mitigation measures - expected promotion of EV adoption.	- Establishing ultra-fast charging stations - Improving battery life - Advancing V2G/V2H connectivity - AI-based charging and price prediction techniques - Smart energy management
Singh et al. [15]	- propose an ANN-based adaptive power management controller for V2G and G2V bidirectional power flow control	- Build a mathematical model of each PV system, storage battery, EV battery, and grid	- Compensation for instability in solar power generation and battery charging status - Manages power flow stably - Supports efficient energy management in EVCS	- Simulation-only validation; no hardware or field deployment verification - Broader robustness under diverse weather, generation-instability, and storage conditions remains untested - Practical implementation and cost-benefit analysis remain future work
Pamulapati et al. [11]	- To ensure the security and reliability of EVCS, propose evciArch, an architectural and semantic model	- Multi-layered structure modeling using ArchiMate based on literature, standards, and reports - Mapping CVE/CWE data with actual vulnerabilities	- Provides a common language for stakeholders - Serves as a foundational tool for security analysis, threat modeling, and policy development	- Early-stage model fails to fully encompass EVCS - Limited CVE/CWE mapping, lack of proven real-time threat detection and response
Li et al. [9]	- Plan EVCS deployment under coupled power-network and transportation-network constraints - Capture interaction between traffic-driven demand and grid feasibility	- MILP formulation for coordinated planning in urban power and transportation networks - Joint optimization under feasibility constraints	- Enables integrated siting/planning decisions beyond single-network assumptions - Provides a tractable optimization framework for coordinated planning	- Depends on modeling assumptions and the quality of coupled-network data - Scalability and calibration for real-world city-scale deployments remain challenging
Cui et al. [4]	- Improve fast-charging station operation under congestion - Incorporate driving demand via demand-based priority for real-time service (QoS)	- Demand-based priority mechanism - Coordinated charging scheme optimizing real-time QoS objectives	- Improves service quality under limited station capacity (as evaluated) - Reflects heterogeneous demand in station-level scheduling	- Requires reliable demand/priority information and policy design - Broader applicability may require integration with storage and grid-side constraints
Hanig et al. [6]	- Quantify national-scale fast-charging adequacy for long-distance travel - Identify persistent corridor/rural gaps under deployment programs	- Consecutive coverage metric (traffic-weighted accessibility within 500 miles) - Scenario analysis for highway-focused expansion	- Translates "coverage" into route-feasibility rather than charger counts - Localizes remaining gaps to support targeted infrastructure investment	- Metric focuses on long-distance feasibility; local access may require complementary metrics - Results are sensitive to threshold and modeling assumptions
Yu et al. [18]	- Evaluate equity and reliability of public EVCS in the United States - Quantify access and reliability disparities across communities	- Large-scale empirical analysis of 470,142 user reviews at census-tract level - Reliability issue characterization based on observed user reports	- Provides evidence on distributional access and day-to-day reliability at scale - Quantifies disparities (e.g., 64% fewer stations; 73% for renters in multi-dwelling units)	- Review-based evidence can be biased by reporting and geographic coverage - Limited visibility into operator-side ground truth and unreported failures

Yousuf et al. [17] recognize EVCS as a complex system integrated with the power system and traffic infrastructure. The spread of EVs poses challenges to the development of EVCS, indicating obstacles such as deterioration of power quality, uncertainty in charging demand, complexity of battery technology, and lack of standardization. The authors review multifaceted approaches to address these challenges, including harmonic filtering, power factor compensation, smart grid integration, battery management, and recycling strategies. The authors comprehensively present the key components required for building an EVCS by analyzing existing studies and structuring them into a Challenges - Response Strategy - Optimization model. Consequently, the authors emphasize that a reliable and efficient charging infrastructure is essential, fast charging stations and battery swapping stations are key solutions to reduce range anxiety and improve charging efficiency. Also, depending on the operating approach of the charging station, it is divided into fixed, mobile, and bidirectional, suggesting flexible solutions that offer complementary utilization methods.

Sarda et al. [12] argue that EVs contribute to reducing carbon emissions in the transportation sector while also contributing to energy security, improving air quality, and expanding the use of renewable energy. The authors systematically analyze charging technology, focusing on this key perspective in the EVCS development process. Specifically, they comprehensively review the practical operational structure, including the technological classification of charging infrastructure (AC/DC-based, grid-connected, off-grid, and hybrid), classification by charging speed (Levels I to IV), and even battery swapping methods. In addition, to address grid integration issues, they address specific technical issues such as power quality, peak load, and voltage imbalance. To mitigate these challenges, they discuss power management systems, charging scheduling, demand response techniques, and renewable energy-based charging station operation, focusing on case studies. The next decade is expected to witness a significant increase in the adoption of EVs driven by technological advancements, improved charging infrastructure, and grid integration. Accordingly, key research topics include the construction of ultra-fast charging stations, enhanced V2G/V2H connectivity to improve battery life, AI-based charging and price prediction techniques, and smart energy management.

Singh et al. [15] address the AI-based power management problem in EVCS. Specifically, they propose an ANN-based adaptive power management controller for bidirectional V2G and G2V power flow control and model the EVCS as a distributed DC microgrid system. This controller optimizes power flow between PV, storage batteries, the grid, and EV batteries, enabling charging stations to function as bidirectional energy hubs (V2G/G2V) rather than simply loads. The authors construct mathematical models of the PV system, storage batteries, EV batteries, and grid, and simulate the performance of the ANN-based controller in a MATLAB/Simulink environment. The authors demonstrate that an ANN-based controller effectively compensates for the highly variable solar power generation and instability of battery charge levels, and effectively manages stable and efficient power flow in EVCSs. In particular, they demonstrate that bidirectional power exchange between EVs and the grid can contribute to the efficient utilization of distributed energy resources and grid stabilization beyond the simple function of charging stations.

Pamulapati et al. [11] propose evciArch, an architectural and semantic model, to ensure the security and reliability of EVCSs. Drawing on literature, standard documents, manufacturer reports, and industry reports, the model represents the EVCS structure from a multi-layered perspective. Based on ArchiMate, it distinguishes between stakeholders, operational applications, and technology layers, expressing the service and data flow between each layer. Moreover, utilizing a Common Vulnerabilities and Exposures (CVE, CWE) database, the authors link the architecture to reported security issues, such as OCPP command injection, privilege escalation, cross-site scripting (XSS), unauthorized network access, and HPGP vulnerabilities based on ISO 15118. The proposed model can serve as a foundational tool for developing security analysis and threat modeling policies, providing a common language for EVCS stakeholders. However, the evciArch model is still in its initial stages and does not fully encompass the entire EVCS landscape. Consequently, CVE/CWE-based vulnerability mapping is limited, making it difficult to demonstrate real-time threat detection and response capabilities in real-world industrial settings. Future research will focus on expanding evciArch and developing a real-time security monitoring system, reflecting empirical data and diverse EVCS operating environments.

Li et al. [9] propose an MILP-based method for coordinated planning of coupled power distribution and transportation networks in urban contexts, where EVCS deployment decisions interact with both grid constraints and traffic/charging behaviors. The study formulates EVCS planning within a joint network setting and presents a tractable MILP formulation to support integrated planning decisions across the coupled domains. From a systems perspective, this work is relevant because it explicitly models EVCS planning under simultaneous power-network and transportation-network feasibility constraints, rather than treating them as separable design problems.

Cui et al. [4] study station-level operation for EV fast-charging and propose a coordinated charging scheme that incorporates driving demand via demand-based priority. The proposed approach allocates available charging power across different priority levels and, within the same priority level, optimizes the charging scheme based on three real-time QoS objectives. The paper reports that the proposed demand-aware coordination improves charging QoS compared to baseline schemes that do not incorporate demand priority, and evaluates robustness under uncertain conditions.

Hanig et al. [6] develop a consecutive coverage metric to quantify national-scale adequacy of fast-charging infrastructure for long-distance travel in the United States. Using this metric, they compute the percent of traffic-weighted roads that are consecutively accessible within 500 miles of each county and assess current coverage as well as projected improvements under highway-focused deployment programs. Their results report that in 2023, 10% of counties had at least 75% minimum viable consecutive coverage, and that if designated highways receive fast chargers, 94% of counties reach at least 75% fast-charger coverage, while remaining gaps are concentrated in rural counties.

Yu et al. [18] examine equity and reliability of public EV charging stations in the United States using large-scale empirical evidence from user-generated reviews (n = 470,142) at the census-tract level. They report that disadvantaged communities have 64% fewer public EVCSs per capita than non-disadvantaged communities, and that this disparity rises to 73% when considering renters in multi-dwelling units. They also report that users in disadvantaged communities and urban areas experience significantly more reliability issues, primarily related to hardware and technical failures. From a systems perspective, these findings motivate evaluating EVCS not only by aggregate deployment volume but also by distributional access and operational reliability.

2.2 Security Perspective

EVCS is implemented as a cyber-physical interface that combines power grid and communication technology, presenting a wide attack surface. Research is underway to enhance this interface structure through vulnerability analysis and integration with IDS and AI technologies to ensure robust security. Table 2 presents a summary of recent research from a security perspective.

Jahangir et al. [7] proposed a new attack model, CMA, targeting EVCS and presented a detection mechanism methodology. In contrast to existing attacks such as sudden surges in electricity demand or periodic switching-based strategies, CMA adopts a different approach. It covertly manipulates user-defined charging start and stop times as well as the requested power. As a result, CMA targets the power market rather than the electric grid, making it a distinctive type of attack. These attacks can be executed without bypassing OCPP's security functions, such as maximum charging speed limits or random delay execution, making them a realistic threat. The authors define 6 types of CMA scenarios and analyze them using real-world datasets. Simulation results show that these attacks can cause direct losses in profitability and market trust. To address this, the authors proposed a real-time monitoring framework utilizing a deep autoencoder-based unsupervised learning (2D-CNN). They present a new threat model that can occur in EVCS environments and improve the effectiveness of a deep learning-based framework for detecting these threats. However, under realistic constraints such as data noise and communication disruptions, the approach exhibits reduced detection efficiency and an increased false positive rate against mixed attack types. Moreover, it reveals a limitation in that the analysis does not extend to standards beyond OCPP.

Aljohani et al. [1] present a mathematical model of the threat of widespread DDoS attacks on EVCS, which is a cyber-physical infrastructure that integrates power-grid operation and communication networks and is considered critical infrastructure for the smart grid. The authors highlight that EVCS can be used as an attack vector. They argue that small perturbations in aggregate EV charging demand can amplify into significant grid disturbances. The attacks were confirmed to cause a range of adverse effects including frequency deviations, voltage

Table 2. Recent research from a security perspective.

Authors	Purpose	Technique	Pros	Challenges/Open issues
Jahangir et al. [7]	- Presents a new threat model for EVCS, CMA. - Analyzes the effectiveness and impact of this attack and proposes a detection mechanism.	- Define 6 CMA scenarios that covertly manipulate user-defined charging start/end times and requested power - Simulations based on real-world datasets - Present a real-time monitoring framework based on unsupervised learning using a deep autoencoder (2D-CNN)	- Highlighting the feasibility of circumventing OCPP security features. - Demonstrating the effectiveness (experimental performance) of a deep learning-based detection framework.	- Detection performance deteriorates due to practical constraints such as communication failures and data noise; false positives increase during mixed attacks. - Exclusion of standards other than OCPP limits generalizability.
Aljohani et al. [1]	- Recognizing EVCS as a core infrastructure within the smart grid - Identifying the threat of large-scale DDoS attacks through mathematical models	- Modeling attack occurrence and intensity using time-varying Poisson processes and Ornstein–Uhlenbeck stochastic processes - Analysis of server congestion and power grid disruption using M/G/1 queues	- Mathematically proven that attacks via EVCS can cause real-world power grid disruptions, including frequency fluctuations, voltage distortion, and generator instability. - Evidence supporting the need for cyber resilience.	- Lack of IDS-based advanced detection strategies - Failure to reflect gaps in actual communication networks - Absence of empirical, large-scale data validation
Dehrouyeh et al. [5]	- A security enhancement plan utilizing TinyML in resource-constrained environments of EVCS and IoT devices is presented.	- Consideration of ISO 15118 and OCPP protocols, as well as DoS, MitM, and malware attack scenarios - TinyML-based IDS and mitigation framework design - ESP32 experimental implementation and performance evaluation	- Real-time threat detection - Bandwidth savings - Energy efficiency - Enhanced privacy protection - Validated as an EVCI security alternative	- Lack of training data - Absence of a unified framework - Limited real-time adaptability - Lack of versatility
Kesavan et al. [8]	- Proposed an ML-based anomaly detection technique for detecting advanced attacks in EVCS and smart grid environments.	- Combining LSTM, Random Forest, SVM, and Autoencoder - Injecting DDoS and data tampering attacks in a smart grid protocol simulation - Applying distributed security updates using federated learning	- Ensures high detection accuracy and low latency - Demonstrates scalability and real-time adaptive security capabilities - Provides an intelligent, adaptive security system	- Simulation-based verification fails to reflect real-world variability. - Inadequate efficiency assessment in resource-constrained environments.
Benfarhat et al. [3]	- Proposed a lightweight, real-time TCN-based intrusion detection system (IDS) to address security vulnerabilities targeting OCPP.	- Application of Temporal Convolutional Networks - Learning long-term time series dependencies through causality and dilation, implementing real-time classification and detection	- Efficient long-term dependency learning - Low computational costs and latency, making it lightweight and suitable for real-time operations - Excellent performance in classifying various attacks	- Performance degrades due to network noise, data bias, and a lack of rare attack samples. - Training data acquisition and generalization remain challenges.
Almadhor et al. [2]	- Designing an IDS for EVCS that is robust against unknown attacks and zero-day attacks using transfer learning to improve detection accuracy and scalability.	- Initialize with pre-trained DNN weights, then apply fine-tuning (transfer learning) to the EVCS-specific dataset. - Reduce computational costs by reducing weight.	- Achieves detection accuracy exceeding 93% - Secures high generalization performance and scalability with low computational costs - Expected to improve practical applicability	- Real-time processing optimization required, lack of large-scale, real-world data - Issues with compatibility with standards (e.g., OCPP) and diversity of operating environments
Nasr et al. [10]	- Propose ChargePrint, a framework for Internet-scale discovery and security analysis of Electric Vehicle Charging Management Systems (EVCMS). - Characterize exposed deployments at scale and report vulnerabilities in deployed management systems.	- Internet-scale discovery and measurement of online EVCMS deployments - In-depth security analysis across multiple implementations - CVE reporting/assignment based on discovered issues	- Enables systematic, large-scale characterization of exposed EVCMS deployments. - Demonstrates substantial real-world insecurity with many vulnerabilities reported.	- Visibility mainly reflects internet-exposed systems; coverage depends on measurement scope. - Continuous platform changes can affect longitudinal reproducibility and patch status.
Sarieddine et al. [14]	- Analyze covert attacks enabled by vulnerabilities in OCPP backend communication with EV charging management systems. - Demonstrate backend-layer weaknesses as a high-leverage attack surface.	- Empirical validation on representative live EVCMS deployments - Backend-focused vulnerability discovery and exploitation analysis - Attack scenario construction based on backend weaknesses	- Shows that scalable attacks can be enabled without compromising each individual charge point. - Motivates threat modeling that explicitly includes backend/management layers.	- Backend diversity complicates generalized mitigation. - Real-world remediation depends on operator patching and monitoring capabilities.
Szakaly et al. [16]	- Conduct a large-scale security measurement study of CCS EV charging deployments across multiple European countries. - Assess implementation gaps between expected security and deployed reality.	- Field measurement across chargers from multiple vendors and manufacturing years - Analysis of TLS/ISO 15118 support and PLC/HomePlug firmware characteristics - Examination of PKI/certificate validation assumptions in deployments	- Provides deployment-grounded evidence of inconsistent TLS adoption and heterogeneous security postures. - Highlights practical gaps that matter for real-world threat assumptions.	- Measurement scope is region/time bounded and may not generalize globally. - Vendor firmware evolution and configuration variance can affect reproducibility.
Sarieddine et al. [13]	- Investigate EV charging mobile applications as an attack surface. - Report design-level weaknesses and authorization issues that can enable remote session hijacking.	- Combined static and dynamic analysis of widely used EV charging mobile apps - Identification of design/authorization weaknesses affecting critical functions - Attack feasibility assessment for session hijacking scenarios	- Expands EVCS threat surface to app–backend APIs and user-facing platforms. - Shows how application-layer issues can translate into infrastructure-level control impact.	- Findings can shift with app updates and vendor patch cycles. - Limited visibility into server-side mitigations and operator response practices.

profile distortions, generator output instabilities, and transient current oscillations. These results imply that securing cyber-resilience is essential as EVCS and smart grids are increasingly digitized and electrified. In conclusion, this study characterizes the probabilistic features of DDoS attacks on EVCS and quantifies their impact on grid stability, thereby emphasizing the necessity of adaptive security mechanisms and real-time defense systems in smart grid environments. However, limitations include that the proposed model does not fully reflect the advanced detection strategies of IDS or the heterogeneous characteristics of actual communication networks, and that there is a lack of large-scale field verification based on empirical data.

Dehrouyeh et al. [5] present an EVCS security solution using TinyML for resource-constrained environments such as charging stations and IoT devices, and examine how TinyML can enhance cybersecurity. The authors identified crucial challenges, such as power, memory capacity, and computational constraints, and discussed corresponding solutions. They propose a detection and mitigation framework that considers standard communication protocols (e.g., ISO 15118, OCPP, etc.) and attack scenarios (DoS, MitM, malware injection, etc.). Additionally, they conducted a case study applying TinyML to an actual EVCS environment and verified its practicality through experimental implementation and performance evaluation based on the ESP32 microcontroller. Applying this method, they demonstrate that real-time IDS and response are possible in resource-constrained environments by integrating various methods such as energy harvesting, privacy-preserving learning, lightweight optimization, and transfer learning. The authors suggest that TinyML can be an effective alternative for EVCS security, offering real-time threat detection, bandwidth reduction, energy efficiency, and enhanced privacy. However, challenges such as insufficient dataset, lack of an integrated framework, and real-time adaptability remain. Future work requires the development of a general-purpose TinyML-based security model that can overcome these limitations.

Kesavan et al. [8] proposed a machine learning-based Anomaly Detection technique based on the Grid Sentinel Framework (AD-GS). This technique addresses the limitations of existing statistical or rule-based methods, which often struggle to detect sophisticated attacks. The proposed technique combines various ML and DL models, such as LSTM, Random Forest, SVM, and Autoencoder, aiming to achieve high accuracy and low latency. Attacks such as DDoS and data tampering are injected in a simulated environment that mimics actual smart grid communication protocols, and the anomaly detection engine's ability to identify and respond to these attacks is evaluated. In addition, by dynamically reflecting security updates across a distributed charging station network through federated learning, the proposed technique demonstrates scalability and adaptive security in near real time. This study contributes to enhancing reliability and resilience by proposing an intelligent adaptive security system in an integrated EVCS–smart grid environment. However, due to the large number of simulation-based verifications, it fails to adequately reflect real-world variability and its effectiveness in resource-constrained environments is inadequate.

Benfarhat et al. [3] proposed a TCN-based IDS to address the security vulnerabilities of OCPP. While existing deep learning techniques are limited in that they either fail to capture time-series dependencies and complex attack patterns or incur high computational costs, TCN efficiently learns long-term dependencies through causal and dilated convolutions, enabling lightweight deployment and real-time performance. This study suggests a strong baseline for lightweight, high-performance security models capable of effectively detecting and classifying various cyberattacks targeting OCPP (DoS, backdoors, data tampering, cryptojacking, etc.). Nevertheless, it demonstrates that detection performance can be degraded by network noise, data bias, and a lack of rare attack samples.

Almadhor et al. [2] propose a transfer learning-based IDS to detect cyber-physical threats to EVCS. Conventional IDSs rely on signatures of known attacks, making them vulnerable to novel or zero-day attacks. To overcome these limitations, they combine deep learning and transfer learning to achieve higher accuracy and scalability. The proposed model achieves a detection accuracy of over 93% by initializing the network with weights from a pre-trained DNN and fine-tuning it on an EVCS-specific dataset. This study demonstrates that an IDS utilizing TL can effectively enhance security in practical EVCS operating environments, achieving higher detection rates and generalization performance at lower computational costs than existing deep learning models. Future research will focus on optimizing real-time performance, securing large-scale/real-world datasets, and ensuring compatibility with standards.

Nasr et al. [10] propose ChargePrint, a framework for Internet-scale discovery and security analysis of Electric Vehicle Charging Management Systems (EVCMS). The study reports identifying 27,439 online EVCS instances instrumented by 44 unique EVCMS implementations, enabling systematic characterization of exposed deployments at scale. Based on in-depth security analysis, the paper reports uncovering 120 zero-day vulnerabilities and notes that more than 20 CVE IDs were assigned, highlighting substantial practical insecurity in deployed management systems.

Sarieddine et al. [14] analyze covert attacks enabled by vulnerabilities in the OCPP backend communication with EV charging management systems. The paper reports empirical validation on 16 representative live EVCMS deployments and discovered six zero-day vulnerabilities in each system. Based on these backend weaknesses, the study discusses multiple attack scenarios that can impact charging operations at scale, emphasizing that backend-layer security is a critical part of the EVCS threat surface.

Szakaly et al. [16] conduct a large-scale security measurement study of chargers implementing CCS across multiple European countries. The study evaluates 325 chargers (manufactured between April 2013 and June 2023, installed as late as May 2024) from 26 manufacturers and reports that only 12% of the analyzed stations implement TLS. The paper also reports an increasing trend in ISO 15118-2 support over time (reaching 70% of chargers manufactured in 2023) and observes that many chargers use outdated firmware for HomePlug modems. In addition, the authors report identifying a PKI design flaw that could allow an attacker with a single valid TLS certificate for any charger to attack communications under the same root CA, indicating practical security gaps in practical CCS deployments.

Sarieddine et al. [13] investigate EV charging mobile applications as an attack surface for EVCS via a combination of static and dynamic analyses across 31 widely used mobile platforms. The paper reports design-level weaknesses including lack of user/vehicle verification and improper authorization checks for critical functions, and reports that 29 out of 31 studied platforms are susceptible to remote charging session hijacking. The study further discusses how such mobile-app vulnerabilities can enable coordinated remote (dis)charging behaviors, shifting the threat model beyond charger-side implementations and protocol-layer protections.

3 Discussion

This paper shows that EVCS cannot be viewed as either grid equipment or IT service in isolation. In practice, EVCS is an end-to-end cyber-physical and socio-technical system: service quality is determined by coupled transportation demand and distribution-grid feasibility, while security risk emerges across the charge point, the backend, management plane, and user-facing applications. In this section, we synthesize the reviewed evidence into assumptions, threats, and vulnerabilities that can be mapped directly to an attack-tree style view. Figures 2 and 3 summarize this evidence by (i) organizing system-level pathways to service failure and (ii) organizing security-level pathways to adversarial impact. In both trees, the OR structure indicates that any branch can be sufficient to realize the root-level outcome under deployment-realistic conditions.

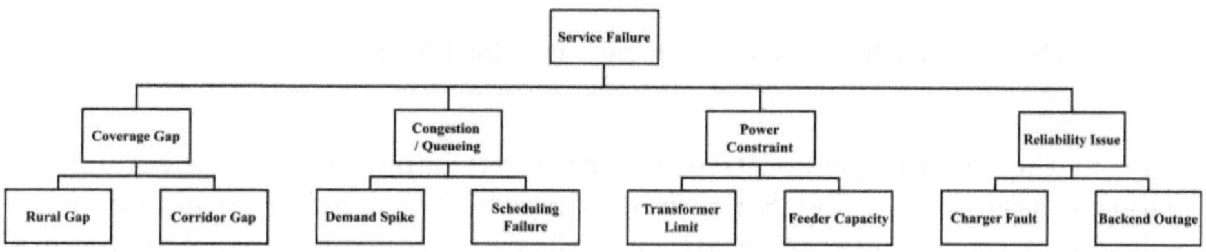

Fig. 2. System-perspective attack tree for EVCS service failure.

From a systems perspective, the key operating assumption is that more chargers do not necessarily ensure adequate service. Service adequacy is constrained by where demand arises and whether the local grid can supply it, which motivates treating the transportation network and the power distribution network as a coupled planning problem rather than separable design tasks [9]. This assumption motivates a service-failure root in the system attack tree, where failures appear as (i) coverage gaps, (ii) congestion and queueing, (iii) power constraints, and

(iv) reliability issues. Coverage gaps are not only a matter of sparse deployment. Measurement work operationalizes adequacy as corridor feasibility for long-distance travel and shows that corridor accessibility can remain limited even under expanding deployment programs, with persistent gaps concentrated in rural regions [6].

Congestion and queueing emerge when demand concentrates in time and space, especially in fast-charging settings, and demand-aware prioritization and coordinated scheduling have been studied as concrete mechanisms to allocate limited charging power while meeting real-time service objectives [4]. Power constraints are repeatedly highlighted as a binding constraint, driven by peak-load and power-quality concerns, grid-integration complexity, and the operational difficulty of supporting high-power charging alongside broader smart-grid objectives [12,17]. Bidirectional operation further strengthens this point by treating EVCS as an active energy hub whose power flow must be controlled under variability rather than as a passive load [15]. Reliability is a primary concern. Empirical evidence based on large-scale user reviews indicates that day-to-day failures (often described as hardware/technical faults) and access can be unevenly realized across communities, which makes reliability and distributional access part of the system problem definition [18]. In attack-tree terms, these studies justify keeping Coverage Gap, Congestion/Queueing, Power Constraint, and Reliability Issue as first-order branches under a service-failure root, because each branch is repeatedly observed or modeled as a direct driver of degraded service.

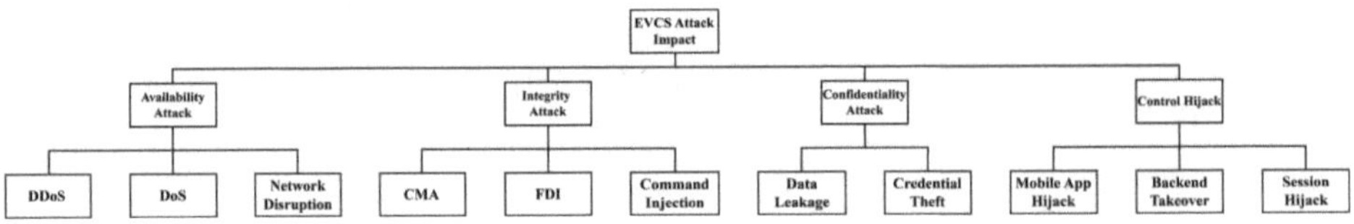

Fig. 3. Security-perspective attack tree for EVCS attack impact.

From the security perspective, the reviewed papers support a second key operating assumption: EVCS risk is best assessed by making trust boundaries explicit and then enumerating attack surfaces by control plane. Architectural modeling work provides a layered view (stakeholders, applications/operations, and technology) and links protocol surfaces to known vulnerability classes, which is useful as a backbone for threat enumeration [11]. Internet-scale discovery and security analysis further indicate that the management backend itself is often exposed and heterogeneous, which motivates treating Internet-facing EV charging management systems as a primary attack surface rather than a secondary concern [10]. This perspective is reinforced by backend-focused analysis showing that vulnerabilities in backend communication (e.g., charge point-backend) and management components can enable covert, scalable attacks without requiring direct compromise of each individual charge point [14]. The threat surface also extends upward: mobile app ecosystems introduce an app–backend control plane, and analysis of EV charging mobile applications reports design and authorization weaknesses that enable remote session hijacking at scale, implying that application-layer flaws can translate into infrastructure-level control impact [13]. At the protocol/deployment layer, measurement of CCS deployments shows that security controls expected by standards are not consistently implemented in the field, which is a practical vulnerability in itself because it widens the feasible set of real attackers beyond what a standards-compliant assumption would suggest [16].

These findings map directly to the security attack tree rooted node defined as EVCS impact. For availability, large-scale and time-varying DDoS modeling frames availability loss as a cyber-physical disturbance problem, rather than as service downtime [1], and OCPP-focused IDS work explicitly targets time-series attack patterns such as DoS-style behaviors and other operationally disruptive attacks [3]. For integrity, CMA concretize manipulation as a realistic threat that targets charging-session parameters and can result in operational and economic impacts under realistic protocol assumptions [7]; architectural and measurement studies further motivate including command-/protocol-surface weaknesses and inconsistent enforcement as integrity-relevant drivers [11,16].

For control hijacking, the evidence is strongest on two planes: mobile-application session hijacking and backend takeover paths [13,14]. Finally, the defense-oriented works clarify an important constraint for the discussion: deploying an IDS is not a one-step solution for EVCS. The proposed defenses are shaped by limited EVCS-specific data and by heterogeneous and resource-constrained deployment environments, which motivates lightweight, on-device approaches [5], temporal models for efficient inference over protocol traffic [3], transfer learning to improve generalization under data scarcity [2], and distributed anomaly detection approaches designed to scale across infrastructures [8].

Taken together, this paper suggests a practical way to write and structure the attack-tree discussion: we treat system perspective service failure as emerging from coverage gaps, congestion, grid feasibility limits, and reliability issues [4,6,9,18], and we treat security perspective impact as emerging from availability disruption, integrity manipulation, and control hijack across the charge point, backend/management, and mobile control planes [1,7,10,13,14,16]. This framing also clarifies the main research direction: EVCS requires an integrated approach in which operational optimization (planning, scheduling and grid-aware control) is evaluated together with security assurance (attack-surface reduction and resource-aware detection), under deployment-realistic assumptions about heterogeneity and imperfect security enforcement [11,16].

4 Conclusion

This paper comprehensively analyzes and summarizes EVCS from both systems and security perspectives. From a systems perspective, EVCS is a multi-layered cyber–physical system that integrates the power grid, transportation infrastructure, energy storage, and charging-station operations into a unified architecture.

Key operational challenges include charging efficiency, power quality stabilization, smart grid integration, battery management, and recycling. Harmonic filtering, charging scheduling, and AI-based power control techniques have been proposed to address these challenges. Several studies argue that EVCS should function as a two-way energy hub, rather than simply a load.

From a security perspective, EVCS serves as a cyber–physical interface between vehicles, the power grid, and communication networks, and it presents a broad attack surface. As a result, various threat models have been reported, including CMA, DDoS, FDI, and MitM. To mitigate these threats, recent studies have proposed AI/ML-based techniques and IDS designs, including TinyML-enabled on-device detection, transfer learning for improved generalization, federated learning for distributed model updates, and TCN-based IDS for time-series attack detection. However, these frameworks suffer from limitations such as limited datasets, resource constraints, and deployment heterogeneity and interoperability constraints. In this context, EVCS deployments must satisfy both operational constraints and security requirements, highlighting the need for a framework that integrates power management algorithms with IDS/AI-based security techniques.

Therefore, future research should focus on designing an integrated framework that includes empirical data-based validation, incorporating heterogeneous communication standards (e.g., OCPP, ISO 15118), hybrid attack response strategies, and economic and policy implications. Accordingly, this study provide a more comprehensive and in-depth analysis to explore the detailed design and practical feasibility of the proposed integrated framework.

References

1. Aljohani, T., Almutairi, A.: Modeling time-varying wide-scale distributed denial of service attacks on electric vehicle charging stations. Ain Shams Eng. J. **15**(7), 102860 (2024)
2. Almadhor, A., et al.: Transfer learning for securing electric vehicle charging infrastructure from cyber-physical attacks. Sci. Rep. **15**(1), 9331 (2025)
3. Benfarhat, I., Goh, V.T., Siow, C.L., Sheraz, M., Chuah, T.C.: Temporal convolutional network approach to secure open charge point protocol (ocpp) in electric vehicle charging. IEEE Access (2025)
4. Cui, D., et al.: Coordinated charging scheme for electric vehicle fast-charging station with demand-based priority. IEEE Trans. Transp. Electri. **10**(3), 6449–6459 (2023)
5. Dehrouyeh, F., Yang, L., Ajaei, F.B., Shami, A.: On tinyml and cybersecurity: Electric vehicle charging infrastructure use case. IEEE Access (2024)
6. Hanig, L., et al.: Finding gaps in the national electric vehicle charging station coverage of the united states. Nat. Commun. **16**(1), 561 (2025)
7. Jahangir, H., Lakshminarayana, S., Poor, H.V.: Charge manipulation attacks against smart electric vehicle charging stations and deep learning-based detection mechanisms. IEEE Trans. Smart Grid **15**(5), 5182–5194 (2024)
8. Kesavan, V.T., Hossen, M.J., Gopi, R., Joseph, E.R.: Anomaly detection with grid sentinel framework for electric vehicle charging stations in a smart grid environment. Sci. Rep. **15**(1), 15774 (2025)

9. Li, K., Shao, C., Hu, Z., Shahidehpour, M.: An milp method for optimal planning of electric vehicle charging stations in coordinated urban power and transportation networks. IEEE Trans. Power Syst. **38**(6), 5406–5419 (2022)
10. Nasr, T., Torabi, S., Bou-Harb, E., Fachkha, C., Assi, C.: Chargeprint: A framework for internet-scale discovery and security analysis of EV charging management systems. In: NDSS (2023)
11. Pamulapati, T., Walker, M., Adu-Duodu, K., Huraysi, T., Ranjan, R., Shah, T.: Architectural and semantic models for ev charging infrastructure. In: 2025 IEEE 25th International Symposium on Cluster, Cloud and Internet Computing Workshops (CCGridW), pp. 117–124. IEEE (2025)
12. Sarda, J., et al.: A review of the electric vehicle charging technology, impact on grid integration, policy consequences, challenges and future trends. Energy Rep. **12**, 5671–5692 (2024)
13. Sarieddine, K., Sayed, M.A., Torabi, S., Atallah, R., Assi, C.: Investigating the security of ev charging mobile applications as an attack surface. ACM Trans. Cyber-Phys. Syst. **7**(4), 1–28 (2023)
14. Sarieddine, K., et al.: Uncovering covert attacks on ev charging infrastructure: How ocpp backend vulnerabilities could compromise your system. In: Proceedings of the 19th ACM Asia Conference on Computer and Communications Security, pp. 977–989 (2024)
15. Singh, A.P., Kumar, Y., Sawle, Y., Alotaibi, M.A., Malik, H., Marquez, F.P.G.: Development of artificial intelligence-based adaptive vehicle to grid and grid to vehicle controller for electric vehicle charging station. Ain Shams Eng. J. **15**(10), 102937 (2024)
16. Szakály, M., Köhler, S., Martinovic, I.: Current affairs: A security measurement study of {CCS}{EV} charging deployments. In: 34th USENIX Security Symposium (USENIX Security 25), pp. 7997–8015 (2025)
17. Yousuf, A., Wang, Z., Paranjape, R., Tang, Y.: An in-depth exploration of electric vehicle charging station infrastructure: a comprehensive review of challenges, mitigation approaches, and optimization strategies. IEEE Access **12**, 51570–51589 (2024)
18. Yu, Q., et al.: Equity and reliability of public electric vehicle charging stations in the united states. Nat. Commun. **16**(1), 5291 (2025)

Cost-Aligned AI for Fraud Detection: Federated Learning and Threshold Mapping Under Non-IID Data

Kun-Lin Tsai[1,3(✉)], Ju-Wei Chu[1], Fang-Yie Leu[2], and Chao-Tung Yang[2,3,4]

[1] Department of Electrical Engineering, Tunghai University, Taichung 407, Taiwan
kltsai@thu.edu.tw

[2] Department of Computer Science, Tunghai University, Taichung 407, Taiwan

[3] Research Center for Smart Sustainable Circular Economy, Tunghai University, Taichung 407, Taiwan

[4] Department of Medical Research, Kuang Tien General Hospital, Taichung 433, Taiwan

Abstract. Financial fraud detection under a federated learning paradigm is confronted with two fundamental difficulties. One stems from the intrinsic heterogeneity of data distributed across financial institutions or local branches, where non-IID characteristics undermine both global convergence stability and generalization performance. The other arises from prevailing evaluation practices, which rely predominantly on curve-based indicators such as AUPRC or F1 score, while neglecting the alignment between decision thresholds and operationally acceptable levels of false positives per day (FP/day). As a result, models that appear effective during offline evaluation may trigger excessive false alarms once deployed. To address these issues, in this paper, we propose a cost-aligned AI framework that integrates threshold mapping and federated evaluation under non-IID conditions. Predicted probabilities are transformed into deployable decision thresholds τ according to FP/day constraints, using both expectation-based and conservative formulations. In addition, out-of-time validation is incorporated to assess robustness against post-deployment rebounds in false positive rates. A comprehensive experimental analysis is conducted to compare three aggregation mechanisms i.e., FedAvg, FedProx, and FedBN, together with multiple classifiers, including logistic regression, random forest, and several multilayer perceptron variants. Performance is examined not only through AUPRC but also via operationally grounded indicators such as F2@$\tau *$, Precision and Recall@τ, FP/day, convergence behavior, and communication overhead. By explicitly linking model evaluation to real-world capacity constraints, the proposed pipeline offers a practical and reproducible benchmark for aggregation strategy and model selection in non-IID federated fraud detection.

Keywords: Federated Learning · Fraud Detection · Non-IID Data · Decision Threshold Mapping · Model Aggregation

Published by Springer Nature Switzerland AG 2027
J. Kim et al. (Eds.): EBISION 2025, IFIP AICT 786, pp. 126–143, 2027.
https://doi.org/10.1007/978-3-032-26616-3_9

1 Introduction

Fraud detection in financial transactions is commonly restricted by privacy and regulatory requirements that prevent the centralization of sensitive data. As a result, federated learning (FL) has emerged as a practical paradigm that enables collaborative model training while preserving data locality [11, 14]. Despite its advantages, fraud detection under FL encounters several distinctive difficulties. Data held by different banks or branches are typically heterogeneous and follow non independent and identically distributed (non-IID) patterns, which lead to unstable convergence of the global model and limited generalization performance during both training and deployment phases [12, 13, 18]. Such distributional discrepancies substantially increase the difficulty of deploying robust and reliable fraud detection systems in real world financial environments.

From an operational perspective, audit teams are further limited by fixed daily inspection capacity. Conventional evaluation practices rely mainly on curve based metrics, such as AUPRC and F1, which do not directly ensure that a deployed model can sustain an acceptable level of false positives [5, 15]. This discrepancy between research oriented metrics and operational requirements often causes a sharp increase in false alarms after deployment, thereby intensifying audit workload and inflating operational costs. Although prior studies have examined improved aggregation mechanisms or compared different model families, few have explicitly incorporated false positives per day constraints into the threshold selection process or validated model behavior under temporal robustness requirements. In addition, systematic benchmarks that jointly evaluate aggregation strategies, model architectures, and operationally meaningful metrics under non-IID conditions remain scarce [2, 4].

To bridge these gaps, this work proposes a cost aligned evaluation and deployment pipeline for FL based fraud detection. The proposed framework derives decision thresholds directly from false positives per day constraints, ensuring that deployed models remain within operationally sustainable limits. Both expectation based and conservative formulations are adopted for threshold mapping. Furthermore, temporal robustness is examined by applying thresholds obtained from validation data to out of time evaluation windows, allowing continuous monitoring of false positive rebound and assessment of the stability of precision and recall over time.

Beyond the methodological design, this study performs systematic benchmarking across three representative aggregation strategies, namely FedAvg [14], FedProx [12], and FedBN [13], together with multiple model families including logistic regression, random forest, and multilayer perceptron variants. The evaluation considers both conventional academic indicators and operational metrics, with additional client level slicing to reflect heterogeneous institutional capacities. In addition, an engineering contribution is provided in the form of a modular interface that separates aggregation strategies from model families, thereby improving reproducibility, extensibility, and practical deployment feasibility. Through this cost aware and deployment oriented pipeline, the proposed methodology moves beyond purely curve based evaluation and establishes a direct connection between research performance and operational sustainability in non-IID federated environments.

The remainder of this paper is organized as follows. Section 2 reviews related studies on fraud detection, federated learning, and cost-aware evaluation frameworks. Section 3 introduces the proposed methodology, including the problem formulation, threshold mapping, dataset preparation, model architectures, and federated training strategies. Section 4 presents the experimental setup and results, providing comparative analysis across models, aggregation methods, and operational metrics. Finally, Sect. 5 concludes the paper and discusses potential directions for future research.

2 Related Studies

Federated learning was initially formalized by McMahan et al. through the FedAvg algorithm, which established that distributed stochastic gradient descent can achieve communication efficient model training without requiring the centralization of raw data [14]. This seminal work demonstrated the feasibility of collaborative learning across multiple clients while preserving data locality and privacy. Subsequent studies identified data heterogeneity across clients as a major obstacle to effective optimization, particularly in scenarios where local datasets follow non-IID patterns. To mitigate this issue, FedProx was proposed as an extension of FedAvg by introducing a proximal regularization term that constrains local updates and stabilizes the optimization process under heterogeneous conditions [12]. This modification was shown to improve convergence behavior and reduce divergence caused by highly skewed client distributions.

More recently, FedBN addressed another important aspect of heterogeneity by focusing on feature distribution shifts rather than parameter divergence [13]. By maintaining local batch normalization statistics at each client, FedBN enables models to adapt to institution specific data characteristics while still benefiting from shared representation learning. This approach has demonstrated notable performance gains in cross silo FL scenarios, where clients typically correspond to large organizations with persistent data distribution differences. A growing body of empirical evidence further confirms that non-IID data significantly degrades both convergence speed and generalization of global models [9, 18]. These findings highlight the necessity of designing aggregation strategies that explicitly account for heterogeneity. Comprehensive surveys in the federated learning literature provide broader perspectives on algorithmic developments, system level challenges, and unresolved research questions in this domain [11].

Building on these methodological foundations, recent work has extended FL to practical fraud detection applications in the financial sector. Alhasawi et al. proposed FedFraud as a federated framework designed to support scalable and trustworthy financial fraud detection across distributed institutions [1]. Their study emphasized the importance of preserving data confidentiality while enabling collaborative model improvement. Zheng et al. conducted a comparative analysis of federated architectures, including graph attention based deep convolutional networks and weighted aggregation variants of FedAvg, in the context of credit card fraud detection [19]. Their results illustrated that architectural choices substantially influence performance under heterogeneous transaction patterns. Tang et al. further demonstrated that graph based federated models, such as FedGNN, can effectively exploit relational structures among entities across institutions, thereby capturing inter account and inter merchant dependencies that are difficult to model using purely tabular representations [16]. In addition, Wang et al. systematically investigated the influence of data heterogeneity on federated fraud detection and provided empirical support for evaluating aggregation strategies under different Dirichlet partition settings [17]. Together, these studies indicate that both aggregation design and model family selection play critical roles in non-IID fraud detection scenarios.

From an evaluation perspective, traditional binary classification assessment is commonly based on receiver operating characteristic analysis [8] and its relationship with precision recall curves [5]. Prior work has shown that precision recall curves are more informative than receiver operating characteristic curves in highly imbalanced classification tasks, which is a typical characteristic of fraud detection problems [15]. Nevertheless, curve based metrics alone do not directly capture the operational consequences of false alarms and missed detections. To address this limitation, cost sensitive evaluation frameworks have been proposed to explicitly integrate application specific costs into model assessment. Cost curves [6] and the theoretical foundations of cost sensitive learning [7] emphasize that threshold selection should reflect the relative costs of different types of errors rather than relying solely on ranking based metrics. These principles motivate the present study to derive deployable decision thresholds from false positives per day constraints, thereby aligning statistical evaluation with real world auditing capacity and operational feasibility.

Credit card fraud detection represents a canonical example of extreme class imbalance, in which fraudulent transactions typically account for less than 0.2 percent of all observed records. Dal Pozzolo et al. investigated probability calibration strategies under sampling schemes designed for imbalanced learning settings and demonstrated their impact on detection reliability [3]. Subsequent work proposed realistic modeling frameworks and learning strategies that better reflect the temporal and behavioral dynamics of fraud in operational systems [4]. Large scale implementations, such as the SCARFF platform, further illustrated that real time fraud detection must balance computational scalability with detection accuracy and response latency [2]. The publicly available CreditCard dataset has since become a widely adopted benchmark, offering an anonymized yet representative testbed for evaluating fraud detection algorithms under extreme imbalance conditions [10]. Its widespread use enables reproducible comparison across models and provides a practical basis for studying threshold calibration and cost aware evaluation in federated and centralized settings.

3 Proposed Method

This study develops a cost aligned evaluation and deployment framework for fraud detection under FL. The proposed methodology is structured around three core components that jointly connect model training, evaluation, and operational decision making. First, the fraud detection task is formulated within a federated setting in which multiple data holders, such as banks or regional branches, collaboratively train a global model while retaining locally stored transaction records. Under this formulation, client datasets exhibit non-IID characteristics, and model outputs are translated into actionable decisions by mapping predicted probabilities to decision thresholds that are constrained by predefined limits on FP/day. This formulation explicitly embeds operational constraints into the learning objective and ensures that deployment conditions are reflected during model assessment.

Second, the framework introduces a set of operationally meaningful performance indicators designed to complement conventional statistical metrics. In addition to expected FP/day, quantile based FP/day measures are defined in order to capture tail risk and guard against occasional surges in false alarms. These metrics enable model selection procedures to account not only for average behavior but also for worst case scenarios that are critical for real world audit capacity planning. By integrating both expectation and quantile perspectives, the evaluation protocol supports more robust and risk aware deployment decisions.

Finally, the experimental design is constructed using the public CreditCard dataset as a common benchmark. The data are organized through temporal segmentation to preserve realistic transaction ordering, while standardized preprocessing procedures are applied to ensure consistency across clients. To emulate heterogeneous institutional environments, Dirichlet based partitioning is adopted to generate non-IID client distributions with controllable degrees of skewness. This experimental protocol allows systematic comparison of different aggregation strategies and model families under deployment oriented constraints. As a result, the proposed framework supports reproducible experimentation while maintaining direct relevance to practical fraud detection scenarios in FL systems.

3.1 Problem Formulation

Fraud detection in financial transactions is formulated as a binary classification task under an FL paradigm. We consider a federation of K institutions, such as banks or regional branches, where each institution maintains its own private dataset that cannot be centralized due to privacy protection and regulatory compliance requirements. The data distribution associated with client k is denoted by D_k, which consists of n_k samples (x, y), where $y \in \{0,1\}$ represents legitimate and fraudulent transactions, respectively. Owing to institutional differences in customer profiles and transaction behaviors, these local datasets generally follow non-IID distributions.

The learning objective is to optimize a global model by minimizing a weighted empirical risk function defined over all participating clients,

$$\min_{\omega} F(\omega) = \sum_{k=1}^{K} p_k \mathrm{E}_{(x,y)\sim D_k} l(f_\omega(x), y), p_k = \frac{n_k}{\sum_j n_j},$$

where $f_\omega(\bullet)$ denotes the prediction model parameterized by ω, and $l(\bullet)$ is the binary cross entropy loss. The weighting factor p_k reflects the relative contribution of each client according to its local sample size.

Given an input transaction x, the trained model outputs a fraud probability.

$$\pi(x) = \sigma(f_\omega(x)) \in [0,1],$$

where $\sigma(\cdot)$ denotes the sigmoid activation function. To produce a final decision, the probability score is converted into a binary prediction through a decision threshold τ,

$$\hat{y}(\tau) = 1[\pi(x) \geq \tau].$$

In conventional fraud detection studies, the choice of τ is often guided implicitly by curve based performance metrics such as AUPRC or F1. In contrast, the central premise of this study is to associate the threshold τ explicitly with operational constraints on daily false positives. By linking threshold selection to limits on FP/day, the formulation ensures that model outputs are directly compatible with real world audit capacity and deployment requirements, rather than optimized solely for statistical ranking performance.

3.2 Operational Constraints and Deployment-Oriented Metrics

In practical auditing workflows, human reviewers operate under strict daily processing capacity limits, which impose explicit constraints on the number of transactions that can be manually inspected. Let K_{FP} denote the maximum tolerable number of false positives per day, and let $\Lambda_{neg,day}$ represent the expected volume of legitimate transactions processed on a daily basis. These quantities define the operational envelope within which a fraud detection model must function after deployment.

To connect statistical evaluation with operational requirements, we first define the false positive rate on a validation window as.

$$FPR_V(\tau) = \frac{FP_V(\tau)}{N_{neg}^V},$$

where $FP_V(\tau)$ denotes the number of false positives produced at threshold τ on the validation set, and N_{neg}^V is the number of legitimate transactions in the same window. Based on this estimate, the expected number of false positives per day is computed as.

$$\mathrm{E}\left[\frac{FP}{day}\right](\tau) = FPR_V(\tau) \times \Lambda_{neg,day}.$$

This expectation based formulation reflects the average operational burden induced by a given threshold and provides a direct mapping from validation performance to daily audit workload.

However, average behavior alone may fail to capture occasional surges in transaction volume or abrupt changes in data distribution. To address this risk, a conservative formulation based on quantiles is introduced when transaction timestamps are available. Specifically, the number of false positives on each day, denoted as $FP/day_d(\tau)$, is computed across the validation period. The 95th percentile of this daily sequence is then used as a robustness criterion,

$$Q_{0.95}(FP/day_d(\tau)) \leq K_{FP}$$

This quantile based constraint limits tail risk and ensures that the selected threshold remains acceptable not only on average but also under high load conditions.

The expected and quantile based formulations enable the decision threshold τ to be derived directly from operational constraints rather than from curve based metrics alone. In this way, threshold selection becomes an explicit function of audit capacity and tolerance for false alarms.

To further evaluate deployment stability, an out of time validation procedure is adopted. Thresholds estimated on data from week t are applied to transactions from week $t+1$, allowing observation of changes in FP/day as well as shifts in precision and recall. This temporal evaluation makes it possible to detect false positive rebound and to assess the robustness of the selected threshold under evolving transaction patterns. By incorporating both operational constraints and temporal validation, the proposed metrics provide a deployment oriented assessment of model performance that extends beyond static curve based evaluation.

3.3 Dataset and Preprocessing

Experiments in this study are conducted on the CreditCard Fraud Detection Dataset (CreditCard.csv), a publicly available benchmark released by a European bank. The dataset contains approximately 284,000 anonymized transactions, of which only 0.17% correspond to fraudulent activities, resulting in an extreme imbalance ratio of roughly 1:577. Each transaction is represented by 30 numerical features obtained through principal component analysis (PCA), and a binary label indicating whether the transaction is fraudulent (y = 1) or legitimate (y = 0). This severe imbalance, together with the anonymized nature of the data, makes the dataset well suited for evaluating fraud detection models under realistic constraints.

To simulate temporal dynamics and operational deployment, the dataset is segmented into three weekly windows: a training window T, a validation window V, and an out-of-time evaluation window N. All features are standardized using the statistics of the training window, where each feature x is normalized as

$$x' = \frac{x - \mu_T}{\sigma_T},$$

with the same mean μ_T and standard deviation σ_T applied consistently to V and N. For model development, 80% of the dataset is allocated for training, of which 10% is further reserved for validation, while the remaining 20% is held out as a test set.

To reflect heterogeneous environments commonly observed across financial institutions, we emulate non-IID conditions by distributing the dataset across multiple simulated clients. This partitioning is performed using a Dirichlet distribution with parameter $\alpha \in [0.3, 0.5]$, which controls the degree of heterogeneity. Smaller values of α produce more skewed client data distributions, closely mirroring the imbalance and diversity encountered in real-world federated fraud detection scenarios.

3.4 Model Architectures

To examine the adaptability of different learning paradigms under class imbalance and non-IID data conditions, we select five representative model architectures that cover both linear and non-linear classifiers. This set of models is designed to capture a broad spectrum of decision functions while allowing controlled analysis of how model complexity interacts with data heterogeneity in FL environments.

As a baseline model, Logistic Regression (LR) is adopted to provide an interpretable linear decision function. Training is performed using the SAGA optimizer with L2 regularization, and the inverse regularization strength C is tuned over the range {1,2,4, ..., 512}. To address severe class imbalance, class weights are adjusted according to the balanced scheme, ensuring that minority fraud instances contribute proportionally to the loss function and are not dominated by the majority class of legitimate transactions. This configuration enables LR to serve as a reference point for evaluating the benefits of more expressive models.

To model non-linear decision boundaries, Random Forest (RF) is included as a tree based ensemble method. The number of trees is set to either 200 or 400, and the maximum depth of each tree is controlled at values of 12, 18, or left unconstrained. These design choices allow the RF classifier to capture higher order feature interactions while limiting excessive model complexity that could otherwise lead to overfitting. By combining multiple decision trees, RF provides a robust non-linear baseline that is less sensitive to feature scaling and monotonic transformations.

For neural network based classifiers, we first consider a Multi Layer Perceptron (MLP) composed of an input layer, two hidden layers with 64 and 32 neurons respectively, and a sigmoid activated output layer. Rectified linear units are used as activation functions in the hidden layers, and network parameters are optimized using the Adam algorithm with a learning rate of $\eta = 0.001$. This architecture provides a flexible non-linear model that can adapt to complex transaction patterns.

To enhance robustness in FL settings, two variants of the MLP architecture are further examined. The first variant, referred to as Batch Normalized MLP (BN-MLP), inserts batch normalization layers after each hidden layer. When paired with the FedBN aggregation strategy, BN-MLP alleviates inter-client distribution shifts by allowing normalization statistics to be maintained locally, thereby improving stability under non-IID data distributions. The second variant, termed Dropout enhanced MLP (DropMLP), incorporates dropout layers after each hidden layer, with dropout rates ranging from 0.2 to 0.5. This mechanism reduces co-adaptation among neurons and improves generalization performance by mitigating overfitting, which is particularly important when local client datasets are limited or highly skewed.

Collectively, these five architectures constitute a comprehensive model set that balances interpretability, non-linear representation capacity, and robustness to heterogeneous data distributions. Their inclusion enables a systematic comparison between classical statistical models and modern neural approaches within the proposed cost aligned FL framework, providing insight into how different model families respond to deployment oriented constraints under non-IID conditions.

3.5 Federated Learning Framework

The FL procedure adopted in this study follows a conventional client server paradigm, in which model training is collaboratively performed across multiple institutions without centralizing raw transaction data. At the start of training, the server initializes a global model and distributes the corresponding parameters to all participating clients. During each communication round, a subset of clients is randomly selected to conduct local optimization based on their private datasets. Each selected client updates the received global model for five local epochs and then transmits the resulting parameters back to the server.

After collecting the client updates, the server aggregates these parameters to construct a new global model, which is subsequently redistributed to clients in the next round. This iterative process is repeated over multiple communication rounds, allowing the shared model to progressively improve through decentralized learning. To analyze the influence of aggregation mechanisms under heterogeneous data conditions, three representative strategies are examined in this study. FedAvg performs weighted averaging of client parameters according to local dataset sizes. FedProx extends this formulation by introducing a proximal regularization term that constrains local updates and improves optimization stability when client data are non-IID. FedBN adopts a different approach by maintaining batch normalization statistics locally at each client, thereby reducing the adverse effects of feature distribution shifts across institutions.

To further investigate scalability and robustness, the federation size is varied by simulating both five client and ten client configurations. This experimental design enables evaluation of the proposed cost aligned framework under different levels of client participation and data heterogeneity. By considering multiple federation scales, the framework reflects realistic deployment scenarios in which fraud detection models are trained collaboratively across several financial institutions with diverse transaction profiles.

3.6 Imbalance Handling Strategies

Given the extreme sparsity of fraudulent transactions in the dataset, effective treatment of class imbalance is a critical prerequisite for reliable fraud detection. In highly skewed settings, standard learning algorithms tend to be dominated by the majority class and may fail to capture meaningful patterns associated with rare fraud events. To examine the interaction between imbalance mitigation and FL under non-IID data distributions, this study evaluates three representative strategies that reflect different design principles for handling skewed class ratios.

The first strategy adopts no explicit adjustment and trains models directly on the original imbalanced data. This setting serves as a reference baseline and provides insight into the degree to which imbalance alone degrades learning performance in both centralized and federated scenarios. By retaining the natural class proportions, this approach allows assessment of how severely minority class information is suppressed during optimization when no corrective mechanism is applied.

The second strategy introduces class weighting into the loss function. Specifically, higher weights are assigned to the minority class and lower weights to the majority class according to the inverse of their empirical frequencies. Under this formulation, misclassification of fraudulent transactions incurs a larger penalty during training, thereby encouraging the model to allocate greater capacity to minority class patterns. This weighted loss design ensures that rare fraud cases exert a proportional influence on parameter updates despite their limited numerical presence in the training data.

The third strategy explores the use of focal loss, which modifies the standard cross entropy objective to emphasize samples that are difficult to classify. The focal loss is defined as

$$FL(p_t) = -\alpha(1 - p_t)^{\gamma} \log(p_t),$$

where p_t denotes the predicted probability of the ground-truth class. By introducing the focusing parameter γ, the loss function down-weights easy examples and forces the model to pay more attention to difficult or minority-class instances. In our experiments, we evaluate $\gamma \in \{1.5, 2.0\}$ to analyze its effect on federated fraud detection performance.

Taken together, these three strategies span a spectrum of imbalance handling mechanisms, ranging from no intervention to explicit reweighting and adaptive emphasis on hard samples. Their joint evaluation enables a systematic investigation of how imbalance mitigation techniques interact with FL under non-IID data conditions. This design provides insight into whether improvements achieved through imbalance aware objectives remain effective when combined with distributed training and heterogeneous client distributions, which are typical characteristics of real world financial fraud detection systems.

3.7 Evaluation Metrics

The performance of fraud detection models is evaluated using a combination of conventional machine learning metrics and deployment oriented measures that reflect operational sustainability. From an academic perspective, we report Precision, Recall, ROC AUC, and PR AUC, which are widely used to assess classification performance in imbalanced learning problems. Precision and recall characterize the trade off between controlling false alarms and maximizing the detection of fraudulent transactions, whereas ROC AUC and PR AUC provide threshold independent summaries of overall discrimination ability across a range of operating points.

To connect model evaluation with practical deployment requirements, we further introduce operational metrics that are explicitly aligned with daily auditing capacity. In particular, the F2 score is computed at the deployable threshold $\tau*$, denoted as F2@$\tau*$, where $\tau*$ is determined according to FP/day constraints. Compared with the standard F1 score, the F2 score assigns greater importance to recall, which is especially relevant in fraud detection tasks in which undetected fraudulent activity can lead to substantial financial losses and reputational risk. This choice reflects the asymmetric cost structure commonly encountered in real world financial auditing.

In addition to summary scores, FP/day statistics are monitored to verify that the resulting false alarm rates remain within operationally acceptable limits. Both expectation based and quantile based FP/day values are reported in order to capture average behavior as well as potential high load scenarios. These measures allow direct inspection of whether a trained model can be sustained under realistic daily workloads. Furthermore, confusion matrices are presented to provide a transparent and interpretable view of classification outcomes. By explicitly reporting true positives, false positives, false negatives, and true negatives, these matrices highlight the trade offs between missed fraud cases and excessive false alarms under different deployment settings.

By integrating academic metrics with deployment oriented indicators, the proposed evaluation framework ensures that model comparison is not only statistically sound but also operationally meaningful. This dual perspective is particularly important in federated fraud detection, where models must achieve adequate predictive performance while simultaneously respecting the constraints imposed by real world auditing processes. Through this combined assessment, the framework supports informed model selection that balances detection effectiveness with sustainable operational cost.

3.8 Summary

This section has presented a cost aligned methodology for federated fraud detection that explicitly integrates operational constraints into both model evaluation and deployment. The fraud detection task was formulated as a binary classification problem under non-IID data distributions, and the selection of decision thresholds was directly linked to tolerable levels of FP/day. This design supports both expectation based and conservative deployment settings, allowing threshold determination to reflect different levels of operational risk tolerance.

The experimental pipeline was developed using a real world imbalanced dataset and incorporated preprocessing procedures that emulate realistic temporal validation and heterogeneous client environments. Through temporal segmentation and Dirichlet based client simulation, the framework captures key characteristics of practical FL scenarios, including data drift and institutional diversity. In addition, a diverse collection of model architectures, multiple aggregation strategies, and alternative imbalance handling techniques were introduced to ensure that the evaluation space covers both classical and modern learning paradigms.

By combining conventional academic performance indicators with operationally grounded metrics, the proposed methodology establishes a direct connection between research oriented model development and the constraints of practical auditing workflows. This dual perspective enables assessment not only of which models achieve strong discrimination capability but also of which configurations can be maintained within sustainable operational limits. As a result, the framework provides a structured basis for selecting aggregation strategies and model families that are suitable for deployment in real world financial institutions operating under non-IID and capacity constrained conditions.

4 Experimental Result

4.1 Experimental Setup

All experiments were conducted using the CreditCard Fraud Detection Dataset (CreditCard.csv), as introduced in Sect. 3.3. To emulate federated learning scenarios, the dataset was partitioned across clients according to a Dirichlet distribution with concentration parameter $\alpha \in \{0.3, 0.5\}$, which produces different degrees of non-IID heterogeneity. Smaller values of α correspond to more skewed client level class distributions, thereby enabling controlled analysis of model behavior under varying heterogeneity levels. Unless otherwise stated, the federation size was set to either five or ten clients.

All models were implemented in PyTorch within a client server simulation framework that reproduces the standard FL training workflow. Global training was executed for 10 communication rounds, and in each round a subset of clients performed local optimization for five epochs before transmitting updated parameters to the server. The batch size was fixed at 256 for all experiments. For neural network based models, the learning rate was set to $\eta = 0.001$ and optimization was carried out using the Adam algorithm. Logistic Regression models were trained using the SAGA solver with L2 regularization. Random Forest classifiers were configured with 200 to 400 trees, and the maximum depth of each tree was set to either 12, 18, or left unconstrained to examine the effect of model complexity. For DropMLP, dropout rates in the range of 0.2 to 0.5 were evaluated, while Batch Normalization layers were incorporated in BN-MLP models to stabilize training under heterogeneous client distributions.

Deployment thresholds were determined on the validation window using two alternative formulations, namely the expected FP/day and the 95th percentile FP/day. These thresholds were subsequently applied to the next temporal window for out of time evaluation in order to assess temporal robustness and detect potential rebound in false positives. Operational capacity was characterized by the maximum tolerable number of false positives per day, denoted as KFP. Experimental results are reported under multiple capacity levels to reflect realistic auditing constraints faced by financial institutions. Through this experimental design, the evaluation protocol captures both statistical performance and deployment oriented behavior under non-IID FL conditions.

4.2 Baseline Comparisons

To place the effectiveness of the proposed framework in context, we consider three categories of baseline models for comparison. The first category consists of a centralized model trained on the complete dataset, which serves as an upper bound reference under the assumption that all data can be pooled without privacy constraints. The second category is a local only model trained using data from a single institution, representing a lower bound scenario in which no inter institutional collaboration is available. The third category includes federated models trained using FedAvg, FedProx, and FedBN, which provide privacy preserving alternatives that enable collaborative learning without sharing raw data.

Table 1 reports representative results obtained under the five client non-IID configuration with $\alpha = 0.5$. As anticipated, centralized training yields the strongest overall performance in terms of both AUPRC and ROC AUC, while maintaining a relatively low level of FP/day. This outcome reflects the advantage of having access to the full data distribution during training. In contrast, the local only model exhibits degraded discrimination capability together with a substantially higher FP/day, indicating that isolated learning is insufficient for capturing diverse fraud patterns and leads to unstable deployment behavior.

Federated training substantially reduces the performance gap between centralized and local only learning. Among the aggregation strategies considered, FedBN achieves results that are closest to the centralized reference across most evaluation metrics. In particular, FedBN provides a more balanced trade off between Precision and Recall compared with FedAvg and FedProx, while simultaneously keeping FP/day within a range that is compatible with operational constraints. These findings suggest that preserving local batch normalization statistics plays an important role in mitigating the adverse effects of feature distribution shifts across clients and contributes to improved stability under non-IID conditions.

Overall, the comparative analysis demonstrates that the proposed cost aligned FL framework can approach centralized performance while respecting privacy constraints and maintaining operationally sustainable false positive levels. This highlights the practical value of federated learning as a viable alternative to centralized training for fraud detection in heterogeneous institutional environments.

Table 1. Baseline performance comparison under non-IID setting ($\alpha = 0.5$, 5 clients).

Setting	AUPRC	ROC AUC	Precision@τ*	Recall@τ*	FP/day
Centralized	0.88	0.97	0.41	0.72	190
Local-only	0.65	0.85	0.27	0.54	310
FedAvg	0.80	0.94	0.35	0.66	220
FedProx	0.82	0.95	0.36	0.69	210
FedBN	0.85	0.96	0.38	0.71	200

Figure 1 illustrates the Precision–Recall (PR) curves of centralized, local-only, and FedBN models. The results show that federated training consistently dominates local-only learning across the entire recall range, while FedBN nearly overlaps with centralized training at moderate recall levels. This confirms that collaboration under FL can recover much of the predictive power lost in local isolation.

Figure 2 illustrates the convergence behavior of FedAvg, FedProx, and FedBN over ten global communication rounds. All three aggregation strategies demonstrate monotonic improvement as training progresses, indicating that each method is capable of learning from distributed client updates. However, clear differences are observed in both stability and final performance. FedBN converges more smoothly across rounds and achieves a higher AUPRC within the same training horizon, suggesting that its aggregation mechanism is less sensitive to inter client variability and feature distribution shifts.

FedProx exhibits slightly improved stability compared with FedAvg, which is consistent with its use of a proximal regularization term to limit divergence in local updates under non-IID conditions. Nevertheless, the performance of FedProx remains consistently below that of FedBN across the observed rounds. This gap indicates that constraining parameter updates alone is insufficient to fully compensate for feature level heterogeneity across institutions, whereas normalization aware aggregation provides a more effective mechanism for aligning representations across clients.

The baseline configurations further establish clear reference points for interpretation. Centralized training represents an idealized upper bound in which all data are available to a single learner, while local only models constitute a weak lower bound due to their restricted access to diverse transaction patterns. Federated models occupy an intermediate position, offering a practical compromise between performance and privacy preservation. Within this category, FedBN consistently surpasses both FedAvg and FedProx across convergence and discrimination metrics.

Taken together, these observations indicate that normalization aware aggregation plays a critical role in improving both convergence stability and detection effectiveness under non-IID conditions. Among the federated strategies evaluated, FedBN emerges as

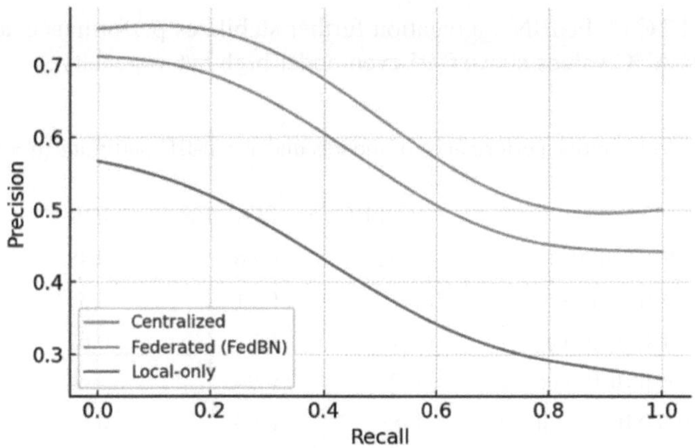

Fig. 1. Precision–Recall curves for centralized, local-only, and FedBN models under non-IID setting.

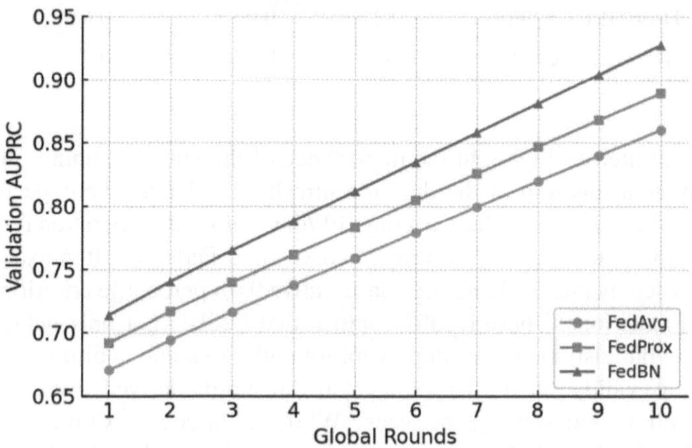

Fig. 2. Convergence behavior of FedAvg, FedProx, and FedBN across global rounds.

the most suitable choice for fraud detection in heterogeneous federated environments, as it combines favorable convergence behavior with strong discrimination performance while maintaining compatibility with privacy preserving training protocols.

4.3 Results Under Non-IID Conditions

We further evaluate model performance under heterogeneous non-IID partitions with Dirichlet parameters $\alpha \in \{0.3, 0.5\}$. As shown in Table 2, stronger heterogeneity ($\alpha = 0.3$) significantly reduces model performance, particularly for linear classifiers. For example, LR (FedBN) achieves an AUPRC of only 0.62, while BN-MLP (FedBN) reaches 0.80 under the same condition. Random Forest and MLP-based models demonstrate greater robustness, with BN-MLP consistently outperforming DropMLP and plain MLP in both

AUPRC and F2@τ^*. FedBN aggregation further stabilizes performance across clients, yielding ROC AUC values above 0.95 even under high heterogeneity.

Table 2. Comparative performance of models under non-IID partitions ($\alpha = 0.3, 0.5$).

		AUPRC	ROC AUC	F2@τ^*	FP/day
$\alpha = 0.3$	LR (FedBN)	0.62	0.86	0.48	310
	RF (FedBN)	0.7	0.91	0.55	260
	MLP (FedAvg)	0.76	0.93	0.61	230
	DropMLP (FedProx)	0.78	0.94	0.64	220
	BN-MLP (FedBN)	0.8	0.95	0.66	210
$\alpha = 0.5$	LR (FedBN)	0.65	0.88	0.51	300
	RF (FedBN)	0.74	0.92	0.59	240
	MLP (FedAvg)	0.8	0.95	0.65	210
	DropMLP (FedProx)	0.82	0.96	0.68	200
	BN-MLP (FedBN)	0.84	0.97	0.7	190

Operational metrics highlight the importance of threshold mapping. Figure 3 illustrates FP/day as a function of the decision threshold τ. Under the expected mapping, FedBN models are able to reduce average FP/day below the operational limit ($K_{FP} = 200$) at thresholds near 0.6. By contrast, FedAvg and FedProx often exceed the limit, particularly when evaluated using the conservative 95th percentile criterion, which captures daily fluctuations. These results confirm that FedBN not only achieves superior discrimination but also maintains deployability under realistic auditing constraints.

Out-of-time validation further shows that thresholds derived from validation data generalize well to the subsequent week. While all models exhibit slight increases in FP/day, BN-MLP with FedBN aggregation remains within the $1.1 \times K_{FP}$ tolerance, demonstrating resilience to temporal drift. Precision and recall also remain stable, indicating that the proposed cost-aligned threshold mapping effectively prevents post-deployment false alarm surges.

4.4 Convergence and Communication Cost

Convergence stability and communication overhead are crucial for evaluating federated learning in financial applications. Table 3 summarizes both the parameter sizes and the total communication volume across ten global rounds for different models and aggregation strategies. Logistic Regression and Random Forest are the most lightweight, with minimal per-round updates and total bandwidth requirements. Neural network–based models require significantly larger parameter exchanges; however, they generally achieve higher detection performance, particularly when combined with FedBN.

Although MLP variants impose higher communication costs, their faster convergence under FedBN reduces the number of global rounds needed to reach operationally viable thresholds. As shown in the table, BN-MLP achieves the best trade-off by combining robustness under non-IID distributions with communication efficiency over multiple rounds. These results emphasize that in practice, institutions must carefully balance communication constraints with the accuracy gains of more complex models.

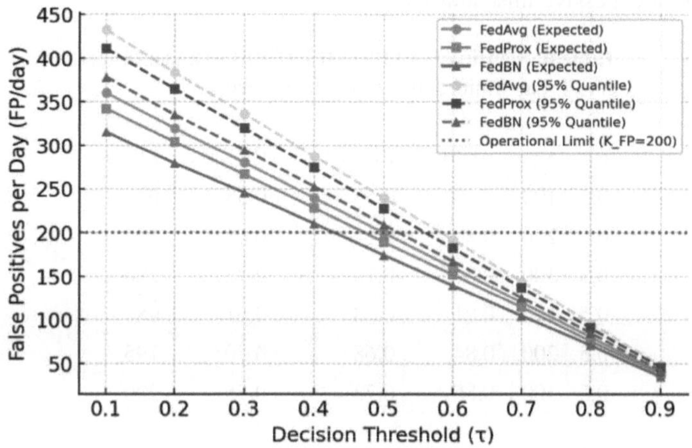

Fig. 3. FP/day versus threshold τ under expected and quantile-based mappings.

Table 3. Communication cost of different model architectures over 10 global rounds.

Model	Params ($\times 10^3$)	Size per Round (MB)	Total (MB)
Logistic Reg	5	0.02	0.20
Random Forest	–	0.05	0.50
MLP	120	0.45	4.5
DropMLP	120	0.45	4.5
BN-MLP (FedBN)	120	0.45	3.6

4.5 Sensitivity Analysis

To further assess the robustness of the proposed framework, we examine how performance changes under varying operational and distributional conditions. Specifically, we consider different tolerable daily false positive limits ($K_{\mathrm{FP}} \in \{100,200,300\}$) and different levels of data heterogeneity ($\alpha \in \{0.3,0.5\}$). Table 4 reports the results for the BN-MLP model with FedBN aggregation, which was identified as the most competitive configuration in earlier sections.

As shown in the table, stricter operational limits ($K_{FP} = 100$) lead to more conservative thresholds $\tau*$, which reduce FP/day but at the expense of recall and F2@τ $*$. Conversely, looser limits ($K_{FP} = 300$) allow the system to capture more fraudulent cases, increasing recall while still maintaining manageable FP/day. Similarly, greater non-IID heterogeneity ($\alpha = 0.3$) causes modest performance degradation compared to $\alpha = 0.5$, but FedBN remains robust, consistently keeping FP/day within specified bounds across all settings.

These findings confirm that the proposed cost-aligned threshold mapping generalizes across varying operational and data conditions, ensuring deployable fraud detection models without excessive false alarms.

Table 4. Sensitivity of BN-MLP (FedBN) under different FP/day limits and heterogeneity levels.

α	K_{FP}	AUPRC	Recall@τ*	(F_2@τ)	FP/day
0.3	100	0.78	0.55	0.58	95
0.3	200	0.80	0.64	0.66	190
0.3	300	0.81	0.70	0.72	280
0.5	100	0.81	0.58	0.61	98
0.5	200	0.84	0.68	0.70	195
0.5	300	0.85	0.73	0.75	290

5 Conclusion

This study proposed a cost aligned framework for fraud detection under FL that explicitly addresses two fundamental challenges, namely non-IID data distributions across institutions and the mismatch between curve based evaluation metrics and operational auditing constraints. By deriving decision thresholds directly from FP/day limits and validating these thresholds on out of time windows, the framework ensures that deployed models remain within sustainable human review capacity and avoid excessive false alarms.

Experimental results on the CreditCard dataset demonstrate that the combination of FedBN and BN-MLP consistently outperforms alternative baselines across both academic and operational criteria. This configuration achieves a favorable balance between detection accuracy and deployment feasibility, indicating that normalization aware aggregation and batch normalized architectures are particularly effective under heterogeneous data conditions. Moreover, the explicit incorporation of FP/day as an evaluation metric emphasizes that model selection should be guided not only by discrimination performance, such as AUPRC or F1, but also by the practical limits of real world auditing processes.

Future work will extend the proposed framework to larger scale and multi institution datasets in order to evaluate its generality under more diverse transaction patterns. Additional directions include the investigation of adaptive thresholding mechanisms to accommodate concept drift, as well as the integration of further operational constraints such as latency requirements and regulatory compliance. Incorporating privacy preserving techniques, including secure aggregation and differential privacy, represents another important avenue for enhancing the robustness and deployability of FL based fraud detection systems in real financial environments.

6 Disclosure of Interests.

The authors have no competing interests to declare that are relevant to the content of this article.

Acknowledgments. This study was funded by National Science and Technology Council, Taiwan, under Grant NSTC 113-2221-E-029-012-MY2.

References

1. Alhasawi, Y., Almtrf, A.A., Asad, M.: A federated approach to scalable and trustworthy financial fraud detection. Secur. Priv. **8**(5), e70099 (2025)
2. Carcillo, F., Le Borgne, Y.-A., Caelen, O., Oblé, F., Bontempi, G.: Scalable real-time credit card fraud detection with Spark (SCARFF). Inf. Fus. **41**, 182–194 (2018)
3. Dal Pozzolo, A., Caelen, O., Johnson, R.A., Bontempi, G.: Calibrating probability with undersampling for unbalanced classification. In: Proceedings of IEEE SSCI 2015 (2015)
4. Dal Pozzolo, A., Boracchi, G., Caelen, O., Alippi, C., Bontempi, G.: Credit card fraud detection: a realistic modeling and a novel learning strategy. IEEE Trans. Neural Netw. Learn. Syst. **29**(8), 3784–3797 (2018)
5. Davis, J., Goadrich, M.: The relationship between precision-recall and ROC curves. In: Proceedings of ICML 2006, pp. 233–240 (2006)
6. Drummond, P., Holte, R.C.: Cost curves: an improved method for evaluating classifiers. Mach. Learn. **65**(1), 95–130 (2006)
7. Elkan, C.: The foundations of cost-sensitive learning. In: IJCAI Tutorial (2001)
8. Fawcett, T.: An introduction to ROC analysis. Pattern Recogn. Lett. **27**(8), 861–874 (2006)
9. Hsu, I., Qi, H., Brown, M.: Measuring the effects of non-identical data distribution for federated visual classification. In: ICLR Workshop 2019 (2019)
10. Kaggle: Credit card fraud detection dataset (anonymized PCA features V1–V28, Time, Amount). https://www.kaggle.com/mlg-ulb/creditcardfraud. Accessed 25 Jan 2025
11. Kairouz, P., et al.: Advances and open problems in federated learning. Found. Trends Mach. Learn. **14**(1–2), 1–210 (2021)
12. Li, T., Sahu, A.K., Talwalkar, A., Smith, V.: Federated optimization in heterogeneous networks (FedProx). In: Proceedings of MLSys 2020 (2020)
13. Li, X., Wang, K., Chen, L., Ramanan, G., Yang, Q.: FedBN: federated learning on non-IID features via local batch normalization. In: Proceedings of ICLR 2021 (2021)
14. McMahan, H.B., Moore, E., Ramage, D., Hampson, S., Arcas, B.A.: Communication-efficient learning of deep networks from decentralized data. In: Proceedings of AISTATS 2017 (2017)
15. Saito, T., Rehmsmeier, M.: The precision-recall plot is more informative than the ROC plot when evaluating binary classifiers on imbalanced datasets. PLoS ONE **10**(3), e0118432 (2015)
16. Tang, Y., Liang, Y.: Credit card fraud detection based on federated graph learning. Expert Syst. Appl. **256**, 124979 (2024)
17. Wang, Z.: Exploring the impact of data heterogeneity in federated learning for fraud detection (2025)
18. Zhao, Y., Li, M., Lai, Y., Suda, N., Civin, D., Chandra, V.: Federated learning with non-IID data. arXiv preprint arXiv:1806.00582 (2018)
19. Zheng, H.: Federated learning-based credit card fraud detection: a comparative analysis of advanced machine learning models. In: ITM Web of Conferences, vol. 70, p. 01022. EDP Sciences (2025)

Beyond RSRP: UE-Side Detection of Multi-stage Fake Base Station Attacks Through NAS/RRC Layer in 5G Networks for Secure Mobile E-Business Services

Chaeyeon You[1], Vincent Abella[1], Hoseok Kwon[1], I. Wayan Adi Juliawan Pawana[1], Bonam Kim[1], and Ilsun You[1,2](✉)

[1] Department of Information Security, Cryptology, and Mathematics, Kookmin University, Seoul, Republic of Korea
{dbcodus326,vincent,hoseok1997,adijuliawan, kimbona}@kookmin.ac.kr

[2] KMU Global Research Center for ICT Convergence Security, Kookmin University, Seoul, Republic of Korea
isyou@kookmin.ac.kr

Abstract. Fake base station attacks enable threats such as denial of service, user tracking, and security downgrades in modern mobile networks. Since many devices remain vulnerable, on-device detection has become an important defense mechanism. However, existing approaches relying on signal-strength metrics such as RSRP become unreliable when attackers manipulate radio conditions or perform protocol-level attacks.

This study proposes an on-device detection framework that incorporates protocol-layer information by analyzing RRC and NAS signaling sequences alongside conventional signal features. Using a self-generated dataset capturing realistic FBS scenarios, we evaluate both classical machine-learning and deep-learning models across multiple feature configurations. Experimental results show that protocol-layer features significantly improve detection accuracy and reduce false positives compared to RSRP-only approaches.

By improving resilience against fake base station attacks, the proposed framework contributes to maintaining reliable mobile connectivity supporting digital transactions and mobile-based e-business services.

Keywords: fake base station detection · 5G security · RRC/NAS protocol analysis · machine learning · mobile network security · E-business security

1 Introduction

A fake base station (FBS) is an attack mechanism that exploits the early access phase of mobile networks to lure a user equipment (UE) into connecting to

Published by Springer Nature Switzerland AG 2027
J. Kim et al. (Eds.): EBISION 2025, IFIP AICT 786, pp. 144–158, 2027.
https://doi.org/10.1007/978-3-032-26616-3_10

an adversary-controlled base station, enabling various protocol manipulation attacks [4,15]. Because the attacker intervenes before security procedures are fully activated in the 4G/5G system architecture [1], FBS attacks can trigger not only simple international mobile subscriber identity (IMSI) collection but also multi-stage threats such as denial of service (DoS), user tracking, and security-level downgrades [11,18].

Beyond privacy leakage, such attacks directly threaten the reliability of mobile digital services that support modern electronic business (E-Business) ecosystems. Mobile commerce, online banking, digital payment platforms, and cloud-based enterprise services rely heavily on uninterrupted and trustworthy mobile connectivity. If a UE is connected to an FBS, attackers may manipulate or interrupt communication sessions, degrade service availability, or intercept traffic, potentially affecting financial transactions and service continuity. Therefore, protecting mobile users against FBS attacks is not merely a network security issue, but an essential prerequisite for maintaining trust in mobile-based e-business services [7,8].

While complementary network-side detection efforts, such as 5G-native NF-based FBS detection using machine learning, have been explored [6], existing UE-side detection techniques based on physical-layer metrics such as RSRP have fundamental limitations in defending against sophisticated multi-stage attacks (MSAs) where attackers manipulate signal strengths or exploit upper-layer protocol procedures [12,13,19]. These vulnerabilities go beyond simple privacy leakage and directly threaten the safety of modern e-business and financial services that rely on trusted mobile connectivity. The main contributions of this study are as follows:

- First, we propose a novel detection methodology that effectively identifies multi-stage fake base station attacks by integrating sequence information from the RRC and NAS protocol layers with traditional RSRP metrics.
- Second, we describe in detail the process of reproducing realistic attack scenarios through a testbed environment and constructing a high-fidelity multi-layer attack dataset based on these scenarios.
- Third, we conduct cross-validation using five dataset configurations combining multi-layer features and six machine learning and deep learning models. Through this evaluation, we empirically demonstrate that the proposed protocol-feature-based detection method significantly outperforms the physical-layer-only method in terms of accuracy and false positive rates.

2 Background

This section covers the core background knowledge required to understand the proposed detection framework. Section 2.1 explains the roles of the RRC and NAS protocols in the 5G NR environment and the flow of handover-based fake base station attacks that exploit them. Section 2.2 analyzes the role and structural limitations of the RSRP metrics predominantly adopted by existing detection techniques. Finally, Sect. 2.3 describes modern multi-stage attack (MSA) scenarios that occur across multiple protocol stages, moving beyond simple identifier collection.

2.1 5G NR RRC/NAS Overview and Malicious Handover Flow

In 5G New Radio (NR) access networks, the RRC and NAS layers manage device attachment, registration, mobility, and security procedures [2,3]. In the `RRC_CONNECTED` state, the UE exchanges data with the serving cell and measures the signal strength of surrounding cells for mobility management. Related studies on strengthening 5G authentication and roaming security further highlight the importance of protecting higher-layer procedures in practical deployments [5,10].

The proposed attack scenario begins with the UE in the `RRC_CONNECTED` state, attached to a legitimate digital unit (DU). The FBS transmits signals with higher strength to be detected by the UE. The UE identifies the FBS signal as the strongest adjacent cell and transmits a `Measurement Report` to the DU [3]. Based on the reported signal quality, the DU makes a `Handover Decision` and transmits an `RRC Connection Reconfiguration` message to the UE to initiate handover to the FBS. The UE synchronizes with the FBS and completes the procedure by transmitting an `RRC Connection Reconfiguration Complete` message.

Upon successful handover, the FBS operates as a legitimate base station and initiates signaling procedures. At the NAS layer, the FBS may transmit an `Identity Request` to collect the IMSI, send `Registration Reject` or `TAU Reject` messages to cause a DoS, or issue a `Security Mode Command (NEA0)` to downgrade security. At the RRC layer, the FBS may terminate the connection using `RRC Release` or disrupt communication through repeated `RRC Reconfiguration` messages [1,2].

Figure 1 illustrates the overall handover-based FBS attack scenario considered in this study.

2.2 Role of RSRP and Its Limitations in FBS Detection

Most UE-side FBS detection approaches rely on layer 1 radio measurements such as RSRP and RSRQ, which can be collected without root privileges [13]. However, RSRP merely reflects received signal strength and can easily be manipulated by adjusting the transmit power of a rogue base station. Moreover, layer 1 metrics do not capture protocol-level manipulations such as injecting registration reject messages, forcing identity request responses, or altering security mode command parameters [11,12]. Consequently, RSRP-based methods fail to detect abnormal state transitions or higher-layer signaling manipulations that are central to modern attacks [15].

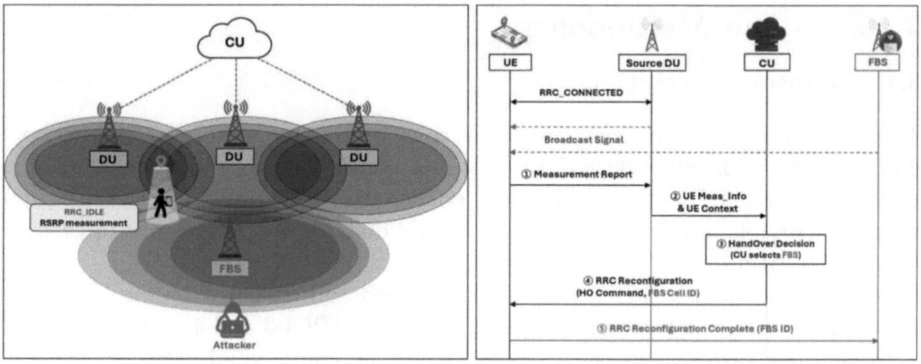

Fig. 1. Overview of the FBS attack scenario.

2.3 Fake Base Stations and Multi-stage Attacks (MSAs)

Recent studies show that FBS attacks have evolved beyond simple IMSI harvesting into multi-phase procedures that manipulate both RRC and NAS signaling [11,15,18]. These multi-stage attacks (MSAs) deliberately modify multiple protocol stages in sequence to drive the UE into an abnormal or vulnerable state. Rather than relying on a single message anomaly, MSAs combine several RRC/NAS procedures to achieve their objectives. Representative MSA types discussed in recent literature include:

- Identity request injection for IMSI exposure, where a NAS identity request is injected at a non-standard point in the procedure to force the UE to transmit its unprotected IMSI [18].
- Registration or tracking area update (TAU) reject manipulation, using abnormal cause values to push the UE into limited service or deregistration states, leading to extended DoS or forced fallback to legacy radio access technologies (RATs) [11].
- Security mode command downgrade, where the attacker alters security negotiation and forces the UE to adopt null encryption (NEA0) or weaker algorithms, exposing subsequent signaling to interception and modification [1,15].
- Abnormal RRC release or reconfiguration, transmitting `RRC Release` or `RRC Reconfiguration` at unnatural timing to prematurely terminate connections or repeatedly trigger reselection, enabling continuous IMSI exposure or repeated DoS cycles [3,11].

These MSAs interfere with (i) the cell selection phase, (ii) NAS registration and authentication procedures, and (iii) security and session management stages [1,2]. Because they span multiple protocol layers and phases, they cannot be detected using single-metric layer 1 indicators such as RSRP. In contrast, RRC/NAS sequences reveal clear abnormal patterns in message ordering, cause values, and procedure invocations [11,19].

3 Data and Methodology

3.1 Dataset Description

The dataset utilized in this study was constructed by combining public open datasets [16] with self-collected data from a controlled laboratory testbed environment. Normal (Benign) traffic was collected in a commercial network environment (PCI 1 and 2), exhibiting an RSRP distribution between −139.7 dBm and −59.6 dBm.

Conversely, attack (FBS) traffic was induced and collected by forcing a handover of the victim UE using a rogue base station (PCI 3 and 4) configured with a higher transmission power (TX = 70) than the commercial network, utilizing srsRAN and Open5GS. The specific attack scenarios were conducted based on the multi-stage attack (MSA) models described previously in Sect. 2.3.

Particularly, to reflect the fake base station attack scenario more realistically, the RSRP values of the rogue and legitimate base stations were designed to overlap between −125 dBm and −90 dBm. This overlapping region accounts for approximately 15–20% of the total FBS samples, effectively reflecting the practical limitation that fake base stations cannot be reliably identified using signal strength alone.

As illustrated in Fig. 2, the experimental setup represents a typical fake base station (FBS) attack scenario involving an attacker (Rogue BS) and a victim (UE). The testbed was built using Open5GS (v2.6.7) [14] as the core network and srsRAN (v3.2.7) [17] for emulating the rogue eNB/gNB. A LibreSDR B220 Mini was employed as the RF front-end to transmit deceptive 5G signals. Data was collected using a rooted OnePlus 9 Pro, which allowed for the extraction of detailed protocol logs via a data logger such as MobileInsight. The specific hardware and software specifications are summarized in Table 1.

The collected data is categorized into three distinct layers based on the protocol stack:

- **RSRP Dataset (Physical Layer):** This dataset contains raw physical signal measurements, including RSRP, RSRQ, and SINR.
- **RRC Dataset (Layer 3 Control):** This dataset captures RRC messages that manage mobility and connection states. It includes critical features such as cell configuration and measurement reports, which are essential for detecting cell spoofing and 5G-to-4G downgrade attacks.
- **NAS Dataset (Layer 3 Non-Access Stratum):** This dataset focuses on NAS signaling messages related to authentication and security. It contains high-level information such as Identity Requests and Authentication Rejects, providing direct evidence of malicious intent during the registration process.

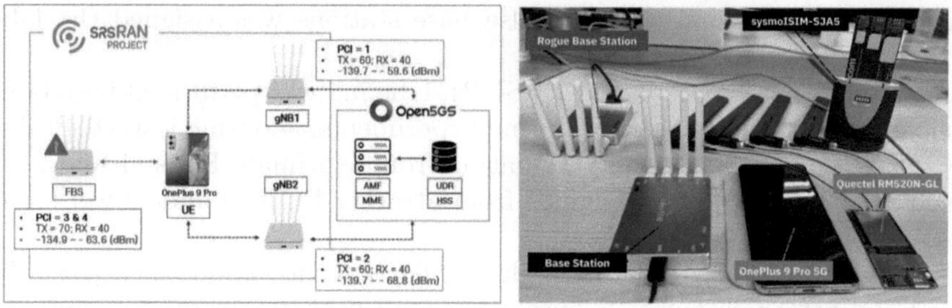

Fig. 2. Architectural overview of the 5G security research testbed.

Table 1. Hardware and Software Specifications of the Experimental Testbed

Category	Component	Specification
Hardware	User Equipment (UE)	OnePlus 9 Pro (Rooted)
	SDR Platform	LibreSDR B220 Mini
	Host PC CPU	Intel Core i5-13600K
	Host PC RAM	64 GB
Software	OS	Ubuntu 24.04 LTS
	Core Network	Open5GS v2.6.7
	RAN Software	srsRAN v3.2.7

3.2 Data Preprocessing and Feature Selection

Before training the detection models, we performed data preprocessing, labeling, and dataset partitioning to distinguish between legitimate and malicious traffic while ensuring fair model evaluation. The collected raw log files in .csv format for the physical (RSRP), RRC, and NAS layers were sorted and normalized based on timestamps to align their procedural flow.

The final merged dataset consists of 8,083 samples. Due to the nature of the controlled testbed environment where multi-stage attacks are continuously induced, attack (FBS) data accounts for 5,971 samples (approximately 73.9%), while normal (benign) data constitutes 2,112 samples. To mitigate this class imbalance, we applied balancing techniques during the model training phase. Subsequently, the entire dataset was transformed into sequential inputs for time-series-based machine learning and deep learning models. We configured the sequence window size to 20 by referencing the optimal length validated in recent literature on fake base station and multi-stage attack detection [11]. These processed sequences were then partitioned to construct the final training and test datasets.

Data Labeling. We adopted a binary labeling scheme for supervised learning tasks. Legitimate base station traffic was assigned the label **0 (Normal)**, while malicious traffic originating from false base stations was assigned the label **1 (Attack)**.

For the physical-layer dataset (RSRP), labeling was performed based on the Physical Cell ID (PCI) observed during experiments, adopting a strategy similar to Nakarmi et al. [13]. Signals originating from legitimate PCIs (1 and 2) were labeled as Normal (0), while signals from attacker PCIs (3 and 4) were labeled as Attack (1).

For the RRC and NAS datasets, data collection was conducted separately for normal and attack scenarios. Consequently, all packets captured during attack experiments were labeled as Attack (1), whereas those obtained during standard operations were labeled as Normal (0).

Dataset Composition and Partitioning. After labeling, datasets were combined and shuffled to avoid temporal or scenario-based bias. To ensure fair model evaluation, the dataset was divided into training, validation, and test sets using an approximate ratio of 80%, 10%, and 10%, respectively. The same partitioning strategy was applied across all feature configurations (RSRP, RRC, NAS, RRC/NAS, and ALL).

Since the amount of traffic captured under normal and attack conditions differed slightly, class imbalance could arise. To mitigate bias toward the majority class, datasets were balanced during training by ensuring comparable numbers of Normal and Attack samples in each batch. This prevents models from favoring the dominant class during optimization.

Feature Construction and Selection. Different feature sets were constructed to evaluate how protocol-layer information influences detection performance. The RSRP dataset contains signal strength measurements representing physical-layer behavior. RRC features capture connection management and configuration procedures, while NAS features represent identity and authentication signaling events.

Combined feature configurations (RRC/NAS and ALL) integrate protocol-layer and signal-level information to reduce ambiguity present in single-layer data. This allows models to capture complementary attack characteristics arising at different protocol layers.

All features were normalized before model training to prevent scale differences from affecting optimization. Sequential inputs were aligned and processed into fixed-length samples to enable consistent input dimensions across different models.

To mitigate high dimensionality and overfitting, we extracted only critical features relevant to FBS characteristics. The selected features focus on signal strength anomalies in the physical layer and procedural irregularities in the RRC and NAS layers. Table 2 summarizes the selected features.

Table 2. Selected Features for False Base Station (FBS) Detection

Layer	Feature Name	Description & Role in Detection
Physical	RSRP	Signal strength (dBm). FBS typically transmits higher power to lure victims.
	RSRQ	Signal quality (dB). High RSRP with low RSRQ indicates potential interference or spoofing.
	Physical Cell ID (PCI)	Identifier for the physical cell. Anomalous or rapidly changing PCIs suggest FBS.
	EARFCN	Frequency channel number. Checks if the frequency band matches the legitimate carrier.
RRC	Tracking Area Code (TAC)	Location area code. FBS uses distinct TACs to trigger Tracking Area Update (TAU) procedures.
	Cell Identity	Unique identifier within the PLMN. Used to verify if the cell belongs to the legitimate network.
	Establishment Cause	Reason for connection request (e.g., *mo-Signalling*). FBS may force specific causes.
	System Information (SIB)	Broadcast information (e.g., SIB1, SIB2). FBS often broadcasts malformed or missing SIBs.
	Release Cause	Reason for connection release. FBS may use causes like *loadBalancingTAURequired* to drop users.
NAS	Mobile Identity Type	Distinguishes between IMSI and TMSI. FBS requests IMSI (permanent ID) instead of TMSI.
	IMSI/TMSI	The actual identity values. Plaintext IMSI transmission is a strong indicator of an IMSI Catcher.
	EMM Cause	Error codes (e.g., #15 *No Suitable Cells*). Critical for identifying DoS attacks.
	Security Header Type	Indicates if the message is integrity protected or sent in plain NAS (Null ciphering).
	Ciphering Algorithm	Encryption algorithm used (e.g., EEA0). FBS forces null encryption (EEA0) to eavesdrop.
	Message Auth Code (MAC)	Integrity check code. Mismatches indicate potential tampering or authentication failure.

Note: Features are categorized into Physical, RRC, and NAS layers based on the LTE protocol stack.

3.3 Model Architecture and Training

This study utilizes both classical machine learning models and deep learning architectures to detect False Base Stations (FBS) by analyzing the time-series evolution of signal strength and the sequential order of protocol messages. Instead of relying on a single complex architecture, we employ a diverse set of algorithms to demonstrate that the discriminative power stems from the intrinsic quality of the proposed features (RSRP, RRC, NAS) rather than the model structure itself. This heterogeneous selection allows us to verify the robustness of the detection method across different levels of model complexity.

- **Random Forest (RF):** RF is an ensemble method that aggregates multiple decision trees to improve generalization. We used RF as a robust baseline for tabular representations derived from RSRP statistics and signaling features.
- **Extreme Gradient Boosting (XGB):** XGB is a gradient-boosted tree model that iteratively fits weak learners to minimize loss. We selected XGB for its strong performance on structured features and its ability to capture non-linear interactions.
- **Support Vector Machine (SVM):** SVM constructs a maximum-margin decision boundary and can model non-linear separation using kernel functions. We included SVM as a representative margin-based classifier for comparison with ensemble methods.
- **Feedforward Neural Network (FNN):** FNN is a multilayer perceptron that learns non-linear mappings from input features to labels. We used FNN to model complex feature interactions on the same input representation as the classical models.
- **Long Short-Term Memory (LSTM):** LSTM is a recurrent neural network designed to address the vanishing gradient problem. We used LSTM to capture sequential dependencies in RSRP logs and ordered NAS/RRC signaling, enabling the distinction between normal mobility patterns and attack sequences.
- **One-dimensional Convolutional Neural Network (1D-CNN):** 1D-CNN applies convolution kernels over sequential input to extract local temporal patterns. We employed 1D-CNN to detect localized anomalies in the signal and protocol stream, such as abrupt RSRP fluctuations or characteristic signaling subsequences.

All models were trained and evaluated consistently across the feature settings to ensure a fair comparison between classical and deep learning approaches, following recent security anomaly detection practices using lightweight learning-based frameworks in other application domains [9].

4 Experimental Results and Analysis

4.1 Experimental Setup and Overview

To conduct a comprehensive evaluation of the proposed FBS detection framework, we employed a total of six detection models, comprising three classical machine learning algorithms (Random Forest, XGBoost, SVM) and three deep learning architectures (FNN, LSTM, CNN). To ensure statistical reliability and mitigate the impact of random initialization, every experimental scenario was executed five times. Consequently, all performance metrics in Tables 3 and 4 are reported as Mean ± Standard Deviation.

As illustrated in Fig. 3, the experimental results confirm our hypothesis. The graph explicitly compares the peak performance of Deep Learning versus Classical ML models, while the solid trend lines indicate the average stability. The consistent hierarchy of performance across all model types confirms that our proposed method is model-agnostic and robust.

4.2 Detailed Performance Analysis

The evaluation was conducted under five distinct feature scenarios: RSRP-only, RRC-only, NAS-only, Combined RRC/NAS, and ALL (including RSRP).

Table 3. Performance Comparison under RSRP, RRC, and NAS Features

Feature	Metric	Model					
		RF	XGB	SVM	FNN	LSTM	CNN
RSRP	Acc	73.56 ± 0.03	72.04 ± 0.36	64.18 ± 0.93	66.84 ± 5.15	62.56 ± 1.53	62.42 ± 1.33
	Prec	77.61 ± 0.28	76.34 ± 0.26	84.69 ± 0.19	79.53 ± 1.01	84.13 ± 0.60	82.02 ± 0.16
	Rec	90.59 ± 0.60	89.78 ± 0.31	63.13 ± 1.39	74.51 ± 10.86	60.63 ± 3.01	62.39 ± 2.51
	F1	83.60 ± 0.10	82.51 ± 0.22	72.33 ± 0.96	76.45 ± 5.55	70.42 ± 1.89	70.84 ± 1.54
RRC	Acc	79.03 ± 0.69	80.30 ± 0.27	52.26 ± 12.45	88.25 ± 0.41	88.85 ± 1.13	88.25 ± 0.94
	Prec	84.76 ± 1.32	79.90 ± 0.45	82.19 ± 2.78	99.79 ± 0.17	99.86 ± 0.20	99.86 ± 0.20
	Rec	79.03 ± 0.69	80.30 ± 0.27	52.26 ± 12.45	87.25 ± 0.30	87.86 ± 1.20	87.19 ± 0.86
	F1	81.09 ± 0.93	79.50 ± 0.34	60.85 ± 8.47	93.10 ± 0.24	93.47 ± 0.70	93.09 ± 0.58
NAS	Acc	90.18 ± 0.33	93.24 ± 0.17	89.22 ± 1.64	96.62 ± 0.25	96.18 ± 0.26	96.47 ± 0.84
	Prec	93.79 ± 0.25	91.94 ± 0.06	93.28 ± 1.13	99.49 ± 0.12	99.38 ± 0.24	99.51 ± 0.09
	Rec	90.18 ± 0.33	93.24 ± 0.17	89.22 ± 1.64	96.87 ± 0.15	96.47 ± 0.42	96.68 ± 0.86
	F1	89.76 ± 0.46	92.14 ± 0.17	88.90 ± 1.74	98.16 ± 0.13	97.91 ± 0.15	98.07 ± 0.47

Table 4. Performance Comparison under Combined Features

Feature	Metric	Model					
		RF	XGB	SVM	FNN	LSTM	CNN
RRC/NAS	Acc	98.61 ± 0.31	99.01 ± 0.10	97.15 ± 0.79	97.35 ± 1.16	98.18 ± 0.83	97.22 ± 1.35
	Prec	99.20 ± 0.49	99.38 ± 0.22	99.66 ± 0.22	99.78 ± 0.18	99.67 ± 0.22	99.78 ± 0.18
	Rec	99.27 ± 0.26	99.53 ± 0.30	97.19 ± 0.91	97.30 ± 1.25	98.32 ± 0.83	97.16 ± 1.43
	F1	99.24 ± 0.17	99.45 ± 0.06	98.41 ± 0.45	98.52 ± 0.66	98.99 ± 0.47	98.44 ± 0.77
ALL	Acc	98.38 ± 0.24	98.97 ± 0.24	97.19 ± 0.18	97.68 ± 0.35	97.98 ± 0.32	98.11 ± 0.20
	Prec	98.81 ± 0.21	99.38 ± 0.18	99.48 ± 0.32	99.31 ± 0.55	99.02 ± 0.24	98.63 ± 0.38
	Rec	99.42 ± 0.24	99.49 ± 0.31	97.41 ± 0.47	98.14 ± 0.87	98.76 ± 0.44	99.31 ± 0.37
	F1	99.11 ± 0.13	99.44 ± 0.13	98.44 ± 0.11	98.72 ± 0.20	98.89 ± 0.18	98.97 ± 0.11

Impact of Individual Feature Layers (RSRP, RRC, and NAS). Using only RSRP features (Scenario 1) results in the lowest detection performance across all models. The best classical model, RF, achieves 73.56% accuracy, while deep learning models remain below 67%. This indicates that signal strength variations caused by normal mobility closely resemble those produced during FBS attacks, making reliable separation based on signal strength alone difficult.

In contrast, when RRC or NAS features are used individually (Scenarios 2 and 3), they demonstrate significantly higher detection rates compared to RSRP-based detection. Notably, the NAS configuration yields strong results, with FNN achieving 96.62% accuracy. This suggests that structured behavioral patterns in protocol control procedures provide more discriminative cues than physical signal attributes.

Analysis of Feature Combination Strategy. The experimental results demonstrate that the Combined RRC/NAS dataset **(Scenario 4)** achieves the highest detection performance (98%–99%), a result attributed to the sequential, multi-layered mechanism of FBS attacks—ranging from RRC connection manipulation to NAS identity theft. By integrating these layers, the model captures the full "attack lifecycle" and causal relationships that are otherwise fragmented during isolated analysis, while simultaneously fusing behavioral anomalies (RRC) with malicious intent (NAS) to form a robust decision boundary. Consequently, once this high-fidelity protocol context is established, the marginal contribution of physical signal strength (RSRP) becomes negligible (Scenario 5), confirming that the core discriminative power resides in the correlation between protocol layers.

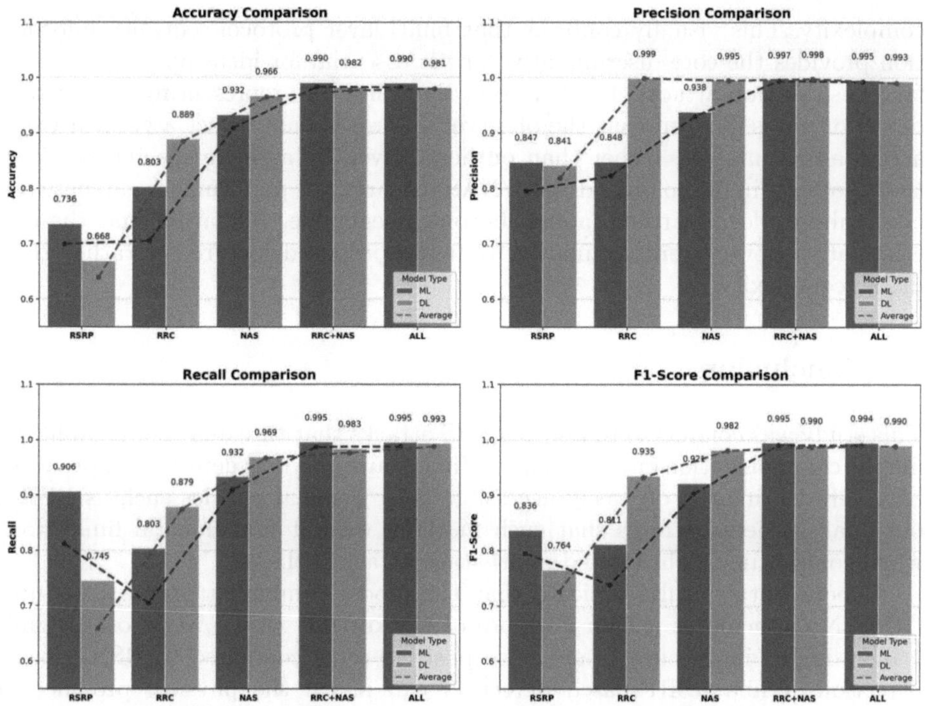

Fig. 3. Comparative analysis of detection performance.

4.3 Comparative Analysis of Model Architectures

Justification for Model Diversity. The strategic adoption of a wide range of algorithms, extending from classical machine learning to deep learning, serves to demonstrate that detection performance is not biased toward specific high-complexity architectures. If the evaluation relied solely on deep learning models, the observed performance gains could be misinterpreted as artifacts of model complexity rather than the quality of the data. However, our experiments confirm that lightweight classical models (e.g., RF, XGB) exhibit the same performance improvement patterns as heavier neural networks.

Quantitative Validation of Model Robustness. Figure 3 visually substantiates this model-agnostic robustness by comparing the peak performance (based on F1-score) of the deep learning group against the classical machine learning group across different feature configurations. As shown in the figure, when relying solely on physical-layer features (RSRP), the maximum performance remains in the low 80% range. However, applying protocol-layer features (RRC or NAS) individually yields a clear performance increase to approximately 93% and 98%, respectively. Most notably, in the combined RRC/NAS scenario, all models achieve a high peak performance of over 99%, regardless of their structural complexity. This visually confirms that multi-layer protocol sequence information provides the core discriminative power essential for identifying multi-stage fake base station attacks. Furthermore, the solid lines representing the average detection rates confirm that the observed improvements reflect a general trend across all six models, rather than outliers driven by a single specific architecture. Notably, in the combined RRC/NAS scenario, the performance gap between classical and deep learning models becomes negligible, validating that the discriminative power stems primarily from the proposed feature set rather than model complexity.

5 Conclusion

This study was conducted to address FBS attacks that threaten the reliability of mobile communication environments. While many previous detection approaches have relied primarily on easily accessible layer 1 signal metrics such as RSRP, our analysis demonstrates that such methods exhibit fundamental limitations when confronting sophisticated multi-stage attacks (MSAs).

Experimental results indicate that the model combining protocol features (RRC/NAS) achieves a high F1-score of up to 0.995 (using XGBoost), significantly improving accuracy and false positive rates compared to RSRP-based detection. While RSRP-based detection can reveal the physical presence of abnormal base stations to some extent, it fails to reliably capture behavior-driven attack patterns such as identity exposure, authentication manipulation, or protocol downgrades.

In contrast, protocol-layer features extracted from RRC and NAS signaling enable reliable detection of attack behaviors through abnormal message sequences and state transitions. When these protocol features are incorporated, both classical machine learning and deep learning models consistently achieve high detection performance, and the performance gap between different model families is minimized. These results empirically demonstrate that protocol-layer information plays a dominant role in practical FBS detection, while signal-strength information serves mainly as auxiliary evidence.

The findings of this study make a significant contribution to increasing user trust by enhancing service availability and communication integrity in modern e-business ecosystems that rely on mobile connectivity, such as digital transactions and online banking. However, the proposed framework requires root privileges on the device to extract lower-layer protocol messages, which restricts its immediate commercial deployment for general users. Therefore, in future work, we plan to improve the practicality of the framework by developing indirect anomaly inference techniques based on non-rooted devices using official Android APIs, alongside model optimization for real-time detection that minimizes device resource consumption.

Acknowledgement. This work was supported by Institute for Information & communications Technology Promotion (IITP) grant funded by the Korea government (MSIP)

(No. 2024-00437252, Development of anti-sniffing technology for mobile communication and AirGap environments).

References

1. 3GPP TS 33.501: Security architecture and procedures for 5G system (release 18). Technical report, 3rd Generation Partnership Project (3GPP) (2024). https://www.3gpp.org/ftp/Specs/archive/33_series/33.501/
2. Non-access-stratum (NAS) protocol for evolved packet system (EPS) (3GPP TS 24.301). Technical report, 3rd Generation Partnership Project (3GPP) (2024). https://www.3gpp.org/ftp/Specs/archive/24_series/24.301/, release 17.6.0
3. NR; radio resource control (RRC); protocol specification (3GPP TS 38.331). Technical report, 3rd Generation Partnership Project (3GPP) (2024). https://www.3gpp.org/ftp/Specs/archive/38_series/38.331/, release 17.4.0
4. CableLabs: False base station or IMSI catcher: what you need to know (2019). https://www.cablelabs.com/blog/false-base-station-or-imsi-catcher-what-you-need-to-know
5. Kwon, H.: 5G-AKA-HPQC: hybrid post-quantum cryptography protocol for quantum-resilient 5G primary authentication with forward secrecy. IEEE Access (2024)
6. Kwon, H.: 5G native network function for false base station detection using machine learning technique. Sensors (2024)
7. Kwon, H.: Evaluating transport layer security 1.3 optimization strategies for 5G cross-border roaming: a comprehensive security and performance analysis. IEEE Access (2024)
8. Kwon, H., et al.: Enhancing roaming security in cloud-native 5G core network through deep learning-based intrusion detection system. CMES Comput. Model. Eng. Sci. (2025)
9. Kwon, H.: Lightweight LLM-based anomaly detection framework for securing IoTMD enabled diabetes management control systems. IEEE J. Biomed. Health Inform. (2025)
10. Won, T., et al.: Towards 6G roaming security: experimental analysis of SUCI-based DoS, cost, and NF stress. IEEE Access (2025)
11. Mubasshir, K.S., Karim, I., Bertino, E.: Gotta detect 'em all: fake base station and multi-step attack detection in cellular networks. In: USENIX Security Symposium (2025). https://arxiv.org/abs/2401.04958, to appear. arXiv:2401.04958
12. Nakarmi, P.K.: Murat: multi-rat false base station detector. Technical report, arXiv/Technical Report (2021). https://arxiv.org/pdf/2102.08780
13. Nakarmi, P.K., et al.: Applying machine learning on RSRP-based features for false base station detection. arXiv preprint (2022). https://arxiv.org/abs/2207.10999
14. Open5GS Project: Open5GS: Open source 5G core and EPC (2019). https://open5gs.org/
15. Park, H., et al.: SMDFbs: specification-based misbehavior detection for false base stations. Sensors **23**(23), 9504 (2023). https://www.mdpi.com/1424-8220/23/23/9504
16. POWDER, P.C.., collaborators: Fake base station and multi-step attack detection in user-side traces (dataset and detection). arXiv/project page (2025). https://arxiv.org/html/2401.04958v3

17. srsRAN Project: srsRAN: 4G/5G software radio suite (2020). https://www.srsran.com/
18. Tucker, T., Marlin, N., et al.: Detecting IMSI-catchers by characterizing identity-exposing behavior. In: NDSS Symposium (2025). https://www.ndss-symposium.org/wp-content/uploads/2025-1115-paper.pdf
19. Wen, H., Porras, P., Yegneswaran, V., Gehani, A., Lin, Z.: 5G-Spector: an O-RAN compliant layer-3 cellular attack detection service. In: NDSS Symposium (2024). https://www.ndss-symposium.org/wp-content/uploads/2024-527-paper.pdf

Toward a Zero Trust Architecture for 6G-Enabled E-Business Ecosystem

Hoseok Kwon[1], Bonam Kim[1], and Ilsun You[1,2](✉)

[1] Kookmin University, Seoul, Republic of Korea
{hoseok1997,kimbona}@kookmin.ac.kr
[2] KMU Global Research Center for ICT Convergence Security, Kookmin University, Seoul, South Korea
isyou@kookmin.ac.kr

Abstract. E-Business Information Systems (EBIS)—encompassing digital payment platforms, e-commerce order management, logistics orchestration, and B2B integration layers—face growing security challenges as they converge with 5G-Advanced and pre-6G ultra-connected environments. Heterogeneous actors and sensitive data flows render traditional perimeter-based models inadequate, requiring continuous verification and adaptive controls. Zero Trust Architecture (ZTA), as defined in NIST SP 800-207, provides a promising paradigm but demands domain-specific adaptation for the unique constraints of mobile networks. This paper bridges the gap between standardization-driven research and practical E-Business security needs. We first present a critical review of prior 5G/6G security surveys, identifying the lack of holistic ZT integration and E-Business domain mapping as key research gaps. Subsequently, we evaluate the applicability of all thirteen candidate solutions outlined in 3GPP TR 33.794 (Release 19) against four criteria—transaction integrity relevance, cross-domain applicability, deployment feasibility, and latency impact—assessing their suitability for digital commerce. We derive operational guidelines for adapting these standardized mechanisms to EBIS environments, with particular attention to deployment path differentiation and regulatory compliance.

1 Introduction

The transition from 5G-Advanced toward sixth-generation (6G) networks is envisioned not merely as an extension of connectivity, but as a hyper-connected platform integrating physical and digital worlds [13,30]. Unlike previous generations focused on data throughput, the pre-6G era—spanning 3GPP Releases 18 through 20—is expected to underpin E-Business ecosystems where digital payments, supply chain coordination, and cross-organizational data exchange converge with mobile infrastructure. In the context of E-Business Information Systems (EBIS)—the integrated platforms that manage these functions along with customer relationship management—this transition is particularly consequential, as next-generation networks will handle increasing levels of sensitive financial and personal data.

J. Kim et al. (Eds.): EBISION 2025, IFIP AICT 786, pp. 159–175, 2027.
https://doi.org/10.1007/978-3-032-26616-3_11

However, the security paradigms inherited from current 5G deployments are increasingly insufficient for this evolving landscape. While 5G introduced robust security features such as Service-Based Architecture (SBA) security and unified authentication [1,3], it essentially relies on a perimeter-based defense model. A critical vulnerability in current mobile networks is the "Implicit Trust" assumption within the Radio Access Network (RAN) and backhaul infrastructure; once a network entity (e.g., gNB or femtocell) is authenticated, it is often trusted for the duration of its operation without continuous re-verification [25].

Critically, attacks exploiting this implicit trust have already resulted in direct financial losses. Rogue base stations—whose real-time detection remains an active challenge [28]—can intercept SMS-based one-time passwords and redirect mobile banking transactions, while SIM-swap attacks have enabled unauthorized access to financial accounts [7,17,22]. These are not theoretical risks—they represent established and growing attack vectors against mobile-dependent services [14,16]. As pre-6G and future 6G networks further integrate E-Business ecosystems where machines conduct autonomous payments, the potential for direct, irreversible financial damage will increase by orders of magnitude. The traditional binary trust model—"Trusted Internal" vs. "Untrusted External"—is no longer viable.

To address these challenges, Zero Trust Architecture (ZTA), grounded in the principle of "Never Trust, Always Verify," has emerged as a necessary paradigm [26]. 3GPP has recognized this necessity, recently initiating studies such as TR 33.794 to enable ZTA within the 5G Core [4,5]. However, current research and standardization efforts predominantly focus on the Core Network (SBA) and cloud-native interfaces, largely overlooking the practical implications for E-Business transaction integrity across the RAN and user-plane data paths. Concurrently, a ten-nation coalition—including South Korea—has issued a joint statement advocating that 6G networks be "Secure, Open, and Resilient by Design" [11], reinforcing the policy imperative for embedded ZT. Most existing surveys either treat ZT as a generic feature or fail to address the specific requirements of E-Business continuity in mobile networks.

In this paper, we bridge this gap by analyzing how the candidate solutions defined in 3GPP TR 33.794 can be operationalized for 6G E-Business ecosystems. Rather than proposing an entirely new architecture, we systematically evaluate the thirteen standardized ZT enablers and derive operational guidelines for their application to EBIS environments. Our specific contributions are as follows:

- A **critical review of prior surveys** that evaluates existing 5G/6G security reviews, identifying the lack of holistic ZT integration and the absence of E-Business domain mapping as key research gaps.
- A **criteria-based suitability assessment** of all thirteen 3GPP TR 33.794 candidate solutions for E-Business, evaluated against four dimensions—transaction integrity relevance, cross-domain applicability, deployment feasibility, and latency impact—to distinguish high-suitability enablers from those with limited applicability.

- **Operational guidelines** that map standardized ZT mechanisms to concrete EBIS building blocks (payment platforms, fraud detection engines, order management systems), with differentiated analysis across deployment paths (external Internet, MEC, network slicing).
- A **critical discussion** of deployment challenges, regulatory compliance (GDPR, PCI-DSS), and the limitations that must be addressed in future implementation and empirical validation.

Unlike prior surveys that treat ZT as a generic concept [8,23] or focus narrowly on O-RAN [6,21], we provide an end-to-end analysis grounded in 3GPP Release 19 standardization with explicit E-Business mapping. We deliberately scope our analysis to 5G-Advanced and pre-6G capabilities (Rel-18/19/20), as these represent the nearest actionable standardization horizon; 6G-specific extensions are discussed as future directions.

2 Related Work: Critical Review of Prior Surveys

As the concept of Zero Trust gains traction in telecommunications, numerous survey papers have attempted to analyze its applicability to 5G and emerging pre-6G networks. However, most existing studies focus either on general security landscapes or strictly on Core Network architectural changes, often overlooking the specific requirements of vertical domains like E-Business. This section classifies existing literature into three categories and identifies the research gaps this paper addresses.

2.1 General 5G/6G Security Surveys vs. Mobile-Native Zero Trust Architecture

Existing literature on next-generation network security can be broadly categorized into two streams, both of which fall short of addressing the specific needs of E-Business ecosystems.

First, **General 5G/6G Security Surveys** [16,25] provide comprehensive overviews of the threat landscape, covering physical layer jamming, AI-enabled attacks, and privacy-preserving techniques. While these studies mention Zero Trust (ZT) as a potential countermeasure, they treat it merely as a high-level principle, lacking a structural analysis of how ZT principles should be enforced across the heterogeneous RAN and Edge environments. More recent surveys [23, 27] have expanded the scope to include ZTA as a dedicated topic for 6G, yet they remain at the conceptual level without mapping to specific 3GPP enablers or vertical-domain requirements.

Second, **SBA-Centric ZT Studies** [4] focus on securing the Core Network by leveraging the SBA. Although they effectively address cloud-native threats (e.g., container security, service mesh), they inherently ignore the "Implicit Trust" vulnerability in the RAN, leaving a critical gap for E-Business scenarios where transactions originate from mobile devices at the network edge.

Meanwhile, a new body of work has emerged around O-RAN Zero Trust [6, 21], proposing xApp-based enforcement at the RAN Intelligent Controller (RIC). While promising for RAN-level security, these studies do not extend their analysis to the Core or Application layers, nor do they address E-Business transaction integrity.

Table 1 contrasts our work with these existing studies, highlighting the necessity of an "End-to-End Trust" model that integrates RAN-level context with business logic.

2.2 The Gap Between Enterprise ZT and Telco ZT

Another critical limitation in current research is the direct application of Enterprise IT Zero Trust models—originally proposed for corporate network perimeters [18] and later codified in NIST SP 800-207 [26]—to mobile networks without sufficient adaptation. As illustrated in Fig. 1, the standard ZTA defined in NIST SP 800-207 operates on a logical framework where the Policy Decision Point (PDP) and Policy Enforcement Point (PEP) govern access based on relatively static attributes [26]. While this centralized model is effective for securing corporate assets in fixed environments, it fails to account for the extreme performance and mobility requirements of next-generation mobile networks [13].

In contrast, the pre-6G E-Business ecosystem is characterized by high mobility, ultra-low latency, and massive heterogeneity [13]. Unlike the identity-centric focus of traditional models, a mobile-native Zero Trust framework must incorporate network-specific contexts—including network slicing, real-time location, and RAN conditions—to protect financial transactions without introducing signaling overhead that violates URLLC constraints.

As summarized in Table 2, this paper differentiates itself by addressing these unique constraints, moving beyond standard IT-centric studies to ensure the infrastructure integrity required for modern digital commerce.

2.3 Critical Limitations of Current Approaches

Despite the extensive literature on 5G and pre-6G security, two fundamental gaps remain unaddressed for E-Business adoption.

Table 1. Comparison of Related Surveys and Research Gap

Category	Focus & Scope	Limitations (Research Gap)
General 5G/6G [16,23,27]	• Broad threat landscape • AI/ML security & Privacy	• Treats ZT as a conceptual feature • Lacks architectural implementation details
SBA-Centric ZT [4]	• **Core Network** focus (3GPP SBA) • Cloud-native security	• **Ignores RAN risks** (e.g., Rogue gNB) • Insufficient for E-Business transaction integrity
O-RAN/RAN-Level ZT [6,21]	• RAN disaggregation security • xApp-based ZT enforcement	• Ignores Core/App layers • No E-Business transaction context
This Work	• **E-Business Ecosystem** in 6G • **End-to-End ZT** (RAN + Core + App)	• **Addresses the Gaps**: Derives operational guidelines for adapting 3GPP ZT enablers to digital commerce.

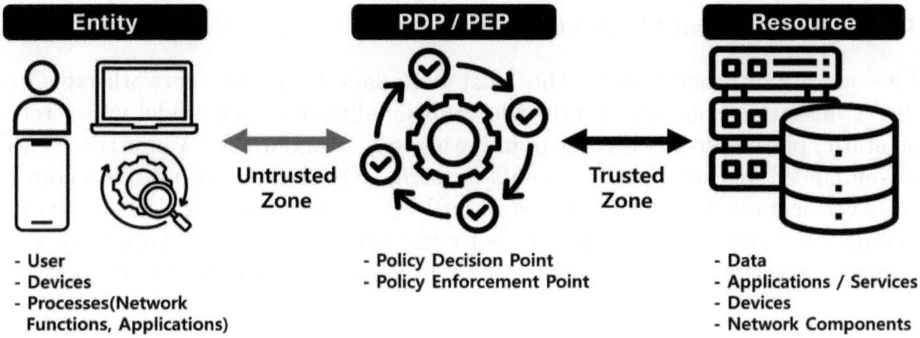

Fig. 1. Logical components of NIST SP 800-207 Zero Trust Architecture [26].

Table 2. Gap Analysis: Enterprise ZT vs. Mobile-Native ZT Requirements for Pre-6G

Feature	Enterprise ZT (Traditional)	Mobile-Native ZT (Required)
Environment	Static (offices, laptops)	**Dynamic & Mobile** (V2X, IoT, XR)
Performance	Human-speed latency	**Ultra-Low Latency (URLLC)**
Trust Scope	Identity & Device Health	**Slice, Location & RAN Condition**
Challenge	Internal Lateral Movement	**Handover & infrastructure integrity**

First, the *Silo Effect between RAN and Core* is a major barrier. Most ZT studies focus exclusively on the SBA in the Core Network, assuming the RAN is merely a transparent data pipe. However, in pre-6G and 6G E-Business scenarios, the RAN Edge is often the first point of contact for financial transactions. Existing perimeter-based models fail to extend the verification phase to the physical link level, leaving the system vulnerable to physical layer attacks such as rogue base stations.

Second, the *Disconnect between Network Security and Business Logic* limits practical application. Current 3GPP standards (e.g., TS 33.501) provide robust connectivity security but lack semantic awareness of the application layer. For instance, a "valid" network connection does not imply a "legitimate" financial transaction. There is a lack of architectural frameworks that correlate network telemetry (e.g., latency, location) with business-level anomalies (e.g., fraud patterns), which is the primary focus of this paper.

3 Operationalizing 3GPP ZT Enablers for Pre-6G E-Business

Rather than treating ZT as a supplementary feature, this section analyzes how the candidate solutions from 3GPP TR 33.794 [5] can be operationalized to address the gaps identified in Sect. 2. We evaluate each solution's applicability to E-Business transaction flows and derive guidelines for their adaptation.

3.1 Architectural Context

The operational model shifts the trust boundary from the "network edge" to the "transaction context." Unlike the traditional 5G security model which relies on static, perimeter-based trust boundaries (e.g., standard AKA and IPsec), the ZT-enhanced architecture for pre-6G enforces dynamic, per-transaction continuous verification. We clarify that standard 5G security features (TS 33.501) are foundational enablers, but they do not constitute a Zero Trust Architecture by themselves without the continuous decision loops described herein (Fig. 2).

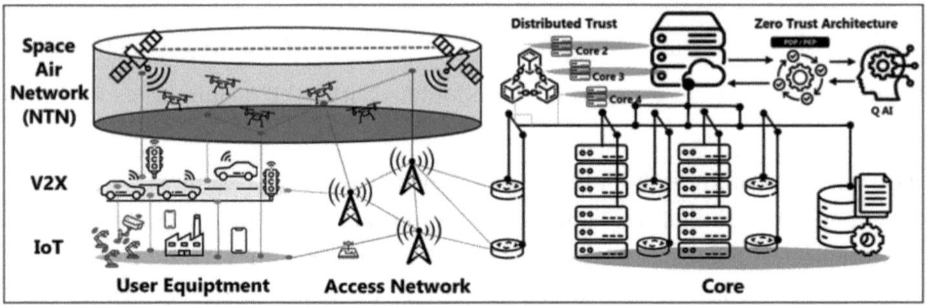

Fig. 2. Mobile-native ZTA with edge-distributed PDP/PEP for pre-6G.

To realize end-to-end ZT, verification must be enforced at three distinct layers:

1. **Radio Layer (RAN):** Verifying physical attributes (location, beam ID) to detect rogue base stations.
2. **Network Layer (SBA):** Monitoring API invocation patterns to detect token theft and lateral movement.
3. **Application Layer (Business):** Validating transaction logic against user behavior profiles and business rules.

3.2 Comprehensive Suitability Assessment of 3GPP TR 33.794 Solutions

To systematically evaluate the thirteen candidate solutions, we define four E-Business suitability criteria. These criteria are synthesized from established ZT assessment frameworks—specifically, NIST SP 800-207's per-request trust evaluation principle [26] and CISA's Zero Trust Maturity Model (ZTMM v2.0) [9], which defines a four-stage maturity progression (Traditional → Initial → Advanced → Optimal) across five pillars—adapted to the specific requirements of mobile E-Business ecosystems:

- **C1: Transaction Integrity Relevance**—Does the solution directly protect the correctness and non-repudiation of financial transactions? (Derived from NIST SP 800-207's per-request trust evaluation tenet.[1])
- **C2: Cross-Domain Applicability**—Is the solution effective across operator, enterprise, and third-party trust boundaries? (Derived from CISA ZTMM's five-pillar framework requiring cross-domain coordination.)
- **C3: Deployment Feasibility**—Can the solution be realized within existing 5G-Advanced NF capabilities (Rel-18/19) without requiring new network elements? (Derived from CISA ZTMM's maturity staging: Traditional → Initial → Advanced → Optimal.)
- **C4: Latency Impact**—Does the solution operate within acceptable latency budgets for real-time E-Business (e.g., URLLC-class payments)? (Derived from the performance overhead considerations acknowledged in both NIST SP 800-207 and 3GPP TR 33.894 [4].)

Solutions rated **High** satisfy at least three of these four criteria; **Medium** solutions satisfy two; **Low** solutions satisfy one or none. In the assessment table, ● denotes a criterion satisfied and ○ denotes not satisfied; inline annotations (e.g., C1×) provide brief justifications for each rating. It is important to note that our mapping is *logical*, not *physical*. We leverage existing Network Functions (e.g., PCF, UPF) to act as Policy Decision/Enforcement Points to minimize architectural changes, but the decision logic within them is augmented with ZT-specific algorithms not present in standard 5G specifications.

Tables 3 and 4 present the complete assessment, categorizing solutions by their suitability for E-Business transaction integrity. For readability, we use the abbreviations FDS (Fraud Detection System) and SEDR (Security Event Data Record) throughout this section. The two tables reflect the logical separation between observability-oriented (*Visibility & Data Exposure*) and action-oriented (*Dynamic Enforcement*) mechanisms in TR 33.794.

Of the thirteen solutions, seven (Sol#1, #2, #7, #8, #11, #12, #13) demonstrate high suitability for E-Business. These solutions address the two critical gaps identified in Sect. 2: they bridge the RAN-Core silo by enabling cross-layer data collection, and they connect network telemetry to business-level enforcement. The remaining six solutions (Sol#3–#6, #9, #10) are primarily designed for intra-operator network management and offer limited direct value for cross-domain E-Business transaction integrity, though they may serve as supporting enablers in specific deployment configurations.

3.3 Mapping to EBIS Building Blocks

To make the operational guidelines concrete, Table 5 maps the high-suitability 3GPP NFs and ZT enablers to typical EBIS components that practitioners will recognize.

[1] In NIST SP 800-207, trust is evaluated on a per-request basis. In the E-Business context, each request corresponds to a discrete financial transaction.

Table 3. Suitability Assessment—Pillar 1: Visibility & Data Exposure (● = satisfied, ○ = not satisfied)

Sol.	Mechanism	E-Business Applicability Analysis	C1	C2	C3	C4	Rating
#1	Net Data Collection	Mapped to **Transaction Log Exporting**. UPF exposes packet drops/latency spikes to FDS to correlate network anomalies with payment failures (C1). Operator-agnostic log format enables cross-domain sharing (C2). Leverages existing UPF counters (C3). Asynchronous export avoids user-plane delay (C4).	●	●	●	●	**High**
#2	Service Data Collection	Complements #1 with service-layer metrics (NF load, response times). Correlates SBA degradation with E-Business SLA violations (C1). Reuses NWDAF subscription APIs (C3). Passive collection imposes no inline latency (C4).	●	●	●	●	**High**
#3	NF Trust Evaluation	Assesses NF trustworthiness via software integrity/patch status. Primarily **intra-operator** (C2×); does not directly verify transaction correctness (C1×).	○	○	●	●	Medium
#4	Trust-based Routing	Routes traffic through higher-trust NF paths. Indirectly protects transaction integrity via path selection (C1). Useful for **premium payment slices** but requires new routing logic not in current NFs (C3×); limited when traffic exits to DN (C2×).	●	○	○	●	Medium
#5	Slice-specific Security	Per-slice security differentiation. Relevant for **dedicated E-Business slices** but does not address intra-slice transaction security (C1×) or cross-operator trust (C2×).	○	○	●	●	Medium
#6	Network Exposure for ZT	Extends NEF for ZT data sharing. Valuable for **Open Banking APIs** across trust boundaries (C2). Does not protect transactions directly (C1×); adds synchronous query overhead for real-time flows (C4×).	○	●	●	○	Medium
#7	API Anomaly Detection	Detects **"Impossible Travel"**: payment token used from distant gNBs simultaneously triggers alarm (C1). Applicable across operator and enterprise domains (C2). Requires synchronous inline analysis on the transaction path (C4×).	●	●	●	○	**High**
#8	UE Behavior Monitoring	Distinguishes legitimate users from **botnets** via passive device pattern analysis (C1). Essential for protecting payment gateway endpoints. Passive monitoring adds no inline latency (C4).	●	●	●	●	**High**

Table 4. Suitability Assessment—Pillar 2: Dynamic Enforcement (● = satisfied, ○ = not satisfied)

Sol.	Mechanism	E-Business Applicability Analysis	C1	C2	C3	C4	Rating
#9	Adaptive Access Control	Adjusts policies by context (C3). Overlaps with existing NSSAAF/PCF mechanisms; **no direct transaction integrity protection** (C1×) or cross-domain reach (C2×), and adds policy evaluation latency (C4×).	○	○	●	○	Low
#10	Continuous Auth.	Re-authenticates UEs on behavioral drift (C3). No direct transaction-level verification (C1×); scoped to single operator (C2×). **Signaling overhead** conflicts with URLLC for real-time payments (C4×).	○	○	●	○	Low
#11	Closed-loop Enforce.	**Automated Quarantine**: on rogue gNB detection (via #1), PCF quarantines session or isolates compromised slice (C1). Pre-authorized policy templates enable sub-ms response (C4).	●	●	●	●	**High**
#12	Short-lived Tokens	**Per-transaction micro-segmentation**. Context-bound cryptographic token neutralizes replay attacks even if intercepted (C1). Applicable across trust domains via standard OAuth 2.0 DPoP extension (C2). Requires PEP↔PDP round-trip for each validation (C4×).	●	●	●	○	**High**
#13	Security Event Record	Standardized async logs across NFs for **interoperable FDS correlation** in multi-vendor environments (C2) [15]. Asynchronous by design, zero inline overhead (C4).	●	●	●	●	**High**

Table 5. Mapping 3GPP ZT Enforcement Points to EBIS Building Blocks

3GPP NF/Role	EBIS Component	ZT Function in E-Business Context
PCF (PDP)	Fraud Rule Engine	Evaluates transaction risk scores; triggers block/allow decisions based on combined network + business signals
UPF (PEP)	Payment Gateway Proxy	Enforces per-transaction token validation at the data plane; blocks suspicious flows before they reach backend ledgers
NWDAF	FDS Analytics Engine	Aggregates network telemetry (Sol#1, #2) with transaction metadata for anomaly detection (Sol#7, #8)
NEF (Sol#6)	Open Banking API Gateway	Exposes scoped network context (location confidence, slice health) to authorized E-Business partners
SEDR (Sol#13)	Audit & Compliance Logger	Provides standardized event records for PCI-DSS audit trails and cross-operator incident forensics

3.4 Deployment Path Differentiation

The applicability of ZT enforcement varies significantly depending on where E-Business transactions are processed. We identify three representative deployment paths, each with distinct trust boundaries and enforcement requirements:

Path A: External Internet (DN Breakout). The UE's transaction traverses the full 5G/6G core (AMF → SMF → UPF) before exiting to the external Data Network where the payment service resides. ZT enforcement is concentrated at the UPF (as PEP) and the PCF (as PDP). Context-Aware Token Binding (Sol#12) is applied at the UPF before the traffic leaves the operator domain. This is the most common path for consumer-facing E-Business (e.g., mobile banking apps, e-commerce). The key challenge is that once traffic exits the operator's UPF, enforcement depends on the E-Business provider's own security stack.

Path B: Multi-access Edge Computing (MEC). The transaction is processed at a MEC platform co-located with the RAN, using UPF Local Breakout to avoid traversing the central core. This path is critical for latency-sensitive E-Business such as in-store contactless payments or V2X toll collection. ZT enforcement must be **distributed to the edge**: the MEC-local PDP must make autonomous decisions using cached policies, as round-trip to the central PCF would negate the latency benefits. Sol#11 (Closed-loop) is particularly important here, as automated response at the edge is the only viable option within URLLC budgets.

Path C: Dedicated Network Slice. A network slice is provisioned exclusively for a financial institution or E-Business consortium, with end-to-end QoS guarantees and isolated resources. Sol#5 (Slice-specific Security Policy) becomes relevant here, as the slice boundary itself serves as an additional trust perimeter. However, ZT principles dictate that intra-slice trust must not be assumed—Sol#7 and Sol#11 remain necessary within the slice to detect compromised NF instances.

Figure 3 illustrates the ZT-enforced transaction flow for Path A, showing how each enforcement point participates in a single payment transaction. The key distinction from standard 5G flows is the insertion of context verification (steps 3–4) and continuous monitoring (step 7) that are not present in baseline TS 33.501 procedures.

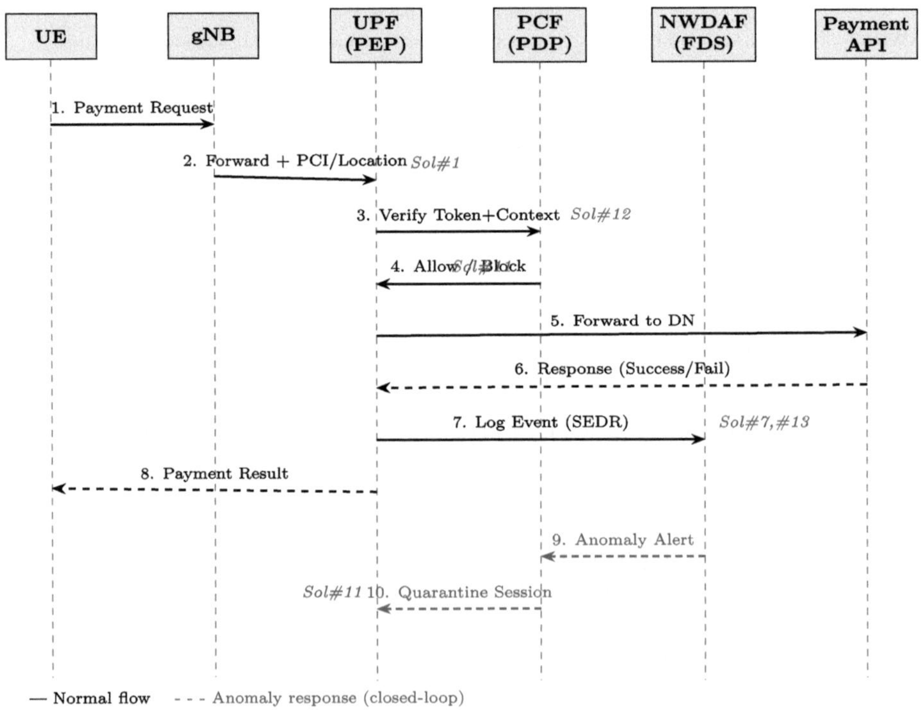

Fig. 3. ZT-enforced payment transaction flow for Path A (External DN).

3.5 Key Operational Guidelines

Based on the comprehensive assessment, we derive two critical enforcement guidelines for E-Business.

3.5.1 Context-Aware Token Binding (Sol#1 + Sol#12)

Traditional OAuth tokens are context-agnostic. We recommend binding the *Physical Cell ID (PCI)* and *user location* to the short-lived access token (Sol#12), leveraging network data collection (Sol#1) as the context source. This ensures that a token obtained at one location cannot be replayed from a different cell, effectively mitigating the "Implicit Trust" vulnerability at the RAN level.

This approach differs from standard 5G re-authentication mechanisms (TS 33.501), which are triggered by timer expiration or mobility events. Context-Aware Token Binding ties verification to the *transaction context* (e.g., the moment of payment initiation), ensuring validation occurs at the exact point of value transfer rather than during routine session maintenance. The binding should be implemented as an optional extension to existing OAuth 2.0 flows [12], building upon the Demonstrating Proof of Possession (DPoP) mechanism [10] to cryptographically bind tokens to the requesting entity, thereby preserving backward compatibility with legacy UEs.

3.5.2 AI-Driven Closed-Loop Response (Sol#7 + Sol#11)

Manual intervention is too slow for pre-6G and 6G financial transaction speeds. We recommend utilizing Sol#7 (API Anomaly Detection) as the trigger and Sol#11 (Closed-loop Enforcement) as the actuator. When the NWDAF-based analytics engine detects an anomaly score exceeding the configured threshold during a transaction request, the PCF executes a "Block" policy at the UPF within the same control-plane signaling round-trip, preventing financial loss before the transaction reaches the core ledger.

For MEC deployments (Path B), the closed-loop must operate locally: edge-cached anomaly models and pre-authorized policy templates enable sub-millisecond enforcement without central PCF involvement. This is essential for maintaining URLLC guarantees while providing meaningful security enforcement.

4 Discussion: Challenges and Limitations

While the operational guidelines derived above provide a pathway for applying 3GPP ZT enablers to E-Business, their practical realization involves significant challenges that we discuss critically.

4.1 Security vs. Ultra-low Latency (URLLC)

One of the core promises of 5G-Advanced and 6G is Ultra-Reliable Low Latency Communication (URLLC). However, the continuous verification mechanism of ZTA inevitably introduces processing overhead. Sol#11 (Closed-loop Enforcement) and Sol#12 (Short-lived Tokens) require frequent signaling between the PEP (User Plane) and PDP (Control Plane). In high-frequency trading or real-time payment scenarios, even marginal delays caused by token validation can be critical. This trade-off is particularly acute for Path B (MEC) deployments, where the latency budget may be as low as 1 ms.

The signaling overhead of Context-Aware Token Binding can be estimated as follows: appending PCI (28 bits), Tracking Area Code (24 bits), and a timestamp (32 bits) yields 84 bits (11 bytes) of raw context. After HMAC-SHA256 binding (32 bytes) and JWS compact serialization overhead (header and Base64url encoding, $\sim$77 bytes), the total addition is approximately 120 bytes per transaction. While the payload overhead is modest relative to typical 5G NAS message sizes ($\sim$500 bytes), the critical latency cost stems from the synchronous

PEP↔PDP round-trip required for each token validation—not the payload size itself. This overhead may further accumulate in massive IoT scenarios (e.g., V2X toll collection generating thousands of micro-transactions per second per cell). Hardware-accelerated token validation at the UPF—leveraging SmartNIC or FPGA-based inline processing—is a prerequisite for production deployment, but its feasibility in pre-6G edge environments remains to be empirically validated.

4.2 Privacy and Regulatory Compliance

Sol#1 and Sol#2 rely on exposing internal network logs and user behavior data to analytics engines (NWDAF). In an E-Business context, this data often contains sensitive financial information and user location history, raising significant regulatory concerns.

Specifically, Sol#1 exposes UE location traces that constitute personal data under GDPR Article 4(1), requiring explicit consent or a legitimate-interest basis for processing. Sol#7's API monitoring may inadvertently capture payment metadata (transaction amounts, merchant identifiers) that falls under PCI-DSS Requirement 3 (Protect Stored Account Data) if persisted in analytics pipelines. Furthermore, cross-border E-Business transactions may trigger data residency requirements under national regulations (e.g., China's PIPL, South Korea's PIPA), complicating centralized NWDAF deployments.

A tiered data minimization strategy is therefore necessary and should be architecturally enforced, not merely recommended:

- **Edge Aggregation (Tier 1):** Raw telemetry is processed at the MEC/edge, producing only anomaly scores and aggregated statistics.
- **Cross-Domain Sharing (Tier 2):** Only anonymized anomaly scores—not raw features—cross trust domain boundaries to reach centralized NWDAF or third-party FDS.
- **Audit Retention (Tier 3):** Sol#13 (SEDR) logs retain only the minimum fields required for PCI-DSS audit compliance, with automated expiration policies.

Privacy-preserving analytics techniques such as federated learning (training anomaly models locally without centralizing raw data) or differential privacy (adding calibrated noise to exported statistics) should be integrated into the data collection layer. However, their impact on detection accuracy in adversarial E-Business environments is not yet well understood and requires dedicated empirical study.

4.3 Adversarial Attacks on AI-Driven Enforcement

The architecture relies on AI/ML for anomaly detection (Sol#7, Sol#11). However, AI models themselves are vulnerable to adversarial manipulation. Sophisticated attackers could inject carefully crafted noise into transaction traffic to deceive the NWDAF into classifying malicious behavior as benign (evasion attacks), or could poison training data over time to degrade model accuracy (poisoning attacks). For a resilient pre-6G E-Business ecosystem, the ZT framework must incorporate AI security measures—including adversarial training, model robustness verification, and ensemble detection—to prevent the security engine itself from being compromised. This remains an open research challenge that intersects with the broader field of trustworthy AI.

4.4 Qualitative Security Analysis

We evaluate the operational guidelines against three critical threat vectors prevalent in the pre-6G E-Business ecosystem.

4.4.1 Defense Against Credential Theft and Replay

In traditional systems, a stolen long-term session key allows an attacker to impersonate a user indefinitely. Context-Aware Token Binding (Sol#12) mitigates this by binding the UE's real-time PCI and beamforming signature to the transaction token. Any attempt to replay the token from a different location or device results in immediate verification failure at the PEP, even if the cryptographic signature remains valid. This is particularly effective against the SIM-swap and fake base station attacks documented in [17,28].

4.4.2 Mitigation of Insider Threats

A compromised internal node (e.g., a hijacked edge server) poses a severe risk under the "Implicit Trust" model. Sol#7 (API Anomaly Detection) monitors the behavioral patterns of internal NFs. If a trusted NF begins making irregular high-frequency queries to financial APIs—indicative of data exfiltration—the NWDAF identifies this deviation from the baseline profile. Sol#11 then triggers an automated policy update to isolate the compromised NF, limiting the scope of impact. The effectiveness of this approach depends on the quality of baseline profiles, which must be established through sufficient observation periods during normal operation.

4.4.3 Resilience Against DDoS on Payment Gateways

Pre-6G and 6G massive IoT environments increase the risk of botnet-driven DDoS attacks. Sol#8 (UE Behavior Monitoring) analyzes signaling patterns at the RAN level, distinguishing human transaction intervals from automated botnet frequencies. The system can preemptively throttle malicious traffic at the Edge UPF (Path B) before it saturates central payment gateways. However, false positive rates in distinguishing legitimate IoT traffic bursts from attack traffic remain a concern that requires empirical calibration.

4.5 Deployment Complexity and Backward Compatibility

Retrofitting ZT into existing 5G-Advanced infrastructure introduces non-trivial deployment challenges that we address through a phased migration strategy fully compliant with 3GPP specifications:

Phase 1 (Near-term, Rel-18/19): Deploy ZT enforcement at the Core only, leveraging existing PCF and UPF capabilities defined in TS 23.501 and TS 23.503 [2]. Sol#7, #11, #12, and #13 can be implemented as software upgrades to existing NFs without architectural changes. E-Business partners integrate via standard NEF/SCEF APIs.

Phase 2 (Mid-term, Rel-19/20): Extend PDP/PEP functions to MEC platforms as 6G edge computing hardware matures. This requires computational resources at cell sites (estimated 2–4 vCPUs per edge PDP instance for real-time anomaly scoring) that may not be available in current macro-cell deployments but are expected in pre-6G and 6G small-cell architectures.

Phase 3 (6G-native, post-2030): Full end-to-end ZT with RAN-level context injection, leveraging 6G-native features such as AI-native air interface and integrated sensing-communication. At this stage, the Radio Layer verification (beam ID, physical layer signatures) becomes operationally feasible. This phase is beyond the scope of current standardization and is identified as a future research direction.

Backward compatibility with Rel-15/16 UEs must be maintained throughout. The proposed Context-Aware Token Binding is designed as an optional extension to existing OAuth 2.0 DPoP flows [10,12], ensuring that non-ZT-capable devices degrade gracefully to standard authentication without breaking service continuity. From a 3GPP compliance perspective, all proposed mechanisms operate within the existing service-based interface (SBI) framework and do not require new protocol definitions—they augment the decision logic within standardized NFs rather than modifying the interfaces between them.

5 Conclusion

This paper analyzed how the Zero Trust enablers defined in 3GPP TR 33.794 can be adapted for pre-6G E-Business Information Systems. While the 3GPP report originally targets network-level trust management within operator domains, our criteria-based assessment of all thirteen candidate solutions revealed that seven demonstrate high suitability for cross-domain E-Business environments. Among these, we recommend the following implementation priority: (1) Sol#12 (Short-lived Tokens) and Sol#13 (Security Event Records) as immediate, low-complexity foundations; (2) Sol#7 (API Anomaly Detection) and Sol#11 (Closed-loop Enforcement) as the core detection-response pair; and (3) Sol#1, #2, and #8 as supporting enablers for comprehensive telemetry. The remaining six solutions are primarily relevant to intra-operator trust management and offer limited direct value for E-Business without additional adaptation.

By mapping these solutions to concrete EBIS building blocks—payment platforms, fraud detection engines, API gateways, and audit systems—and differentiating across three deployment paths (external DN, MEC, dedicated slice), this work provides actionable guidelines for practitioners seeking to integrate ZT principles into pre-6G digital commerce. The analysis also identified critical challenges: the latency-security trade-off for URLLC-bound transactions, regulatory compliance complexities involving GDPR and PCI-DSS, adversarial risks to AI-driven enforcement, and the phased deployment strategy required for backward compatibility with existing 5G infrastructure.

Several limitations of this work must be acknowledged. First, the suitability assessment is qualitative; quantitative evaluation through simulation or testbed implementation is necessary to validate the feasibility and overhead of the proposed guidelines. Second, the EBIS component mapping assumes a generalized E-Business architecture; domain-specific adaptations (e.g., for healthcare payments vs. supply chain finance) may require further refinement. Third, the interaction effects between multiple simultaneously deployed solutions (e.g., Sol#7 + Sol#11 + Sol#12) have not been formally analyzed for potential conflicts or emergent behaviors.

Future work will focus on four concrete directions: (1) prototyping the Context-Aware Token Binding mechanism on an O-RAN-compliant testbed to measure end-to-end latency overhead, (2) developing and evaluating federated anomaly detection models that comply with the tiered data minimization strategy, and (3) conducting a formal security analysis of the closed-loop enforcement chain under adversarial conditions. (4) While this paper focuses on application- and network-layer ZT enablers from TR 33.794, the ZT principle of minimizing implicit trust extends to the underlying authentication protocol layer as well [24]. Incorporating forward secrecy into 5G-AKA [29] and extending it to hybrid post-quantum key agreement [19] would complete the cryptographic foundation of the proposed architecture, ensuring that compromise of long-term credentials does not cascade to past sessions—a complementary defense-in-depth measure. A comprehensive formal verification and empirical evaluation of the EAP-AKA' protocol family under these evolving requirements is provided in [20]. As 6G standardization matures beyond Rel-20, extending these guidelines to incorporate 6G-native features (AI-native air interface, integrated sensing-communication) represents a natural continuation of this work.

References

1. 3GPP. Ts 33.501: Security architecture and procedures for 5G system. Technical report, 3GPP (2022). V17.0.0
2. 3GPP. Ts 23.503: Policy and charging control framework for the 5G system. Technical report, 3GPP (2024). V18.6.0
3. 3GPP CT. Ts 23.501: System architecture for the 5G system (5GS). Technical report, 3GPP (2024). V18.6.0.
4. 3GPP SA3. Tr 33.894: Study on applicability of the zero trust security principles in mobile networks (release 18). Technical report, 3GPP (2023). V18.0.0

5. 3GPP SA3. Tr 33.794: Study on enablers for zero trust security (release 19). Technical report, 3GPP (2025). V19.1.0
6. Abdalla, A.S., Moore, J., Adhikari, N., Marojevic, V.: ZTRAN: prototyping zero trust security xApps for open radio access network deployments. IEEE Wirel. Commun. **31**(2), 66–73 (2024)
7. Bhavana, S.U., Miriam, D.D.H., Rene Robin, C.R.: Understanding the implications of SIM card swap fraud in India: a comprehensive study. In: 2024 International Conference on Communication, Computing and Internet of Things (IC3IoT), pp. 1–8 (2024)
8. Chen, X., Feng, W., Ge, N., Zhang, Y.: Zero trust architecture for 6G security. IEEE Network **38**(4), 224–232 (2024)
9. CISA. Zero trust maturity model, version 2.0. Technical report, Cybersecurity and Infrastructure Security Agency (2023). Revised April 2023
10. Fett, D., Campbell, B., Bradley, J., Lodderstedt, T., Jones, M., Waite, D.: Oauth 2.0 demonstrating proof of possession (DPoP). RFC 9449 (2023)
11. Governments of Australia, Canada, Czech Republic, Finland, France, Japan, Republic of Korea, Sweden, United Kingdom, United States. Joint statement endorsing principles for 6G: Secure, open, and resilient by design (2024). https://www.ntia.gov/other-publication/2024/joint-statement-endorsing-principles-6g-secure-open-and-resilient-design. Ten-nation joint statement released at Mobile World Congress, Barcelona
12. Hardt, D.: The oauth 2.0 authorization framework. RFC 6749 (2012)
13. ITU-R. IMT-2030 Framework for 6G Mobile Systems (2023). https://www.itu.int/en/ITU-R/study-groups/rsg5/rwp5d/imt-2030/. Accessed 30 Sept 2025
14. Jover, R.P., Marojevic, V.: Security and protocol exploit analysis of the 5G specifications. IEEE Access **7**, 24956–24963 (2019)
15. Kent, K., Souppaya, M.: Guide to computer security log management. Technical report, NIST SP 800-92 (2006)
16. Khan, R., Kumar, P., Jayakody, D.N.K., Liyanage, M.: A survey on security and privacy of 5G technologies: potential solutions, recent advancements, and future directions. IEEE Commun. Surv. Tutor. **22**(1), 196–248 (2020)
17. Kim, M., Suh, J., Kwon, H.: A study of the emerging trends in SIM swapping crime and effective countermeasures. In: 2022 IEEE/ACIS 7th International Conference on Big Data, Cloud Computing, and Data Science (BCD), pp. 240–245 (2022)
18. Kindervag, J.: No more chewy centers: introducing the zero trust model of information security. Technical report, Forrester Research (2010)
19. Ko, Y., Pawana, I.W.A.J., You, I.: 5G-AKA-HPQC: hybrid post-quantum cryptography protocol for quantum-resilient 5G primary authentication with forward secrecy. arXiv preprint arXiv:2502.02851 (2025)
20. Kwon, H., Ko, Y., Pawana, I.W.A.J., You, I.: Toward quantum-safe 6G mobile networks: a survey on EAP-AKA' family with formal security analysis and empirical evaluation. IEEE Trans. Consum. Electron. (2025)
21. Mehrban, A., Abou El Houda, Z., Moudoud, H., Le, L.B.: Integrating zero trust architecture in O-RAN: a comprehensive survey and analysis. IEEE Open J. Commun. Soc. **6**, 10465–10495 (2025)
22. Mutabazi, P., Ndalama, F.E., Taenaka, Y.: Mitigating SIM swap fraud in mobile money platforms in SSA: a zero trust identity and access management architecture. In: IEEE International Conference on Information and Communication Technology (ICT), pp. 1–6. IEEE (2025)

23. Nahar, N., Andersson, K., Schelén, O., Saguna, S.: A survey on zero trust architecture: applications and challenges of 6G networks. IEEE Access **12**, 94753–94764 (2024)
24. Norrman, K., Sahlin, B., Smeets, B., Thormarker, E., Fogelström, E.: 6G security – drivers and needs. Technical report, Ericsson (2024). White Paper GFTL-24:000588
25. Porambage, P., Gür, G., Osorio, D.P.M., Liyanage, M., Gurtov, A., Ylianttila, M.: The roadmap to 6G security and privacy. IEEE Open J. Commun. Soc. **2**, 1094–1122 (2021)
26. Rose, S., Borchert, O., Mitchell, S., Chandramouli, R.: Zero trust architecture. Technical report, NIST Special Publication 800-207 (2020)
27. Scalise, P., Boeding, M., Hempel, M., Sharif, H., Delloiacovo, J., Reed, J.: A systematic survey on 5G and 6G security considerations, challenges, trends, and research areas. Future Internet **16**(3), 67 (2024)
28. Wen, Y.-T., et al.: Real-time rogue base stations detection system in cellular networks. In: Advanced Information Networking and Applications (AINA 2024). Lecture Notes on Data Engineering and Communications Technologies, vol. 204, pp. 465–474. Springer (2024)
29. You, I., Kim, G., Shin, S., Kwon, H., Kim, J., Baek, J.: 5G-AKA-FS: a 5G authentication and key agreement protocol for forward secrecy. Sensors **24**(1), 159 (2024)
30. Zhang, Z., et al.: 6G wireless networks: vision, requirements, architecture, and key technologies. IEEE Veh. Technol. Mag. **14**(3), 28–41 (2019)

E-Business

Foundations for Explainable Fraud Detection in Emerging eSIM and Mobile Payment Ecosystems

Vincent Abella[1], Jhury Kevin Lastre[1,2], Bonam Kim[1], and Ilsun You[1,3](✉)

[1] Department of Information Security, Cryptology, and Mathematics, Kookmin University, Seoul, South Korea
{vincent,lavelliane,kimbona}@kookmin.ac.kr
[2] OWASP Cebu, Cebu City, Philippines
jhurykev.lastre@owasp.org
[3] KMU Global Research Center for ICT Convergence Security, Kookmin University, Seoul, South Korea
isyou@kookmin.ac.kr

Abstract. As mobile payments evolve toward Embedded Subscriber Identity Module (eSIM)-enabled ecosystems, financial institutions face a pressing question: can Explainable Artificial Intelligence (XAI) techniques proven for credit card fraud detection adapt to emerging threats in converging payment-telecommunications infrastructures? The eSIM technology introduces distinct attack vectors, including SIM swap fraud, unauthorized provisioning, and man-in-the-middle attacks during activation, that existing systems were not designed to address, while regulatory demands for transparent AI decisions remain constant. This study presents the Risk Understanding in Monetary Intelligence (RUMI) framework, which integrates supervised models, SHapley Additive exPlanations (SHAP)-based interpretability, and TinyLlama-1.1B for natural language explanations. Dual-domain evaluation validates the approach on real-world credit card data, yielding a receiver operating characteristic area under the curve (ROC-AUC) of 0.997, and provides preliminary evidence of adaptability to synthetic eSIM infrastructure (ROC-AUC: 1.000). SHAP-based analysis reveals behavioral patterns dominating payment fraud and cryptographic attributes driving eSIM security, offering complementary intelligence for converged protection strategies. The framework addresses payment fraud and explainability challenges central to e-commerce and mobile commerce operations.

Proceedings of the 1st IFIP WG 8.4 International Symposium on E-Business Information Systems Evolution (EBISION '25), Article No. 65.
J. Kim et al. (Eds.): EBISION 2025, IFIP AICT 786, pp. 179–196, 2027.
https://doi.org/10.1007/978-3-032-26616-3_12

Keywords: eSIM Security · Mobile Payments · Fraud Detection · Explainable Artificial Intelligence · Small Language Models · Payment Security Foundations · e-commerce

1 Introduction

The boundaries between financial services and telecommunications infrastructure continue to blur. As mobile payments transition from card-based transactions to Embedded Subscriber Identity Module (eSIM)-enabled ecosystems, financial institutions confront a critical question: *can fraud detection systems designed for traditional payment technologies adapt to converged payment-telecommunications landscapes?*

E-commerce transactions are predominantly card-not-present, making fraud detection a critical operational requirement for online merchants and payment processors. Traditional credit card fraud detection reflects decades of refinement, with sophisticated machine learning models achieving strong performance on card-present and card-not-present transactions [7]. These systems, however, were architected for a different threat model. Payment credentials remain relatively static, device identity is peripheral, and the telecommunications layer serves primarily as transport infrastructure.

The eSIM technology may significantly alter these assumptions. Unlike physical cards with fixed credentials, eSIMs enable dynamic remote provisioning, on-device profile switching, and deep integration between payment credentials and telecommunications identity. This convergence introduces attack vectors that traditional systems were not designed to address (SIM swap fraud, unauthorized provisioning, man-in-the-middle attacks during activation). The distributed nature of eSIM provisioning spans mobile network operators, eSIM management platforms, and payment service providers, creating complex trust relationships where fraudulent activity may manifest across domain boundaries. Mobile payments represent a growing share of e-commerce transactions, and eSIM-enabled devices are increasingly used for mobile commerce and in-app payments.

Meanwhile, regulatory demands for transparent, auditable Explainable Artificial Intelligence (XAI) systems are intensifying. Financial regulators and telecommunications authorities increasingly require that automated security decisions be explainable to auditors, interpretable by operational teams, and justifiable to affected users. Organizations therefore face a dual challenge: they need sophisticated detection capabilities to identify evolving fraud patterns while simultaneously providing clear explanations for flagged transactions.

Rather than developing separate fraud detection systems for each domain, this study explores whether XAI principles proven effective for credit card fraud detection can provide architectural foundations for eSIM payment security. The Risk Understanding in Monetary Intelligence (RUMI) framework integrates supervised models, SHapley Additive exPlanations (SHAP)-based feature attribution, and Small Language Model explanation generation. Credit card fraud serves as the validation anchor on real-world data. Synthetic eSIM infrastructure tests adaptability to different feature spaces (behavioral patterns vs. cryptographic attributes). This work makes four contributions:

- **Unified cross-domain XAI pipeline:** A common detection and explainability pipeline applied independently across behavioral payment fraud and cryptographic eSIM security, demonstrating that SHAP's model-agnostic design operates without architectural modification across fundamentally different feature spaces.
- **Dual-domain empirical benchmark:** A performance comparison of supervised (Random Forest, XGBoost) and unsupervised (Isolation Forest) approaches evaluated across real-world credit card and synthetic eSIM data, providing reproducible baselines for future payment-telecommunications security research.
- **Cross-domain SHAP attribution study:** A feature importance analysis across two semantically distinct threat domains (behavioral payment patterns and cryptographic eSIM protocol attributes), demonstrating the applicability of model-agnostic explainability to converged security environments.
- **Natural language explanation prototype:** Integration of TinyLlama-1.1B with SHAP attribution to generate structured, human-readable explanations for flagged transactions, providing a prototype for cost-efficient, on-premise explanation generation applicable across both security domains.

2 Background

2.1 eSIM Technology and Payment Convergence

Embedded Subscriber Identity Module (eSIM) technology enables remote profile provisioning via the GSM Association's (GSMA) Remote SIM Provisioning (RSP) specification, supporting over-the-air profile management and eliminating physical SIM swapping [1,8]. Payment systems require strong identity verification and credential protection. Convergence with eSIM is emerging despite limited work directly combining payment transactions with provisioning [11]. SIM provisioning protocols (mutual authentication, profile download via Subscription Manager-Data Preparation Plus (SM-DP+) servers, RSP workflows) form building blocks for payment integration [2]. Trust coordination among mobile network operators, device vendors, payment providers, and regulators presents ongoing challenges for converged deployments.

Recent RSP protocol analysis reveals vulnerabilities including absence of perfect forward secrecy and man-in-the-middle susceptibility [16], underscoring the need for rigorous verification in payment-critical deployments. Securing inter-network communication in 5G roaming scenarios presents additional challenges [18]. Emerging quantum computing threats necessitate hybrid post-quantum cryptographic approaches for long-term resilience [17].

2.2 eSIM Threat Landscape for Payment Systems

Threats at the eSIM-payment boundary fall into three classes. *Identity takeover*: SIM swap fraud enables attackers to transfer phone numbers to attacker-controlled eSIMs and intercept SMS-based two-factor authentication codes for banking and payment platforms. eSIM swaps can be executed remotely, reducing attacker exposure [8]. *Provisioning infrastructure*: Compromised SM-DP+ servers could inject malicious profiles. Man-in-the-middle attacks during profile download could intercept tokens or modify contents. Rogue local profile assistants could exfiltrate payment credentials from eSIM secure elements [2,8,11]. *Cross-domain correlation*: Attackers may correlate telecommunications metadata (cell tower connections, roaming patterns, profile switching) with payment patterns to identify high-value targets or detect when victims are unreachable for fraud alerts.

Traditional credit card fraud detection systems, optimized for transaction-level behavioral anomalies, lack visibility into these telecommunications-layer threats. This limitation motivates the dual-domain approach.

2.3 Regulatory Landscape for Explainable AI

Financial institutions deploying AI-based fraud detection face evolving mandates for explainability and transparency. The EU AI Act (2024) classifies fraud detection as high-risk, requiring transparency and human oversight [14]. The General Data Protection Regulation Article 22 mandates meaningful information about automated decision logic [20]. The Payment Services Directive 2 requires Strong Customer Authentication, balancing security with customer friction at checkout [27]. U.S. regulations (Equal Credit Opportunity Act, Fair Credit Reporting Act, Federal Reserve SR 11-7) require specific reasons for adverse actions and model documentation [15]. Telecommunications regulations (Federal Communications Commission SIM swap protections, European Electronic Communications Code) create jurisdictional overlap [9,10]. Collectively, these mandates require individual-level explanations, model documentation, human review mechanisms, and audit trails.

3 Related Work

3.1 Fraud Detection for Payment and Telecommunications Security

Mobile payment fraud detection employs hybrid deep learning [32], temporal Long Short-Term Memory (LSTM) architectures [28], boosted machine learning (ML) with expert rules [29], and graph convolutional networks [30]. Deep learning approaches have demonstrated effectiveness for securing roaming scenarios in cloud-native 5G core networks, where recurrent architectures such as gated recurrent unit and LSTM achieve strong performance in detecting rare but high-impact attacks in inter-Public Land Mobile Network signaling [25]. ML techniques also enable detection of infrastructure-level threats such as false base stations [24]. Key challenges for eSIM integration include device identity spoofing, data sparsity for new profiles, real-time latency constraints, and privacy compliance.

3.2 Explainable AI and Natural Language Explanation Generation

Supervised methods (Random Forest, XGBoost, LightGBM) with synthetic minority over-sampling technique balancing outperform simple classifiers for imbalanced fraud detection [4,7,12,34]. Integration of XAI via SHAP and local interpretable model-agnostic explanations (LIME) provides interpretability required for regulatory compliance [3,5]. Deployment challenges include real-time latency, adversarial robustness, privacy preservation, and explanation fidelity.

Small Language Models (SLMs) offer efficiency and lower latency compared to Large Language Models (LLMs) for generating security explanations in constrained environments [33]. Lightweight LLMs have also demonstrated effectiveness in anomaly detection tasks [26]. However, deploying language models in security contexts requires careful oversight to ensure accuracy, prevent sensitive information leakage, and maintain auditability [22].

A gap remains: existing XAI-based fraud detection frameworks are predominantly single-domain, addressing payment transaction anomalies without extending to telecommunications-layer threats such as eSIM provisioning attacks. Prior work typically stops at feature attribution and does not integrate natural language explanation generation for non-technical stakeholders. The proposed RUMI framework addresses both gaps by applying a unified XAI pipeline across payment and eSIM security domains and coupling SHAP attribution with an SLM to produce human-interpretable narratives.

4 Proposed Framework

The RUMI framework provides a unified architecture for credit card fraud (validation domain) and eSIM infrastructure (adaptability domain), integrating supervised models (Random Forest, XGBoost), Isolation Forest as an unsupervised baseline, SHAP-based interpretability, and TinyLlama for natural language explanation generation.

4.1 Dataset Description and Preprocessing

The evaluation employs dual-domain validation across traditional payment systems and emerging eSIM infrastructure. The eSIM evaluation relies on synthetic data rather than production network traffic, limiting direct generalization to real-world deployments.

Credit Card Fraud Detection Dataset. The Credit Card Fraud Detection dataset [31] contains 284,807 transactions with 492 fraudulent instances (0.17% imbalance). Each record includes 28 Principal Component Analysis (PCA)-derived features (V1–V28), transaction amount, and timestamp. A stratified 80/20 train-test split (random_state = 42) was used, keeping the test set imbalanced to reflect deployment conditions. The training partition was rebalanced by undersampling legitimate transactions to reduce class imbalance, yielding 36,030 records. Supervised models were trained on the balanced set. Isolation Forest was fit on legitimate transactions only. All features were z-score normalized.

eSIM Infrastructure Security Dataset (Synthetic). A synthetic dataset of 5,000 SM-DP+ server transactions was generated using RSP ASN.1 specifications from pySim [23]. The dataset contains 17 attributes capturing HTTP metrics, GSMA SGP.22 protocol states, and performance indicators across three protocol phases (initiateAuthentication 60%, authenticateClient 25%, getBoundProfilePackage 15%). The 90%-10% normal-anomalous split includes five balanced anomaly categories: protocol violations, authentication failures, resource exhaustion, malformed ASN.1 structures, and transaction mismatches. While protocol-compliant, this synthetic data cannot fully capture the complexity, temporal dependencies, and adversarial patterns present in real-world eSIM infrastructure.

4.2 Feature Engineering

The credit card domain uses anonymized principal components (V1–V28), transaction amount, and timestamp with z-score normalization. The eSIM domain transforms 17 base attributes into 33 features. These incorporate protocol-specific knowledge: logarithmic response time transformations log(1 + response_time_ms), binary indicators for extreme latencies, and HTTP status code categorization (2xx success, 4xx client errors, 5xx server errors) aligned with GSMA SGP.22 specifications. This dual-domain approach revealed complementary intelligence: behavioral patterns dominated credit card fraud detection while certificate-based authentication and protocol compliance drove eSIM security.

4.3 Anomaly Detection Models

Unsupervised (Isolation Forest) and supervised (Random Forest, XGBoost) approaches were evaluated on both datasets using ROC-AUC, Average Precision (AP), F1-score, and Precision@K. Isolation Forest serves as a well-validated baseline. Supervised models leverage labeled data. Findings for Isolation Forest should not be generalized to all unsupervised methods.

4.4 Model Hyperparameters

Hyperparameters were chosen to balance efficiency and detection performance. All configurations use `random_state=42` for reproducibility.

Isolation Forest. `n_estimators=400`, `max_samples='auto'`, `contamination=0.01`. Training on legitimate transactions only from the balanced set.

Random Forest. `n_estimators=400`, `max_depth=None`, `min_samples_split=4`, `min_samples_leaf=2`, `class_weight=None`.

XGBoost. `n_estimators=600`, `max_depth=6`, `learning_rate=0.05`, `subsample=0.9`, `colsample_bytree=0.9`, `eval_metric='aucpr'`, `tree_method='hist'`.

4.5 Explainable AI Integration (SHAP)

To make model predictions interpretable, the framework integrated SHAP, which attributes each feature's contribution to a prediction. The SHAP method decomposes the model output into a baseline expectation plus additive feature contributions:

$$f(x) = \phi_0 + \sum_{j=1}^{d} \phi_j(x), \tag{1}$$

where $\phi_0 = \mathbb{E}[f(X)]$ is the expected output and $\phi_j(x)$ is the Shapley value of feature j for instance x.

The Shapley value itself is defined as:

$$\phi_j(x) = \sum_{S \subseteq F \setminus \{j\}} \frac{|S|!\,(|F| - |S| - 1)!}{|F|!} \Big(f_{S \cup \{j\}}(x) - f_S(x) \Big), \tag{2}$$

ensuring a fair allocation of contributions across all features.

Implementation. The TreeSHAP algorithm is applied for efficient exact computation on tree-based models. Locally, SHAP explains why a transaction is flagged. Globally, $\mathbb{E}[|\phi_j|]$ highlights the most influential features.

Algorithm 1. SHAP Integration for Fraud Detection

1: Train model (Isolation Forest, Random Forest, or XGBoost) on preprocessed dataset
2: Select background dataset (sample of training data)
3: **for** each transaction x in test set **do**
4: Compute SHAP values $\phi_j(x)$ using TreeSHAP
5: Rank features by $|\phi_j(x)|$
6: Store top-k features as explanation object
7: **end for**
8: Aggregate SHAP values for global feature importance

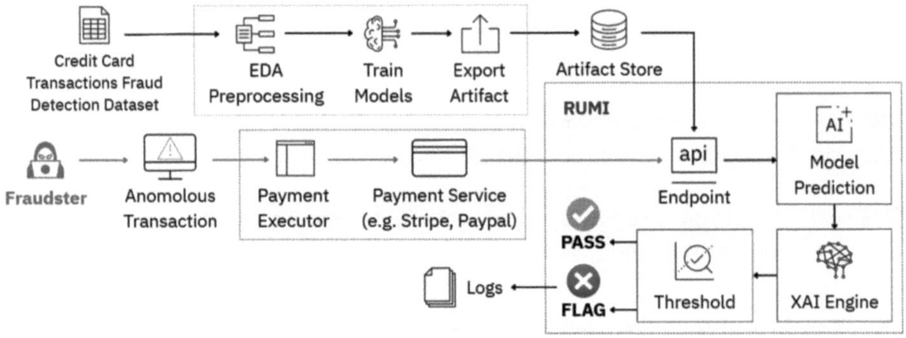

Fig. 1. RUMI framework architecture: establishing methodological foundations for explainable fraud detection applicable to emerging eSIM payment ecosystems.

4.6 Architecture Overview

Figure 1 illustrates the RUMI architecture. A unified pipeline processes both credit card and eSIM data through identical detection, classification, and explainability workflows.

4.7 Natural Language Translation with TinyLlama-1.1B

To make SHAP outputs accessible to non-technical stakeholders, the framework integrates **TinyLlama-1.1B** to transform structured attributions into plain-language narratives.

TinyLlama integration. The SHAP contributions are extracted via TreeSHAP and top-k features mapped to human-readable descriptors, forming explanation objects $\mathcal{E}(x) = \{\texttt{tx\_id}, \hat{p}(x), \texttt{[feature signals]}\}$. These are serialized into natural-language prompts for TinyLlama-1.1B [33], selected for deployability on standard hardware, small memory footprint, and on-premise compatibility. The model generates concise explanations with a consistent three-part structure: a risk summary, bullet-point reasons, and recommended actions. Generation is configured at a maximum of 256 tokens and temperature 0.7 to balance output coherence and lexical variation. Post-processing filters technical jargon and ensures privacy compliance. Inference averages approximately 1.2 s per explanation on CPU in the benchmark setup. Latency varies with hardware and is acceptable for asynchronous processing.

Cost Considerations. SLMs such as TinyLlama offer substantial cost advantages over LLMs: the 1–10B parameter range enables lower inference costs and memory footprints than 70B+ models, supporting on-premise deployment on commodity hardware without cloud API dependencies [19]. Explanations are generated only for flagged transactions, keeping token volume modest and supporting cost efficiency and data privacy requirements common in financial services.

Runtime Deployment. The framework exposes a FastAPI service for single and batch scoring. Transactions are preprocessed, scored by the selected model, and compared against a configurable threshold (default 0.5). Explanations are generated only for *FLAG* transactions. The API returns model type, fraud score, decision, and narrative in JSON (Fig. 2).

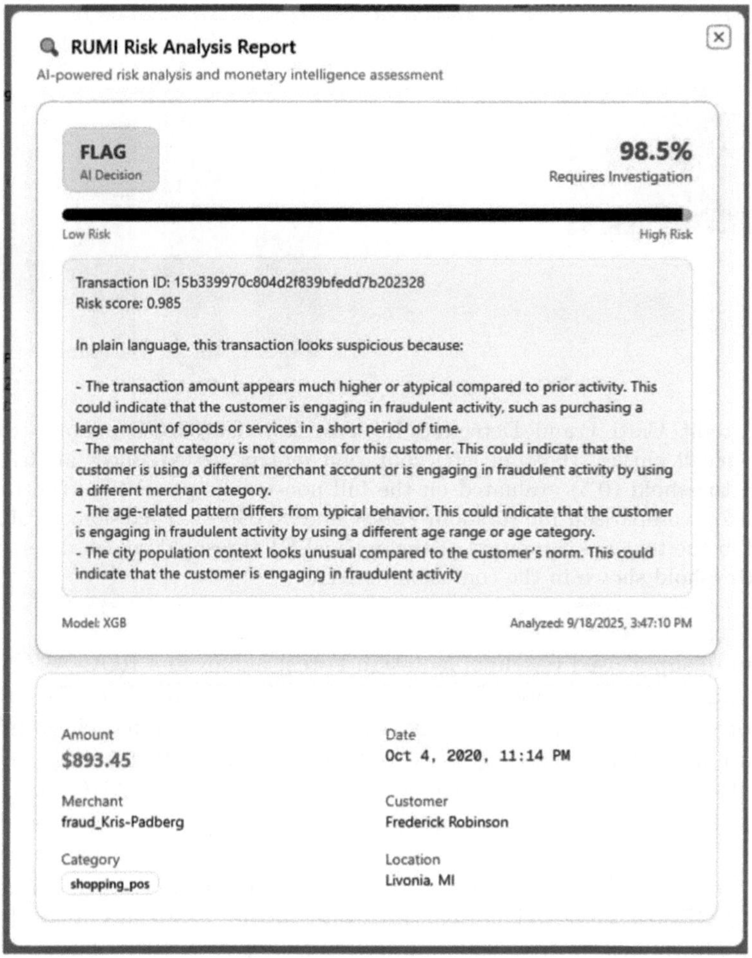

Fig. 2. A Next.js application with FastAPI interface for running RUMI fraud detection simulations.

5 Results and Discussion

5.1 Results

Credit Card Fraud Detection Results. Figure 3 summarizes evaluation results across all three models.

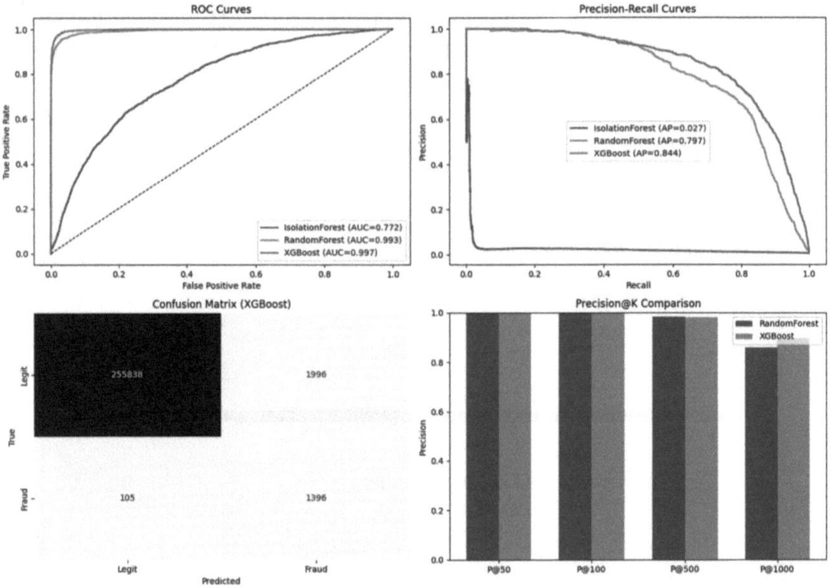

Fig. 3. Credit Card Fraud Detection Results: (top left) ROC curves, (top right) precision-recall curves, (bottom left) confusion matrix for XGBoost at default classification threshold (0.5) evaluated on the full non-training partition, (bottom right) Precision@K comparison for Random Forest and XGBoost. Precision, recall, and F1 reported in the text are computed at the optimal F1 threshold, which differs from the default threshold shown in the confusion matrix.

As an unsupervised baseline, Isolation Forest achieved a ROC-AUC of 0.772, AP of 0.027, and F1-score of 0.216 (precision 0.180, recall 0.270), reflecting limitations of unsupervised anomaly detection under extreme class imbalance. Random Forest attained a ROC-AUC of 0.993 and AP of 0.797 (F1-score 0.739). The XGBoost model delivered the strongest results: ROC-AUC of 0.997, AP of 0.844, F1-score of 0.777, outperforming other approaches across all major metrics.

The Precision@K analysis demonstrates practical utility: both Random Forest and XGBoost achieved perfect precision at $K = 50$ and $K = 100$, with precision above 98% at $K = 500$ and above 85% at $K = 1000$. These results are specific to the evaluated dataset and may vary in production.

eSIM Infrastructure Security Results (Synthetic Data). Cryptographic protocol compliance replaced behavioral patterns as the primary detection signal. Figure 4 shows the ROC-AUC comparison across models for SM-DP+ server transaction analysis.

Table 1 summarizes the metrics.

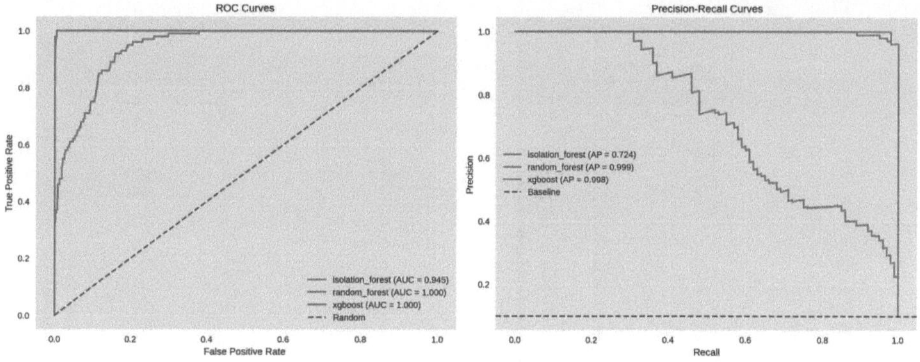

Fig. 4. eSIM Anomaly Detection Performance: ROC-AUC comparison across models for SM-DP+ server transaction analysis

Table 1. eSIM Infrastructure Anomaly Detection Performance

Model	Precision	Recall	F1-Score	ROC-AUC
Isolation Forest	0.587	0.610	0.598	0.945
Random Forest	0.917	1.000	0.957	1.000
XGBoost	0.926	1.000	0.962	1.000

Both Random Forest and XGBoost attained perfect recall and ROC-AUC of 1.000 (XGBoost precision 0.926 vs. 0.917). Results should be interpreted cautiously given synthetic data, balanced class distribution (10% vs. 0.17% in credit cards), and absence of real-world adversarial complexity (Sect. 6).

Cross-Domain SHAP Analysis. Section 4 established that behavioral patterns dominate credit card fraud detection. For the eSIM domain, Fig. 5 presents the SHAP explainability analysis for both Random Forest and XGBoost.

Table 2 lists the top eSIM features by SHAP importance. Client certificate presence is most influential (average 1.780). The large differences between Random Forest and XGBoost (e.g., `client_cert_present`: 0.127 vs. 3.433) reflect different scaling of SHAP values across tree-based models.

Unified Performance Assessment. Table 3 summarizes cross-domain performance. Direct comparison is limited by differing class distributions and synthetic data (Sect. 6).

5.2 Discussion

Observations on Cross-Domain XAI Applicability. The results provide preliminary evidence that a unified XAI pipeline can operate across payment and telecommunications security domains without architectural modification,

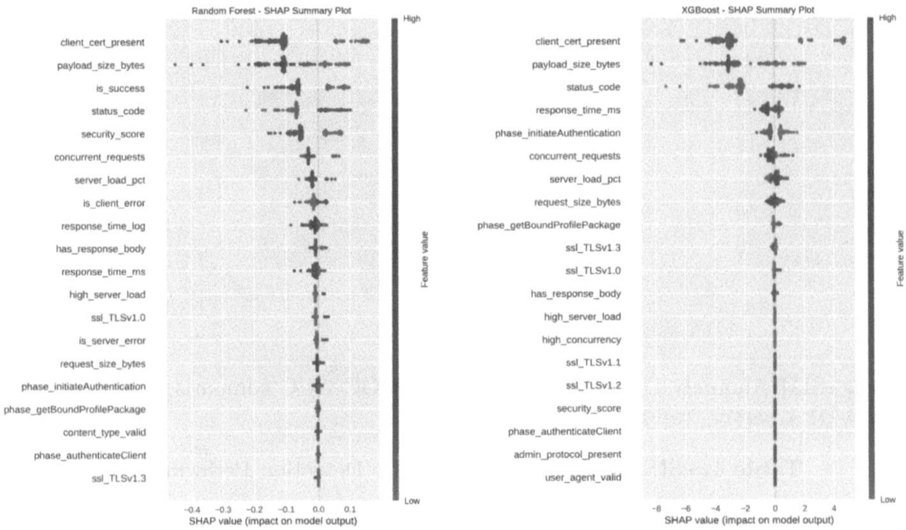

(a) eSIM Random Forest SHAP (b) eSIM XGBoost SHAP

Fig. 5. SHAP explainability analysis for eSIM infrastructure security models

Table 2. Top eSIM Infrastructure Features by SHAP Importance

Feature	Random Forest	XGBoost	Average
client_cert_present	0.127	3.433	1.780
payload_size_bytes	0.105	2.415	1.260
status_code	0.068	2.050	1.059
response_time_ms	0.009	0.451	0.230
phase_initiateAuthentication	0.003	0.426	0.215

Table 3. Cross-Domain Performance Validation: Traditional Payments vs eSIM Infrastructure

Security Domain	Model	Precision	Recall	F1-Score	ROC-AUC
Credit Card Fraud	Isolation Forest	0.180	0.270	0.216	0.772
	Random Forest	0.719	0.759	0.739	0.993
	XGBoost	0.811	0.744	0.777	0.997
eSIM Infrastructure	Isolation Forest	0.587	0.610	0.598	0.945
	Random Forest	0.917	1.000	0.957	1.000
	XGBoost	0.926	1.000	0.962	1.000

Note: Precision, recall, and F1 for supervised models are reported at the optimal F1 threshold.

reflecting SHAP's model-agnostic design. Supervised models outperformed Isolation Forest in both contexts. Isolation Forest's higher performance on eSIM data (0.945 vs. 0.772 ROC-AUC) aligns with literature on class-balance sensitivity. The SHAP attribution mechanism provides interpretable outputs in both domains (Table 4), which may help meet regulatory requirements in converged systems.

Complementary Intelligence for Hybrid Threat Landscapes. Table 4 indicates the two domains provide *complementary* rather than redundant intelligence. As payment credentials migrate to eSIM secure elements, the proposed approach could accommodate both threat types while maintaining explainability.

Table 4. Cross-Domain Feature Intelligence: Complementary Security Focus Areas

Security Domain	Primary Features	Security Focus
Credit Card Fraud	Behavioral patterns (V1–V28)	Transaction anomalies
	Transaction amount	Spending behavior
	Temporal patterns	Activity timing
eSIM Infrastructure	Certificate presence	Authentication integrity
	Protocol compliance	Communication security
	Payload characteristics	Data integrity

Human-Interpretable XAI at Scale. The TinyLlama-1.1B model produced structured natural language explanations for flagged transactions in both domains without domain-specific fine-tuning, each following the same three-part structure (risk summary, feature signals, recommended actions). This consistency across semantically distinct domains suggests that structured prompt engineering is sufficient for basic cross-domain applicability. The on-premise deployment model and flagged-only explanation policy keep inference overhead modest (Sect. 4). The explanations have not been assessed for accuracy, completeness, or analyst trust by domain experts, and TinyLlama-generated text for technically dense eSIM protocol violations may be limited by general-domain training. Formal evaluation by professional fraud analysts remains necessary (Sect. 6).

Scalability Considerations. The FastAPI implementation achieved approximately 500 transactions per second in preliminary single-node benchmarks on commodity hardware, potentially sufficient for mid-sized processors but requiring horizontal scaling for enterprise volumes (10,000+ transactions per second). Model inference executes in milliseconds. The SHAP component adds 10–50 ms overhead per transaction. With explanations limited to flagged transactions

(Sect. 4), traffic requiring language model inference remains modest. Scaling strategies include horizontal load distribution, caching, memoizing SHAP explanations, and optimized inference engines. Production requires monitoring for concept drift, A/B testing, and explainability audit logs for regulatory compliance.

Architectural Implications. The framework indicates that organizations could build unified security frameworks rather than maintaining separate systems for payment and eSIM security, though these benefits require empirical validation in production.

Operational Workflow Integration. When a transaction is flagged, the framework generates a risk score, SHAP contributions, and a TinyLlama narrative. Level 1 analysts review explanations first, then SHAP details if needed. Level 2 investigators access waterfall plots and historical patterns. Explanations guide focus (e.g., certificate dominance directs attention to provisioning logs), and analyst decisions feed back into retraining.

Adversarial Considerations. Fraud detection is adversarial: attackers may manipulate features to evade classification. Tree-based models are often considered more robust to small perturbations than neural networks in some settings [6] but remain vulnerable to coordinated manipulation. The present evaluation does not include adversarial robustness testing. Mitigations include limiting explanation granularity, adding noise to SHAP values, rate limiting, and model diversity. Concept drift monitoring and retraining are necessary as fraud patterns evolve.

Deployment Recommendations. A phased deployment is recommended: (1) shadow mode (no decision impact), (2) hybrid mode (alerts supplement existing detection), and (3) primary mode (framework as main system with legacy fallback). Each phase should include success criteria and rollback procedures. Threshold calibration should consider review capacity, fraud loss tolerance, and customer experience. Organizations should establish explanation governance and maintain daily monitoring, quarterly retraining, and A/B testing. Dual-domain deployment should maintain separate model versions and coordinate threshold setting.

Cost-Benefit Considerations. False positives often exceed the cost of undetected fraud: industry estimates indicate approximately \$118 billion in false declines annually in the U.S. versus approximately \$9 billion in actual fraud [13]. Although absolute figures have likely shifted with e-commerce growth and EMV adoption, the disparity persists as a structural challenge for e-commerce businesses where card-not-present transactions dominate [21]. A majority of manually reviewed transactions are ultimately approved as legitimate. Reducing unnecessary reviews is therefore as important as improving detection accuracy.

The framework's 100% precision at $K = 50$ and $K = 100$ on credit card data may translate to operational savings. For example, a queue of 16,000 alerts at 20 reviews/hour and $50/hour requires approximately 800 analyst-hours. Prioritizing the top-100 (all genuine fraud) reduces this to five hours, an estimated $40,000 savings per cycle [21]. Similar prioritization logic applies to eSIM provisioning security [8]. TinyLlama's SLM-scale inference keeps explanation overhead low [19].

6 Limitations

6.1 Synthetic Data Limitations

As noted in Sect. 4, the eSIM evaluation relies on synthetic data. The protocol-compliant dataset does not fully capture real-world adversarial behavior, temporal dependencies, or operational noise. The reported metrics (1.000 ROC-AUC) should be interpreted as proof-of-concept. Validation on real SM-DP+ server logs would strengthen deployment readiness, though access remains constrained by commercial sensitivity and privacy regulations.

6.2 Explanation Quality Limitations

TinyLlama-generated explanations have not yet been quantitatively evaluated by domain experts. Formal assessment of fidelity, analyst trust, and decision-making impact would strengthen confidence (see Sect. 7). Planned evaluation includes structured surveys with professional fraud analysts using standardized protocols.

6.3 Technical and Methodological Limitations

The use of SHAP requires expensive approximations for deep learning. Supervised learning presents cold-start challenges and may not generalize to previously unseen fraud types. Model scope is limited to tree-based architectures.

6.4 Evaluation Methodology Limitations

All reported results are based on a single stratified train-test split (`random_state=42`). No cross-validation or bootstrap confidence intervals were computed. Performance metrics may vary across different random partitions, particularly in the credit card domain where the small number of fraudulent instances (492 across the full dataset) amplifies sampling variance in the test set. Cross-validation is recommended before production deployment decisions.

7 Conclusion

This work presents evidence that a unified XAI pipeline, applied independently on each domain, can operate across behavioral payment fraud and cryptographic eSIM security without architectural modification. On real-world credit card data, XGBoost achieved 0.997 ROC-AUC and Random Forest achieved 0.993 ROC-AUC. Supervised approaches consistently outperformed the Isolation Forest baseline in both domains. The eSIM result (1.000 ROC-AUC) should be interpreted as proof-of-concept given synthetic data, a higher anomaly rate (10% vs. 0.17%), and the absence of real-world adversarial complexity. The SHAP-based analysis revealed complementary feature patterns (Table 4): behavioral attributes dominate credit card fraud detection while cryptographic protocol compliance drives eSIM anomaly detection. The TinyLlama-1.1B model generated structured natural language explanations for flagged transactions across both domains without domain-specific fine-tuning, providing a prototype for cost-efficient, on-premise explanation generation.

Both explanation quality and eSIM performance require further validation. Nevertheless, this work offers a methodological starting point for unified, explainable security frameworks in converging payment-telecommunications ecosystems. Future research directions include: (1) validation on production eSIM network data to assess real-world performance beyond synthetic protocol simulations, (2) advanced class imbalance strategies (synthetic minority over-sampling with edited nearest neighbors, focal loss, dynamic thresholding) to improve minority-class recall, (3) adaptation of XAI techniques to eSIM-specific patterns including device identity and multi-stakeholder trust relationships, (4) systematic evaluation of explanation fidelity, consistency, and robustness against adversarial perturbations, and (5) usability studies with professional fraud analysts using structured evaluation protocols to address the explanation quality limitations noted in Sect. 6.

Acknowledgment. This work was supported by Institute of Information & Communications Technology Planning & Evaluation (IITP), South Korea, grant funded by the Korea government (MSIT) (No. RS-2024-00398312, Development of Quantum Security Based Device Identification and Test Verification Technologies for 5G Non-Public Network).

References

1. Abu, A.S, Peltonen, A., Sethi, M., Aura, T.: Security analysis of the consumer remote sim provisioning protocol. ACM Trans. Priv. Secur. **27**(3), 36 (2024). https://doi.org/10.1145/3663761
2. Ahmed, A.S., Peltonen, A., Sethi, M., Aura, T.: Security analysis of the consumer remote sim provisioning protocol. ACM Trans. Priv. Secur. **27**(3), 1–36 (2024). https://doi.org/10.1145/3663761
3. Awosika, T., Shukla, R.M., Pranggono, B.: Transparency and privacy: the role of explainable ai and federated learning in financial fraud detection (2023)

4. Chang, V., Ali, B., Golightly, L., Ganatra, M.A., Mohamed, M.: Investigating credit card payment fraud with detection methods using advanced machine learning. Information **15**(8) (2024). https://doi.org/10.3390/info15080478
5. Chavakula, S.J., Albert, C.A.J., Ebenezer, E., Bhagat, M.H., Mahamuni, C.V.: Explainable AI (XAI) using SHAP and LIME for financial fraud detection and credit scoring. In: 2025 International Conference on Advanced Computing Technologies (ICoACT), pp. 1–8 (2025). https://doi.org/10.1109/ICoACT63339.2025.11005238
6. Chen, H., Zhang, H., Boning, D., Hsieh, C.J.: Robust decision trees against adversarial examples. In: Proceedings of the 36th International Conference on Machine Learning (ICML), pp. 1122–1131 (2019). https://proceedings.mlr.press/v97/chen19m.html
7. Dastidar, K.G., Caelen, O., Granitzer, M.: Machine learning methods for credit card fraud detection: a survey. IEEE Access **12**, 158939–158965 (2024). https://doi.org/10.1109/ACCESS.2024.3487298
8. ENISA: Embedded sim ecosystem, security risks and measures. Technical report, European Union Agency for Cybersecurity (2023). https://www.enisa.europa.eu/publications/embedded-sim-ecosystem-security-risks-and-measures
9. European Union: Directive (EU) 2018/1972 establishing the european electronic communications code (2018). https://eur-lex.europa.eu/legal-content/EN/TXT/?uri=CELEX:32018L1972
10. Federal Communications Commission: Protecting consumers from sim swap and port-out fraud. Report and Order, FCC 23-95, WC Docket No. 21-341 (2023). https://www.fcc.gov/document/protecting-consumers-sim-swapping-and-port-out-fraud
11. GSMA: RSP technical specification (SGP.22 v3.0). Official document, GSMA (2023). https://www.gsma.com/solutions-and-impact/technologies/esim/gsma_resources/sgp-22-v3-0/
12. Gupta, S., Varshney, T., Verma, A., Goel, L., Yadav, A.K., Singh, A.: A hybrid machine learning approach for credit card fraud detection. Int. J. Inf. Technol. Proj. Manage. **13**, 1–13 (2022). https://doi.org/10.4018/IJITPM.313420
13. Javelin Strategy & Research: Addressing the threat of false positive declines. Technical report, Javelin Strategy & Research (2018). https://javelinstrategy.com/research/addressing-threat-false-positive-declines
14. Jozak, T.: 2024 EU AI act: a detailed analysis (2025). https://papers.ssrn.com/sol3/papers.cfm?abstract_id=5196856
15. Knight, E.: AI and machine learning-based credit underwriting and adverse action under the ECOA. Bus. Fin. L. Rev. **3**, 236 (2019). https://gwbflr.org/knight/
16. Ko, Y., Lastre, J.K., Kwon, H., You, I.: Revisiting the M2M remote sim provisioning protocol: a comprehensive security and performance analysis. Alex. Eng. J. **135**, 1–19 (2026). https://doi.org/10.1016/j.aej.2025.12.049. In press
17. Ko, Y., Pawana, I.W.A.J., You, I.: 5G-AKA-HPQC: hybrid post-quantum cryptography protocol for quantum-resilient 5G primary authentication with forward secrecy (2025). https://doi.org/10.48550/arXiv.2502.02851
18. Lastre, J.K., Ko, Y., Kwon, H., You, I.: Evaluating transport layer security 1.3 optimization strategies for 5G cross-border roaming: a comprehensive security and performance analysis. Sensors **25**(19) (2025). https://doi.org/10.3390/s25196144
19. Lu, Z., et al.: Small language models: survey, measurements, and insights (2024)
20. Malgieri, G.: Automated decision-making in the EU member states: the right to explanation and other "suitable safeguards" in the national legislations. Comput.

Law Secur. Rev. **35**(5), 105327 (2019). https://papers.ssrn.com/sol3/papers.cfm?abstract_id=3233611
21. Mastercard: What do inefficient manual fraud reviews really cost you? (2024). https://www.mastercard.com/us/en/news-and-trends/Insights/2024/manual-fraud-review-cost.html
22. Nazzal, M., Khalil, I., Khreishah, A., Phan, N.H.: PromSec: prompt optimization for secure generation of functional source code with large language models (LLMs). In: Proceedings of the 2024 ACM SIGSAC Conference on Computer and Communications Security (CCS 2024), pp. 2266–2279. ACM (2024). https://doi.org/10.1145/3658644.3690298
23. Osmocom Project: pySim: a python tool to explore and program SIMS/USIMS/ISIMS. https://github.com/osmocom/pysim
24. Park, H., Astillo, P.V.B., Kim, T., You, I.: 5g native network function for false base station detection using machine learning technique. Inf. Syst. Front. (2025). https://doi.org/10.1007/s10796-025-10614-1
25. Pawana, I.W.A.J., Abella, V., Lastre, J.K., Ko, Y., You, I.: Enhancing roaming security in cloud-native 5G core network through deep learning-based intrusion detection system. CMES - Comput. Model. Eng. Sci. **145**(2), 2733–2760 (2025). https://doi.org/10.32604/cmes.2025.072611
26. Pawana, I.W.A.J., Astillo, P.V., You, I.: Lightweight LLM-based anomaly detection framework for securing IoTMD enabled diabetes management control systems. IEEE J. Biomed. Health Inform. 1–12 (2025). https://doi.org/10.1109/JBHI.2025.3577604
27. Qahfarrokhi, S.S.: Security challenges in mobile payments: the EU's approach. Mod. Technol. Law J. **1**(1), 1–15 (2025). https://mtlj.usc.ac.ir/article_220147_en.html
28. Sampietro Saquicela, J.L., Bermúdez Herrera, L.A., Morejón Hidalgo, V.P., Cajas Cajas, V.E., De Los Ángeles Ponce Villacis, P., Rodríguez Arboleda, V.E.: Credit card fraud detection using bidirectional LSTM with attention mechanism on sequential spending behavior. In: 2025 Second International Conference on Intelligent Technologies for Sustainable Electric and Communications Systems (iTech SECOM), pp. 1–7 (2025). https://doi.org/10.1109/iTechSECOM64750.2025.11307600
29. Sun, Q., Tang, T., Chai, H., Wu, J., Chen, Y.: Boosting fraud detection in mobile payment with prior knowledge. Appl. Sci. **11**(10), 4347 (2021). https://doi.org/10.3390/app11104347
30. Tam, D.S.H., Lau, W.C., Hu, B., Ying, Q.F., Chiu, D.M., Liu, H.: Identifying illicit accounts in large scale e-payment networks: a graph representation learning approach (2019)
31. ULB Machine Learning Group: Credit card fraud detection dataset. https://www.kaggle.com/datasets/mlg-ulb/creditcardfraud
32. Verma, S., Dhar, J.: Credit card fraud detection: a deep learning approach (2024)
33. Zhang, P., Zeng, G., Wang, T., Lu, W.: TinyLLaMA: an open-source small language model (2024)
34. Zheng, Q., Yu, C., Cao, J., Xu, Y., Xing, Q., Jin, Y.: Advanced payment security system: XGBoost, LightGBM and smote integrated (2024)

Knowledge-Driven E-Business in Cultural Heritage: A Framework for Design and Evaluation

Angelo Lorusso[1](✉), Federico Martusciello[2], Henry Muccini[2], Giusy Strollo[3], and Alfredo Troiano[4]

[1] DISAMIS, University of Salerno, Fisciano, SA, Italy
alorusso@unisa.it
[2] University of L'Aquila, L'Aquila, Italy
federico.martusciello@graduate.univaq.it,
henry.muccini@univaq.it
[3] DICiv, University of Salerno, Fisciano, SA, Italy
g.strollo9@studenti.unisa.it
[4] NetCom Group, Napoli, Italy
a.troiano@netcomgroup.eu

Abstract. Cultural heritage institutions implement E-business information systems to integrate enjoyment, economic sustainability, and public purpose. This study presents a comprehensive framework that systematically connects cultural data (shared models and vocabularies, digitally described content) with operational processes (bookings, online sales, membership, and public relations) through integration utilising documented interfaces and event exchange. This approach produces a distinctive information model that connects objects, individuals, locations, and events, while also quantifying the impact of architectural decisions on measurable outcomes: data quality and alignment, service response times, booking completion rates, membership renewal rates, and decreased absenteeism. The methodological component establishes reproducible protocols for collecting and analysing evidence, considering seasonality and contextual factors, while incorporating data protection and accessibility standards throughout the design process. We examine the anticipated outcomes and ramifications for sustainability, experiential quality, and system governance.

1 Introduction

Cultural heritage institutions, including museums, archives, libraries, and archaeological sites, are currently operating in a context where digital technology increasingly influences economic sustainability models and cultural enjoyment (Colace et al., 2025). Beyond the basic digitization of collections, there is an increasing demand for E-Business Information Systems (EBIS) that can amalgamate cultural content, transactional processes, and analytical tools into a unified ecosystem: encompassing time-slot ticketing, e-commerce, copyright management, subscriptions/memberships, image licensing, and

Published by Springer Nature Switzerland AG 2027
J. Kim et al. (Eds.): EBISION 2025, IFIP AICT 786, pp. 197–212, 2027.
https://doi.org/10.1007/978-3-032-26616-3_13

online educational programs (Cantone et al., 2023; Grimaldi et al., 2022; Vega-Gorgojo, 2024). Notwithstanding the advancement of standards for asset description (e.g., CIDOC CRM, IIIF, SKOS/RDF), technical and scientific literature remains deficient in providing a comprehensive framework for orchestrating the complete life cycle of data and services in a composable, measurable, and reproducible manner, while integrating cultural interfaces and E-business subsystems amidst compliance constraints (privacy, accessibility) and resource limitations (capacity, budget, skills) (Colace et al., 2018; Nishioka & Nagasaki, 2021).

Two fundamental reasons exist for this. Cultural institutions must diversify their revenue streams and optimize operational processes while maintaining their public mission; concurrently, they must guarantee the quality of cultural data and semantic consistency, essential for interoperability, discovery, knowledge reuse, and research (Casillo, Colace, Gaeta, et al., 2025). The conflict between these two goals is evident in the amalgamation of disparate silos (repository/DAM, IIIF servers, LOD graphs, ticketing, e-commerce, CRM, LMS), frequently characterized by incompatible technologies and data models. This leads to elevated integration expenses, inadequate traceability of information flows, challenges in assessing impact (both cultural and economic), and, often, technological lock-in (Pellegrino et al., 2022).

This article presents a cohesive architectural and methodological framework for applying EBIS to cultural heritage. The initial step involves implementing an API-first and event-driven architecture, segmented into specialized layers (cultural, transactional, integration, channels, governance) and interconnected via formal contracts and semantic mappings. Consequently, we develop a formal graph model that integrates cultural entities and transactional events with explicit typology and temporality, facilitating cross-analysis (provenance ↔ visitor journey) while maintaining compliance with museum standards (Sanderson, 2024). We propose an evaluation workflow that delineates datasets (public, synthetic, and anonymized real cases), metrics, and experimental protocols to assess: integration effort; query performance; operational outcomes (conversion, membership renewal, no-shows); and adherence to accessibility and privacy standards (De Simone et al., 2022; Yap et al., 2024).

Economic sustainability, interoperability, privacy and regulatory compliance, and scientific reproducibility are the four project constraints against which our approach is evaluated. Interoperability necessitates precise alignment with ontologies and vocabularies (e.g., mapping IIIF to CIDOC CRM, SKOS for thesauri), whereas privacy mandates minimization, granular consent, and privacy-preserving analytical methodologies. Sustainability necessitates explicit cost models and the minimization of integration debt; reproducibility demands the availability of shared datasets, pipelines, and metrics to facilitate equitable comparisons among architectural alternatives (e.g., monolithic versus composable) (Gaeta et al., 2025a; Huang et al., 2023). Notwithstanding the existing research on digital libraries, knowledge graphs, and descriptive standards, the following domains remain underexplored: the systematic integration of the cultural semantic layer with E-business subsystems; the cohesive formalization of entities and events for cross-domain analytics; the quantitative evaluation of architectural impacts on KPIs under realistic constraints (capacity, seasonal demand, queue management); and the intentional incorporation of ethical-legal requirements (GDPR, accessibility) into technical workflows (Clarizia et al., 2020; Gaeta et al., 2024; Zhang, 2022).

This work seeks to establish a cohesive framework for E-Business Information Systems in cultural heritage, wherein semantic content modelling underpins the integration of transactional subsystems and facilitates subsequent analysis and reporting. This context presents a composable architectural framework with API-first and event-driven integration, incorporating roles, permissions, and comprehensive traceability. It also establishes a typed and temporal graph model that aligns with CIDOC CRM and IIIF, enhancing them with events throughout the user journey (booking, visit, purchase, renewal) (Davis & Heravi, 2021). The work presents an experimental protocol featuring operational and interoperability metrics, underpinned by a controlled synthetic dataset and guidelines for utilising anonymized real cases. Ultimately, it examines the anticipated outcomes and their ramifications for sustainability, governance, and the ethical design of systems, emphasizing how the tenuous connection between the semantic domain and the operational domain can enhance information quality and service performance. This methodology facilitates the systematic and reproducible examination of the correlation between architectural decisions and quantifiable results (e.g., enhancement in conversion rates prompted by time slots and contextual upselling). Practically, it offers cultural institutions a framework to minimize the total cost of ownership, enhance user experience (particularly regarding accessibility), and facilitate content circulation within national and international ecosystems (e.g., aggregators, thematic portals) while maintaining control and compliance.

While API-first and event-driven integration are established architectural patterns, this work contributes a framework that makes the coupling between semantic cultural modelling and operational EBIS outcomes explicit, measurable, and reproducible. The key novelty is to treat identifiers, mappings, and event traces as first-class analytical variables, enabling a typed temporal graph that links cultural entities to user-journey events with provenance and version references, and an evaluation workflow that connects architectural and semantic decisions to comparable KPIs under realistic constraints (seasonality, capacity, compliance). Concretely, the paper provides:

- A layered semantic–operational integration blueprint for CH EBIS, including governance and compliance-by-design controls.
- A typed temporal event-enriched information model aligned with CIDOC CRM/IIIF/SKOS that links cultural entities to transactional and interaction events.
- A reproducible evaluation protocol defining dimensions, metrics, and experimental designs to quantify interoperability, integration effort, performance, and funnel outcomes.

The document is organized as follows: the "Related Work" section delineates standards, architectural patterns, and contemporary practices within the field; the "Proposed Workflow" section narratively outlines the phases, participants, and artifacts, supplemented by a diagram illustrating data and event flows; the "Expected Results and Discussion" section articulates testable hypotheses and examines their technical and ethical ramifications; lastly, the "Conclusions and Future Developments" section encapsulates the contributions and suggests a research roadmap, emphasizing online optimization, inter-institutional federation, and bias auditing.

2 Related Work

The digital transformation of cultural heritage arises from three converging elements: semantic modelling and interoperability of cultural data; advanced digital applications (imaging/annotations, federated discovery); and integration with E-business subsystems (ticketing, e-commerce, membership/CRM). The body of work on digital libraries and knowledge organisation has established standards and practices for description; however, the operational integration of the semantic layer with transactional processes continues to be the primary technical and organisational challenge. CIDOC CRM advocates for event-centric modelling of works, agents, places, and processes at the reference ontology level, facilitating alignment among diverse archives and maintaining provenance throughout the data transformation and mediation process. This method is deemed essential for achieving semantic interoperability in museum metadata.

SKOS formalises concepts, hierarchical and associative relationships for thesauri and taxonomies with minimal ontological commitment, a design rationale facilitating its adoption and interoperability between various systems, which is essential in cultural heritage aggregation pipelines. The RDF/OWL expression and the presence of SPARQL endpoints constitute the technological framework for LOD/knowledge graphs within the cultural domain (Baker et al., 2013; Casillo, Colace, Lorusso, et al., 2025a; 2025b).

IIIF has emerged as the definitive standard for disseminating high-resolution images, multi-resource sequences/manifests, and interoperable annotations in imaging and advanced applications. The literature in this domain outlines its objectives, APIs, and advantages for interoperability and application reuse, with extensive implementation in prominent libraries and museums. IIIF facilitates zooming, comparison, storytelling, and extensions to audiovisual and three-dimensional content; however, it does not inherently address licensing and the integration of transactional metadata, which are persistent architectural challenges (Haller et al., 2018; Snydman et al., 2015).

Regarding knowledge graphs and open aggregation, Europeana has provided metadata as Linked Open Data in EDM, showcasing tangible benefits (dereferenceable URIs, SPARQL, connections to external resources such as GeoNames/GEMET/DBpedia) while simultaneously confronting the challenges of quality and heterogeneity characteristic of large-scale aggregation (granularity, coverage, licenses) (Cecere et al., 2025; Isaac & Haslhofer, 2013).

Recent studies in CH + KG demonstrate that relational search methodologies on semantic graphs can provide elucidated connections and discovery pathways that surpass mere keyword retrieval, featuring explanation patterns that identify intriguing connections and facilitate explanations in natural language—a valuable viewpoint for cultural discovery and engagement (Hyvönen & Rantala, 2021).

Cultural institutions employ E-business information systems, including ticketing suites for time-slot and capacity management, e-commerce platforms for bookshops, merchandising, and print-on-demand services, CRM and marketing automation for segmentation and multi-channel journeys, and Learning Management Systems for educational purposes. The trend in information systems/software architecture is transitioning from monolithic structures to microservices and event-driven architecture (EDA) to attain decoupling, targeted scalability, and diminished time-to-market. Mapping studies on microservices encapsulate patterns, taxonomies, and trade-offs (such as service granularity, observability, and versioning) and apply to CH domains characterized by frequent integrations and multiple suppliers (Pahl & Jamshidi, 2016). Recent empirical evidence regarding EDA in enterprise information systems demonstrates quantifiable effects on performance and scalability during real-time and fluctuating traffic conditions, such as those encountered in advance ticket sales or major exhibitions, thereby supporting bus/event streaming implementation to mitigate strong interdependencies among components (Cabane & Farias, 2024).

The implementation of EBIS in CH necessitates privacy-by-design and accountability in compliance with the GDPR (including granular consent, data minimization, DPIA, and retention), as well as digital accessibility of platforms (websites/apps) in accordance with WCAG 2.2 (W3C Recommendation of 5 October 2023, featuring new success criteria). In the cultural sector, accessibility constitutes a public obligation: recent research indicates inconsistent implementation and persistent obstacles at museum locations, advocating for ongoing evaluations and collaborative design with individuals with disabilities (Kruczek et al., 2023). Technical literature suggests employing privacy and data protection by design tools utilising knowledge graphs to depict consent and autonomously verify compliance (regulatory obligations → technical/organisational measures → code), yielding reproducible results in analogous domains and transferable to EBIS processes (bookings, accounts, telemetry) (Chhetri et al., 2022).

Traditionally, digital libraries have assessed metadata quality and search efficacy; from an EBIS standpoint, operational KPIs (conversion rates, membership renewals, absenteeism) and impact metrics (accessibility, reach, and reuse) are relevant. It is advisable to employ online controlled experiments (A/B) for features/UI and quasi-experiments, such as Difference-in-Differences (DiD) with staggered treatments, adhering to established guidelines and econometric updates to prevent negative weights and prohibited comparisons. These methods are pertinent for isolating the impact of architectural or policy decisions (e.g., implementation of time slots, reminders) on observed outcomes (Callaway & Sant'Anna, 2021; Kohavi et al., 2020; Roth et al., 2023).

The technological foundation is established (CIDOC/SKOS/RDF, IIIF, EDM; microservices/EDA; WCAG 2.2; GDPR-compliant tools), yet the literature identifies four operational deficiencies: an absence of unified models that systematically connect cultural entities and E-business events within a queryable and provenance-aware graph; a lack of vendor-agnostic guidelines for transitioning from monolithic to composable systems in the public sector; insufficient shared benchmarks and replicable datasets addressing interoperability, performance, and outcomes under realistic constraints (capacity, seasonality, queues); and the need for technical-organizational playbooks that incorporate accessibility and privacy by design into the DevOps cycle and KPI assessment. The proposed workflow in the subsequent section addresses these deficiencies through reproducible phases (semantic ingestion, mapping, API/event integration, analytics, reporting), standardised metrics, and integrated compliance controls.

Based on the limitations identified in existing approaches, we derive a set of explicit. requirements guiding the proposed framework:

- R1 – Semantic continuity: cultural entities and operational events must be linked through stable identifiers and shared semantics.
- R2 – Observability: all relevant interactions must generate traceable and versioned events.
- R3 – Composability: subsystems must evolve independently without breaking analytical continuity.
- R4 – Measurability: architectural and semantic decisions must be evaluable through comparable metrics.
- R5 – Compliance by design: privacy and accessibility constraints must be enforced at process level.

3 Proposed Workflow

The suggested workflow is predicated on the notion that the digital value chain in cultural heritage arises from the tenuous interconnection between two historically distinct domains: the semantic-cultural domain (models, vocabularies, manifests) and the transactional domain (bookings, payments, membership). The glue is an API-first, event-driven integration layer that disseminates stable identifiers, versioned messages, and reproducible transformations. This results in an observable and measurable ecosystem that adheres to ethical and legal standards. Figure 1 illustrates these blocks and their interactions.

The initial focus is on the semantic structuring of the informational legacy. Descriptive catalogues and authority files explicitly delineate entities and events (works, agents, places, processes) and are supplemented by interoperable manifests for multimedia resources. This standardization is not an ultimate goal; it renders content citable and composable by other subsystems by offering shared keys, temporal context, and interpretative rules. The cultural graph and manifests serve as a "common lexicon" for the architecture, providing a clear reference point.

The operational domain is integrated into this lexicon. Slot reservation, e-commerce, membership frameworks, and communication channels reveal public, versioned interface agreements and disseminate domain events (e.g., booking.created, order.fulfilled, membership.renewed). Their responsibility is not to reproduce cultural knowledge, but to utilize it as necessary (e.g., to create a contextual offering) and to transmit signals when notable transactions or interactions occur. In this interaction, the minimization of personal data and the traceability of consent are constant principles: only essential information is conveyed, and the purposes are restricted.

The integration layer serves as a pivotal connection between the two domains. Operational events are aligned with cultural entities via semantic-operational transformations and linking protocols: a booking is not an isolated occurrence but is connected to the pertinent object, exhibition, and location; a membership renewal may be correlated with usage patterns and preferences, consistently in pseudonymized form. This layer contains a registry of schemas for messages and events, along with compatible versioning practices, enabling the ecosystem to evolve seamlessly while ensuring the reproducibility of experiments and measurements.

The user experience on public channels (website, app, kiosks) is enhanced by this unification: interoperable visualizers utilize manifests, search merges facet-based navigation with graph projections, and purchase processes amalgamate content and services.

Every significant interaction produces events that revert to the integration layer, completing an initial learning cycle. Simultaneously, a measurement pathway converts events into pre-established indicators (conversion, renewal, no-show, mapping coverage, adherence to accessibility standards), maintaining the connection with versions of schemas, vocabularies, and contracts. This link is essential: it enables us to differentiate the impacts of an architectural modification from those resulting from seasonality or content, and to retroactively reconstruct the circumstances under which a specific measurement was generated.

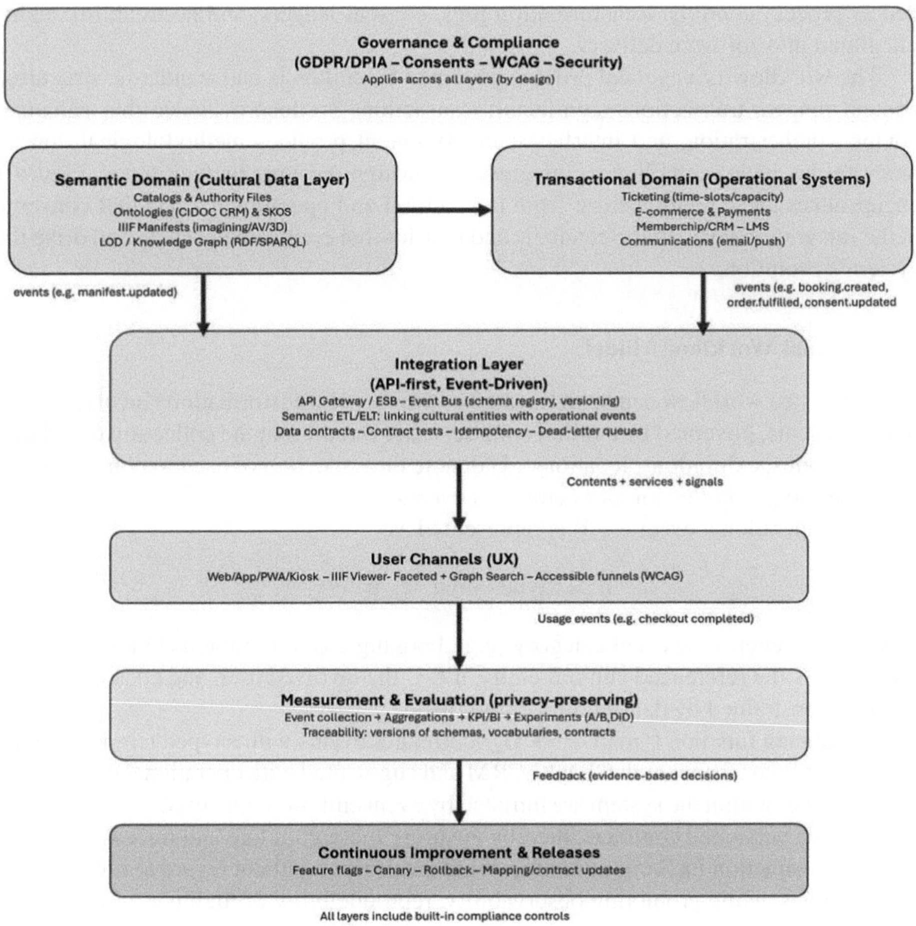

Fig. 1. The proposed workflow scheme has an API-first, event-driven integration layer with versioned schemas that lets the semantic-cultural domain (graph and manifest) and the transactional domain (reservations, e-commerce, membership) exchange identifiers and events. Public channels use content and services and send usage signals. A measurement subsystem turns events into reproducible indicators and helps with continuous improvement, with compliance checks built in at every process step.

The cycle concludes with ongoing enhancement driven by empirical evidence. New features or policies, such as modifications in time-slotting, contextual suggestions, and messaging alterations, are implemented in a regulated manner (feature flags, canary). The effects are assessed using suitable experimental designs (controlled experiments for localized changes; quasi-experiments for process alterations), and the resultant decisions exert a retroactive influence on both the semantic domain (mapping updates, enrichments, vocabulary restructuring) and the operational domain (contract evaluation, new orchestration protocols). Compliance constraints—data protection, consent management, accessibility—are not assessed retrospectively at each stage, but are embedded as process controls: transformation logs, consent ledgers, and accessibility audits integrated into software delivery.

The workflow is a cyclical process governed by contracts and standards: structured content renders transactions significant; transactions produce evidence that enhances content, orchestration, and interfaces; measurement provides methodological consistency to the cycle; compliance, integrated by design, ensures its legitimacy. Figure 1 encapsulates these relationships: from the cultural and operational strata that converge at the integration level, to the channels and metrics that complete the cycle and drive the system's evolution.

3.1 Formal Workflow Model

The suggested workflow can be delineated as a series of transformations involving entities and events, governed by explicit contracts. Let C represent the collection of cultural entities (items, exhibitions, locations), U denote the collection of pseudonymized users, and E signify the collection of operational events.

Each operational event $e \in E$ is represented as:

$$e = \langle \text{type}, \ \text{time}, \ c, \ u, \ \text{ctx} \rangle$$

where type denotes the event category (e.g., booking.created), time its temporal occurrence, $c \in C$ the referenced cultural entity, $u \in U$ the involved user, and ctx a contextual payload constrained by data-minimization rules.

A mapping function f_map: E → G_t correlates events with a typed temporal graph G_t, which is consistent with CIDOC CRM and augmented with operational event types. State changes within the system are initiated by event emissions and used by downstream services via versioned contracts, thereby ensuring loose coupling and traceability.

This abstraction facilitates thinking about the process without regard to implementation specifics, while promoting observability, reproducibility of findings, and regulated system evolution.

3.2 Governance, Versioning, and Maintainability

The system's enduring sustainability depends on clear governance structures. Schemas, APIs, and event types are governed by a registry that facilitates semantic versioning and ensures backward compatibility. Disruptive modifications require simultaneous schema implementation and controlled migration phases to maintain analytical consistency.

Semantic drift is mitigated by regularly validating mappings against reference ontologies and controlled vocabularies, employing coverage thresholds and consistency assessments. Mapping updates are versioned and associated with metric assessments, enabling attribution of observed changes to either semantic or operational factors.

Compliance standards are integrated into processes rather than applied retrospectively. Consent provenance is documented as event metadata, data minimization is implemented at the integration layer, and accessibility audits conforming to WCAG 2.2 are incorporated into release processes. These techniques facilitate maintainability, accountability, and consistent evaluation throughout time.

4 Expected Results and Discussion

The proposed workflow is expected to have measurable effects on two closely related levels: first, the quality and interoperability of cultural information (semantic consistency, traceability, observability); second, the operational results related to use and economic sustainability (conversion, capacity management, loyalty). The idea is that semantic formatting of content, which is linked to API-first and event-driven integration, is not just a technological change but a change in the information model. Identifiers and relationships become shared contracts between the cultural and transactional domains, and events in the usage channels are reported in the knowledge graph with context and provenance.

In the near future, we expect semantic mapping coverage to go up and integration costs to go down. The first can be measured by the ratio of fields mapped to reference ontologies or vocabularies to the subset of fields that are relevant to use cases. The second can be measured by the number of person-days needed for connectors, mapping, and testing for the same functional scope. Once fully operational, stable contracts and a registry scheme are available to lower integration debt and allow for gradual evolution without any problems. This has indirect benefits for time-to-market and pipeline reliability. In systems with peaks in demand, like pre-sales and temporary exhibitions, event-driven orchestration also aligns to reduce perceived latency along the funnel. Architectural decoupling lets critical parts be isolated and selectively scaled, stabilising the p95 latency of queries that combine cultural content and transactional data.

When semantic modelling and consumption channels come together, they change how people act. Systematically using interoperable manifests and search engines that use faceted navigation and graph projections makes it easier to make informed decisions about buying and participating, reducing friction during the selection and payment phases. The conversion rate can be defined in numbers as

$$\mathrm{Conv} = \frac{\mathrm{order}}{\mathrm{unique\ visitors}},$$

while no-show for slot reservations is

$$\mathrm{No} - \mathrm{show} = \frac{missedreservations}{\mathrm{total\ reservations}}$$

An anticipated rise in conversion is attributed to contextual suggestions and enhanced clarity of information. At the same time, a decrease in no-shows results from reminders and more transparent presentations of capacity and schedules. A favourable effect on loyalty is also conceivable: the (pseudonymized) integration of events throughout the journey facilitates pertinent communications and membership proposals that correspond with actual usage trends, potentially enhancing the renewal rate in the medium term. Accessibility functions as a systemic quality variable: intentionally incorporating WCAG criteria into release cycles typically diminishes abandonment at crucial stages (such as forms and payment), broadening the effective user base without imposing technical obstacles.

Empirical validation necessitates an experimental design aligned with the characteristics of the intervention. For localised modifications to the interface or messaging, a controlled online experiment is suitable; for process alterations (e.g., the introduction or restructuring of slots), a quasi-experiment utilising temporal or cohort control groups is advisable, such as in the form of difference-in-differences (DiD). In a basic two-period framework, the mean impact of the treatment can be articulated as

Y represents the principal metric (e.g., conversion) and the bars denote averages across observational units. Results reporting must encompass point estimates and 95% confidence intervals, alongside effect sizes articulated in percentage points or relative reduction, with adjustments for multiple comparisons when assessing various variants. The traceability of schema, vocabulary, and contract versions guarantees the replicability of analyses and the accurate interpretation of deviations and regressions.

The anticipated effects rely on specific operational assumptions: demand is not entirely restricted by capacity during most observation periods; the initial quality of semantic mapping is adequate to prevent interpretative leakage; and the levels of consensus permit minimal orchestration (reminders, confirmations) without surpassing data minimisation limits. Estimating effects of exogenous shocks (such as blockbuster exhibitions, tariff alterations, or weather conditions) necessitates appropriate controls, including homogeneous cohorts, temporal blocking, or available instrumental variables. Threats to validity persist and require meticulous consideration, notably selection bias (experiments conducted on more digitised segments) and semantic drift resulting from vocabulary evolution. Both issues can be alleviated through ex-ante stratification, subgroup analysis, intent-to-treat methodologies, and automatic mapping validation.

The approach supports user-centric analysis by relating interaction events to cultural context, thereby going beyond mere operational efficiency. This enables the use of adaptive personalization techniques (such as contextual recommendations and accessibility-aware interfaces) while still keeping your identity secret. You can measure engagement metrics such as dwell time per entity, recurring visits, and cross-channel transitions without adding new data collection points.

Integrating enhanced interoperability, adaptive orchestration, and stringent measurement aligns cultural objectives with economic sustainability without compromising the former for the latter. Moderate conversion enhancements, reduced no-shows, and improved WCAG compliance on essential pages can exert considerable macroeconomic impacts on project life cycles. At the same time, diminished integration efforts liberate resources for more valuable pursuits (curation, education, research). The generalizability of archives and libraries is substantial due to the similarity in their semantic and search components; conversely, the impact on funnels is contingent upon the transactional intensity and nature of the services provided.

4.1 Evaluation Dimensions and Metrics

To delineate the suggested framework beyond qualitative anticipations, we establish a series of evaluation dimensions and corresponding metrics. These dimensions show that the framework has two sides: semantic interoperability and operational performance. They also make it possible to compare it to other EBIS designs in similar situations like in Table 1.

Table1. Evaluation Dimensions and Metrics

Dimension	Metric	Definition	Baseline for comparison
Semantic interoperability	Mapping coverage	Ratio between mapped fields and fields relevant to supported use cases	Flat or ad-hoc metadata
Semantic interoperability	Traceability depth	Avg. Number of provenance links per entity/event	Isolated system logs
Integration effort	Integration cost	Person-days required for integration and evolution	Point-to-point integration
System performance	p95 latency	95th percentile response time for mixed semantic/transactional queries	Monolithic EBIS
Operational effectiveness	Conversion rate	Orders/unique visitors	Content-only funnel
Operational effectiveness	No-show rate	Missed reservations/total reservations	No reminders or slot visibility
Engagement & loyalty	Membership renewal rate	Renewals/expiring memberships	Generic CRM campaigns
Governance & compliance	WCAG adherence	Percentage of WCAG 2.2 success criteria met	Manual post-hoc audit

The expected results discussed in the remainder of this section refer explicitly to the dimensions and metrics defined above, which serve as analytical lenses for interpreting the effects of the proposed workflow.

4.2 Simulation-Based Feasibility Assessment

To enhance anticipated outcomes through preliminary operational validation, we conducted a simulation-based feasibility evaluation. The objective of this assessment is to ascertain the internal consistency of the framework, the observability of specified metrics, and the capacity to evaluate alternative architectural configurations under controlled conditions, rather than to exhibit statistically significant gains.

A synthetic dataset was created to replicate cultural entities (collections, exhibitions, places), user pathways (browsing, booking, visiting, renewing), and operational limitations (time slots, capacity constraints, seasonal demand). Event streams were generated based on time-dependent arrival rates, with demand surges synchronized to simulated exhibition launches. All user identifiers were pseudonymized, and only the essential personal attributes for event correlation were included.

Two baseline configurations were simulated: a content-centric EBIS, in which cultural data and transactional logs are loosely interconnected, and the proposed semantic-operational framework, in which events are explicitly associated with cultural entities via stable identifiers and versioned mappings. Identical demand and capacity profiles were utilized for both configurations.

The simulation validated that the proposed architecture facilitates the systematic aggregation of all measures delineated before, encompassing mapping coverage, p95 latency at peak demand, conversion rate, and no-show rate. Furthermore, the clear traceability across events, schemas, and mappings enabled the isolation of changes in architectural or semantic configurations from seasonal influences, facilitating equitable comparisons between alternatives.

This assessment does not assert performance superiority; however, the results indicate the framework's feasibility, the lack of structural bottlenecks in the event flow, and the appropriateness of the evaluation protocol for forthcoming empirical studies utilising real or anonymized institutional data.

5 Conclusions and Future Outcomes

This study presents a cohesive framework for E-Business Information Systems in the context of cultural heritage, demonstrating that the loose coupling between the semantic-cultural domain and the transactional domain, facilitated by an API-first and event-driven integration layer, can yield quantifiable advantages in interoperability, data quality, and operational outcomes. The initial premise is that the persistent implementation of open standards (event-oriented ontologies, controlled vocabularies, interoperable manifests) is not solely a technological adjustment, but represents a deliberate selection of knowledge architecture: identifiers, relationships, and events transform into stable agreements upon which to coordinate services, channels, and measurement. The reference scheme (Fig. 1) serves not as a detailed diagram but as a representation of the conceptual constraints that unify the components—content, transactions, analysis, and compliance—within a continuous improvement cycle.

From a scientific perspective, the primary contribution lies in elucidating three interrelated connections that are frequently addressed in isolation: the semantic continuity between cultural descriptions and usage events; the quantifiability of architectural impacts on observable metrics (conversion rates, no-show instances, membership renewals, p95 latency, mapping coverage); the intentional incorporation of ethical and legal constraints (privacy, accessibility) as process controls rather than retrospective evaluations. The discourse on anticipated outcomes delineated feasible orders of magnitude and replicable evaluation frameworks, elucidating assumptions and potential threats to validity. The image indicates that even modest enhancements in operational metrics and a decrease in integration efforts can substantially influence economic sustainability and user quality without undermining the cultural mission.

From a theoretical standpoint, the suggested framework can be understood through the lens of digital ecosystem governance, in which cultural institutions serve as coordinators of semantic, operational, and regulatory resources. In this way, the framework enables dynamic capabilities by allowing services and knowledge assets to be reconfigured continuously within the limits of ethics and institutions.

Nonetheless, constraints and margins of uncertainty persist. The efficacy of the workflow is contingent upon the calibre of the initial semantic mapping, adherence to schema versioning, and the implementation of comprehensive observability practices. Moreover, external factors (seasonality, major exhibitions, pricing strategies, climatic conditions) can disrupt the effects assessment. To address these factors, it is imperative to compile a corpus of benchmarks that includes datasets (public, synthetic, and anonymised real cases), contract specifications, and experimental protocols, thereby enabling equitable comparisons among architectural alternatives across various contexts.

Future advancements are progressing along four interrelated trajectories. A more comprehensive formalisation of the graph model, incorporating uncertainties, data quality, and detailed provenance, to enhance causal analysis and result interpretability and secondly, incorporating online optimisation techniques (e.g., dynamic capacity management with fairness and transparency constraints) alongside ethical safeguards and metrics reconciling economic and social goals. Third, the experimentation with inter-institutional federations utilising verifiable credentials and distributed access policies aims to facilitate content and signal sharing while maintaining data control; this approach necessitates the standardisation of domain events and interoperability testing among providers(Gaeta et al., 2025b). Fourth, creating tools for reproducibility (data catalogues and schemas, a schema registry with evolutionary compatibility, notebooks, and packages for KPI calculation) that facilitate peer review and production adoption.

Special consideration must be given to equity and prejudice in recommendation and funnel orchestration systems. In the cultural domain, the visibility and dissemination of content are not impartial: selection and recommendation mechanisms can exacerbate disparities between renowned works and obscure material, between dominant and minority languages, and between central and marginal locations. The path ahead necessitates clear criteria for procedural fairness, regular audits of models, and the engagement of relevant communities in establishing quality metrics—broadening the by-design principle from privacy to fairness.

The roadmap encompasses pilot projects across diverse institutions (museums with fluctuating demand, libraries with robust digital services, archives with enduring mandates) to evaluate the generalizability of the workflow and refine the orchestration mechanisms. The development of an operational playbook, encompassing sample contracts, event taxonomies, WCAG checklists, and DPIA models, is proposed to facilitate organisations with diverse resources in transitioning incrementally from monolithic to composable architectures.

In conclusion, the thesis posits that semantic interoperability, reactive integration, and rigorous evaluation are not merely compatible with the objectives of cultural institutions but rather a natural extension of them within the modern digital ecosystem. The proposal presented herein establishes a methodological and technical framework for designing cultural information systems that are transparent, quantifiable, and accountable. The release of supplementary materials—summary datasets, sample configurations, KPI definitions, and audit guides—is essential for establishing a community of practice that can evolve swiftly, adhering to transparency and user protection principles.

References

Baker, T., Bechhofer, S., Isaac, A., Miles, A., Schreiber, G., Summers, E.: Key choices in the design of Simple Knowledge Organization System (SKOS). J. Web Semant. **20**, 35–49 (2013). https://doi.org/10.1016/j.websem.2013.05.001

Cabane, H., Farias, K.: On the impact of event-driven architecture on performance: an exploratory study. Futur. Gener. Comput. Syst. **153**, 52–69 (2024). https://doi.org/10.1016/j.future.2023.10.021

Callaway, B., Sant'Anna, P.H.C.: Difference-in-Differences with multiple time periods. J. Econometr. **225**(2), 200–230 (2021). https://doi.org/10.1016/j.jeconom.2020.12.001

Cantone, A.A., et al.: Contextualized experiential language learning in the metaverse. In: Proceedings of the 15th Biannual Conference of the Italian SIGCHI Chapter, pp. 1–7 (2023). https://doi.org/10.1145/3605390.3605395

Casillo, M., Colace, F., Gaeta, R., Lorusso, A., Pellegrino, M.: Artificial intelligence in archaeological site conservation: trends, challenges, and future directions. J. Comput. Appl. Archaeol. **8**(1), 224–241 (2025). https://doi.org/10.5334/jcaa.207

Casillo, M., Colace, F., Lorusso, A., Santaniello, D., Valentino, C.: Integrating physical and virtual experiences in cultural tourism: an adaptive multimodal recommender system. IEEE Access **13**, 28353–28368 (2025). https://doi.org/10.1109/ACCESS.2025.3539205

Cecere, L., Grimaldi, M., Lorusso, A., Marra, A., Stoia, F.: Immersive urban planning: evaluating park safety perception with digital twins and metaverse simulation. Sustainability **17**(17), 7608 (2025). https://doi.org/10.3390/su17177608

Chhetri, T.R., Kurteva, A., DeLong, R.J., Hilscher, R., Korte, K., Fensel, A.: Data protection by design tool for automated GDPR compliance verification based on semantically modeled informed consent. Sensors **22**(7), 2763 (2022). https://doi.org/10.3390/s22072763

Clarizia, F., et al.: A multilevel graph approach for rainfall forecasting: a preliminary study case on London area. Concurr. Comput. Pract. Exp. **32**(8). https://doi.org/10.1002/cpe.5289

Colace, F., Gaeta, R., Lorusso, A., Pellegrino, M., Santaniello, D.: New AI challenges for cultural heritage protection: a general overview. J. Cult. Herit. **75**, 168–193 (2025). https://doi.org/10.1016/j.culher.2025.07.019

Colace, F., Lombardi, M., Pascale, F., Santaniello, D., Tucker, A., Villani, P.: MuG: a multi-level graph representation for big data interpretation. In: 2018 IEEE 20th International Conference on High Performance Computing and Communications; IEEE 16th International Conference on Smart City; IEEE 4th International Conference on Data Science and Systems (HPCC/SmartCity/DSS), pp. 1408–1413 (2018).https://doi.org/10.1109/HPCC/SmartCity/DSS.2018.00233

Davis, E., Heravi, B.: Linked data and cultural heritage. J. Comput. Cult. Herit. **14**(2), 1–18 (2021). https://doi.org/10.1145/3429458

De Simone, M.C., Lorusso, A., Santaniello, D.: Predictive maintenance and structural health monitoring via IoT system. In: 2022 IEEE Workshop on Complexity in Engineering (COMPENG), pp. 1–4 (2022). https://doi.org/10.1109/COMPENG50184.2022.9905441

Gaeta, A., Loia, V., Lorusso, A., Orciuoli, F., Pascuzzo, A.: Computational analysis of Information Disorder in Cognitive Warfare. Online Social Netw. Media **48**, 100322 (2025). https://doi.org/10.1016/j.osnem.2025.100322

Gaeta, A., Loia, V., Lorusso, A., Orciuoli, F., Pascuzzo, A.: Towards a LLM-based intelligent system for detecting propaganda within textual content. Comput. Electr. Eng. **128**, 110765 (2025). https://doi.org/10.1016/j.compeleceng.2025.110765

Gaeta, A., Loia, V., Orciuoli, F.: An explainable prediction method based on Fuzzy Rough Sets, TOPSIS and hexagons of opposition: applications to the analysis of Information Disorder. Inf. Sci. **659**, 120050 (2024). https://doi.org/10.1016/j.ins.2023.120050

Grimaldi, M., Giordano, C., Graziuso, G., Barba, S., Fasolino, I.: A GIS-BIM approach for the evaluation of urban transformations: a methodological proposal. WSEAS Trans. Environ. Dev. **18**, 247–254 (2022). https://doi.org/10.37394/232015.2022.18.26

Haller, A., et al.: The modular SSN ontology: a joint W3C and OGC standard specifying the semantics of sensors, observations, sampling, and actuation. Semantic Web **10**(1), 9–32 (2018). https://doi.org/10.3233/SW-180320

Huang, Y.Y., Yu, S.S., Chu, J.J., Fan, H.H., Du, B.B.: Using knowledge graphs and deep learning algorithms to enhance digital cultural heritage management. Herit. Sci. **11**(1), 204 (2023). https://doi.org/10.1186/s40494-023-01042-y

Hyvönen, E., Rantala, H.: Knowledge-based relational search in cultural heritage linked data. Digital Schol. Human. **36**(Supplement_2), ii155–ii164 (2021). https://doi.org/10.1093/llc/fqab042

Isaac, A., Haslhofer, B.: Europeana Linked Open Data – data.europeana.eu. Semant. Web **4**(3), 291–297 (2013). https://doi.org/10.3233/SW-120092

Kohavi, R., Tang, D., Xu, Y.: Trustworthy Online Controlled Experiments. Cambridge University Press, Cambridge (2020). https://doi.org/10.1017/9781108653985

Kruczek, Z., Gmyrek, K., Ziżka, D., Korbiel, K., Nowak, K.: Accessibility of cultural heritage sites for people with disabilities: a case study on Krakow museums. Sustainability **16**(1), 318 (2023). https://doi.org/10.3390/su16010318

Nishioka, C., Nagasaki, K.: Understanding IIIF image usage based on server log analysis. Digital Schol. Human. **36**(Supplement_2), ii210–ii221 (2021). https://doi.org/10.1093/llc/fqab040

Pahl, C., Jamshidi, P.: Microservices: a systematic mapping study. In: Proceedings of the 6th International Conference on Cloud Computing and Services Science, 137–146 (2016). https://doi.org/10.5220/0005785501370146

Pellegrino, M.A., Scarano, V., Spagnuolo, C.: Move cultural heritage knowledge graphs in everyone's pocket. Semant. Web **14**(2), 323–359 (2022). https://doi.org/10.3233/SW-223117

Roth, J., Sant'Anna, P.H.C., Bilinski, A., Poe, J.: What's trending in difference-in-differences? A synthesis of the recent econometrics literature. J. Econometr. **235**(2), 2218–2244 (2023). https://doi.org/10.1016/j.jeconom.2023.03.008

Sanderson, R.: Implementing linked art in a multi-modal database for cross-collection discovery. Open Libr. Human. **1**(1) (2024). https://doi.org/10.16995/olh.15407

Snydman, S., Sanderson, R., Cramer, T.: The international image interoperability framework (IIIF): a community & technology approach for web-based images. Arch. Conf. **12**(1), 16–21 (2015). https://doi.org/10.2352/issn.2168-3204.2015.12.1.art00005

Vega-Gorgojo, G.: LOD4Culture: easy exploration of cultural heritage linked open data. Semant. Web **15**(5), 1563–1592 (2024). https://doi.org/10.3233/SW-233358

Yap, J.Q.H., Kamble, Z., Kuah, A.T.H., Tolkach, D.: The impact of digitalisation and digitisation in museums on memory-making. Curr. Issue Tour. **27**(16), 2538–2560 (2024). https://doi.org/10.1080/13683500.2024.2317912

Zhang, L.: Empowering linked data in cultural heritage institutions: a knowledge management perspective. Data Inf. Manag. **6**(3), 100013 (2022). https://doi.org/10.1016/j.dim.2022.100013

Ontology-Grounded Fact-Checking for E-Commerce: A Neuro-Symbolic, Claim-Centric Approach

Mario Casillo[1(✉)], Liliana Cecere[2], Angelo Gaeta[3], Marco Lombardi[1], Angelo Lorusso[3], and Giusy Strollo[4]

[1] DiSPaC, University of Salerno, Fisciano, SA, Italy
{mcasillo,malombardi}@unisa.it
[2] DIIn University of Salerno, Fisciano, SA, Italy
lcecere@unisa.it
[3] DISAMIS, University of Salerno, Fisciano, SA, Italy
{agaeta,alorusso}@unisa.it
[4] DICiv, University of Salerno, Fisciano, SA, Italy
g.strollo9@studenti.unsia.it

Abstract. Misinformation in e-business—discounts based on volatile prices, fictitious stock levels, erroneous certifications, and implausible delivery commitments—erodes trust, competition, and regulatory adherence. This study introduces EBFN-Detect, a neuro-symbolic framework for claim-centric verification that incorporates a domain ontology (EBFN-O), a commercial knowledge graph, and natural language processing models. The pipeline extracts claims from diverse sources, conducts entity linking for products, brands, and sellers, retrieves ontology-guided evidence (RAG on KG), and assesses truthfulness by integrating a claim-evidence aware classifier with symbolic verifications of temporal consistency, price plausibility, and regulatory compliance. The output generates calibrated probabilities and verifiable explanations derived from supported or refuted chains with provenance. The work delineates the method, introduces EBFN-O in accordance with schema.org/GoodRelations/PROV-O, presents a multi-source corpus annotated at three tiers (claim, linking, truth) with reproducible guidelines, describes a RAG + KG pipeline featuring transparent fusion and calibration, and proposes an evaluation protocol that integrates metrics of accuracy, retrieval quality, and explanatory utility. Consequently, EBFN-Detect demonstrates enhancements in macro F1 and Brier/ECE relative to pure neural baselines, exhibiting significant benefits in time-sensitive scenarios and in categories characterized by substantial variant ambiguity, thereby delineating a feasible approach to dependable, traceable, and contestable verification in digital commerce.

Keywords: Knowledge Graphs · Explainable Artificial Intelligence · Probability Calibration

Published by Springer Nature Switzerland AG 2027
J. Kim et al. (Eds.): EBISION 2025, IFIP AICT 786, pp. 213–230, 2027.
https://doi.org/10.1007/978-3-032-26616-3_14

1 Introduction

The growing digitization of promotional and sales channels has heightened the exposure of consumers and economic agents to potentially deceptive content. Misinformation in e-business is evident through unrealistic discount calculations based on inflated reference prices, availability claims unsupported by actual inventory, improper use of trademarks or certifications, non-compliant delivery assurances and return policies, and unsubstantiated technical performance assertions. These practices erode trust in marketplaces, incur compliance costs and sanction risks, and, most importantly, distort competition (Colace, Lombardi, Pascale, & Santaniello, 2018a; Gaeta et al., 2024; Grimaldi et al., 2022; Kotonya & Toni, 2020). This study adopts a claim-centric perspective, defining a "claim" as a verifiable assertion about entities within the domain—product, brand, seller, or offer. We classify claims along a truth axis comprising "true," "false," "misleading," and "unverifiable," with the intermediate category encompassing instances where the statement is partially accurate yet presented out of context or in a misleading manner(Casillo et al., 2024; Jiang et al., 2020).

Technological advancements in neural NLP have enhanced the efficacy of text classification; however, they exhibit limitations in scenarios necessitating semantic grounding, numerical-temporal reasoning, and traceable explanations. Standard e-business verifications rely on the exact correspondence between text and entities (SKUs, variants, bundles), jurisdictional and temporal validity constraints, and access to diverse evidence, including unstructured documents, semantic markup (e.g., JSON-LD), historical pricing data, commercial policies, and comparison pages(Gaeta et al., 2025b; Karpukhin et al., 2020). The dynamic nature of promotional language introduces drift phenomena that necessitate robust systems to manage variation in style and communication strategies (Cantone et al., 2023; Gaeta et al., 2025a; Wu et al., 2020).

This research is motivated by the necessity to integrate accuracy, transparency, and robustness: a system is required to identify deceptive statements prevalent in transactional contexts consistently; concurrently, decisions must be explicable and subject to challenge to facilitate internal audits, consumer protection, and regulatory oversight, while minimizing costs associated with complaints, penalties, and erosion of trust.

To tackle these challenges, we propose EBFN-Detect, a neuro-symbolic framework that amalgamates a domain ontology and a knowledge graph with contemporary NLP models (Colace, Lombardi, Pascale, Santaniello, et al., 2018b). The primary concept is to integrate the extraction of claims and their association with a knowledge graph alongside semantically guided evidence retrieval (Retrieval-Augmented Generation on graph) and an assessment of veracity achieved by amalgamating neural signals with symbolic rules that delineate constraints of temporal consistency, price plausibility, and regulatory compliance (Cicalese et al., 2024; Colace et al., 2019; Graziuso et al., 2020). This integration enhances the precision and calibration of predictions while generating verifiable explanations through chains of evidence that substantiate or contradict each assertion, facilitating informed audits and disputes (De Simone et al., 2022).

The objectives of this work are fourfold and interrelated: to define and release EBFN-O, an ontology for misinformation in e-business that aligns with established vocabularies (schema.org, GoodRelations, PROV-O) to ensure interoperability and traceability; to construct a multi-source annotated corpus that distinctly differentiates between claim extraction, ontological linking, and truth labeling; to design and assess an architecture that integrates RAG on knowledge graphs with neural classifiers and symbolic checks to achieve explainable and accurately calibrated decisions; and finally, to establish a comprehensive benchmark with metrics for classification, calibration, and evidence retrieval, supplemented by ablation studies and robustness tests to isolate the contributions of individual components.

The proposal facilitates immediate applications. Proactive validation of commercial assertions and subsequent diminution of grievances and sanctions; enhanced consumer transparency through verifiable elucidations; assistance for regulatory bodies with comprehensive traceability of origins. The following chapters delineate related work, methodology, ontology, data collection/annotation decisions, the evaluation protocol accompanied by error analysis, an ethical discourse highlighting primary limitations, and ultimately, the conclusions alongside prospects for real-world implementation.

In addition to being accurate, e-commerce fact-checking systems must work in environments with many users, an unstable market, and differing rules across businesses. Product catalogs change quickly, promotional language changes constantly, and compliance rules vary from one place to another and from one moment to the next. These traits put purely data-driven methods to the test because they typically lack clear ways to handle changes in regulations, time limits, and differences across entities. This study addresses scalability with a modular design that separates knowledge graph updates, ontology evolution, and neural retraining. This allows for gradual adaptation to new goods, markets, and legal settings without the need for complete system retraining.

The principal premise of this work is that neither neural-only nor symbolic-only solutions are sufficient to facilitate effective claim verification in digital commerce. Neural models are robust to changes in language, but they struggle with consistency in numbers, validity over time, and grounding in rules. On the other hand, symbolic techniques are easy to understand and accurate, but they aren't strong against changes in language or missing information. EBFN-Detect is specifically designed to fill this gap by integrating claim-evidence neural inference with ontology-driven retrieval and symbolic consistency tests. This way, each part can make up for the others' weaknesses.

Taken together, this work positions ontology-grounded, neuro-symbolic fact-checking as a scalable and extensible foundation for trustworthy verification in e-commerce, and lays the groundwork for future public benchmarks and cross-market evaluations in this domain.

2 Related works

The way research is done on identifying misinformation and automated fact-checking has evolved. It has moved from being centred on documents and phrases to being centred on claims. It also uses systems that retrieve and verify evidence. The previous approach treated disinformation as a single textual classification issue, achieving favourable results on general datasets, but proving vulnerable when associating with real entities or requiring temporal or numerical reasoning (Clarizia et al., 2020; Zhou & Zafarani, 2021). The claim-centric approach has led to the development of benchmarks and pipelines in which the assertion serves as the analytical unit and truth is evaluated based on external evidence, as demonstrated by FEVER (Thorne et al., 2018). However, most resources continue to focus on news and politics, paying little attention to the transactional contexts characteristic of e-business.

At the same time, organised knowledge has become increasingly crucial in retrieving evidence and reasoning: knowledge graphs reduce the hallucination of neural models and improve retrieval precision, especially when entity linking is a fundamental part of the process (Hogan et al., 2022). KG-augmented methodologies combine entity linking, structured queries, and neural networks on graphs to disseminate signals among entities and relations (Schlichtkrull et al., 2018), as well as embeddings such as ComplEx for link prediction. However, the integration of e-business is still limited: encyclopedic graphs effectively represent generic entities, but often fail to encapsulate commercial specifics (SKUs, bundles, time-sensitive offers) or the connection between promotional assertions and their regulatory and market origins(Guha et al., 2016; Hepp, 2008).

Advancements in Transformers have facilitated hybrid strategies in which the neural component is 'grounded' by retrieval-augmented pipelines: evidence obtained from document engines or graphs informs generation or classification, thereby reducing reliance on text statistics alone. However, structural issues persist, including the precise alignment of mentions with product, brand, and seller identities, the explicit consideration of temporal factors such as price validity and promotional periods, numerical plausibility concerning historical data, and modelling compliance regulations that differ by jurisdiction. These elements are crucial to e-business, yet they are rarely formalised as symbolic constraints during decision-making (Hogan et al., 2022; Schlichtkrull et al., 2018).

Another issue is explainability and calibration: although techniques and generated explanations improve readability, their accuracy concerning the decision-making process is often questioned. At the same time, metrics such as ECE and Brier score are sometimes disregarded, despite their importance when confidence scores affect operational workflows (Atanasova et al., 2020; BRIER, 1950).

In high-stakes situations like marketplaces, it is crucial that the estimated probability accurately represents the actual risk, and that the explanations are verifiable and traceable (Baker et al., 2013; BRIER, 1950; CHESÑEVAR et al., 2006).

The literature offers essential components—claim-centric verification, KG-enhanced retrieval, ontological standards for commerce, and methods for explainability and calibration—yet reveals a deficiency at the convergence of these domains within e-business. The primary deficiencies pertain to the absence of claim-centric datasets with verifiable provenance and distinct claim categories (price, availability, certifications), the nascent application of ontologies as a cohesive and explicable reasoning framework, and the insufficient focus on calibration in actual decision-making contexts. The proposed framework precisely occupies this domain, integrating ontology and commercial knowledge graphs to facilitate retrieval and consistency verification, amalgamating neural and symbolic elements for truthfulness assessment, and ensuring decision-making is auditable via chains of evidence.

3 Methodology

The proposed methodology, EBFN-Detect, integrates neural and symbolic components within a pipeline comprising distinct yet closely interconnected steps. The concept involves treating each statement as an object extracted from the text, grounding it concerning domain entities and constraints, and verifying it against pertinent and traceable evidence. The pipeline (Fig. 1) initiates with the ingestion of sources (advertisements, product pages, social commerce, comparison sites, press releases), wherein each document is normalized (HTML/JSON-LD), deduplicated, and augmented with temporal and provenance metadata. At this juncture, any semantic markups (e.g., Product, Offer, AggregateOffer, or ClaimReview) are converted into candidate triples and associated with a "commercial" knowledge graph encompassing products, brands, sellers, offers, and domain regulations.

The EBFN-Detect pipeline is structured as a modular sequence of components, each with well-defined inputs, outputs, and functions. This modularization is deliberate: it facilitates reproducibility, permits focused ablation research, and allows individual components (e.g., entity linking, evidence retrieval, symbolic validation) to develop autonomously in response to domain drift or regulatory modifications. Each module can be assessed independently, whereas the end-to-end pipeline simulates authentic deployment scenarios.

We implement a claim extraction module on the standardized text, functioning in two phases: a language model (seq2seq or classifier with span extraction) detects sentences containing verifiable assertions, followed by a refiner that nominalizes the content into a structured format, delineating the propositional component (e.g., 'Product X is 70% off until Sunday') and semantic arguments (entities, quantities, dates, conditions). This representation is transmitted to semantic linking, which correlates mentions with entities in the graph (SKU, variants, merchants, campaigns) utilizing a hybrid engine: A primary stage of dense/lexical retrieval narrows down the candidates, while a neural reranker functions pairwise between the mention and the entity profile; in cases of ambiguity, the system prefers resolutions that align with binding attributes (category, brand, region, time frame).

Upon alignment of the claim, the system commences ontology-driven evidence retrieval. In this context, formal knowledge functions as a "semantic filter": the category of the assertion (price, availability, certification, delivery promise, returns, warranty) dictates the permissible sources and the constraints that must be adhered to (e.g., for a discount, the validity of the reference price within a prior timeframe; for a delivery promise, the geographical scope of the courier; for a certification, the inclusion of the certificate in recognized registries). The retrieval integrates structured queries on the graph (for relationships and attributes) with document searches on a textual index; the outcomes are consolidated into a "file" of evidence containing citations, timestamps, and provenance chains.

Claim-evidence verification is conducted under specific supervision, wherein each claim is linked to a definitive truth label and a carefully selected array of corroborating and contradicting evidence. Claims are manually marked for validity (true, false, misleading, unverifiable), whereas evidence snippets are selected as both essential and adequate for verification. During training, the model encounters both gold evidence and challenging negative evidence from similar products or offers, thereby promoting the differentiation between ostensibly credible but erroneous reasons.

Negative sampling is deliberately regulated to mitigate misleading correlations and enhance robustness. For each assertion, negative examples include evidence from closely related SKUs, variation configurations, or offerings that are temporally mismatched. Furthermore, slight alterations in numerical values (such as discount rates or prices) and variations in promotional language are implemented, thereby preventing the model from relying on superficial lexical or numerical heuristics.

The veracity estimate is obtained from the amalgamation of two signals. The initial component is neural: a claim-evidence aware model assesses the coherence between the assertion and the evidence set, generating a distribution of labels (true, false, misleading, unverifiable). The second is symbolic: a compilation of checks that conducts deterministic or probabilistic validations on domain rules, numerical and temporal consistency, and regulatory adherence. These evaluations produce comprehensible scores (e.g., "reference price unstable for N days" or "lack of certificate in the official registry"), which are consolidated through a straightforward yet transparent fusion function (e.g., a linear combination with optimized weights, or supervised logistic stacking). To render the score applicable in decision-making, we implement a post-hoc calibration that adjusts the estimated probabilities to correspond with the observed empirical frequency, ensuring that thresholds and escalation policies accurately represent actual risk.

The ultimate truth score is derived by integrating neural and symbolic information through a clear, transparent fusion methodology. Let p_n(y|c,e) represent the probability distribution of labels generated by the claim-evidence neural classifier, and let s_k(c) signify the outputs of symbolic validations (e.g., temporal validity, pricing plausibility, regulatory compliance), normalized within the interval [0,1]. The conclusive decision score is calculated using a supervised fusion function, executed as either a linear combination or logistic stacking, with parameters derived from the development set.

Explanations are produced by compiling a succinct claim-oriented 'evidence set': the pipeline identifies multiple representative pieces of evidence and connects them through ontological relations (supports/refutes/derivedFrom/validDuring), thereby constructing a coherent narrative that substantiates the conclusion (e.g. "the 70% reduction is predicated on a price that exhibits instability within the designated timeframe," supplemented by references to excerpts and price charts). When the neural model and symbolic evaluations are inconsistent, the system underscores the divergence and denotes considerable doubt, favoring human review.

Post-hoc probability calibration is applied to the fused model output to ensure that predicted confidence scores accurately reflect empirical correctness. Calibration is conducted on a reserved validation set using standard methodologies and is assessed using the Brier score and Expected Calibration Error. Calibration is applied to the entire hybrid decision function rather than solely to the neural component, ensuring that symbolic constraints are fully incorporated into the final confidence estimates.

Explanations are produced by compiling a concise, evidence-based set of claims that demonstrate both neurological significance and symbolic validation. Each explanation clearly relates the claim with chosen evidence snippets via ontological relations (e.g., supports, refutes, validDuring), supplemented by provenance metadata and a compilation of activated symbolic checks. When neurological and symbolic signals conflict, this discrepancy is highlighted in the explanation, facilitating uncertainty-aware human evaluation instead of mandated automation.

The neural models are trained using a composite objective that integrates classification loss, semantic robustness terms (contrastive learning on challenging negatives from similar products), and, when applicable, a penalty for inadequate calibration. To prevent spurious dependencies, the sampling of negative evidence is regulated: for each claim, pertinent yet inconclusive documents are incorporated, and realistic perturbations (promotional paraphrases, minimal numerical variations) are introduced to enhance resilience against pattern shortcuts. The symbolic component is constructed as a versioned knowledge base: the rules are articulated in declarative format, evaluated through property-based testing on synthetic scenarios, and subjected to canary assessment using simulated real traffic to guarantee that domain evolution (new campaigns, revised legal terms) does not impair performance.

From an infrastructural perspective, the knowledge graph is refreshed via regular ETL processes and quality assurance measures (consistency of identifiers, sameAs relations with external catalogs, management of variants). Entity IDs and page versions facilitate traceability: every decision is reproducible as queries on the graph and indexes are documented alongside the temporal snapshot of the sources. Ultimately, to reduce operational application, the system output comprises the label, the calibrated probability, a structured explanation with citations, and a collection of symbolic flags indicating the checks that have been passed or failed; this framework enables both automation (e.g., obstructing high-risk campaigns) and effective human auditing.

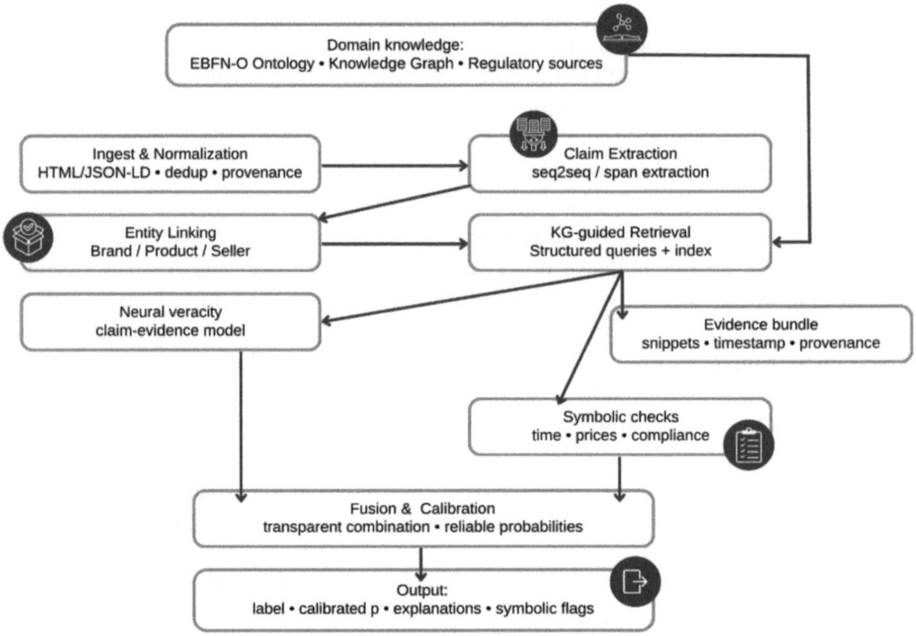

Fig. 1. Pipeline of EBFN-Detect.

4 Support Ontology

The EBFN-O ontology delineates the concepts and relationships essential for validating standard e-business assertions, preserving connections to sources, context, and constraints for each decision-making process. The core is distinctly claim-centric: each claim pertains to one or more entities within the domain (product, brand, seller, offer) and is associated with evidence that substantiates or contradicts it, maintaining its provenance and temporal relevance. To guarantee interoperability, EBFN-O conforms to recognized vocabularies: schema.org for products, offers, and ClaimReview; GoodRelations for commercial attributes and offer classifications; PROV-O for traceability; AIF for the supports/refutes argumentative framework; SKOS for taxonomy administration (claim types, product categories, source types). The design prioritizes three attributes: (i) Verifiability—each supporting or refuting arc must be substantiated by quotable excerpts and provenance metadata (URI, timestamp, version); (ii) Explicit constraints—temporal factors, pricing, and regulatory compliance are depicted as inspectable relationships and attributes; (iii) Minimal assumption—elementary axioms that facilitate consistency reasoning without enforcing obscure inferences.

The competency questions that direct EBFN-O exemplify our domain: What evidence substantiates or contradicts a discount claim for a particular product within a defined jurisdiction and temporal framework? Has the reference price utilized in the promotion remained consistent for the designated duration? Does the delivery commitment align with logistics capabilities and shipping terms? Addressing these inquiries necessitates classes including Claim, Evidence, Product, Offer, Price, Promotion, Certification, Jurisdiction, Regulation, Source, and MediaItem, along with relationships such as claimsAbout, supports, refutes, derivedFrom, validDuring, hasPrice, hasReferencePrice, soldBy, and sameAs. A statement like "–70% off Product X until Sunday" will be based on the accurate SKU, supplemented with the promotional timeframe, associated with historical pricing data, and verified against the criteria establishing the validity of the price reference.

The ontology facilitates reproducible queries by offering SPARQL query patterns on graphs that integrate structured searches (e.g., obtaining all supporting/refuting evidence along with associated derivedFrom and validDuring) alongside filters for jurisdiction and temporal intervals. The commercial knowledge graph utilized by EBFN-O is informed by product, brand, and seller identities, which correspond to external catalogs (via sameAs) and temporal versions of pages, ensuring verifications align with the web's state at the time of the assertion.

The corpus is constructed by amalgamating various authentic sources: advertising creatives, social commerce posts, product pages, promotional landing pages, official brand press releases, blogs, feeds, price comparison sites, technical data sheets, and fact-checking pages featuring ClaimReview. The ingestion process consolidates formats (HTML, JSON-LD, PDF), implements deduplication and normalization, extracts temporal metadata, preserves snapshots and original URIs for complete reproducibility, and retrieves existing semantic markup (e.g., Product/Offer/AggregateOffer). Without complete markup, automated extraction processes obtain entities, numerical attributes (such as prices, discount percentages, and quantities), and temporal references, which are subsequently aligned with the commercial knowledge graph.

To mitigate bias and leakage, sampling encompasses various product categories, price ranges, and publication channels, while restricting the occurrence of multiple variants of the same product within a single partition. Each document includes metadata specifying language, country/jurisdiction, collection timestamp, and, when applicable, page version.

Annotation occurs in three synchronized phases. Initially, claim extraction involves the annotator identifying the minimal span that conveys a verifiable assertion and documenting a normalized format (subject–predicate–arguments), while also noting the claim type (price, availability, certification, delivery promise, returns/warranty, performance) and contextual elements (date(s), conditions, geographical area). Secondly, ontological linking: the textual reference is anchored to Product/Brand/Seller/Offer within the graph, incorporating pertinent attributes such as hasPrice/hasReferencePrice, validDuring, inJurisdiction, soldBy, and clarifying ambiguities between SKUs and variants. Third, truth labeling: the assertion is categorized as true, false, misleading, or unverifiable; in cases of dishonesty, the specific factor is identified (e.g., improper calculation basis, lack of context, variant ambiguity, etc.). Every annotation must comprise at least two pieces of evidence accompanied by verifiable citations and a chain of origin (PROV) to facilitate auditing and reanalysis.

An external reviewer assesses Quality through dual annotation and conflict resolution; we evaluate concordance using Cohen's κ or Krippendorff's α for both the claim type and the truth label. Persistent ambiguities necessitate revisions to the guidelines with illustrative positive and negative examples. Regarding compliance, we implement data minimization, pseudonymization of personal data, and a restricted retention policy in accordance with the GDPR; all removal and anonymization decisions are documented in the provenance graph.

The train/dev/test split is conducted by source and product family to enhance robust evaluations, minimizing spurious correlations and promoting generalization. A typical configuration comprises 10,000 documents in the training set (approximately 25,000 claims), 2,000 in the development set (approximately 5,000 claims), and 2,000 in the test set (approximately 5,000 claims), ensuring balanced distributions by claim type and language. Alongside fundamental statistics (document/claim count, average length, label distribution), we will provide metrics on linking coverage (percentage of claims with disambiguated entities), evidence completeness (evidence per claim), and temporal latitude (frequency of verifications necessitating historical data) (Table 1).

Table 1. Competency Questions (CQs)

ID	Question
CQ1	What evidence supports or refutes a claim of a **discount** on a product in a specific **time frame** and **jurisdiction**?
CQ2	Has the **reference price** used to declare the discount remained **stable** for the period required by applicable legislation?
CQ3	Is a **delivery promise** consistent with the stated **logistical coverage, geographical area**, and **conditions**?
CQ4	Is the use of a **certification/mark** supported by a **record in the official register** and is it **valid** for the period indicated?
CQ5	Are the statements regarding **availability** ('in stock') consistent with the seller's **historical stock data** and **lead times**?
CQ6	Are there any **numerical inconsistencies** (unit price vs quantity; discount vs final price) that make the claim **misleading**?

4.1 Error Assessment and Analysis

The assessment of the EBFN-Detect system seeks to quantify predictive accuracy, evidence retrieval quality, probability calibration, and explanatory utility in realistic operational contexts in a balanced fashion. Data partitioning adheres to criteria based on source and product family to prevent overly optimistic estimates, thereby minimizing spurious correlations between training and testing data and promoting generalization to analogous yet distinct domains. All outcomes are presented as means and standard deviations across various seeds, with confidence intervals derived from bootstrap methods and statistical comparisons between models conducted using non-parametric tests when applicable.

To contextualize the evaluation results, EBFN-Detect is compared with two alternative configurations: a neural-only baseline that relies solely on the claim-evidence neural classifier without ontology-guided retrieval or symbolic validation, and a symbolic-only baseline that employs ontology-driven retrieval and rule-based validation without neural inference. All configurations use identical claim extraction and entity linking components, facilitating standardized and equitable comparisons.

Ground truth is defined as the set of human-assigned veracity labels for each extracted claim (true, false, misleading, or unverifiable), determined through a three-tier annotation procedure involving double annotation and dispute resolution. Evaluation relies on gold labels and gold evidence established during this process. To calculate accuracy, recall, precision, and macro- and micro-F1 scores, the predicted claim label is compared with the gold veracity label at the claim level.

For retrieval evaluation, ground truth consists of a set of gold evidence specific to each claim. During annotation, each claim is associated with a limited number of evidence snippets deemed necessary and sufficient by annotators to support or refute the claim, along with metadata such as source URI, timestamp, and excerpt boundaries. Retrieval metrics such as Precision@k, Recall@k, and nDCG@k are computed by comparing the ranked list of retrieved items to this gold evidence set. A retrieved item is considered relevant if it satisfies the matching criterion described below and corresponds to a gold evidence snippet or its parent document.

Criterion for matching. When excerpt IDs are provided, relevance matching is done at the snippet level. If not, it is done at the document level using source URL/version identifiers. When several snippets come from the same document, relevance is counted only once at the document level for retrieval metrics that operate on documents, and once for each snippet for metrics that operate on snippets. This standard ensures that categorisation and retrieval scores are based on veracity labels and evidence that people have checked and can be traced and repeated.

The primary metric for veracity classification is the macro F1 score, selected to equilibrate potentially imbalanced classes such as misleading and unverifiable, supplemented by AUC-ROC for a threshold-independent perspective and micro F1 for overall performance assessment. Given that the system's decisions initiate subsequent actions (campaign suspension, human audit, request for correction), probability calibration is pivotal: we employ the Brier score as a comprehensive metric of probabilistic accuracy and assess the Expected Calibration Error through adaptive binning, supplemented by reliability diagrams that illustrate the disparity between average confidence and empirical frequency. Calibration is conducted post-hoc on the fusion model to represent the behavior of the entire system rather than solely the neural component. It is also validated within specific subgroups (product category, language, jurisdiction) to detect systematic variations.

Probability calibration is crucial for evaluation, as verification results directly affect subsequent actions such as campaign suspension or human auditing. Consequently, the Brier score and Expected Calibration Error are considered primary measures, and calibration is consistently applied across all assessed configurations to facilitate meaningful comparisons.

Evidence retrieval is assessed independently to analyze errors: for each claim, we examine precision@k and nDCG@k concerning a minimal set of snippets identified as necessary and sufficient by the annotators; furthermore, we evaluate recall in greater detail to gauge potential coverage. The quality of explanations is evaluated on two dimensions: fidelity and utility. Fidelity is assessed by examining the alignment between the signals that influenced the decision (activated symbolic rules, significant neural evidence) and the elements presented to the user; usefulness is evaluated through a double-masked human judgment in which expert annotators determine whether the outcome seems justified and verifiable based on the explanations provided. When there are discrepancies between internal reasoning and the provided explanation, the system is deemed under-explained, even if the prediction is accurate, as transparency is essential in regulated environments.

The test defines robustness by incorporating adverse conditions derived from actual instances: promotional paraphrases featuring lexical and rhetorical variations, numerical micro-perturbations altering discounts and prices by minimal percentage points, temporal shifts undermining the validity of promotional windows, and out-of-distribution scenarios in novel product categories. In these situations, we document the relative decline of the primary metrics and the fluctuations in calibration, intending to discern where symbolic rules mitigate the vulnerabilities of the neural model and where, conversely, excessive constraints yield false negatives.

Ablation studies delineate the contributions of various components: by excluding the knowledge graph and retaining solely neural classification, the effects of grounding can be assessed; by omitting symbolic controls, reliance on domain rules can be evaluated; by turning off structured retrieval and substituting it with text-only search, the deficit resulting from the lack of ontological constraints can be quantified. Every configuration undergoes identical calibration protocols to guarantee comparability; when the F1 difference is minimal yet significantly enhances the Brier score and ECE, we favor the better-calibrated variant, as it is more appropriate for systems with fluctuating operating thresholds and priorities.

Ablation experiments underscore the significance of each component. Eliminating ontology-guided retrieval predominantly reduces evidence precision, whereas deactivating symbolic checks results in higher false positives and inferior calibration, despite comparable macro F1 scores. These findings affirm that accuracy alone is inadequate to define system behavior in high-stakes e-commerce environments.

Error analysis provides a quantitative assessment by identifying prevalent failure types and their underlying causes. The initial group pertains to entity ambiguity, characteristic of products with closely resembling variants: linking errors result in the acquisition of accurate evidence for an incorrect SKU, yielding deceptive outcomes; in such instances, the incorporation of distinguishing attributes (capacity, color, bundle) in the entity profile mitigates confusion. A second category pertains to temporal dynamics: the disparity between the page timestamp and the discount regulatory window may render a claim seemingly valid that was not valid at the time of publication; thus, the explicit indication of validity throughout the entire evidence chain is essential. A third category pertains to numerical reasoning: discrepancies arising from rounding, taxes, or ancillary costs omitted from the final price may cause the neural model to classify true outcomes as false erroneously; the resolution entails the application of symbolic rules to standardize the calculation basis. A considerable number of errors arise from explanations that, while formally accurate, are deemed inadequate by annotators. Modifying the evidence selector to prioritize more self-sufficient snippets and contextually relevant citations enhances utility without affecting the decision-making process.

Ultimately, qualitative analysis of verification results indicates that hybrid explanations exhibit greater stability and auditability. Symbolic limitations offer clear rationales for regulatory or temporal infractions, but neural evidence selection underpins language diversity. This combination enhances the transparency and contestability of choices in expert evaluations.

5 Discussions and Limitations

Implementing EBFN-Detect in e-business environments necessitates stringent oversight of privacy, equity, transparency, and governance, alongside a comprehensive understanding of technical and operational constraints. Data collection adheres to the minimization principle: only the information essential for claim verification is obtained, retention periods are established, and accesses and modifications are monitored. The traceability of origin, structured with PROV, renders each verification auditable yet necessitates vigilance to prevent re-identification; consequently, quotable excerpts are segregated from comprehensive snapshots, modifying visibility according to usage. Fairness is evaluated through disaggregated assessments by product category, language, and channel; when discrepancies arise, adjustments are made for subgroups, and human intervention is implemented in areas of heightened uncertainty. Ontology is a focal point: taxonomies and mappings are versioned and documented to mitigate market or linguistic bias, and modification proposals are accepted via a formal review process.

Scalability in practical e-commerce settings presents issues that surpass mere dataset size. Product catalogs, pricing strategies, and advertising language evolve continually, leading to domain and temporal drift. EBFN-Detect tackles these dynamics using a modular architecture that separates ontology updates, knowledge graph refreshes, and neural model retraining. This design enables the system to slowly adapt to new products, markets, and regulatory changes without necessitating complete pipeline retraining.

Cost of deployment and workflow integration. Operationally, implementing EBFN-Detect necessitates both computational and organisational planning. Hybrid verification introduces additional costs for accessing knowledge graphs, evaluating symbolic rules, and calibrating model layers. However, these costs are predictable and modular. Neural inference efficiency improves with batch processing, while symbolic checks operate on structured attributes of limited complexity. In high-traffic systems, verification can be incorporated as an asynchronous service within existing moderation pipelines. Comprehensive hybrid validation is reserved for claims that exceed predefined risk thresholds.

The objective of workflow integration is to facilitate more accessible governance. The system output includes a label, a calibrated confidence score, activated symbolic constraints, and structured evidence references. These outputs enable seamless integration with audit dashboards and case management systems. EBFN-Detect does not replace existing moderation processes; rather, it introduces a decision-support layer that prioritises claims for review and reduces manual labour requirements.

Effort required to extend the ontology. Expanding EBFN-O to new markets or product categories is resource-intensive but feasible. Ontology evolution primarily involves incorporating new claim types, regulatory constraints, and entity attributes, while maintaining alignment with schema.org, GoodRelations, and PROV-O. Incremental addition of extensions is supported, as symbolic rules are parameterised and versioned, ensuring that existing verification logic remains unaffected. Ontology maintenance remains challenging, particularly in domains with rapidly changing rules or highly specific product taxonomies, and requires periodic expert review.

The combination of neural inference with ontology-guided retrieval and symbolic validation incurs greater computational overhead than neural-only models. This cost is mitigated through a layered execution strategy: lightweight pre-filters handle low-risk claims, while comprehensive hybrid verification is applied only beyond adjustable risk limits. The caching of recurrent evidence queries and materialized graph views further decreases latency in high-throughput situations.

Operational transparency entails that each decision is accompanied by a quantified probability, a verifiable rationale, and a disclosure of any informational deficiencies; individuals disputing the decision may present supplementary evidence, and the appeals results are integrated into the learning process to rectify persistent error patterns. Governance distinctly delineates the analytical engine from enforcement policies: the obstruction or moderation of campaigns is externally regulated, whereas modifications to ontology and graph undergo a request for alteration, review, and non-regression testing, with temporal versioning of the regulatory sources implemented.

Symbolic validation standards are tailored by country and time, allowing the framework to adapt to diverse regulatory requirements. Regulatory sources and constraints are versioned within the ontology, facilitating historical verification and mitigating errors arising from legislation revisions. In the absence of jurisdiction-specific norms or when they are vague, the system deliberately reduces confidence and highlights ambiguity for human evaluation instead of imposing possibly invalid limits.

There are definitive technical constraints. Regulations can be delicate: overly stringent rules produce false negatives, while excessively vague ones diminish their discriminatory efficacy. Synthetic test suites and progressive releases with canaries are therefore maintained. Domain drift—page formats, promotional language, regulatory frameworks—necessitates ongoing monitoring, regular retraining, and validity assessments for expiring claims. Numerical reasoning regarding prices and discounts is influenced by implementation specifics (rounding, taxes, additional costs): the symbolic element standardizes calculation foundations and clarifies assumptions, diminishing ambiguity among reference price, discount percentage, and final price. Reliance on external data, such as certification registries or stock feeds, results in delays and information deficiencies; in the absence of updates, the system generates conditional outcomes and refrains from excessively aggressive automation. Ultimately, adversarial risks exist, such as "price pulsing" or duplications with micro-linguistic variations, which are mitigated through anti-gaming controls, inter-source correlations, and semantic de-duplication.

Notwithstanding these benefits, numerous constraints persist. The efficacy of ontology grounding depends on the comprehensiveness and recency of structured sources, which can vary across product categories and markets. Numerical reasoning about prices and discounts depends on implementation specifics, including taxes, rounding policies, and additional costs, which necessitate clear normalization assumptions. Furthermore, adversarial tactics such as swift price changes or subtle language alterations might temporarily erode system trust, necessitating ongoing surveillance and adjustments to regulations.

Operational scalability necessitates a graph that is continuously updated through incremental ETL, curated sameAs alignments, and temporal page versions, alongside a stratified approach: employing light pre-filters for typical scenarios, conducting thorough checks beyond the risk threshold, and utilizing caching and materialized views for recurring evidence. All decisions are reproducible due to the documentation of queries, snapshots, and version parameters alongside the output. The roadmap anticipates the implementation of multilingual and multimodal extensions (including creative images, comparison tables, and visual badges), the enhancement of structured sources and ontological alignments, the fortification of numerical normalizations, and a regular red-teaming initiative to evaluate the system against real-world manipulation scenarios. This approach integrates specific practices—data minimization, disaggregated assessments, verifiable explanations, appeal mechanisms, and formalized governance—with a continuous improvement cycle that acknowledges existing limitations and converts them into a verifiable action plan.

These constraints immediately shape a pragmatic roadmap. Future enhancements encompass comprehensive multilingual and cross-market assessments, incorporation of multimodal evidence (e.g., photos, badges, comparison tables), improved numerical normalization, and ongoing red-teaming against actual manipulation tactics. The simultaneous introduction of a public, claim-focused benchmark for e-commerce verification would facilitate reproducible comparisons and promote additional study in this field.

6 Conclusions and Future Outcomes

This study introduced EBFN-Detect, a neuro-symbolic methodology for validating assertions in e-business, integrating domain ontology, knowledge graphs, and NLP models to generate precise, calibrated, and elucidated decisions. The salient characteristic is the transition from "isolated" textual classification to a claim-centric methodology, anchored in domain entities and constraints, and substantiated by verifiable evidence. The EBFN-O ontology offers the lexicon and constraints necessary to correlate discounts, availability, certifications, and delivery promises to queryable frameworks; the knowledge graph operationalizes these frameworks, facilitating a semantically informed retrieval that diminishes ambiguity and enhances the relevance of the evidence. Integrating neural elements and symbolic controls facilitates navigation through the ambiguities inherent in promotional marketing. At the same time, probabilistic calibration renders the outputs applicable in decision-making processes with varying thresholds and priorities. The methodological contribution includes a data quality initiative: a three-tier annotated corpus (claim, linking, truth) and an evaluation protocol that assesses not only accuracy and AUC but also Brier score, ECE, retrieval quality, and the utility of explanations, alongside robustness analysis and error taxonomy. The proposal incorporates operational practices concerning privacy, fairness, transparency, and governance, essential for adoption in regulated environments, alongside its technical components.

A principal result of this research is the assertion that explainability can be regarded as a primary design target instead of an afterthought. The framework establishes verification judgments based on clear evidence chains and symbolic limitations, facilitating traceable, contestable, and auditable results that comply with regulatory and governance standards in digital commerce.

Experimental findings indicate that the proposed hybrid design provides quantifiable advantages beyond mere precision. Compared with neural-only settings, EBFN-Detect demonstrates persistent improvements in macro F1 while significantly reducing mis-calibration, as evidenced by lower Brier scores and Expected Calibration Error. These advancements are especially pertinent in e-commerce environments, since confidence assessments directly affect automated moderation and auditing processes.

Future advancements proceed along three interrelated trajectories. The primary focus is on coverage: broadening the system to encompass additional languages and markets, incorporating multimodal signals (such as creative images, graphic badges, comparison tables, and screenshots with advanced OCR), and enhancing structured sources, including certification registers and vertical industry catalogs, to augment the breadth and precision of retrieval. The second aspect pertains to the rationality of reasoning: enhancing numerical standardization for pricing, discounts, and units of measurement; implementing anti-gaming mechanisms and inter-source correlations to mitigate strategies like price pulsing; investigating counterfactual explanations and more nuanced measures of uncertainty to provide the label with credible alternatives and absent conditions. The third guideline pertains to operational maturity: implement systematic retraining and drift monitoring, formalize synthetic and canary testing before each release, establish a closed-loop system of contestation and learning that converts appeals into new annotated examples; concurrently, design controlled studies (A/B) to assess the impact on complaints, audit durations, and erroneous removal rates, thereby informing the system's evolution with empirical evidence. In the future, a public, claim-oriented benchmark tailored to e-business, featuring traceable provenance and distinct product categories, is essential for consolidating results and enabling transparent method comparisons.

In conclusion, EBFN-Detect illustrates that integrating explicit knowledge and statistical learning is not merely an architectural decision, but a necessity for transitioning fact-checking from the "news" domain to the mechanisms that regulate trust in digital commerce. The trajectory is evident: enhanced structured and multimodal data, improved normalization; increased declarative reasoning, superior verifiability; augmented measures of uncertainty, enhanced usability. The objective is to develop a system that determines its veracity upon encountering any assertion while elucidating the rationale, degree of confidence, and supporting evidence—representing a tangible advancement towards a more transparent, competitive, and dependable e-business environment.

This study indicates that scalable fact-checking in e-commerce necessitates the amalgamation of structured knowledge, statistical learning, and explicit reasoning. EBFN-Detect offers a definitive implementation of this idea and lays the groundwork for forthcoming public benchmarks, cross-market assessments, and industrial integration. The proposed framework serves not as a definitive solution, but as an adaptable reference architecture for reliable, evidence-based verification in digital marketplaces.

References

Atanasova, P., Simonsen, J.G., Lioma, C., Augenstein, I.: Generating fact checking explanations. In: Proceedings of the 58th Annual Meeting of the Association for Computational Linguistics, pp. 7352–7364 (2020).https://doi.org/10.18653/v1/2020.acl-main.656

Baker, T., Bechhofer, S., Isaac, A., Miles, A., Schreiber, G., Summers, E.: Key choices in the design of Simple Knowledge Organization System (SKOS). J. Web Semant. **20**, 35–49 (2013). https://doi.org/10.1016/j.websem.2013.05.001

Brier, G.W.: Verification of forecasts expressed in terms of probability. Monthly Weather Rev. **78**(1), 1–3 (1950). https://doi.org/10.1175/1520-0493(1950)078<0001:VOFEIT>2.0.CO;2

Cantone, A.A., et al.: Contextualized experiential language learning in the metaverse. In: Proceedings of the 15th Biannual Conference of the Italian SIGCHI Chapter, pp. 1–7 (2023). https://doi.org/10.1145/3605390.3605395

Casillo, M., Colace, F., Lorusso, A., Santaniello, D., Valentino, C.: A multilevel graph approach for IoT-based complex scenario management through situation awareness and semantic approaches. J. Reliable Intell. Environ. **10**(4), 395–411 (2024). https://doi.org/10.1007/s40860-024-00224-0

Chesñevar, C., et al.: Towards an argument interchange format. Knowl. Eng. Rev. **21**(4), 293–316 (2006). https://doi.org/10.1017/S0269888906001044

Cicalese, F., Grimaldi, M., Fasolino, I.: The Applicability of the Urban Digital Twin in the Detailed Choices of the Urban Plan, pp. 211–220 (2024). https://doi.org/10.1007/978-3-031-54118-6_20

Clarizia, F., et al.: A multilevel graph approach for rainfall forecasting: a preliminary study case on London area. Concurr. Comput. Pract. Exp. **32**(8) (2020). https://doi.org/10.1002/cpe.5289

Colace, F., De Santo, M., Lombardi, M., Santaniello, D.: CHARS. In: Proceedings of the 1st ACM International Workshop on Technology Enablers and Innovative Applications for Smart Cities and Communities, pp. 58–61 (2019).https://doi.org/10.1145/3364544.3364830

Colace, F., Lombardi, M., Pascale, F., Santaniello, D.: A multilevel graph representation for big data interpretation in real scenarios. In: 2018 3rd International Conference on System Reliability and Safety (ICSRS), pp. 40–47 (2018).https://doi.org/10.1109/ICSRS.2018.8688834

Colace, F., Lombardi, M., Pascale, F., Santaniello, D., Tucker, A., Villani, P.: MuG: A multilevel graph representation for big data interpretation. In: 2018 IEEE 20th International Conference on High Performance Computing and Communications; IEEE 16th International Conference on Smart City; IEEE 4th International Conference on Data Science and Systems (HPCC/SmartCity/DSS), pp. 1408–1413 (2018). https://doi.org/10.1109/HPCC/SmartCity/DSS.2018.00233

De Simone, M.C., Lorusso, A., Santaniello, D.: Predictive maintenance and Structural Health Monitoring via IoT system. In: 2022 IEEE Workshop on Complexity in Engineering (COMPENG), pp. 1–4 (2022). https://doi.org/10.1109/COMPENG50184.2022.9905441

Gaeta, A., Loia, V., Lorusso, A., Orciuoli, F., Pascuzzo, A.: Computational analysis of Information Disorder in Cognitive Warfare. Online Social Netw. Media **48**, 100322 (2025). https://doi.org/10.1016/j.osnem.2025.100322

Gaeta, A., Loia, V., Lorusso, A., Orciuoli, F., Pascuzzo, A.: Towards a LLM-based intelligent system for detecting propaganda within textual content. Comput. Electr. Eng. **128**, 110765 (2025). https://doi.org/10.1016/j.compeleceng.2025.110765

Gaeta, A., Loia, V., Orciuoli, F.: An explainable prediction method based on Fuzzy Rough Sets, TOPSIS and hexagons of opposition: applications to the analysis of Information Disorder. Inf. Sci. **659**, 120050 (2024). https://doi.org/10.1016/j.ins.2023.120050

Graziuso, G., Grimaldi, M., Mancini, S., Quartieri, J., Guarnaccia, C.: Crowdsourcing data for the elaboration of noise maps: a methodological proposal. J. Phys: Conf. Ser. **1603**(1), 012030 (2020). https://doi.org/10.1088/1742-6596/1603/1/012030

Grimaldi, M., Giordano, C., Graziuso, G., Barba, S., Fasolino, I.: A GIS-BIM approach for the evaluation of urban transformations: a methodological proposal. WSEAS Trans. Environ. Dev. **18**, 247–254 (2022). https://doi.org/10.37394/232015.2022.18.26

Guha, R.V., Brickley, D., Macbeth, S.: Schema.org. Commun. ACM **59**(2), 44–51 (2016). https://doi.org/10.1145/2844544

Hepp, M.: GoodRelations: an ontology for describing products and services offers on the web, pp. 329–346 (2008). https://doi.org/10.1007/978-3-540-87696-0_29

Hogan, A., et al.: Knowledge graphs. ACM Comput. Surv. **54**(4), 1–37 (2022). https://doi.org/10.1145/3447772

Jiang, Y., Bordia, S., Zhong, Z., Dognin, C., Singh, M., Bansal, M.: HoVer: a dataset for many-hop fact extraction and claim verification. In: Findings of the Association for Computational Linguistics: EMNLP 2020, pp. 3441–3460 (2020). https://doi.org/10.18653/v1/2020.findings-emnlp.309

Karpukhin, V., et al.: Dense passage retrieval for open-domain question answering. In: Proceedings of the 2020 Conference on Empirical Methods in Natural Language Processing (EMNLP), pp. 6769–6781 (2020).https://doi.org/10.18653/v1/2020.emnlp-main.550

Kotonya, N., Toni, F.: Explainable automated fact-checking: a survey. In: Proceedings of the 28th International Conference on Computational Linguistics, pp. 5430–5443 (2020). https://doi.org/10.18653/v1/2020.coling-main.474

Schlichtkrull, M., Kipf, T.N., Bloem, P., van den Berg, R., Titov, I., Welling, M.: Modeling Relational Data with Graph Convolutional Networks, pp. 593–607 (2018). https://doi.org/10.1007/978-3-319-93417-4_38

Thorne, J., Vlachos, A., Christodoulopoulos, C., Mittal, A.: FEVER: a Large-scale dataset for fact extraction and VERification. In: Proceedings of the 2018 Conference of the North American Chapter of the Association for Computational Linguistics: Human Language Technologies, vol. 1 (Long Papers), pp. 809–819 (2018). https://doi.org/10.18653/v1/N18-1074

Wu, L., Petroni, F., Josifoski, M., Riedel, S., Zettlemoyer, L.: Scalable zero-shot entity linking with dense entity retrieval. In: Proceedings of the 2020 Conference on Empirical Methods in Natural Language Processing (EMNLP), pp. 6397–6407 (2020). https://doi.org/10.18653/v1/2020.emnlp-main.519

Zhou, X., Zafarani, R.: A survey of fake news. ACM Comput. Surv. **53**(5), 1–40 (2021). https://doi.org/10.1145/3395046

Emerging Technology

ShockShot: Enhancing Mixed Reality Immersion Through Real-Time Multisensory Physical Feedback

Bogyu Choi, Ungsik Kim, Sumin Yeon, Sang-Min Choi, and Suwon Lee(✉)

Gyeongsang National University, Jinju-si, Gyeongsangnam-do, South Korea
{chlqhrb876,blpeng,sumin.yeon,jerassi,leesuwon}@gnu.ac.kr

Abstract. This paper proposes ShockShot, a haptic system that incorporates a real gunpowder-based firing mechanism to deliver an immersive and realistic shooting experience in a mixed reality (MR) environment. Unlike conventional haptic devices that simulate recoil using vibration motors or electromagnetic force, ShockShot adopts the structural principles of a real firearm to provide embodied, multisensory feedback. The system synchronizes firing and reloading actions with the virtual environment, enabling integrated tactile, visual, and olfactory stimuli, including muzzle flash, smoke, and the scent of gunpowder. A shock sensor is used to precisely detect firing timing, and a six-degrees-of-freedom controller ensures accurate motion tracking and alignment with MR content. To evaluate its effectiveness, a user study (N = 17) compared ShockShot with commercially available gun-shaped haptic devices. The results demonstrated that the integration of realistic tactile, visual, and olfactory feedback significantly enhanced user immersion and satisfaction without increasing fatigue. These findings indicate that incorporating real physical mechanisms into MR systems can extend beyond conventional digital feedback, strengthening experiential realism and highlighting the potential of multisensory interaction for next-generation immersive applications.

Keywords: Firearm Interaction · Mixed Reality · Multisensory Feedback · Haptic Feedback · Real-world Recoil · Olfactory Interfaces · Physical-Virtual Synchronization

1 Introduction

Mixed reality (MR) integrates digital and physical environments, enabling real-time interactions with virtual objects [1]. Rapid developments in MR are offering immersive experiences across various domains, including gaming [2,3], education [4], and training simulations [5]. Beyond technological advancement, MR is increasingly positioned as a core infrastructure for emerging digital commerce ecosystems, particularly within immersive content platforms and experience-driven service markets. As immersive technologies become integral to the digital

Published by Springer Nature Switzerland AG 2027
J. Kim et al. (Eds.): EBISION 2025, IFIP AICT 786, pp. 233–251, 2027.
https://doi.org/10.1007/978-3-032-26616-3_15

economy, enhancing user engagement and experiential realism has become a key competitive factor in e-business environments.

Current MR developments are predominantly focused on audiovisual integration, which forms the bedrock for immersive experiences and enhanced realism. However, in digital content markets—especially gaming and interactive entertainment—user retention, monetization potential, and platform differentiation increasingly depend on the depth of embodied interaction. To further enrich user engagement and strengthen the commercial viability of MR-based services, sensory components such as haptic and force feedback are increasingly being incorporated into MR systems [6–9]. This development is evidenced by a growing body of research aimed at blurring the boundaries between virtual environments and the real world through haptic technologies [10–13].

Haptic feedback plays a crucial role in enabling realistic physical interactions within virtual environments [14–16]. It encompasses tactile and force feedback mechanisms that simulate physical sensations when users interact with virtual objects [17]. In immersive digital marketplaces—such as MR gaming platforms—enhanced haptic realism not only improves experiential quality but also contributes to perceived value, willingness to pay, and long-term user engagement. Numerous devices have been developed to provide haptic feedback in virtual first-person shooter (FPS) environments [18–21]. For instance, Su et al. [18] developed a haptic device that simulates recoil using vibrations, and Pamungkas et al. [21] developed a device that utilizes force feedback.

Although these methods effectively stimulate the sense of touch, they fall short of fully replicating the sensation of real-world physical interactions [22–25]. Specifically, gun-shaped haptic devices employed in MR shooting games frequently fail to reproduce the sensory complexity associated with actual firearm use [26,27]. Existing devices utilize vibration motors [18] to mimic recoil or solenoids [24,28] to deliver electromagnetic force; however, these devices do not adequately simulate the physical experience of firing an actual firearm. This limitation constrains the experiential differentiation of MR shooting platforms in competitive digital content markets.

Therefore, we propose ShockShot, a novel haptic device that utilizes a gunpowder-based firing mechanism to enhance immersion in the MR environment. In contrast to existing artificial feedback methods [29], ShockShot is designed to replicate the structure and operational principles of real guns, thereby allowing users to experience sensory feedback that closely resembles reality. From an e-business perspective, this approach strengthens experiential authenticity, which can serve as a strategic differentiator in immersive content platforms and location-based MR entertainment services. The system incorporates a lightweight, sensor-based design that accurately detects the movement of the gun and synchronizes it with the MR environment. This approach underscores the significance of tactile feedback in MR, particularly through the establishment of a streamlined reloading process optimized for speed and calibration, a pivotal component of immersive interaction and user-centered service design.

Figure 1 shows an overview of the ShockShot system and its usage in an MR FPS environment. This integration supports more intuitive and natural interaction with the virtual environment, providing a novel MR shooting experience that overcomes the limitations of conventional haptic devices and expands the commercial potential of immersive MR applications.

To assess the efficacy of ShockShot, a user study (N = 17) was conducted comparing its sensory effect with that of a commercially available gun-shaped haptic device within the same MR shooting game environment. Participants conducted a comparative experiment with ShockShot and a commercially available gun-shaped haptic device. ShockShot received favorable evaluations in terms of enjoyment, user satisfaction, and immersion. These findings suggest that enhanced haptic realism may positively influence user engagement metrics that are critical in digital entertainment markets.

The key contributions of this paper are as follows:

1. Proposing a ShockShot system that utilizes a real gunpowder-based firing mechanism.
2. Developing a physical mechanism that mirrors the use of a real gun, achieving synchronization with the MR environment.
3. Providing a more realistic shooting experience by integrating various sensory elements, thereby expanding the scope of sensory feedback in MR applications and highlighting its implications for immersive digital commerce ecosystems.

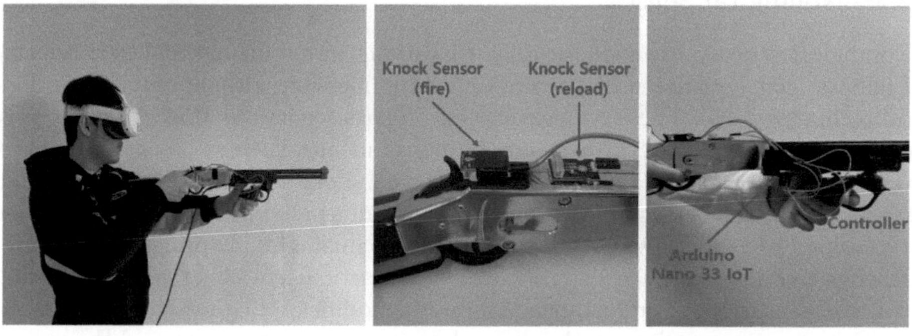

Fig. 1. ShockShot provides immersive sensation in mixed reality first-person shooter environments using a real gunpowder-based firing mechanism.

2 Related Work

2.1 Gun-Shaped Haptic Device

Gun-shaped haptic devices are designed to enhance the user's physical experience by replicating the form factor and handling characteristics of real firearms.

These devices aim to preserve the ergonomic and tactile characteristics of real guns, thereby facilitating more natural and intuitive interactions within virtual environments [30]. Early studies have shown that such devices can significantly improve immersion in virtual reality (VR) applications, particularly in scenarios involving firearm interaction [31].

Various gun-shaped haptic devices have been developed to incorporate various physical feedback mechanisms [18,20,22,23,26,27,32–34], providing a high-fidelity reproduction of the sensory experiences encountered during firearm operation, such as firing, recoil, and reloading. For example, recoil-based devices mimic the mechanical recoil of a firearm when the trigger is pulled, eliciting a physical response in the user's hand. Rahimi et al. [19] proposed a technique to adjust recoil intensity, whereas Wei et al. [20] proposed a haptic device that simulates both trigger pull force and recoil. Additional haptic feedback, such as vibrations and impact forces, further enhances the shooting sensation, making it more immersive and realistic in applications including virtual training, gaming, and simulation.

Despite notable advancements in this field, existing gun-shaped haptic devices primarily focus on simulating recoil [18,19,22,23] and maintaining realistic form factors. However, these efforts often result in a discrepancy in realism when compared to actual firearms. Furthermore, the reloading mechanisms are often oversimplified or abstracted, reducing the overall fidelity and realism of user interactions.

2.2 Nondigital Senses

Nondigital sensory experiences refer to various forms of physical and sensory feedback that enhance user perception and immersion without relying on digital technology [35]. These experiences encompass sensations that are inherently challenging to replicate through purely digital means, such as physical textures, temperature variations, tangible weight, and olfactory stimuli. By engaging these senses, users are better able to perceive and interpret virtual environments as extensions of reality. Among the available technologies, haptic and pressure-sensing technologies have been identified as particularly effective in delivering realistic sensations. For instance, vibration modules and pressure sensors can simulate tactile experiences, thereby enhancing user engagement and the overall sense of realism [36].

A growing body of research has recently emerged that explores the integration of nondigital sensory elements—beyond sight and hearing—into VR systems [28,37–43]. The integration of tangible physical elements helps mitigate the perceptual gap between real and virtual worlds, facilitating a more natural and immersive experience. This enhanced sense of presence, characterized by heightened authenticity and sensory richness, remains challenging to achieve through audiovisual stimuli alone. As noted in [40], nondigital multisensory feedback serves as a crucial conduit between the digital and physical domains, enhancing realism in virtual environments. Furthermore, [43] highlighted that the incorporation of olfactory stimuli significantly contributes to user immersion in MR settings.

These strategies can also be applied to FPS environments. Key nondigital sensory elements in such contexts include the actual weight of weapons, visible smoke, the smell of gunpowder, and the manual reloading process. These elements are important for enhancing the immersion and realism of the virtual experience. However, most existing research has focused on tactile and pressure-focused nondigital sensation with relatively few studies exploring the integration of other sensory modalities beyond sight and hearing. Consequently, significant limitations exist in integrating VR systems capable of delivering complex, multisensory experiences that are analogous to reality. Moreover, the effective and natural implementation of additional sensory elements—such as smell, temperature, and humidity—poses technical difficulties [25]. Consequently, a key challenge lies in formulating strategies for the seamless and effective integration of these supplementary sensory components within FPS environments to achieve a truly multifaceted and immersive user experience.

3 ShockShot Design

3.1 Overview

In this study, we propose ShockShot, a haptic device that uses a real gunpowder-based gun to provide a more realistic and immersive shooting experience in an MR environment. By integrating the physical structure and operational processes of a gunpowder gun into an MR environment, ShockShot enables users to experience multiple types of sensory feedback, including muzzle flashes, explosion sounds, the smell of gunpowder, and visible smoke.

Given that ShockShot incorporates a real gunpowder-based firing mechanism, safety and ethical considerations were integrated into the system design from the earliest development stages. The device was engineered for use exclusively within controlled environments under strict operational protocols. Clear visual distinctions from actual firearms, restricted access procedures, and supervised usage conditions were implemented to prevent misuse and unintended risks. Additionally, the system is intended solely for research and immersive simulation purposes, not for recreational weapon replication. By embedding safety-oriented design principles at the architectural level, ShockShot aims to balance enhanced realism with responsible technological deployment.

Users operate the gunpowder-based device by physically holding it and either pulling the trigger or performing the reloading process. The device is equipped with two sensors: one to detect the moment of firing and another to detect the reloading action. These sensor signals are transmitted wirelessly to the MR application via an Arduino, enabling immediate updates to bullet firing and magazine status within the virtual environment.

In contrast to systems that rely on virtual crosshairs or automatic aim correction, ShockShot utilizes the actual direction of the gun barrel and the user's line of sight, resulting in a heightened level of realism. While this approach may present a learning curve for novice users, it significantly enhances immersion by closely mirroring real-world shooting dynamics.

3.2 Enhance Sensory Feedback

The objective of this research is to enhance user immersion through the development of ShockShot, thereby providing a level of sensory realism that closely approximates a real shooting experience. Conventional haptic devices, which typically provide tactile feedback through vibration motors [21] or solenoid-based recoil mechanisms [24,28], fall short in replicating multisensory elements such as physical mass, odor, smoke, and actual sound generated by the firing of real gunpowder. In contrast, ShockShot is developed to provide a comprehensive sensory experience by employing an authentic gunpowder gun.

From a visual perspective, ShockShot allows users to experience the raw flash and smoke generated by ignited gunpowder, providing a significantly deeper level of immersion than virtual particle effects, which are limited to screen-based representations. Additionally, the dynamic movement and volume of smoke emitted during use further enhance the realism of the FPS environment.

Olfactory stimulation constitutes an essential sensory element that cannot be replicated by existing digital effects. The distinctive scent created by igniting gunpowder activates the user's olfactory senses, significantly enhancing the sense of realism and distinguishing the experience from conventional audiovisual-based feedback. This olfactory element plays a pivotal role in deepening user immersion in the virtual environment, addressing a longstanding limitation of conventional VR/MR shooting experiences, where the sense of smell has historically been excluded.

Complementing the olfactory feedback, the auditory experience delivers the explosive and impact sounds resulting from gunpowder combustion, providing a level of realism that digital sound alone struggles to achieve. The intensity and character of the sound vary depending on the auditory environment (e.g., indoors versus outdoors). Consequently, the ability to experience the unaltered auditory characteristics of a real gunpowder gun contributes to a more three-dimensional immersive auditory experience.

The manual reloading mechanism serves as the culminating element of this multisensory feedback system. In conventional MR shooting games, reloading is typically reduced to a simple button press or gesture. However, ShockShot restores the full physicality of loading real gunpowder, imparting the tension and realism associated with the use of a real weapon. The reloading process involves a series of deliberate actions—feeling the weight of the firearm, handling the ammunition, and inserting the gunpowder—fostering a deep state of engagement. This comprehensive physical interaction further blurs the boundary between the virtual and real worlds, offering users a uniquely immersive and authentic experience.

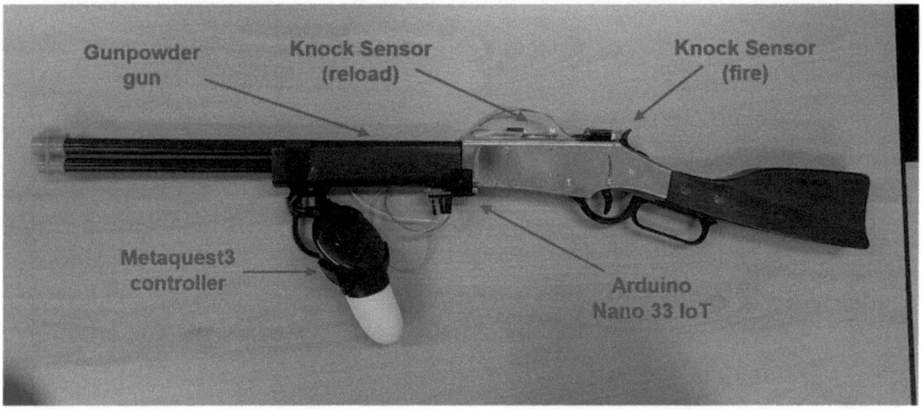

Fig. 2. ShockShot prototype.

4 System Implementation

4.1 Hardware Implementation

Figure 2 shows the prototype of ShockShot. The hardware configuration consists of an Arduino Nano 33 IoT, two knock sensors, a gunpowder gun, and a Meta Quest 3 controller. The Arduino Nano 33 IoT facilitates communication between the knock sensors and the head-mounted display (HMD). Consistent with the capabilities of other Arduino-based devices [44–46], the prototype utilizes Bluetooth low energy (BLE) communication to reduce battery consumption and extend operational duration. The Arduino was powered directly via the HMD, although battery operation was also supported as an alternative configuration. Meta Quest 3 served as the HMD platform. The final dimensions of the ShockShot prototype were $(W, D, H) = (70, 16, 8)$cm.

ShockShot uses a gun that fires gunpowder to provide users with an experience that closely replicates handling a real firearm. Upon discharge, the gun emits both a flash and an audible report, and the physical reloading process can be performed authentically. This setup enables users to engage with the full range of sensory feedback—including visual, auditory, and olfactory stimuli. To mitigate the necessity for modifications to the firearm's exterior or internal structure, the knock sensor and electronic components are mounted on a custom removable mount positioned on the top or side of the gun that can be attached to the exterior.

Gunfire System. In the ShockShot system, it is important that the real gun fires in real time within the virtual environment. To achieve this synchronization, a knock sensor was affixed to the location shown in Fig. 3, with the objective of accurately capturing the precise moment of firing. If the sensor is attached as illustrated, it fails to operate correctly due to internal resistance encountered as the trigger moves from the position illustrated in Fig. 3(a) to that in Fig. 3(b).

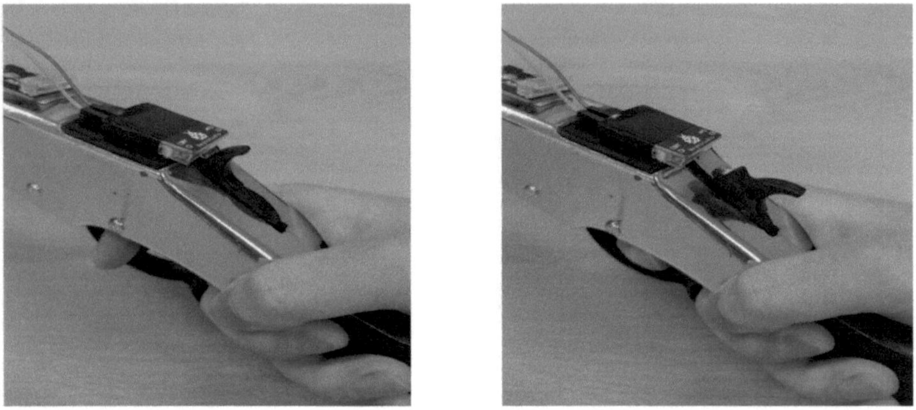

(a) (b)

Fig. 3. Fire process: (a) state before and after firing and (b) state during firing.

However, when the trigger is fully pulled, it moves forward rapidly, delivering a strong impact to the knock sensor. This is immediately followed by the discharge of the gunpowder-based gun. Since the interval between the sensor activation and the actual firing is extremely short, the firing event is reflected in the virtual world in real time, allowing users to witness the shot instantaneously.

(a) (b)

Fig. 4. Reload process: (a) state before and after reloading and (b) state during reloading.

Reload System. In the ShockShot system, a physical reloading system was developed to enhance realism. Conventional reloading methods relied on button presses or gesture-based inputs [14,35,47]. However, the gesture-based method eventually diverged from the actual reloading motion, diminishing the sense of realism because it cut through open air. To address these concerns, ShockShot incorporates a reload system using a shock sensor positioned in the location depicted in the accompanying illustration. Reloading is initiated by the movement of a protruding black plastic part during the transition from Fig. 4(a) to Fig. 4(b). As this movement begins, the shock sensor detects the impact, and the software registers the reloading action accordingly. After that, the user replaces the gunpowder and closes the black plastic part. While a slight temporal gap exists between the physical and virtual reloading processes, this does not affect system performance, as firing is disabled during reloading.

6DOF Estimation. Estimating 6DOF in the ShockShot system is important for accurate tracking. To achieve this, a controller was utilized. However, incorporating the controller risked compromising certain aesthetic elements of the system, particularly those contributing to its realism. To address this challenge, the controller was positioned on the vertical handle of the actual firearm. Aiming aids such as crosshairs or raycasts were deliberately omitted to maintain the authentic feel of the firearm. Given that zeroing accuracy varies significantly in the absence of such aids, the system allowed the user's left hand some freedom in controlling the movement of the firearm.

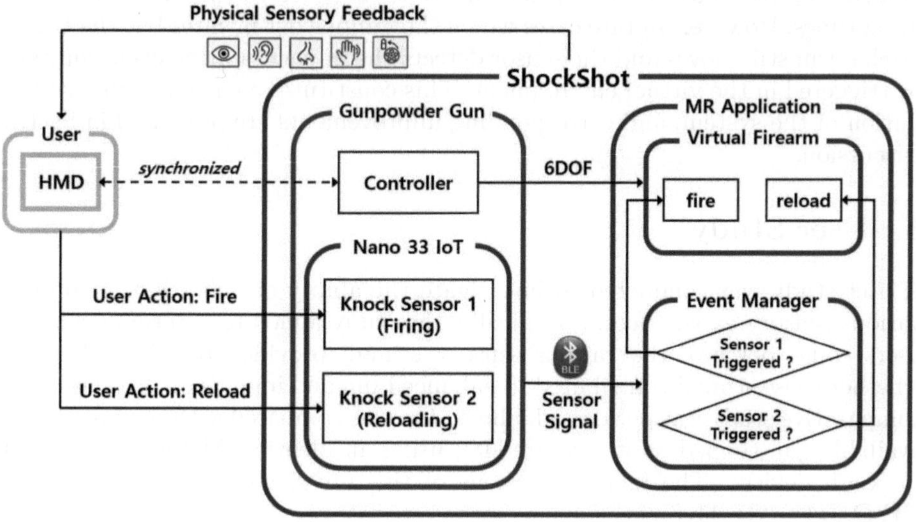

Fig. 5. System workflow.

4.2 Software Implementation

Arduino Firmware. Figure 5 shows the workflow of the ShockShot system. The device is equipped with a knock sensor that converts the physical impact generated by the movement of the gun into a digital signal. The Arduino Nano 33 IoT is programmed to receive this signal in real time and immediately transmit a BLE notification upon detecting a firing or reloading event. To ensure reliability, the system design incorporates internal resistance and an event debounce mechanism to minimize the effects of microvibrations and external noise. A threshold-based triggering mechanism is employed such that only significant impacts are registered as valid events. The system achieves an average latency of 1–2 ms from sensor input to BLE transmission. From the user's perspective, this results in a seamless integration of physical trigger action and digital signal response, creating the impression of an instantaneous response to user input.

MR Application. When the user fires and the event is detected by the knock sensor, the data are transferred via the Arduino's BLE module, and the bullet is immediately fired within the game engine. A similar process is followed during reloading, with the software simultaneously updating the current number of bullets. This dynamic is analogous to the physical behaviour of real gunpowder guns, where a new charge must be physically loaded to enable firing, thus enabling a natural and intuitive interaction aligned with the VR experience. The 6DOF data, provided by the controller, are received in real time to continuously update the position and direction of the gun within the MR application. From the user's perspective, the firing and reloading systems are perceived as immediate, with minimal perceptible difference between the physical and virtual firing times. However, in rare cases where the gunpowder misfires but the trigger mechanism still moves and the sensor detects the impact, a firing event may still be triggered in the virtual environment. This constitutes a current technical limitation of the system, and corresponding improvements are presented in Sect. 6, Discussion.

5 User Study

A user study was conducted to investigate the ability of ShockShot to provide various sensory experiences. Specifically, the study aimed to determine whether users could perceive the various sensory stimuli provided by ShockShot and whether these stimuli contributed to enhanced fun and immersion. To this end, a comparative study was performed. ShockShot was compared with a commercially available gun-shaped haptic device [48], using an identical MR gaming process for both devices. The final dimensions of the gun-shaped haptic device were $(W, D, H) = (41, 11, 8)$cm.

5.1 Participants

An experiment was conducted with 17 participants, comprising 13 males and 4 females, aged between 22 and 26 years (M = 24.2, SD = 1.1). Participants'

Fig. 6. Gun-shaped haptic device.

prior VR experience was categorized into three levels: high (currently using VR), medium (previously used VR), and low (only briefly experienced VR). We also surveyed participants with prior experience firing a real gun to assess perceived realism; a total of 12 participants reported having done so. Each participant received a reward of approximately $10.

Table 1. Survey questionnaire.

No.	Aspect	Question
1	Fun	How much fun did you have while playing?
2	Satisfaction	How satisfied are you with the feedback provided?
3	Fatigue	How fatigued were you while playing?
4	Immersion	How immersive were you while playing?
5	Preference	Which device is preferred?

5.2 Design

We used the gun-shaped haptic device shown in Fig. 6 to evaluate the enhancement of the sensory experience provided by ShockShot. For a fair comparison, we excluded conventional recoil-based haptic devices because the real gunpowder gun used in ShockShot produces minimal recoil. Instead, we used software-based effects such as muzzle flash and smoke particles to ensure consistency across both systems. Although comparing ShockShot with a real gun would have been ideal, we eliminated that as a realistic problem. Participants were asked to respond to four questions comparing the two methods using a 5-point Likert scale (1 = strongly disagree to 5 = strongly agree). Table 1 shows the questions used in the survey. In addition to rating these items, respondents were asked to indicate their preferred method—ShockShot or the commercial gun-shaped haptic device—and were invited to provide any additional comments.

Fig. 7. Participant's view in user test.

5.3 Procedure

ShockShot was previously tested in a user study involving a defense game where participants were tasked with shooting flying monsters with a gun. The monsters, represented as carnivorous beetles, were sourced from freely available assets. Participants played the game until they had fired 24 shots (8×3), which required two reloads. Before beginning, the experimenter explained the entire procedure, including safety precautions, and demonstrated how to aim, fire, and reload the gun. The recommended posture is shown in Fig. 7. Participants then donned the HMD, and the two experimental conditions using the commercial gun-shaped haptic device and ShockShot were conducted in a counterbalanced order.

As the experiment progressed, the monsters advanced toward the participant. For the convenience of the participants, monsters appeared only within a 30° horizontal and 20° vertical field of view from the user's point of view. Each participant fired a total of 24 rounds (8×3), reloading twice during the game. The experiment using the commercial haptic device lasted approximately 3 min, whereas the ShockShot trial took approximately 7 min. Upon completing the two experiments, participants filled out a survey. The entire session lasted approximately 25 min per participant.

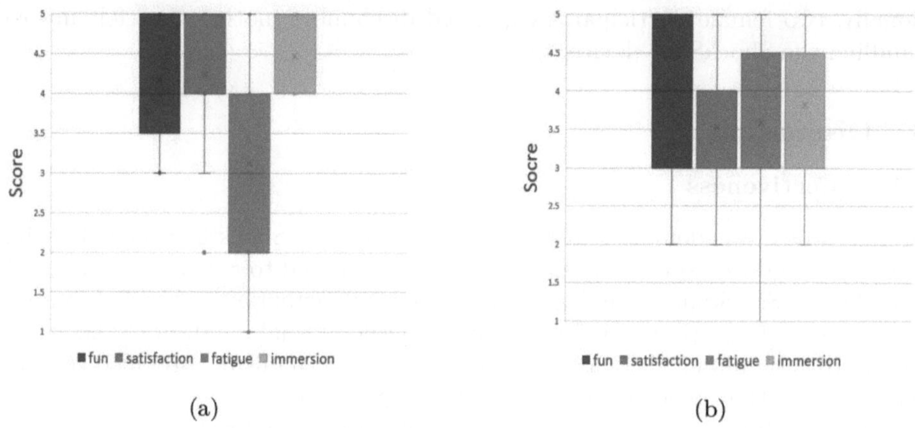

Fig. 8. Survey results: (a) ShockShot and (b) gun-shaped haptic device.

5.4 Results

Subjective Scores. Figure 8 shows the results of the questionnaires evaluating fun, realism, fatigue, and immersion. The mean scores are visible as 'x' in the diagram for reference. The fatigue score was corrected such that higher values indicated lower fatigue and were thus considered better. As the Shapiro–Wilk test [49] indicated non-normal distribution across all measures, the Wilcoxon signed-rank test [50] was employed for statistical tests. The ShockShot group scored higher in all areas except fatigue. Notably, ShockShot had a significant effect on satisfaction ($p < 0.05$, $r = 0.543$) and immersion. Immersion ($p < 0.005$, $r = 0.681$), the primary focus of the study, showed a particularly significant result. In addition, no significant difference was found in fatigue between the two groups ($p > 0.05$), alleviating concerns about physical strain. However, no significant difference was observed in the fun factor ($p > 0.05$). In contrast, users with prior VR experience ($N = 7$) showed a significant difference in the fun factor ($p < 0.05$, $r = 0.782$). Suggesting that first-time VR users might have perceived the VR experience itself as sufficiently fun.

Subjective Comments. Participants were asked to provide additional comments on the ShockShot system. A majority of participants reported positively that ShockShot enhanced their sense of immersion (eight participants) and realism (three participants), with several noting that the reloading process contributed positively to this immersive experience. However, two participants felt that the reloading process was time-consuming and detracted from the overall immersion.

Regarding device preference, 11 participants preferred ShockShot, whereas six preferred the gun-shaped haptic device, as shown in Fig. 8. Those who preferred the commercial haptic device cited the quicker firing process (two participants) and found ShockShot to be overly complicated (two participants). Additionally, two female participants expressed discomfort, noting they felt uneasy handling the ShockShot device.

6 Discussion

6.1 Effectiveness

In this study, we demonstrated the effectiveness of ShockShot in enhancing immersion and realism in MR environments. Compared to a commercially available device, ShockShot significantly improved user experience, highlighting the importance of multisensory integration. Tactile, visual, auditory, and olfactory feedback—along with an authentic reloading mechanism—provided realistic physical cues that deepened engagement and presence.

These findings extend prior work on multisensory feedback by showing how authentic physical interactions can overcome the limitations of visually driven haptic devices. While the current evaluation focused on firearm-based scenarios, future studies should examine broader applications to validate this approach further.

6.2 Limitations and Future Work

However, the proposed system has several limitations that warrant further research. First, accurately detecting gunpowder misfires remains a significant challenge. In the present study, a knock sensor was used to detect firing events; however, in real shooting situations, trigger movement can occur even when the gunpowder fails to ignite. As a result, the knock sensor may still send a signal, falsely registering a firing event in the virtual environment. This problem not only significantly affects the user experience but also reduces the reliability of the system, which is particularly critical for applications such as combat training. Consequently, more sophisticated detection technologies are needed. While optical detection methods using muzzle smoke or flash are potential alternatives, they are susceptible to environmental variables such as ambient lighting or visual obstructions—and may fail entirely when no smoke is produced. Acoustic-based solutions, however, face challenges in distinguishing signals when multiple users are engaged simultaneously. Therefore, future research should focus on building a multisensor fusion system that integrates information from various sources—such as muzzle flash sensors and pressure sensors—or devising real-time monitoring techniques for gunpowder ignition status to minimize false positives.

Second, while the reloading process clearly enhances immersion, it can also be perceived as cumbersome and disruptive by some users. Greater realism in mimicking real-world reloading processes often results in longer execution times and more complex movements, which may overwhelm beginners or casual users. Herein, several participants reported that the reloading sequence was excessively long, leading to a temporary break in immersion. This finding highlights the need to balance "immersion" with "convenience". To address this, future designs could incorporate adjusted reloading mechanisms, such as simplified mechanics in casual modes or automated processes, allowing users to select the appropriate level of realism based on their preferences and skill levels. Ensuring a flexible reloading process would allow the ShockShot platform to accommodate a broader range of users while maintaining both realism and efficiency.

Finally, although ShockShot shows considerable potential, its deployment must be accompanied by strict safety protocols and ethical guidelines. Because the system closely resembles real firearms, clear differentiation from actual weapons, controlled usage environments, and responsible application domains are essential to prevent misuse and to address broader societal concerns related to firearm simulation.

7 Conclusion

In this study, we introduced ShockShot, a haptic device designed to integrate firearm-like interactions into MR environments to enhance immersion and realism. Unlike conventional gun-shaped haptic devices that rely on vibration or force feedback, ShockShot adopts the structural principles of a real firearm and a gunpowder-based firing mechanism to deliver multisensory feedback, including muzzle flash, smoke, scent, and a reloading system. By narrowing the gap between physical and virtual interaction, ShockShot enables a more embodied MR shooting experience.

A user study ($N = 17$) comparing ShockShot with a traditional haptic device showed that ShockShot significantly increased immersion and user satisfaction without excessive fatigue. Participants positively evaluated the integration of physical, audiovisual, and olfactory feedback, which contributed to a more lifelike experience. These findings suggest that enhancing multisensory realism can increase experiential value in immersive environments. By incorporating real physical mechanisms into virtual systems, this work demonstrates a promising direction to advance tactile realism and strengthen the engagement potential of MR applications.

Acknowledgment. This work was supported by the Learning & Academic research institution for Master's·PhD students, and Postdocs (LAMP) Program of the National Research Foundation of Korea (NRF) grant funded by the Ministry of Education (No. RS-2023-00301974).

References

1. Milgram, P., Kishino, F.: A taxonomy of mixed reality visual displays. IEICE Trans. Inf. Syst. **77**(12), 1321–1329 (1994)
2. Hu, B.A., Zhang, Y., Hao, S., Tao, Y.: MOFA: multiplayer omnipresent fighting arena. In: ACM SIGGRAPH 2024 Immersive Pavilion, SIGGRAPH 2024. Association for Computing Machinery, New York (2024). https://doi.org/10.1145/3641521.3664414

3. Kim, S.Y., Choi, D.S., Jeon, K.J.: A motion and haptic system for immersive games. In: Han, Y.H., Park, D.S., Jia, W., Yeo, S.S. (eds.) Ubiquitous Information Technologies and Applications. LNEE, vol 214, pp. 905–914. Springer, Dordrecht (2013). https://doi.org/10.1007/978-94-007-7411-2_113
4. Wu, Y., You, S., Guo, Z., Li, X., Zhou, G., Gong, J.: Mr. brick: designing a remote mixed-reality educational game system for promoting children's social & collaborative skills. In: Proceedings of the 2023 CHI Conference on Human Factors in Computing Systems, pp. 1–18. ACM (2023).https://doi.org/10.1145/3544548.3580758
5. LaViola, J., Williamson, B., Brooks, C., Veazanchin, S., Sottilare, R., Garrity, P.: Using augmented reality to tutor military tasks in the wild. In: Proceedings of the Interservice/Industry Training Simulation & Education Conference, Orlando, Florida (2015)
6. Richard, P., Birebent, G., Coiffet, P., Burdea, G., Gomez, R., Langrana, J.: Effect of frame rate and force feedback on virtual object manipulation. Presence: Teleoper. Virtual Environ. **5**(1), 95–108 (1996). https://doi.org/10.1162/pres.1996.5.1.95
7. Vinnikov, M., Allison, R.S., Fernandes, S.: Gaze-contingent auditory displays for improved spatial attention in virtual reality. ACM Trans. Comput.-Hum. Interact. (TOCHI) **24**(3), 1–38 (2017). https://doi.org/10.1145/3057850
8. Grubert, J.: Mixed reality interaction techniques. arXiv preprint arXiv:2103.05984 (2021)
9. Gao, B., Shao, T., Tu, H., Ma, Q., Liu, Z., Han, T.: Exploring bimanual haptic feedback for spatial search in virtual reality. IEEE Trans. Visual Comput. Graphics **30**(5), 2422–2433 (2024). https://doi.org/10.1109/TVCG.2024.3372045
10. Fan, C.A., et al.: SpinShot: optimizing both physical and perceived force feedback of flywheel-based, directional impact handheld devices. In: Proceedings of the 37th Annual ACM Symposium on User Interface Software and Technology, UIST 2024. Association for Computing Machinery, New York (2024). https://doi.org/10.1145/3654777.3676433
11. Hashimoto, T., Hirao, Y.: Selfrionette: a fingertip force-input controller for continuous full-body avatar manipulation and diverse haptic interactions. In: Proceedings of the 37th Annual ACM Symposium on User Interface Software and Technology, UIST 2024. Association for Computing Machinery, New York (2024). https://doi.org/10.1145/3654777.3676409
12. Speicher, M., Hall, B.D., Nebeling, M.: What is mixed reality? In: Proceedings of the 2019 CHI Conference on Human Factors in Computing Systems, CHI 2019, pp. 1–15. Association for Computing Machinery, New York (2019). https://doi.org/10.1145/3290605.3300767
13. Ikeda, T., Fujita, K., Ogawa, K., Takashima, K., Kitamura, Y.: LooptBot: representing continuous haptics of grounded objects in room-scale VR. In: Proceedings of the 37th Annual ACM Symposium on User Interface Software and Technology, UIST 2024. Association for Computing Machinery, New York (2024). https://doi.org/10.1145/3654777.3676389
14. Shi, Y., Shen, G.: Haptic sensing and feedback techniques toward virtual reality. Research **7**, 0333 (2024). https://doi.org/10.34133/research.0333
15. Feick, M., Biyikli, C., Gani, K., Wittig, A., Tang, A., Krüger, A.: VoxelHap: a toolkit for constructing proxies providing tactile and kinesthetic haptic feedback in virtual reality. In: Proceedings of the 36th Annual ACM Symposium on User Interface Software and Technology, UIST 2023. Association for Computing Machinery, New York (2023). https://doi.org/10.1145/3586183.3606722

16. Zhang, H., Zhu, L., Xiang, Y., Zheng, J., Song, A.: Haptic rendering of neural radiance fields. In: Proceedings of the 36th Annual ACM Symposium on User Interface Software and Technology, UIST 2023, Association for Computing Machinery, New York (2023). https://doi.org/10.1145/3586183.3606811
17. Zhang, Z., Li, J., Yan, Z., Nishida, J., Peng, H.: JetUnit: rendering diverse force feedback in virtual reality using water jets. In: Proceedings of the 37th Annual ACM Symposium on User Interface Software and Technology, UIST 2024. Association for Computing Machinery, New York (2024). https://doi.org/10.1145/3654777.3676440
18. Su, Y., Nai, W., Sun, X., Sun, Z.: Design and modeling of an ungrounded haptic gun that simulates recoil using asymmetric force. In: 2021 IEEE World Haptics Conference (WHC), pp. 361–366 (2021). https://doi.org/10.1109/WHC49131.2021.9517202
19. Rahimi, A., Zhou, J., Haghani, S.: A VR gun controller with recoil adjustability. In: 2020 IEEE International Conference on Consumer Electronics (ICCE), pp. 1–2. IEEE (2020). https://doi.org/10.1109/ICCE46568.2020.9043008
20. Wei, L., Zhou, H., Nahavandi, S.: Haptically enabled simulation system for firearm shooting training. Virtual Reality **23**, 217–228 (2019). https://doi.org/10.1007/s10055-018-0359-6
21. Pamungkas, D.S., Ward, K.: Electro-tactile feedback system to enhance virtual reality experience. Int. J. Comput. Theory Eng. **8**(6), 465–470 (2016)
22. Komori, S., Ishikawa, T.: A research on a feedback device to represent gun recoil in a virtual reality game. In: Proceedings of the 2024 ACM Conference on Virtual Reality Software and Technology (VRST 2024), pp. 1–5 (2024). https://doi.org/10.1145/3657547.3657553
23. Rahimi, A., Patel, H., Ajmal, H., Haghani, S.: The design and implementation of a VR gun controller with haptic feedback. In: 2019 IEEE International Conference on Consumer Electronics (ICCE), pp. 1–2. IEEE (2019). https://doi.org/10.1109/ICCE.2019.8661983
24. Raza, A., Hassan, W., Jeon, S.: Pneumatically controlled wearable tactile actuator for multi-modal haptic feedback. IEEE Access **12**, 59485–59499 (2024). https://doi.org/10.1109/ACCESS.2024.3376753
25. Chapman, A.: Haptic feedback in virtual reality: an investigation into the next step of first person perspective presence. Ph.D. thesis, University of Lincoln Lincoln, UK (2019). https://doi.org/10.24385/lincoln.24326122
26. Sinclair, M., et al.: Three haptic shape-feedback controllers for virtual reality. In: 2018 IEEE Conference on Virtual Reality and 3D User Interfaces (VR), pp. 777–778. IEEE (2018). https://doi.org/10.1109/VR.2018.8446624
27. Choi, I., Ofek, E., Benko, H., Sinclair, M., Holz, C.: Claw: a multifunctional handheld haptic controller for grasping, touching, and triggering in virtual reality. In: Proceedings of the 2018 CHI Conference on Human Factors in Computing Systems, pp. 1–13. ACM (2018). https://doi.org/10.1145/3173574.3174268
28. Chen, D.K., Chossat, J.B., Shull, P.B.: HaptiVec: presenting haptic feedback vectors in handheld controllers using embedded tactile pin arrays. In: Proceedings of the 2019 CHI Conference on Human Factors in Computing Systems, CHI 2019, pp. 1–11. Association for Computing Machinery, New York (2019). https://doi.org/10.1145/3290605.3300401
29. Divekar, R.R., Kephart, J.O., Mou, X., Chen, L., Su, H.: You talkin' to me? A practical attention-aware embodied agent. In: Lamas, D., Loizides, F., Nacke, L., Petrie, H., Winckler, M., Zaphiris, P. (eds.) INTERACT 2019. LNCS, vol. 11748, pp. 760–780. Springer, Cham (2019). https://doi.org/10.1007/978-3-030-29387-1_44

30. Krompiec, P., Park, K.: Enhanced player interaction using motion controllers for first-person shooting games in virtual reality. IEEE Access **7**, 124548–124557 (2019). https://doi.org/10.1109/ACCESS.2019.2938167
31. Hermann, T., Burkard, A., Radicke, S.: Virtual reality controller with directed haptic feedback to increase immersion. In: VISIGRAPP (2: HUCAPP), pp. 203–210 (2020)
32. Strasnick, E., Holz, C., Ofek, E., Sinclair, M., Benko, H.: Haptic links: bimanual haptics for virtual reality using variable stiffness actuation. In: Proceedings of the 2018 CHI Conference on Human Factors in Computing Systems, CHI 2018, pp. 1–12. Association for Computing Machinery, New York (2018). https://doi.org/10.1145/3173574.3174218
33. Striker VR: Striker VR haptic VR gun (2024). https://www.strikervr.com/. Product
34. BeswinVR: MAG P90 gun controller VR rifle Xbox one, PS4pro, HTC vive, oculus, windows mixed reality (2024). https://www.beswinvr.com/. Product
35. Sutherland, I.E.: The ultimate display. In: Proceedings of the IFIP Congress, New York, vol. 2, pp. 506–508 (1965)
36. Jiang, X., Wang, F., Li, Y., Tao, L., Xi, Q., Wu, J.: A multimodal haptic rendering system combining force and vibrotactile feedback. IEEE Sens. J. **24**(12), 19167–19174 (2024). https://doi.org/10.1109/JSEN.2024.3397391
37. Chen, J., Fu, S., Liao, Z., Xiao, X., Qu, H., Lv, J.: RobotFire: a multisensory VR simulator for fire training with robot-assisted smoke and temperature simulation. In: Proceedings of the 17th International Symposium on Visual Information Communication and Interaction, VINCI 2024. Association for Computing Machinery, New York (2024). https://doi.org/10.1145/3678698.3687173
38. Baus, O., Bouchard, S.: Exposure to an unpleasant odour increases the sense of presence in virtual reality. Virtual Reality **21**(1), 59–74 (2017). https://doi.org/10.1007/s10055-016-0291-0
39. Dinh, H.Q., Walker, N., Hodges, L.F., Song, C., Kobayashi, A.: Evaluating the importance of multi-sensory input on memory and the sense of presence in virtual environments. In: Proceedings IEEE Virtual Reality (Cat. No. 99CB36316), pp. 222–228. IEEE (1999). https://doi.org/10.1109/VR.1999.756955
40. Tewell, J., Ranasinghe, N.: A review of olfactory display designs for virtual reality environments. ACM Comput. Surv. **56**(11), 1–35 (2024). https://doi.org/10.1145/3571794
41. Narumi, T., Nishizaka, S., Kajinami, T., Tanikawa, T., Hirose, M.: Augmented reality flavors: gustatory display based on edible marker and cross-modal interaction. In: Proceedings of the SIGCHI Conference on Human Factors in Computing Systems, pp. 93–102. ACM (2011). https://doi.org/10.1145/1978942.1978958
42. Harley, D., Verni, A., Willis, M., Ng, A., Bozzo, L., Mazalek, A.: Sensory VR: smelling, touching, and eating virtual reality. In: Proceedings of the Twelfth International Conference on Tangible, Embedded, and Embodied Interaction, pp. 386–397. ACM (2018). https://doi.org/10.1145/3173225.3173251
43. Melo, M., Gonçalves, G., Monteiro, P., Coelho, H., Vasconcelos-Raposo, J., Bessa, M.: Do multisensory stimuli benefit the virtual reality experience? A systematic review. IEEE Trans. Visual Comput. Graphics **28**(2), 1428–1442 (2020). https://doi.org/10.1109/TVCG.2020.3030465
44. Yao, K., et al.: A fully integrated breathable haptic textile. Sci. Adv. **10**(42), eadq9575 (2024). https://doi.org/10.1126/sciadv.adq9575

45. Li, D., et al.: Touch IoT enabled by wireless self-sensing and haptic-reproducing electronic skin. Sci. Adv. **8**(51), eade2450 (2022). https://doi.org/10.1126/sciadv.ade2450
46. Chan, J., Torah, R.: E-textile haptic feedback gloves for virtual and augmented reality applications. Eng. Proc. **15**(1) (2022). https://doi.org/10.3390/engproc2022015001
47. Silpasuwanchai, C., Ren, X.: Designing concurrent full-body gestures for intense gameplay. Int. J. Hum. Comput. Stud. **80**, 1–13 (2015). https://doi.org/10.1016/j.ijhcs.2015.02.010
48. System, C.: 3D vibration motor module haptic vibration module. 11st. https://www.11st.co.kr/products/7294435742. Product
49. Shapiro, S.S., Wilk, M.B.: An analysis of variance test for normality (complete samples). Biometrika **52**(3–4), 591–611 (1965)
50. Wilcoxon, F.: Individual comparisons by ranking methods. In: Kotz, S., Johnson, N.L. (eds.) Breakthroughs in Statistics. Springer Series in Statistics, pp. 196–202. Springer, New York (1992). https://doi.org/10.1007/978-1-4612-4380-9_16

Feasibility of Cryptocurrency JavaScript Mining for Micro Payments

Fajar Purnama(✉), I. Wayan Adi Juliawan Pawana, and Adi Panca Saputra Iskandar

Udayana University, Bali, Indonesia
{fajarpurnama,adijuliawanpawana,adipanca}@unud.ac.id

Abstract. Cryptocurrency mining has existed for more than a decade. In 2017, JavaScript-based web mining enabled cryptocurrency mining directly within web browsers. However, this innovation was widely misused through unauthorized execution of mining scripts on users' devices, a practice known as cryptojacking. This paper proposes a legitimate and consent-based application of JavaScript web mining as a payment mechanism. Unlike cryptojacking, the proposed system operates with explicit user consent, where customers compensate merchants by performing cryptocurrency mining tasks through their web browsers. A prototype file-selling web application was developed to evaluate the technical feasibility of this concept. Experimental results demonstrate that energy consumption increases with hash rate but varies significantly across device types. For example, the Acer Aspire E14 consumed 28 W above idle to reach 60 hps, while the Orange Pi Plus 2e consumed only 3.1 W to achieve 7.5 hps, indicating sublinear energy–performance scaling. The power-to-hash efficiency ratio ranged from 0.106 to 0.466 W/hps across tested devices, where lower values indicate higher efficiency. Desktop-class CPUs achieved higher throughput but lower efficiency, whereas single-board computers demonstrated better per-hash efficiency despite limited performance. Network measurements further indicated data rates between 7–12 kbps for 100–250 hps, suggesting additional bandwidth considerations. Overall, the feasibility of JavaScript mining payments depends on the balance between mining throughput, energy efficiency, and regional electricity cost. The findings highlight that device characteristics significantly influence fairness and practicality in mining-based payment ecosystems.

Keywords: cryptocurrency · JavaScript · web miner · mining pool · CoinIMP · Mintme · micropayment

A. P. S. Iskandar—The authors used chatgpt.com and gemini.google.com for latex formatting including the tables, pseudocodes, and flowcharts, also elaborations which are explained in detail in Acknowledgment section.

Published by Springer Nature Switzerland AG 2027
J. Kim et al. (Eds.): EBISION 2025, IFIP AICT 786, pp. 252–280, 2027.
https://doi.org/10.1007/978-3-032-26616-3_16

1 Introduction

Cryptocurrency mining began with the introduction of Bitcoin as a peer-to-peer electronic cash system by Satoshi Nakamoto [1]. Since then, blockchain-based cryptocurrencies have attracted significant attention from researchers, governments, and industry practitioners. Today, blockchain technology is widely recognized across academic, industrial, and governmental communities. The public generally refers to blockchain-based peer-to-peer cash systems as cryptocurrencies. Mining activity gained widespread public attention in 2011 [2], shortly after Bitcoin obtained a measurable market price [3]. The possibility that personal computers could generate digital assets attracted significant public interest.

Shortly thereafter, cryptocurrency mining evolved into multiple variations [4]. Mining can be performed on different hardware platforms, including central processing units (CPU), graphics processing units (GPU), application-specific integrated circuits (ASIC), field-programmable gate arrays (FPGA), and ARM-based architectures such as mobile devices and single-board computers. There are also mining on different software such as on desktop, mobile, and now on the browser utilizing JavaScript programming language. Without installing anything except the browser, anybody can visit any JavaScript mining website and start mining cryptocurrencies. Afterwards JavaScript mining became known as one form of cryptocurrency web mining.

Immediately, web mining was used as an alternative method of donation from the website visitors. It is a web mining conducted by the visitors on behalf of the beneficiary, recipients, or the receiver of the donation. In other words, the visitors mined the cryptocurrency for the website owners. The problem lies in the execution of asking donation through web mining. The ethically acceptable implementation requires explicit user consent before mining activities begin. Controversial implementations include cases where mining begins automatically despite the presence of a notice, or where users are informed but mining starts before explicit consent is granted, even if an option to stop is provided. A definite misconduct is that mining without giving notice to the visitors which in other words the mining is hidden without the visitors knowledge. The worst is using the lots of the visitors' resources which led to web mining labeled as cryptojacking [5].

It is unfortunate that cryptocurrency web mining today is widely known as a malware while there are potential positive innovation of this cryptocurrency web mining. One of the potential positive innovation is proposed on this manuscript and that is cryptocurrency JavaScript web mining as a method of payment. Merchants can sell digital and physical items only and accept the cryptocurrency web mining conducted by the customers in this case the website visitors a form of payment. The merchant can set the price as they normally would and the customers will mine cryptocurrency on the website until the mining result reached the price set by the merchant. However this manuscript shows that this method currently is more suitable for micro payments even though other sales are possible. This manuscript investigates how web-based cryptocurrency mining could function as an alternative payment system.

To align this study with the broader E-Business Information Systems (EBIS) domain, this work positions JavaScript-based mining payment as a microtransaction layer that can be embedded into existing online service architectures. Within EBIS frameworks, it may serve as an alternative or complementary payment gateway, particularly for low-value digital content or users lacking access to conventional financial infrastructure. From a security and trust perspective, modern EBIS platforms increasingly require payment and service mechanisms that are resilient, transparent, and verifiable by design. Recent research has emphasized the importance of cryptographic robustness, hybrid post-quantum security, and formal verification in next-generation communication and service infrastructures [6–8]. In addition, security enhancement approaches in cloud-native, roaming-enabled, and transport-layer–optimized environments highlight the necessity of intelligent detection and protocol-level analysis to preserve service continuity and transactional trust [9–11]. Formal and practical evaluations of authentication and provisioning protocols further indicate that early-stage vulnerabilities can directly affect service availability and economically driven interactions [12,13]. In this context, the proposed cryptocurrency web mining–based payment mechanism is positioned as an exploratory EBIS component whose feasibility must be assessed not only from an economic standpoint, but also in terms of transparency, user consent, and computational trust.

2 Background on Cryptocurrency and Value

2.1 Genesis and Technical Architecture

The digitization of the financial sector predates cryptocurrency by several decades. By the late 1990s, online banking and payment processors like PayPal had already build the concept of transferring value over the internet. However, these systems remained fundamentally centralized, relying on trusted intermediaries (banks) to maintain ledgers and prevent the "double-spending" problem.

The paradigm shifted in 2008 following the global financial crisis, which eroded public trust in centralized financial institutions. In response, an unknown entity operating under the pseudonym Satoshi Nakamoto published the Bitcoin whitepaper [1]. The Bitcoin community's vision was to create a peer-to-peer electronic cash system that operated independently of central banks or government authorities.

To achieve this decentralized consensus, Bitcoin incorporate several existing technologies into its architecture:

1. **Distributed Ledger (Blockchain):** A public, immutable database shared across all nodes in the network, ensuring transparency.
2. **Peer-to-Peer (P2P) Network:** A decentralized communication architecture [14] that allows participants to propagate transactions directly without a central server where the illustration is on Figure 1 showing that all nodes must have a copy of the ledger.
3. **Cryptographic Hashing (SHA-256):** The Secure Hash Algorithm defined in FIPS 180-2 [15], used to chain blocks together and secure the integrity of the ledger where the technical architecture is shown on Fig. 2.

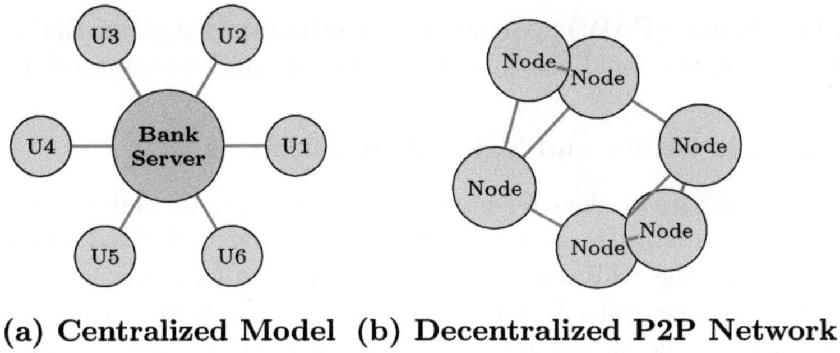

Fig. 1. Comparison of network topologies: (a) Traditional finance relies on a central authority to clear transactions. (b) Bitcoin utilizes a mesh network where every peer participates in validation.

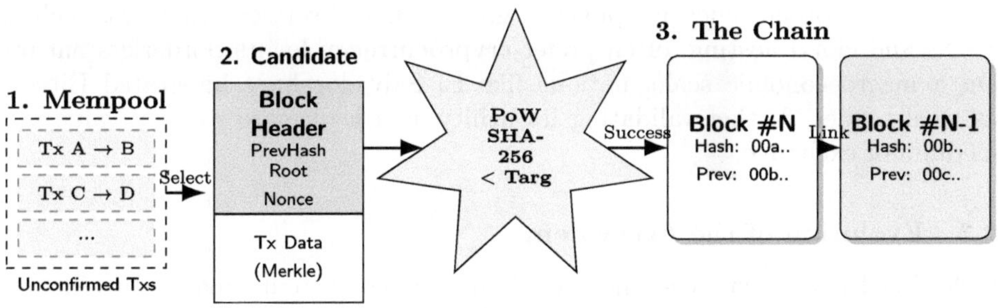

Fig. 2. The Bitcoin Technical Architecture: Transactions are aggregated into a candidate block, where miners perform Proof-of-Work to cryptographically link it to the existing blockchain.

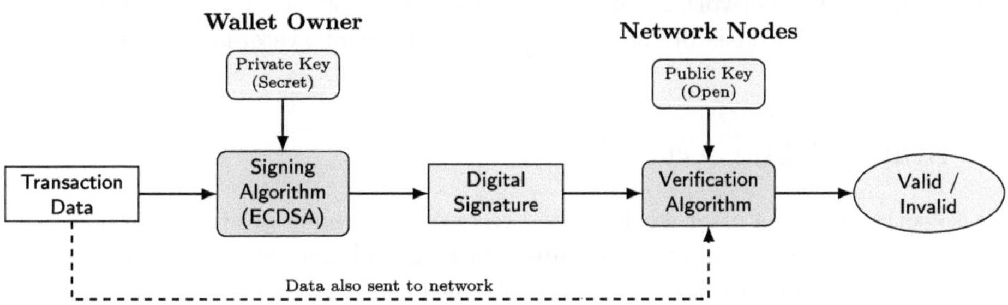

Fig. 3. The Digital Signature Process (ECC): The private key generates a signature for the transaction data. The network uses the corresponding public key to verify authenticity without ever seeing the private key.

4. **Elliptic Curve Cryptography (ECC):** A public-key cryptosystem proposed by Koblitz [16] and Miller [17], utilized here (via the secp256k1 curve) to generate digital signatures that prove ownership of funds illustrated on Fig. 3.

5. **Proof-of-Work (PoW):** A consensus mechanism based on Hashcash [18], requiring computational energy expenditure to validate transactions.

2.2 Economic Utility and Value Proposition

Unlike fiat currencies backed by national governments or digital banking balances backed by institutional credit, Bitcoin's value is derived initially from social consensus—the willingness of a community to exchange goods and services for it. Fundamentally, Bitcoin functions as a commodity money. Its value is underpinned by the significant cost of its production (energy and hardware wear). This scarcity, combined with its utility as a censorship-resistant medium of exchange, incentivizes merchants and users to adopt it.

In the contemporary economy, this utility has expanded beyond speculative trading. Major payment processors (e.g., MoonPay, BitPay) allow online retailers to accept cryptocurrency for physical goods. Digital service providers, such as VPNs and cloud hosting, often prefer cryptocurrency for its borderless nature. On a macroeconomic scale, nations like El Salvador have integrated Bitcoin as legal tender, further validating its utility as a legitimate store of value and medium of exchange.

2.3 Evolution of the Ecosystem

Following Bitcoin's success, the cryptocurrency ecosystem expanded to include thousands of alternative assets ("altcoins"). Notable examples include Ethereum, which introduced programmable smart contracts, and Monero, which focused on privacy. However, regardless of their specific utility, the majority of these early cryptocurrencies relied on the same fundamental mechanism to issue new coins and secure their networks: *mining*. This reliance on computational work for security forms the basis of the mining-based payment systems discussed in this study.

3 State of The Art

This section reviews prior work related to cryptocurrency mining, browser-based JavaScript mining, mining pools, and existing web monetization models. The objective is to position the proposed mining-based payment mechanism within the broader landscape of technical implementations and online economic systems. The following subsections progressively narrow the discussion from general mining principles to payment-related applications.

From the authors knowledge, there are currently three forms of monetizations which are donations, advertisements, and cryptocurrency web minings summarized on Fig. 4. It shows the time flow from cryptocurrency mining to this method cryptocurrency mining for payment which are cryptocurrency mining → browser-based JavaScript mining → web monetization mechanisms → applications such as donation, captcha, and payment. The detail explanation are on following subsections.

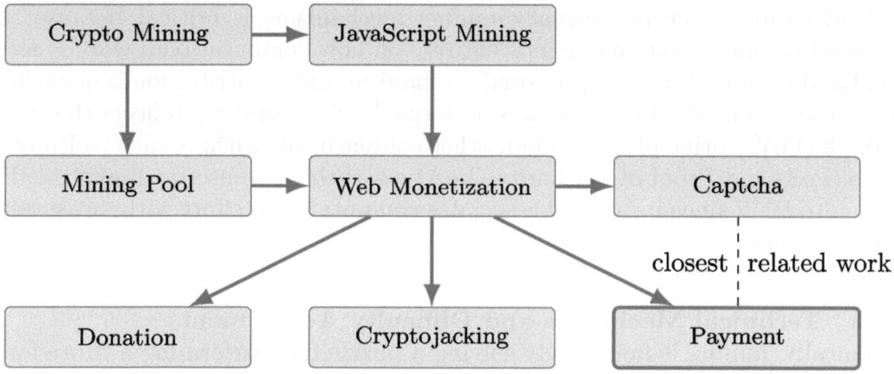

Fig. 4. State of the art diagram overview.

3.1 Cryptocurrency Mining

Understanding cryptocurrency mining mechanisms is important because the proposed payment system depends on how computational work is measured and rewarded. This is relevant because in the proposed payment mechanism, user contribution is measured through the amount of work (hashes) performed, which directly reflects the Proof of Work (PoW) principle. Although other consensus algorithms such as Proof of Stake (PoS) and Proof of Authority (PoA) exist, this manuscript limits discussion to Proof of Work (PoW) since it directly associates computational effort with measurable value.

3.1.1 Concept and Analogy

The term mining is literally taken from the physical labor of people mining in real physical mines. It costs the laborers energy in order to obtain valuable resources. For cryptocurrency mining, the laborers are computers using their computing powers to solve complex cryptography in order to obtain cryptocurrencies. Most of the general public forgot that cryptocurrency mining is not free. The author explained in the author's previous manuscript [19] that basic costs of cryptocurrency mining other than the initial capital of hardware and software are electricity usage cost and data usage cost which is usually Internet connection usage cost.

For the general public, mining is the easiest term to explain while in actual, it is the process of securing the decentralized distributed blockchain network [20]. Different from the traditional information system where the topology is clustered star tree, decentralized distributed blockchain information system the topology is mesh. Every node within the network holds a copy of the ledger and the problem lies in how to have general agreement (consensus) within the network regarding of which version of the blockchain ledger is valid. Therefore, honest nodes are busy maintaining that consensus but rewarded with cryptocurrency in exchange.

Understanding cryptocurrency mining mechanisms is critical because the proposed payment system depends entirely on how computational work is measured and rewarded. In this proposed mechanism, user contribution is quantified through the number of valid hashes performed, which directly reflects the Proof of Work (PoW) principle. Although other consensus algorithms such as Proof of Stake (PoS) and Proof of Authority (PoA) exist, this manuscript limits the discussion to PoW since it directly associates computational effort with measurable economic value.

3.1.2 Technical Mechanics and Difficulty Adjustment

Technically, mining is not merely solving a puzzle but performing a brute-force search for a hash output that meets a specific difficulty target. Back in Fig. 2, a miner constructs a block header B containing the previous block's hash, a timestamp, and a Merkle root of transactions. The miner then iterates a variable called a *nonce* n through a cryptographic hash function H. The goal is to find an n such that the resulting hash value is strictly less than a network-defined target T in Eq. 1:

$$H(B \parallel n) \leq T \tag{1}$$

The target T is a 256-bit integer that serves as a dynamic threshold. There is an inverse relationship between the target and the mining *difficulty* (D) Eq. 2:

$$D = \frac{T_{max}}{T_{current}} \tag{2}$$

where T_{max} is the maximum possible target (lowest difficulty). As T decreases, the probability of finding a valid hash decreases. In hexadecimal representation, a smaller T requires the hash to begin with a specific number of leading zeros. For example, a hash starting with '0000...' represents a smaller numerical value than one starting with '00AB...'.

To maintain a consistent block generation time (e.g., 10 min for Bitcoin), the network employs a Difficulty Adjustment Algorithm. If the total network hashrate increases, blocks are found too quickly; the protocol automatically lowers T (increasing difficulty) to compensate. Conversely, if miners leave the network, T increases to make mining easier. This self-regulating mechanism ensures the economic stability of the payment system regardless of the number of active miners.

3.1.3 Hashing Algorithms: SHA-256, Lyra2, and GhostRider

Different cryptocurrencies utilize different hashing algorithms (H) to achieve consensus. Bitcoin utilizes the SHA-256 (Secure Hash Algorithm 256-bit) family. SHA-256 is purely computational; it requires negligible memory but executes simple arithmetic operations at extreme speeds, leading to the dominance of Application-Specific Integrated Circuits (ASICs).

In contrast, the experiments in this study utilize MintMe (formerly Webchain) and Raptoreum, which employ ASIC-resistant algorithms designed for consumer hardware. MintMe employs the Lyra2 algorithm proposed by Simplicio Jr. et al. [21]. Lyra2 is designed to be "memory-hard", meaning its execution time is strictly bound by memory access latency rather than pure processor clock speed. The algorithm utilizes a tunable memory matrix to create a bottleneck that ASICs cannot easily optimize. Additionally, the study incorporates Raptoreum, which utilizes the GhostRider algorithm [22]. Unlike static algorithms, GhostRider employs an "algorithmic switching" technique, randomly cycling through different hashing functions (derived from the x16r and Cryptonight families) on a per-block basis. This approach specifically targets the CPU's L3 cache and memory bandwidth.

These designs are crucial for browser-based mining because:

1. **Egalitarian Distribution:** By targeting RAM (Lyra2) and L3 Cache (GhostRider), they reduce the efficiency gap between consumer CPUs and specialized hardware.
2. **Browser Compatibility:** Modern JavaScript engines (V8, SpiderMonkey) and WebAssembly (WASM) are increasingly optimized for memory operations, allowing these algorithms to run with reasonable efficiency on standard laptops and mobile devices compared to pure compute-heavy algorithms.

3.1.4 Decentralized Topology

Finally, the purpose of this work is to maintain the integrity of a decentralized topology. In Fig. 1, unlike traditional clustered star-tree information systems (e.g., banking servers), a blockchain exists as a mesh network. Every node holds a copy of the ledger. Mining solves the problem of consensus in this mesh: honest nodes expend resources to maintain the correct version of the ledger and are rewarded with cryptocurrency, creating an economic incentive for honesty.

3.2 JavaScript Cryptocurrency Web Mining

The first Bitcoin mining software was written in C++ as a desktop software. This means that it opens possibilities to write the mining software using other programming language. In 2017, CoinHive released a mining software in JavaScript which enables mining on the web browser [23]. Unlike desktop mining which runs at near-hardware performance, browser-based mining operates under JavaScript runtime limitations, making it less efficient but more accessible. Not long afterwards, many website provides services for mining cryptocurrency on the web browser. Without additional software installations, the users only need to visit the websites on their web browser, input their cryptocurrency wallet address, and start mining [24]. It is important to understand that the scope of this manuscript is limited to JavaScript cryptocurrency web mining which means not including other types of cryptocurrency mining. Typical browser mining hashrates range from tens to hundreds of hashes per second, several magnitudes lower than native miners, thus limiting its practicality to micro-payments or low-value exchanges.

The viability of browser mining depends heavily on the underlying hashing algorithm. Early implementations targeted the **CryptoNote** protocol (used by Monero), which relied on the *CryptoNight* algorithm. CryptoNight was designed to be "ASIC-resistant" and CPU-friendly, utilizing 2 MB of L3 cache—a requirement that matched consumer CPUs well.

Initially, these miners were written in **asm.js**, a strict subset of JavaScript optimizable by browsers. However, as mining difficulty increased and algorithms evolved—such as the memory-hard **Lyra2**, the virtual-machine based **RandomX**, or the algorithmic switching of **GhostRider**—pure JavaScript became insufficient due to its lack of native 64-bit integer support and garbage collection pauses. Modern browser miners, including the MintMe and Raptoreum implementations used in this study, utilize **WebAssembly (WASM)**. WASM provides a compact binary format that runs at near-native speed, enabling these complex, cache-intensive algorithms to function efficiently in a client-side environment. Typical browser mining hashrates range from tens to hundreds of hashes per second (H/s). While this is magnitudes lower than native GPU/ASIC mining, it is sufficient for the micro-payment models proposed in this work.

3.3 Mining Pool

CoinHive did not survived but there is another JavaScript mining software provider called CoinIMP [25]. Currently is difficult to find working source code for JavaScript cryptocurrency web mining. Due to the authors' limited time two experiments are conducted which are proprietary solution using CoinIMP and a custom open-source miner from MintMe desktop miner. CoinIMP provides a vast library to implement JavaScript cryptocurrency mining on any website for mining MintMe coin formerly known as Webchain which the important component needed for the JavaScript mining payment execution is the amount of hashes generated by the customers and a dashboard showing the amount MintMe received based on the customers' hashes for the merchant. However, CoinIMP's web miner is currently a black box which is why a custom open-source miner for MintMe as well is tried on this work.

The mining on CoinIMP is through its own mining pool. Since the nature of Proof of Work mining is that higher computing power that could generate more hashes per second tends to obtain more of the mining reward, smaller miners tend to join together into a mining pool to compete with these parties with high computing powers [26]. Mining pool is like a mining group where the group and not individually obtains the mining reward. The problem afterwards, is how to distribute the mining rewards to each members of the group. The generally accepted method of distribution is based on the computing power or hashes generated by each members. Those with higher hashes generated receives higher rewards while those with lower hashes generated received lower rewards. This is still preferred by smaller miners because mining alone or solo for them tends to be almost impossible to obtain rewards because they lose competition with the larger miners.

For the open-source experiments in this study, specific stratum endpoints were utilized to validate the architecture. The customized Raptoreum web miner (adapted from [27]) was configured to submit shares to the `raptoreum.zone` mining pool. Conversely, the self-compiled MintMe WASM miner was connected via the custom Python proxy to the official `pool.webchain.network`. In both instances, the proxy server maintained the persistent TCP Stratum connection to these pools, while the browser clients communicated with the proxy via WebSockets, ensuring valid share submission and difficulty adjustment.

3.3.1 The Necessity of Pooled Mining

Not limited to CoinIMP but well operating mining pool is necessary to guarantee payment value to the merchant. Since rewards in PoW mining are competitive and random, there is no guarantee that merchants can receive cryptocurrency when the customer mines. Thus, the use of a mining pool is not only computationally advantageous but also economically necessary to ensure predictable value transfer in the payment process. Therefore the scope of this manuscript is limited to the necessary utilization of mining pools.

Both implementations rely on a **Mining Pool** architecture. In a Proof-of-Work system, mining is a Poisson process where finding a block is statistically rare. A solo miner using a browser (CPU) might not find a block for years, resulting in zero revenue based on Eq. 3.

$$P(winning) = \frac{h_{browser}}{H_{network}} \tag{3}$$

Since $h_{browser} \ll H_{network}$, the probability approaches zero.

To solve this variance problem, miners aggregate their computational power into a pool [26]. The pool treats the search for a block as a granular task, assigning easier "share difficulties" to individual miners. When a browser finds a nonce satisfying this lower difficulty (a "share"), it submits it to the pool. The pool then credits the miner proportionally. This mechanism is economically essential for a payment system: it converts the "lottery-like" nature of solo mining into a steady stream of "micro-earnings" that allows the merchant to be paid in real-time as the customer browses.

3.3.2 Shares and Payment Verification

A critical distinction in this architecture is the difference between *hashes* and *shares*. A "hash" is a single iteration of the cryptographic algorithm performed locally by the browser. Based on Eq. 4, a "share" is a hash that meets a specific difficulty threshold set by the pool, which is significantly easier than the network's block difficulty.

$$T_{network} \ll T_{pool} < H(B \parallel n) \tag{4}$$

While the browser generates continuous hashrate (e.g., 50 H/s), the pool has no visibility into this local activity. The pool only receives data when the browser finds a nonce that satisfies the pool's target (T_{pool}). Consequently, the "Current Hashrate" displayed on mining dashboards (such as CoinIMP or the prototype's interface) is not a real-time measurement of processor cycles. Based on Eq. 5, it is a probabilistic estimate calculated derived from the submission frequency of valid shares:

$$H_{estimated} = \frac{D_{share} \cdot 2^{32}}{\Delta t} \tag{5}$$

where Δt is the time interval between submitted shares. This explains the phenomenon observed during experimentation where the displayed hashrate remains at zero until the first share is found. For the proposed payment system, this implies that the unit of account cannot be "time spent on site" or "raw CPU usage", but must be the valid share count. The merchant is guaranteed payment only for verified shares, making the "Pay-Per-Share" (PPS) model the only viable economic structure for browser-based micro-payments.

3.4 Online Monetizations

Previously, there were already many forms of monetizations for the website owners to generate income for their website but can be generally divided into two. The first one is donation transfers where the website owners post their bank and/or digital wallet accounts on their website. One of the earliest request for donation was from Wikipedia asking for donation through Paypal in 2005 [28]. The second one is advertisements (ads) where web owners allows any form of ads on their website and get paid by the advertisement owners. The most popular platform among bloggers or individual website owners is Google Adsense [29]. JavaScript cryptocurrency web mining adds another form of online monetizations and became the third one where the visitors mines cryptocurrency on behalf of the website owners. Unlike donations or ads which rely on financial transfer or user attention, cryptocurrency web mining monetizes computational work, converting visitors' processing power into value for the merchant.

Table 1. Comparison of Online Monetization and Payment Methods

Method	Customer Account	Merchant Account	Privacy	User Action	Value Type
Donation	Required	Required	High (depends on channel)	Active (transfer)	Currency
Advertisement	Not required	Required	Low (tracking common)	Passive (viewing)	Attention
cryptocurrency web mining	Not required	Required	Medium to High	Passive (computing)	Computation

From the authors knowledge, there are currently three forms of monetizations which are donations, advertisements, and cryptocurrency web minings summarized on Table 1. All three requires the merchant have accounts on each respected forms. While the customers requires having their own accounts for donation method, both advertisement and cryptocurrency web mining method requires no setup from the customers rendering them more simple than the donation method. For privacy, all three are technically possible but currently there are very few to almost no existing platform that provides them except for the cryptocurrency web mining.

Cryptocurrency web mining as a form of monetization is already a well known topic. Most research on this topic discusses security, ethics, or browser performance [30]. At least from the authors knowledge Never once mention about economic feasibility or payment systems.

3.5 Online Payments

Today there are many online payment methods but almost all of them requires account setup from both the merchants and the customers. For banks and other parties related to national governments requires to follow the know your customer (KYC) [31] practice which at least filling the form, providing identity card, email address, and phone number, also there are some strict countries requiring proof of address. Other than those usually only requires account setup but customers needs to handle the balance top up themselves. However, advertisement and cryptocurrency web mining only requires the merchant to setup an account or create their own platform while there are no setup requirements for the customers. Therefore for setup on the customers advertisement and cryptocurrency web mining are the most convenient. If the computational contribution from visitors can be reliably measured and valued, it may serve as an implicit form of payment—without requiring explicit account setup or currency transfer.

3.6 The Micropayment Challenge

The limitations of traditional payment infrastructure are most acute in the context of *micropayments*—transactions involving very small sums of money (typically under $1.00 or even fractions of a cent).

3.6.1 Economic Inefficiency of Fiat Rails

Traditional payment networks (e.g., Visa, Mastercard, PayPal) rely on a fee structure that typically includes a fixed base fee plus a percentage of the transaction value (e.g., $0.30 + 2.9%). This pricing model renders micropayments economically non-viable. For instance, purchasing a digital file for $0.10 would incur a processing fee greater than the item's value, resulting in a net loss for the merchant.

3.6.2 Use Cases and the "Mental Transaction Cost"

Despite these technical barriers, the demand for micropayments is growing in the Web 3.0 economy. Common use cases include pay-per-view content like reading a single news article without purchasing a monthly subscription, digital assets like purchasing low-cost in-game items, skins, or wallpapers, API monetization which is paying for a single API call or data request (e.g., weather data or stock quotes), and file downloads like One-time access to PDFs, software, or media files (the primary use case of this study). Beyond the financial fees, micropayments suffer from "mental transaction costs". Users are psychologically unwilling to undergo a complex checkout process (entering credit card details) for a trivial purchase. Browser-based mining addresses both barriers: it facilitates fractional value transfer without fixed fees and removes the mental friction of checkout, making it uniquely positioned to solve the micropayment problem.

3.7 Limitation

Unfortunately, JavaScript cryptocurrency web mining became a controversy because most website owners misused it. Awarely or unawarely, most of the website owners execute the JavaScript cryptocurrency web mining without the visitors' consent. Therefore up until today, JavaScript cryptocurrency web mining is considered as a malware called cryptojacking derived from the hijacking which means the visitors' computer are hijacked to perform mining by the hijackers which is the website owner in this case. This became one of the main reasons why JavaScript cryptocurrency web mining did not develop much where most of the articles published professionally and all other online contents including news, magazines, and blogs are about analysis and defending against cryptojacking [32]. There are very few to almost no developers in this field, which is why although the prototype introduced in this manuscript may not be impressive but the JavaScript mining as a method of payment is probably new.

3.8 Novelty

The closest only work in the world related to JavaScript mining as a method of payment is probably Coinhive's Captcha [33]. Therefore, this article is probably the first if not one of the first in the world to introduce this method. While previous works focus on detecting and preventing unauthorized mining, this manuscript explores how a transparent and consensual browser mining process could function as a legitimate payment method. The novelty of this work lies not in the mining algorithm itself but in its application as a voluntary, measurable, and browser-based micro-payment mechanism.

4 Method and Experiment

4.1 General JavaScript Mining Payment Method

The process of JavaScript mining as a method of payment is very straightforward, as shown in Fig. 5. Basically, the merchant sets the amount of payment units the customer has to generate through JavaScript cryptocurrency web mining where in this manuscript payment units can be total hashes, total shares, or hybrid. Once the customer generates enough, the goods and/or services are delivered. The source code for the program should be derived from Algorithm 1. This mechanism effectively turns computational work into a measurable form of digital payment, where the customer's processing power serves as the medium of exchange instead of conventional currency.

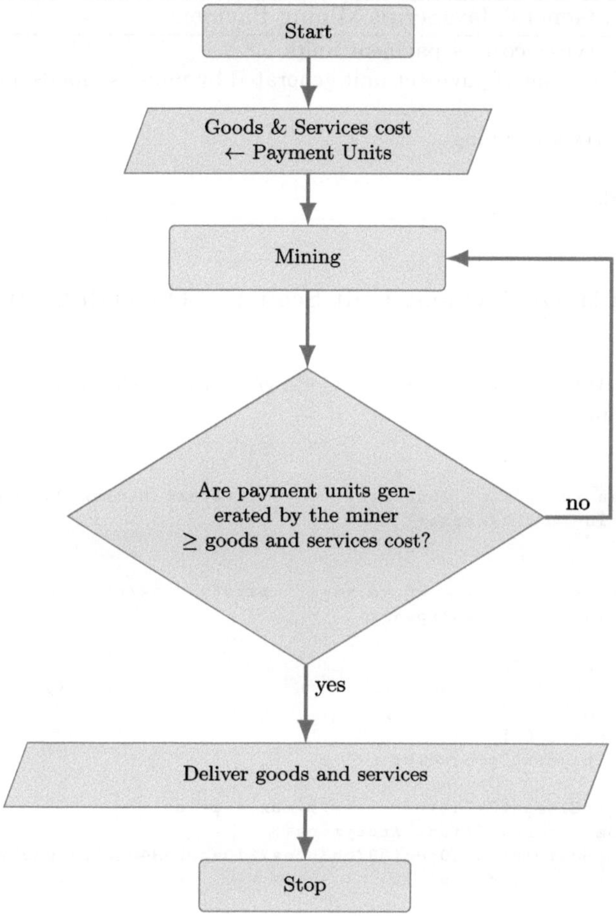

Fig. 5. General JavaScript mining as a payment flowchart.

4.2 Practical Source Code

As written in Subsect. 3.3.2, both total hashes and total shares can be used as payment units but each have their own advantages and disadvantages. The advantage for using total hashes is for the customers where the customers have a clear calculation of the time they need to mine with their available resource and the disadvantage is for the merchant where the merchant is not guaranteed to receive shares which is essential for payment. Vice versa the advantage of using total shares is the guarantee for merchants to receive payment and the disadvantage is for the customer where the probability of generating shares is actually random where increasing resource to increase hash generated per second only increases the probability of finding the shares.

Algorithm 1. General JavaScript Mining Payment

```
goods and services cost ← payment units
while total amount of payment unit generated by miner < goods and services cost do
    cryptocurrency mining
end while
deliver goods and services
```

4.2.1 Total Hash Payment Unit Scenario Through Coinimp

Listing 16.1. HTML and JavaScript Code of Total Hash Payment Unit Scenario Through Coinimp

```
<html>
    <p>
        <button id="button" onclick="start()">Start Mining Payment</button>
        <span id="hps"></span>
    </p>
    <p>
        <progress id="progress" value="0" max="100"></progress>
        <span id="hashes"></span>
    </p>
    <p id="the_file"></p>
<script src="https://www.hostingcloud.racing/QgkD.js"></script>
<script>
    const price = 2000;
    let mining_payment_progress;
    let hps;
    document.getElementById("progress").max = price;
    var _customer = new Client.Anonymous(
        '0f01ab5d9f918554840bde1897be3bfae2370ac9b5940da9e4abb572df9591df',
        { throttle: 0, c: 'w' }
    );
    function start() {
        _customer.start();
        setInterval(inprogress, 250);
    }
    function inprogress() {
        document.getElementById("button").innerHTML = "In␣Progress";
        hps = _customer.getHashesPerSecond();
        document.getElementById("hps").innerHTML = hps + "␣hashes/second";
        mining_payment_progress = _customer.getTotalHashes();
        document.getElementById("hashes").innerHTML =
            mining_payment_progress + "/" + price + "␣hashes";
        document.getElementById("progress").value = mining_payment_progress;
        if (mining_payment_progress >= price) {
            _customer.stop();
            document.getElementById("button").innerHTML = "Complete";
            document.getElementById("the_file").innerHTML =
                "<a␣href='file.zip'>Download␣File</a>";
        }
    }
</script>
</html>
```

This is a scenario where a website owner sells a file and receives payment through browser-based mining. The implementation, shown in Listing 16.1, uses simple HTML and JavaScript: the file link is hidden, a button starts the CoinIMP mining process, and once sufficient hashes are generated, the mining stops and the link becomes visible. A progress bar indicates mining progress as payment status. In practice, the required hashes depend on the product price and the customer's device performance, while the progress bar visually shows how close the payment is to completion and when the file becomes accessible.

4.2.2 Total Shares Payment Unit Scenario Through Custom Cpu-Web-Miner

Listing 16.2. HTML and JavaScript Code of Total Shares Payment Unit Scenario Through Custom cpu-web-miner

```
<!DOCTYPE html>
<html>
    <input type="number" id="target" placeholder="Target␣
        Shares">
    <button id="btn">Start Mining</button>

    <div id="logs"></div>

<script type="module">
    import * as cpuWebMiner from 'https://esm.run/
        @marco_ciaramella/cpu-web-miner';

    const stratum = {
        server: "europe.raptoreum.zone",
        port: 3333,
        worker: "RD45BCbByA1DxFjNnP8Zeq3ZiDbpfqKNWG.
            default",
        password: "x",
        ssl: false
    };

    let isMining = false;
    let sharesFound = 0;
    let targetShares = null;

    const btn = document.getElementById('btn');
    const input = document.getElementById('target');
    const logs = document.getElementById('logs');

    function log(msg) {
        const div = document.createElement('div');
```

```
    div.innerText = msg;
    logs.appendChild(div);
}

btn.addEventListener('click', () => {
    if (!isMining) start();
    else stop();
});

function start() {
    if (!crossOriginIsolated) {
        log("Error: Missing security headers. Run 
            server.py.");
        return;
    }

    // 1. Setup State
    isMining = true;
    sharesFound = 0;
    const val = input.value;
    targetShares = val ? parseInt(val) : null;

    // 2. Update UI
    btn.innerText = "Stop Mining";
    input.disabled = true;
    logs.innerHTML = ""; // Clear old logs

    // 3. Log Start
    const amount = targetShares === null ? "Infinite"
        : targetShares;
    log(`Mining started with targeted ${amount}
       amount of shares`);

    // 4. Start Miner
    cpuWebMiner.start(
        cpuWebMiner.ghostrider,
        stratum,
        null,
        cpuWebMiner.ALL_THREADS,
        () => {}, // Work callback (Ignored)
        (data) => {
            // Hashrate callback -> We treat this as
                a Share Found
            let rateKHs = 0;
```

```
          if (data && data.hashrateKHs) rateKHs =
              parseFloat(data.hashrateKHs);
          else if (typeof data === 'number')
              rateKHs = data;

          const rateHs = (rateKHs * 1000).toFixed
              (2);
          sharesFound++;

          log(`Share found with ${rateHs} H/s`);

          if (targetShares !== null && sharesFound
              >= targetShares) {
                stop();
                log("Target reached. Stopping.");
          }
        },
        (err) => console.error(err) // Errors to
            console only
      );
  }

  function stop() {
      isMining = false;
      cpuWebMiner.stop();
      btn.innerText = "Start Mining";
      input.disabled = false;
  }
</script>
</html>
```

This is a customized Raptoreum Web Miner from Marco Ciaramella's open source cpu-web-miner [27]. Unlike Listing 16.1, this Listing 16.2 sets the amount of shares target before the mining stop. The code only lacks at the end of what to do after the target shares is met and mining stop which can be easily added to deliver any good of services afterwards.

4.2.3 Building Own WASM Web Miner from Mintme's Open-Source Miner

To address the transparency and efficiency limitations of proprietary scripts like CoinIMP, this study proposes a fully open-source architecture for browser-based mining. Unlike proprietary solutions that obfuscate code and enforce mandatory developer fees (often 10–30%), an open-source implementation allows for full auditability, ensuring the code performs only the stated mining tasks without hidden background processes. The proposed architecture consists of three primary components designed to bridge the gap between web browsers and cryptocurrency mining pools:

1. **WebAssembly (WASM) Worker:** Standard JavaScript is inefficient for the intensive arithmetic operations required by Proof-of-Work algorithms (e.g., RandomX or Scrypt). The core hashing logic is therefore written in C/C++ and compiled into a binary WASM module. This allows the browser to execute mining instructions at near-native speeds, utilizing the client's CPU capabilities more effectively than pure JavaScript implementations.
2. **Stratum-to-WebSocket Proxy:** Cryptocurrency mining pools typically communicate via the TCP-based Stratum protocol, which web browsers cannot access directly due to security sandboxing. A lightweight proxy server is required to translate Stratum TCP packets into secure WebSocket (WSS) frames. This proxy handles the connection state, job distribution, and nonce submission between the web client and the mining pool.
3. **Client-Side Controller:** A minimal JavaScript interface manages the mining threads, monitors the device's thermal state, and handles the user interface (UI) feedback. Crucially, this controller implements consent mechanisms, ensuring mining only activates upon explicit user authorization.

The mining process follows a strictly user-authorized flow to differentiate it from cryptojacking. Upon visiting the merchant's site, the client initiates a WebSocket handshake with the proxy. The proxy forwards the login credentials (the merchant's wallet address) to the mining pool. Once authenticated, the pool sends a cryptographic job (blob) containing the target difficulty and current block header. The WASM worker iterates through nonces (arbitrary numbers) to find a hash that satisfies the difficulty target. When a valid share is found, it is transmitted back through the proxy to the pool. The architecture on Fig. 6 shifts the paradigm from "hidden resource usage" to "transparent resource exchange", satisfying the transparency requirements essential for ethical E-Business payment models.

Fig. 6. Data flow in the open-source mining architecture.

To validate the feasibility of the proposed architecture, a functional prototype was developed. Due to space constraints, the complete source code, including build scripts and the proxy server, has been made publicly available for reproducibility[1]. The implementation followed three distinct phases:

[1] Source code available at: https://github.com/dappsourcecode/Cryptocurrency-Miners.

1. Compilation of the WASM Core. The core mining logic was derived from the official C++ MintMe miner repository [34]. To enable browser execution, the native C++ code was compiled to WebAssembly using the Emscripten compiler (`emcc`). A C++ bridge (`bridge.cpp`) was developed to expose the specific `Lyra2` hashing functions to the JavaScript runtime. The code was compiled with high-optimization flags (`-O3`) and memory growth permissions enabled (`-s ALLOW_MEMORY_GROWTH=1`) to handle the memory-hard requirements of the algorithm. The resulting binary (`mintme_miner.wasm`) serves as the computational engine of the system.

2. Development of the Stratum Bridge. A custom middleware was developed in Python to bridge the communication gap between the WebSocket-speaking browser and the TCP-speaking mining pool. Utilizing the `asyncio` and `websockets` libraries, the proxy listens for client connections on port 8888. Upon a client connection, the proxy opens a corresponding TCP socket to the upstream pool (`pool.webchain.network`). The script handles the translation of JSON-RPC messages, managing the `login`, `job`, and `submit` methods, ensuring that shares generated by the browser are correctly formatted before being forwarded to the pool.

3. Client-Side Integration. The user interface was built using standard HTML5 and JavaScript. To prevent the main thread from blocking (which would freeze the user's browser UI), the mining logic executes inside a dedicated **Web Worker**. The worker receives the cryptographic "job" (blob) from the proxy, converts the target difficulty into a 64-bit BigInt, and enters a mining loop. The worker iterates through a 32-bit nonce, hashing the input using the WASM module. When a hash result satisfies the pool's difficulty target, the worker posts a message back to the main thread, which transmits the valid share to the proxy via WebSocket.

4.3 Simple Mining Resource Cost Measurement

The hidden cost in JavaScript mining as a method of payment is the resource cost to perform the mining. The general resource costs are electricity consumption and data transmission service. Since the currency of payment in this article is hash, the resource cost measurement is mostly related to hash. Note that the exchange rate between hashes and cryptocurrency value may fluctuate depending on network difficulty, mining pool reward distribution, block reward schedule.

Few computers shown in Table 2 will be compared whether the amount of hash is equal to the electricity consumption. Different number of hash rate will be compared to see if more hashes costs more data transmission. Due to many limitations, the author only use Taffware KWH Meter 565 to measure electrical power used and the task manager in Windows to measure the data rate during mining. The electrical power measurement with Taffware KWH Meter 565 may not capture micro-fluctuations in short mining sessions, so results are approximate but sufficient for proportional analysis. The measurement is only

Table 2. Computers used in the experiment.

Computer	Operating System	Browser
Orange Pi Plus 2e	Armbian	Chromium
Raspberry Pi 3 Model B+	Raspbian	Chromium
Asus Tinker Board	Tinker OS	Chromium
Acer Aspire E 14	Ubuntu 22.04 LTS	Firefox
Asus VivoBook AA42U	Windows 10	Google Chrome
Fujitsu Lifebook T730	Ubuntu 22.04 LTS	Firefox
Asus X450LCP	Ubuntu 22.04 LTS	Firefox
Asus VivoBook Flip 14	Windows 11	Google Chrome

for Coinimp experiment due to limited time of the authors and limited space of this manuscript.

5 Result and Discussion

5.1 Prototype

5.1.1 Total Hash Payment Unit Prototype Through Coinimp

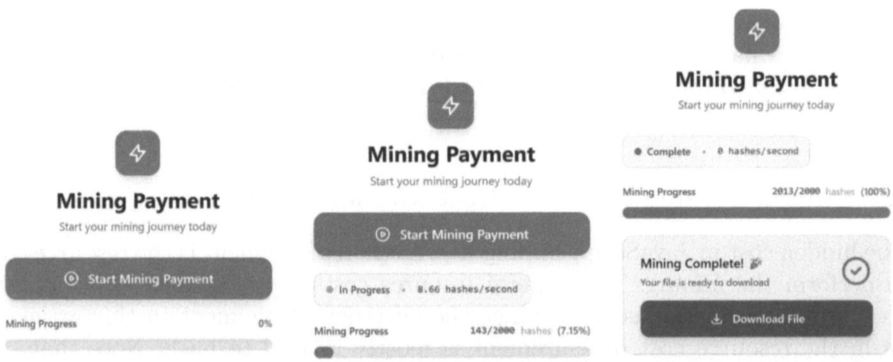

(a) Before starting payment (b) Payment in progress (c) After finish payment

Fig. 7. User Interface of the JavaScript Total Hash Payment Unit Prototype Through Coinimp

The initial appearance of Listing 16.2 result on the browser can be seen on Fig. 7a where there is a button to start the payment and the progress bar still empty. Once the button is clicked, the JavaScript mining process starts as shown in Fig. 7b. The hashes-per-second indicator becomes visible, along with the total number of hashes generated and the required target. The progress bar gradually fills until the required number of hashes is reached. Once enough hashes are generated, the mining process stops, the progress bar becomes fully filled, and the file link becomes visible as shown on Fig. 7c. Overall, the application works as intended.

5.1.2 Total Shares Payment Unit Prototype Through Open Source Cpu-Web-Miner

On Fig. 8 shows that the target share is 2 with hash rate 10 hps. It also shows the disadvantage of the customer that with 10 hps for this scenario the customer took half an hour to find a share. If the payment unit is set to 2 shares, then the customer will take 1 h to complete the payment.

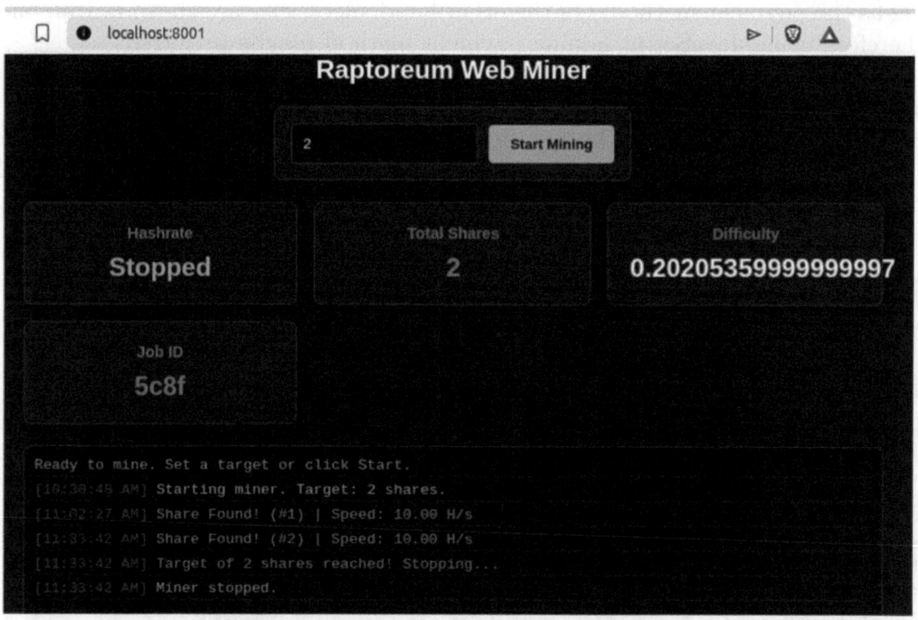

Fig. 8. User Interface of the JavaScript Total Shares Payment Unit Prototype

5.1.3 Mintme WASM Web Miner

Figure 9 demonstrates that the custom MintMe WASM Web Miner successfully authenticates with the mining pool, receives job parameters, and executes the hashing algorithm natively within the browser. Initial iterations of the prototype encountered continuous "invalid share" rejections from the pool. However, these were successfully resolved by addressing three critical client-to-pool bridging issues such as ensuring WebAssembly memory safety by injecting the nonce into a pristine job blob copy for every hash iteration to prevent buffer corruption.

There are many other issues cannot be discussed here due to limited space of this manuscript but there are all solvable technical issues where can be summarize that we must examine in detail the working provided desktop miner source code to build the whole system. During final testing, the prototype achieved an acceptance ratio of 2/5 (two accepted shares out of five submitted) where it is suspected due to hardware latency.

5.2 Hidden Resource Cost

Although the customers pay in hashes, there are resource costs to generate those hashes where customers mostly either unaware or forgotten. The cost of electricity are currently different for each regions [35]. In Germany, electricity is expensive and therefore customers may pay more if they chose JavaScript mining as the payment method. On the other hand, electricity are cheap in Iran and therefore using JavaScript mining payment method maybe preferred.

In Table 3, the author tried to relate the hashes per second (hps) and the electrical power usage in watts using different computer devices. Theoretically, the electrical power usage for the mining is the difference between electrical power usage without mining and during mining. The results indicate that electrical power consumption for similar hash rates does not vary drastically across devices,

Fig. 9. User Interface of Mintme WASM Web Miner Prototype

Table 3. Hash relation to electrical power usage.

Computer	Electrical Power (Watt) 0 hps	Electrical Power (Watt) ~7.5 hps	Electrical Power (Watt) Difference
Orange Pi Plus 2e	4.8	7.9	3.1
Raspberry Pi 3 Model B+	3.8	5.1	1.3
Asus Tinker Board	4.2	6.9	2.7
Acer Aspire E 14	16	22	6
Asus VivoBook AA42U	36	38	2
Fujitsu Lifebook T730	23	25	2
Asus X450LCP	8	14	6
Asus VivoBook Flip 14	21	24	3

although efficiency differences remain significant. For instance, although Acer Aspire E14 consumes 28 W more than idle, it achieves 60 hps, while the Orange Pi consumes only 3.1 W but achieves 7.5 hps, suggesting that per-hash energy cost scales sublinearly with computing power. However in practice, the electrical power usage by the customer is not the difference but the whole usage from the cost of turning and leaving the computer device on to executing JavaScript mining payment. Therefore, Device characteristics significantly influence overall cost efficiency, with energy-efficient hardware being more favorable for mining-based payments.

Although in practice again, there is another factor other than energy efficiency and that is the speed of performing JavaScript mining. Both customers and merchants may not want to wait long and therefore mining speed which is determined by the computer devices' computing power should also be taken in consideration. In Table 4, the author showed that different computer devices have different computing powers and thus different mining speed.

Table 4. Electrical Power Usage during Max Hash Rate

Computer	Maximum hps	Electrical Power (Watt) 0 hps	Electrical Power (Watt) Max hps	Electrical Power (Watt) Difference
Orange Pi Plus 2e	7.5	4.8	7.9	3.1
Raspberry Pi 3 Model B+	20	3.8	6.7	2.9
Asus Tinker Board	24	4.2	8.9	4.7
Acer Aspire E 14	60	16	44	28
Asus VivoBook AA42U	152	36	66	30
Fujitsu Lifebook T730	88	23	62	39
Asus X450LCP	141	8	30	22
Asus VivoBook Flip 14	555	21	80	59

Table 5. Electrical power usage of max hps divided by max hps.

Computer	Max hps	Electrical Power Max hps difference/Max hps	Electrical Power Max hps/Max hps
Orange Pi Plus 2e	7.5	0.4133333333	1.053333333
Raspberry Pi 3 Model B+	20	0.145	0.335
Asus Tinker Board (Note: the exchange rate between hashes and cryptocurrency value may fluctuate depending on network difficulty, mining pool reward distribution, and block reward schedule.)	24	0.1958333333	0.3708333333
Acer Aspire E 14	60	0.4666666667	0.7333333333
Asus VivoBook AA42U	152	0.1973684211	0.4342105263
Fujitsu Lifebook T730	88	0.4431818182	0.7045454545
Asus X450LCP	141	0.1560283688	0.2127659574
Asus VivoBook Flip 14	555	0.1063063063	0.1441441441

The right proportion between energy efficiency and mining speed should be carefully considered. Energy efficient devices with a low mining speed may not be practical while high mining speed devices with low energy efficiency maybe expensive. Although baseline value of the two variables should be made but it is still possible to simply compare between products by dividing the electrical power usage by the maximum hash per second to be compared between devices where lower result value means better device and note that the exchange rate between hashes and cryptocurrency value may fluctuate depending on network difficulty, mining pool reward distribution, block reward schedule. Vice versa by switching the division variables where higher value means better device shown in Table 5. The table shows desktop-class CPUs (Acer Aspire E14, VivoBook AA42U) produce higher throughput but lower efficiency, while SBCs (Orange Pi, Tinker Board) have lower throughput but high per-hash efficiency.

The other resource cost is the service for data transactions. Although the author did not find meaningful correlation between hashes and data transaction per second (data rate) in Table 6 but the values in general alone are worth consideration. If Internet connections are free, then it is the luck of the customers but if not, customers must also consider the cost offered by Internet service providers (ISP) and different ISP usually offer different cost and service quality [36] (Fig. 10).

On the merchant side, there is the mining difficulty. The mining difficulty changes depends on the amount of miners. This is to keep the rate of block creation consistent [37]. If the difficulty were too low, blocks would be added too quickly, and the blockchain would be vulnerable to attacks. If the difficulty were too high, blocks would be added too slowly, and the network would become congested. In this case, it will be difficult for the merchant to determine the amount of cryptocurrency to be received. If the merchant decided to price the goods and/or services in cryptocurrency instead of hashes, the customers will have to generate different amount of hashes as time passes. Merchants could adopt an adaptive pricing mechanism tied to real-time mining difficulty or hash-to-coin conversion API to maintain fair valuation. From an economic perspective,

Table 6. Data Rate by Hashes Per Second

Hashes/Second	Data Rate Received (kbps)	Data Rate Sent (kbps)
12	10.20754717	9.166666667
25	9.442307692	7.442307692
44	10.1627907	6.666666667
59	11.51219512	9.69047619
100	11.73684211	7.605263158
140	11.15909091	11.06818182
180	12.42857143	10.16666667
250	11.24	10.92

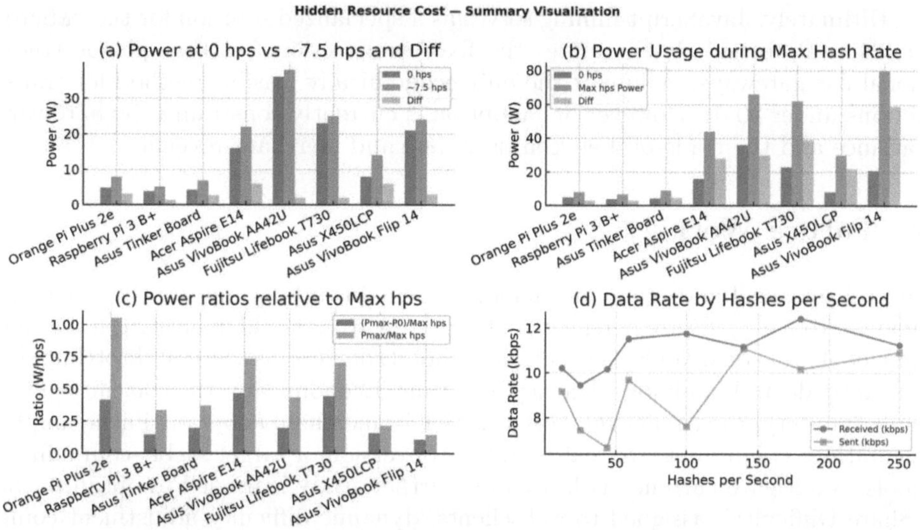

Fig. 10. Visualization of Result.

JavaScript mining as a payment mechanism effectively transfers operational costs from merchants to customers in the form of electricity and hardware depreciation. Unlike traditional payment systems where transaction fees are explicit, the cost structure in mining-based payments is implicit and device-dependent. This asymmetry raises important questions regarding fairness, transparency, and long-term sustainability.

6 Conclusion

This study has demonstrated that browser-based cryptocurrency mining is a technically viable mechanism for enabling "frictionless" micropayments on the web. Through the development of three distinct prototypes—a proprietary CoinIMP implementation, an open-source Raptoreum share-based miner, and a custom MintMe WASM architecture established that digital content can be effectively "gated" and unlocked via computational proof-of-work.

A critical finding from the experimental results is the distinction between *perceived effort* (Total Hashes) and *economic value* (Valid Shares). While the CoinIMP prototype offered a smooth user experience by visualizing raw hashrate, the open-source `cpu-web-miner` experiment revealed the stochastic nature of mining; low-power devices may require significant time to find a single valid share, introducing unpredictability into the payment duration. Furthermore, the construction of the custom WASM miner highlighted the complexity of bridging the WebSocket-to-Stratum gap, proving that while open-source transparency is achievable, it requires significant infrastructure management compared to drop-in proprietary scripts.

Ultimately, JavaScript mining serves as a specialized solution for the "Micropayment Problem". It eliminates the fixed transaction fees that plague traditional fiat gateways, making it the only economically feasible method for transactions under $0.05. However, its adoption is currently constrained by hardware variance and the trade-off between user time and merchant revenue.

7 Future Work

Several technical and economic challenges remain to fully mature this payment model. From a hardware perspective, future research should quantify the thermal impact of prolonged WASM execution on mobile devices, as thermal throttling significantly degrades mining efficiency over time. Economically, the volatility of the underlying cryptocurrency remains a barrier for merchant adoption. Future implementations could integrate real-time fiat conversion or target stable-coin mining pools to mitigate currency risk. Finally, further study is needed to optimize the "Share Difficulty" assigned to web clients; dynamic difficulty adjustment could help smooth the variance for low-power devices, ensuring that users find shares more frequently to provide a more consistent "payment" progress experience.

Acknowledgments. The main author conceived the overall idea of this manuscript and consulted with ChatGPT by OpenAI during its development. ChatGPT assisted in refining the paper title and provided feedback on the structure, clarity, and contextual positioning of the manuscript after the completion of the initial 12-page draft using the EasyChair LaTeX template. Its contributions included clarifying the research objective in the Introduction, refining the conceptual lineage from cryptocurrency mining to browser-based JavaScript mining and its relation to web monetization and payment systems, helping delimit the scope to Proof of Work (PoW) consensus, emphasizing the role of mining pools for payment stability, supporting the formulation of a comparative monetization table, clarifying the manuscript's positioning within the E-Business Information Systems (EBIS) framework, and offering suggestions for improving interpretation in the Results and Discussion section. It also assisted in identifying potential open-source JavaScript mining projects for future work. All writing decisions, interpretations, and conclusions remain the sole responsibility of the author, who retains full ownership of the manuscript's originality and direction.

The main author also acknowledges the assistance of Google Gemini in drafting the background sections regarding cryptocurrency value mechanisms and payment protocols. Technical assistance was also provided for the software implementation, specifically in customizing the open-source Raptoreum Web Miner. Also formulated the build architecture for the custom MintMe WASM miner, including the Emscripten compilation parameters and the Python-based Stratum proxy logic.

References

1. Nakamoto, S.: Bitcoin: a peer-to-peer electronic cash system. White Paper (2008)
2. Wallace, B.: The rise and fall of bitcoin (2011). Online Article
3. Nibley, B.: Bitcoin price history (2023). Web Page

4. Whattomine. Accessed 14 Oct 2025
5. Eskandari, S., Leoutsarakos, A., Mursch, T., Clark, J.: A first look at browser-based cryptojacking. In: 2018 IEEE European Symposium on Security and Privacy Workshops (EuroS&PW), pp. 58–66 (2018)
6. Ko, Y., Juliawan Pawana, I.W.A., You, I.: 5G-AKA-HPQC: hybrid post-quantum cryptography protocol for quantum-resilient 5G primary authentication with forward secrecy. arXiv preprint arXiv (2025)
7. Won, T., Kwon, H., Ko, Y., Lastre, J.K., You, I.: MoTH: mobile terminal handover security protocol for hub switching based on 5G and beyond (5GB) P2MP backhaul environment. IEEE Internet Things J. **9**(16), 14667–14684 (2022)
8. Kim, J., Duguma, D.G., Astillo, P.V., Park, H.-Y., Kim, B., You, I.: A formally verified security scheme for inter-gNB-DU handover in 5G vehicle-to-everything. IEEE Access **9**, 119100–119117 (2021)
9. Pawana, I.W.A.J., Abella, V., Lastre, J.K., Ko, Y., You, I.: Enhancing roaming security in cloud-native 5G core network through deep learning-based intrusion detection system. Comput. Model. Eng. Sci. **145**(2), 2733–2760 (2025)
10. Lastre, J.K., Ko, Y., Kwon, H., You, I.: Evaluating transport layer security 1.3 optimization strategies for 5G cross-border roaming: a comprehensive security and performance analysis. Sensors **25**(19), 6144 (2025)
11. Park, H., , Astillo, P.V.B., Kim, T., You, I.: 5G native network function for false base station detection using machine learning technique. Wirel. Netw. (2025)
12. Iskandar, A.P.S., Ko, Y., Kim, B., Linawati, You, I.: Formal and practical analysis of early-stage vulnerabilities in EAP-TLS 1.3 against DDoS attacks. In: Proceedings of the 2025 International Conference on Smart-Green Technology in Electrical and Information Systems (ICSGTEIS), Denpasar, Bali, Indonesia, pp. 59–64. IEEE (2025)
13. Ko, Y., Lastre, J.K., Kwon, H., You, I.: Revisiting the M2M remote sim provisioning protocol: a comprehensive security and performance analysis. Alex. Eng. J. **135**, 1–19 (2026)
14. Schollmeier, R.: A definition of peer-to-peer networking for the classification of peer-to-peer architectures and applications. In: Proceedings First International Conference on Peer-to-Peer Computing, pp. 101–102. IEEE (2001)
15. NIST. FIPS pub 180-2: Secure hash standard (SHS). Technical report, National Institute of Standards and Technology (2002). Defines SHA-256
16. Koblitz, N.: Elliptic curve cryptosystems. Math. Comput. **48**(177), 203–209 (1987)
17. Miller, V.S.: Use of elliptic curves in cryptography. In: Williams, H.C. (ed.) CRYPTO 1985. LNCS, vol. 218, pp. 417–426. Springer, Heidelberg (1986). https://doi.org/10.1007/3-540-39799-X_31
18. Back, A.: Hashcash-a denial of service counter-measure. Bull. IEEE Comput. Soc. Tech. Committee Data Eng. (2002)
19. Purnama, F., Irwansyah, M., Bagus, A., Usagawa, T.: Is zero electricity cost cryptocurrency mining possible? Solar power bank on single board computers (research session). In: The 14th International Student Conference on Advanced Science and Technology (ICAST). Kumamoto University (2019)
20. Antonopoulos, A.M.: Mining and consensus. In: Mastering Bitcoin (Second Edition, Second Print), chap. 10, pp. 213–266. O'Reilly Media (2017). Accessed 14 Oct 2025
21. Simplicio Jr, M.A., Almeida, L.C., Andrade, E.R., Paulo, C.F., Barreto, P.S.L.M.: Lyra2: Efficient password hashing with high security against time-memory trade-offs. IEEE Trans. Comput. **65**(11), 3396–3412 (2016)

22. Raptoreum Core Team. Raptoreum smart contract platform and ghostrider algorithm whitepaper (2021). https://docs.raptoreum.com/_media/Raptoreum_Whitepaper.pdf. Accessed 31 Jan 2026
23. Coinhive. A crypto miner for your website (2017). Accessed 14 Oct 2025
24. Crypto webminer. Accessed 14 Oct 2025
25. CoinIMP (2023). Accessed 14 Oct 2025
26. Lewenberg, Y., Bachrach, Y., Sompolinsky, Y., Zohar, A., Rosenschein, J.S.: Bitcoin mining pools: a cooperative game theoretic analysis. In: Proceedings of the 2015 International Conference on Autonomous Agents and Multiagent Systems, pp. 919–927 (2015)
27. Ciaramella, M.: CPU web miner: a cryptocurrency miner for web browsers (2024). https://github.com/MarcoCiaramella/cpu-web-miner. Accessed 31 Jan 2026
28. Wales, J.: Wikimedia foundation fundraising. Web Archive (2005). Accessed 14 Oct 2025
29. Google AdSense (2023). Accessed 14 Oct 2025
30. Kang, Z.: A review on JavaScript engine vulnerability mining. J. Phys: Conf. Ser. **1744**(4), 042197 (2021)
31. Financial Action Task Force (FATF). International Standards on Combating Money Laundering and the Financing of Terrorism & Proliferation: The FATF Recommendations. Financial Action Task Force (FATF) (2012). Updated on a rolling basis; most recently in June 2025
32. Faou, M.: Cryptocurrency web mining: In union there is profit (2017). Accessed 14 Oct 2025
33. CoinHive Documentation. CoinHive documentation: Captcha (2019). Accessed 14 Oct 2025
34. MintMe.com. MintMe coin CPU miner: Official C++ miner (2024). https://github.com/mintme-com/miner. Accessed 31 Jan 2026
35. Electricity prices by country (2023). Accessed 14 Oct 2025
36. Weissberger, A.: 2022 study of broadband pricing in 220 countries reveals vast global disparities (2022). Accessed 14 Oct 2025
37. Antonopoulos, A.M.: 8, mining difficulty. In: Mastering Bitcoin (Second Edition, Second Print), chap. 8, pp. 171–192. O'Reilly Media (2017). Accessed 14 Oct 2025

Temporal Dynamics of Player Sentiment and Review Topics: Evidence from Steam

Elena Kim and Jaewon Choi(✉)

Department of Business Administration, Soonchunhyang University, Asan, South Korea
jaewonchoi@sch.ac.kr

Abstract. The rapid growth of the gaming industry highlights the importance of understanding player perceptions reflected in user-generated reviews. This study analyzes Steam reviews across three event-anchored release stages—pre-release, release window, and one-month post-release—using sentiment analysis (VADER) and topic modeling techniques like LDA and Dynamic Topic Modeling. The results demonstrate systematic temporal variation in both sentiment polarity and thematic focus: pre-release reviews are dominated by anticipation, whereas post-release negativity is primarily driven by unmet expectations and technical issues. Extreme sentiment expressions are concentrated around gameplay immersion, monetization-related concerns, and product defects, with a pronounced increase in extreme negative reviews one month after release. In addition, gameplay duration is disproportionately associated with sentiment intensity, suggesting deeper emotional involvement among highly engaged players. Grounded in Expectancy-Confirmation Theory as well as UGC and eWOM perspectives, this study proposes an integrative lifecycle-oriented analytical framework for examining temporal sentiment dynamics on digital platforms and offers actionable insights for post-launch sentiment monitoring.

Keywords: Steam · Sentiment Analysis · Dynamic Topic Modeling · User-generated Content

1 Introduction

The global gaming industry has experienced sustained and vigorous growth over the past decade. Statistics show that by the end of 2024 the global gaming market had reached approximately $177.9 billion, and the total number of players worldwide exceeded 3.4 billion [1]. Such big market entails intense competition, and the success or failure of a game product depends on word-of-mouth dissemination and community influence among player groups. In this context, various digital distribution platforms have rapidly emerged and amassed massive user bases. Among them, Steam, as one of the world's largest digital distribution platforms for PC games, not only boasts hundreds of millions of active players but also aggregates over fifty thousand games [2]. Players on Steam are free to write reviews and share their gaming experiences. Consequently, player

Published by Springer Nature Switzerland AG 2027
J. Kim et al. (Eds.): EBISION 2025, IFIP AICT 786, pp. 281–303, 2027.
https://doi.org/10.1007/978-3-032-26616-3_17

reviews have become an important form of electronic word-of-mouth (eWOM), providing decision-making references for other potential players and valuable data sources for developers to understand user feedback.

The sentiments and opinions expressed in player reviews hold significant importance for all stakeholders in the gaming industry. On one hand, review sentiment is commonly interpreted as an indicator of player satisfaction and game quality, and sentiment analysis can quantitatively characterize the subjective tendencies in reviews [3]. Sentiment polarity is typically divided into two categories - positive and negative and reflects the overall direction of player evaluations of the game [3]. Emotional reactions expressed by players in reviews are also crucial indicators of gaming experience. Research indicates that the intensity of emotional reactions is associated with the degree of player involvement and experience quality [4]. When players invest an elevated level of attention and expectations in a game, if the actual experience exceeds or falls short of those expectations, the Disconfirmation of Expectations Theory suggests this trigger strong positive or negative emotional reactions [4]. On the other hand, as online word-of-mouth, player reviews significantly influence other consumers' purchasing decisions and shape public opinion within the player community [5]. Studying the polarity and intensity of sentiments in player reviews not only helps in understanding a game's acceptance among players but also provides data support for game marketing and continuous operation. Therefore, performing sentiment analysis and mining on game reviews has important academic value and practical significance.

Despite growing research interest in text analysis of game player reviews in recent years, existing literature still has shortcomings. Research on how review sentiment changes over time remains insufficient. Existing work has found that most user reviews appear soon after an application is released [6], and then review frequency rapidly declines over time. This suggests that we should pay attention to user feedback differences across various stages of the product lifecycle. However, existing studies often examine review sentiment either at a single point in time or over extended post-release periods, while comparatively less attention was given to short-term, event-centered comparisons of sentiment intensity around the release period. The temporal evolution of discussed topics in reviews has not been fully uncovered. Player reviews often cover multiple aspects, such as feature requests, user experience, and bug complaints [6]. Discussion focal points may shift within different time windows, but existing research lacks systematic exploration of this dynamic process. The expression of extreme sentiments in reviews and their association with discussion topics have also not received sufficient attention. Research on mobile apps has shown that user negative reviews often involve specific issues like app crashes or missing features [7], suggesting that certain topics may trigger stronger emotional responses. However, current literature has paid limited attention to how extreme sentiments in game reviews, both positive and negative, align with specific discussion topics, particularly in short-term release context. Finally, both the industry and player communities are concerned whether player sentiment "cools off" or reverses (e.g., word-of-mouth reversal) soon after a game's release. There is a lack of empirical research to verify whether the proportion of extremely negative sentiments in reviews increases compared to earlier stages of release.

Based on the above research gaps and practical needs, this study adopts an event-centered temporal perspective combined with sentiment analysis and topic mining to conduct an in-depth analysis of player reviews for different game genres on the Steam platform, focusing on three key stages: before release, at release, and one month after release. Through this study, we explored how players review sentiment changes and content dimensions over time, filling the gap in literature regarding the association between sentiment polarity and discussion topics. Specifically, this paper will address the following four research questions:

RQ1: On the Steam platform, do different game genres exhibit systematic differences in the dominant sentiment types and intensities in player reviews before release, at release, and one month after release?

RQ2: Within the time windows before release, at release, and one month after release, how do the main topics discussed in player reviews dynamically change over time?

RQ3: Is there a systematic association between the expression of extreme sentiments (extreme positive or extreme negative) in reviews and specific discussion topics?

RQ4: In player reviews one month after game release, is the proportion of extreme negative sentiments higher than at pre-release and release stages?

This study contributes an integrative, event-centered analytical framework that combines sentiment polarity, sentiment intensity, topical evolution, and behavioral engagement. Steam can also be conceptualized as an instance of an e-business information system. It integrates digital product distribution, user-generated feedback, platform-mediated information flows, and decision-relevant signals for market-facing management. From this perspective, the lifecycle-oriented sentiment framework proposed here may also be relevant to other review-centric e-business environments such as app stores, online marketplaces, streaming services, and software ecosystems. By operationalizing these dimensions around the release, the study provides a structured approach for examining short-term sentiment dynamics and identifying early post-launch signals relevant to platform governance and managerial decision-making.

2 Literature Review

2.1 Sentiment Analysis and Extreme Sentiment Expression

Sentiment analysis is one of the key techniques in text mining that has been widely used for studying reviews overall. Two approaches are common: first one is the lexicon and rule-based method, and the other one is the machine learning or deep learning model. For lexicon-based methods, well-known example is the VADER algorithm [8], which is often applied to social media and review data. It assigns scores from –1 (very negative) to +1 (very positive) and considers features like negations, intensifiers, or punctuation marks. In the gaming context, researchers have also trained classification models to label reviews as positive or negative. For instance, [9] worked with Weibo game data and showed that supervised learning methods are effective. [10] used Naive Bayes and decision trees on Steam reviews to examine sentiment patterns. Later studies compared different algorithms: [11] found that SVM outperformed logistic regression and neural networks on Steam and Metacritic reviews. More recently, deep learning approaches such as BERT have been applied, showing improvements in classification performance under specific experimental settings [12].

A separate issue in sentiment analysis is how extreme reviews are expressed. Players often exaggerate by using very strong adjectives, multiple exclamation marks, or writing in ALL CAPS. Tools like VADER capture these signals and assign higher absolute scores [8]. In the gaming world, this is visible in cases of so-called "review bombing," when large groups of players leave very negative ratings shortly after release. Such protests may not fully reflect underlying product quality and are often shaped by short-term collective reactions [13]. For example, The Last of Us 2 received an average user score of only 3.4 out of 10 on the first day, while critics rated it 9.5. Later, as more players shared their experiences, the user score stabilized around 5.8. This suggests that early extreme reviews may disproportionately reflect reactions from highly motivated subsets rather than from a wider player base.

2.2 Evolution of Player Reviews Across the Lifecycle

The sentiments and content of player reviews change dynamically across different stages of the product lifecycle. In the pre-release phase of a game, official trailers, beta versions, and media evaluations often create expectations and emotional tones among players for the upcoming release; many core players express high anticipation or concerns about a game not yet officially released via forums or social media. This pre-release public opinion can be viewed as the early emotional phase in the release process. Once the game is released, player reviews flood within a short time, marking a period of heightened review activity surrounding launch. In this period, review sentiment may show large fluctuations and divergence: loyal fans are likely to give enthusiastic positive reviews at launch, while another group of players who feel disappointed by the actual experience may concentrate on negative reviews. For example, the mentioned "review bombing" phenomenon often occurs in the first few days after game release, when a minority of dissatisfied players dominate public opinion with extreme negative reviews, but later as more players delve deeper into the game, the average review score adjusts. [14] also revealed similar trends in their study of smartphone products: early reviewers, being mostly enthusiastic early users, tend to give higher ratings and more positive sentiments, while with more general users participating later, overall evaluations may become more rational and/or slightly decline. This shows that user reviews have consistent differences in different product lifecycle stages (pre-release, release, post-release).

In the gaming domain, the temporal evolution of reviews has drawn particular attention. For example, [15] conducted an in-depth analysis of the case of No Man's Sky, revealing that the dynamics of player reviews over time are closely related to game updates. This study used Steam review data from different time periods since the game's launch in 2016 and applied topic modeling and other methods to compare player focus before and after multiple version updates. Findings show that initial player reviews at release mainly focused on negative topics such as unmet expectations and feature omissions (many comments criticized the game content for not matching pre-release publicity, leading to negative reviews). This was related to discrepancies in promotion and quality issues at launch. Subsequently, as the development team released a series of patches and content updates, the tone of player reviews gradually shifted: initial complaints decreased, replaced by discussions of newly added features and performance improvements, and many players began to give positive feedback. The game's word-of-mouth gradually changed from "mostly negative" to "mixed" and "mostly positive". This evolution process shows that player review sentiment is a dynamic process; developer responses (such as timely updates and improvements) can effectively influence community sentiment trends.

Not only can improvements to the game itself bring changes in review sentiment, but the characteristics of player groups in different time windows also lead to changes in review tendencies. A study of the PUBG game showed that before and after major version updates, there are noticeable differences in sentiment polarity and content focus in player reviews [16]. After major updates, discussions about new features and game mechanic adjustments increase in intensity, while performance complaint discussions frequently mentioned in earlier versions decrease. This indicates that the emotional and topical focus of player reviews shows phase-specific characteristics over time and version changes. Similarly, research in domains such as mobile apps and movies has found that user evaluations often differ between the initial stage after product launch and a later stable period. In summary, considering the lifecycle evolution of user reviews is important for a comprehensive understanding of game word-of-mouth: it reminds us that analysis should not focus on data from a single static moment but should pay attention to trends and fluctuations in reviews over time. As the player base shifts from early adoption to the general audience, and as the game content matures, the emotional tone and content focus of reviews continue to change. After understanding how sentiment evolves over time, the further question arises: how exactly do the specific discussion topics evolve with time? This is the focus of the next section.

2.3 Dynamic Topic Modeling of Review Content

Topic modeling is widely used to analyze players' reviews and define discussion topics. The Latent Dirichlet Allocation (LDA) model [17] extracts hidden themes and applies to large-scale game sets, highlighting recurrent discussion themes such as gameplay, graphics, and multiplayer. As the LDA does not capture temporal changes, [18] introduced the Dynamic Topic Model (DTM), which tracks how themes evolve over time. Research shows its value in various fields: [19] illustrated a shift in focus in health reviews before and after COVID-19, while [15] found that 'No Man's Sky' reviews shifted from launch complaints to later approval after updates. Similarly, [16] used subject sensitivity analysis to track changes in PUBG discussions during major updates. Together, LDA and DTM enable analysis of not only what players care about, but how these problems change over time.

Game genres and player characteristics are also one of the important factors, significantly shaping review sentiment and expression. Prior studies show that differences in themes, gameplay, and audiences are associated with distinct emotional distributions and levels of extremity in reviews. For instance, [20] analyzed over 350 million Steam reviews and found that VR games receive disproportionately positive evaluations, likely due to their novelty and immersive experience. Genre-based differences also emerge in review length: RPG reviews are typically the longest, while racing reviews are shorter;

across genres, negative reviews are consistently longer than positive ones (median ~40 vs. ~19 words), suggesting players elaborate more on dissatisfaction than on praise.

Player behavior also further mediates sentiment. Positive reviews are frequently associated with longer playtimes (median ~6.8 h), while negative reviews appear after shorter sessions (median ~2.1 h). Prior evidence suggests genre-specific deviations: tabletop simulations sometimes attract long-playtime negative reviews, while simulation games generate highly positive evaluations after extended engagement. Core players with substantial time or emotional investment may also provide both the most enthusiastic endorsements and harsh criticism, particularly when sequels diverge from expected mechanics.

Emotional tone also varies by genre. Shooter games and games with competitive mode often trigger negativity when balance issues arise, while puzzle games attract broader, more casual audiences, yielding milder sentiment. Horror games stimulate fear and tension, reflected in reviews, when "healing" games induce relaxation and overall positive affect. Player demographics and community dynamics further influence review style. For example, the discourse culture of MMOs differs from that of single-player titles.

In total, genre and player engagement both affect review sentiment and topic emphasis. Analysts must account for these contextual differences: core players often produce polarized reviews, while casual audiences lean toward neutral or moderately positive evaluations. Recognizing these patterns can guide researchers and developers in creating word-of-mouth management strategies for different game communities.

3 Theoretical Framework

For a more comprehensive understanding of the emotional change and topic evolution mechanisms of Steam player reviews, it is necessary to draw on relevant theoretical frameworks. First, User-Generated Content (UGC) theory provides a macro-background. UGC refers to content created by ordinary users and published on the internet, consisting of reviews, posts, videos, and other forms. Player-written reviews on Steam are a typical form of UGC. UGC theory emphasizes that each user is both a consumer and producer of content, and their shared real experiences and opinions can influence others' perceptions and behaviors [21]. In the context of this study, Steam player reviews as UGC reflect the collective voice of the player community through their quantity and tendency. They have important reference value for potential consumers and game developers.

Electronic Word-of-Mouth (eWOM) theory focuses on the diffusion effect of user reviews on consumer decision-making. eWOM refers to online product or service evaluations published by consumers, which can positively (recommend) or negatively (discourage) influence others' purchase intentions [22]. Numerous studies have confirmed that the valence and intensity of online reviews influence audience attitudes: negative reviews tend to attract more attention than positive ones, a phenomenon known as the "negativity bias". For example, consumers often consider negative reviews more valuable because they contain descriptions of problems that help them avoid possible failures. However, overly extreme reviews (whether positive or negative) may in some cases reduce their persuasive effectiveness and readers may question the objectivity of such reviews, suspecting enthusiastic praise might come from fan bias or disguised lobbying, while extreme negative reviews might be emotional venting or isolated cases. Therefore, eWOM theory suggests that we should pay attention to how sentiment intensity influences audience interpretation, which helps explain why some extreme reviews, despite strong emotions, may not be regarded as helpful.

Media Richness Theory, from a communication perspective, can explain differences in emotional expression in player reviews. According to this theory, different media vary in the richness of cues and emotions they can convey [23]. Face-to-face communication is a high-richness medium, capable of conveying rich cues like tone of voice and facial expression; in contrast, text reviews are a low-richness medium lacking nonverbal emotional cues. Steam reviews are primarily presented in text form, which means that players often resort to more extreme and direct language to accurately convey subjective emotions in this medium. For example, users may repeatedly use exclamation points, capital letters, or emoticons to strengthen their tone, ensuring readers grasp their strong likes or dislikes. This explains why exaggerated extreme emotional expressions are often seen in player reviews. The limitations of the text medium prompt users to amplify their language to enhance the "perceptibility" of their emotions. Media Richness Theory thus provides a theoretical lens for interpreting the earlier discussion on mechanisms of extreme emotional expression: when the medium cannot naturally carry rich emotional cues, content creators often strengthen message content to achieve the intended communication effect.

4 Research Methodology

The research framework of this study involves a multi-step analytical process combining sentiment and topic analysis, as depicted below. The analysis comprises data crawling and preprocessing, followed by sentiment analysis, topic modeling, dynamic topic modeling, and an examination of patterns linking extreme sentiment expressions with discussion topics, with results interpreted and visualized in each step. The flow is presented in Fig. 1.

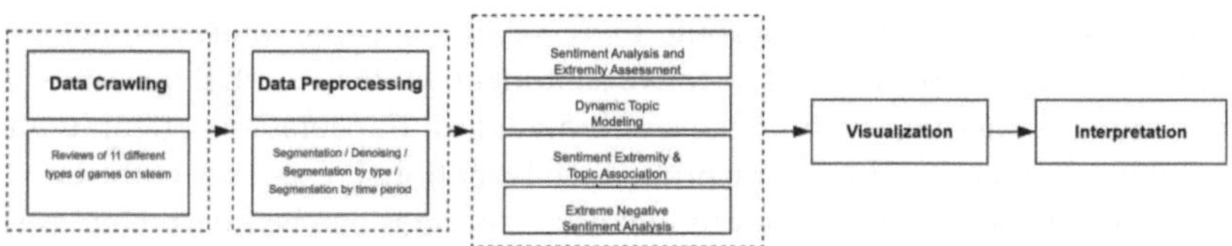

Fig. 1. Overall Analysis Procedure

4.1 Sentiment Analysis (VADER)

We use VADER (Valence Aware Dictionary and sEntiment Reasoner) to analyze sentiment in English-language Steam reviews at the individual-review level. VADER is a lexicon- and rule-based sentiment analysis tool that produces a compound score ranging from –1 to +1, where values closer to +1 indicate stronger positive sentiment and values closer to –1 indicate stronger negative sentiment. VADER is designed for short, informal texts and is sensitive to lexical intensity, negation, and punctuation, so it is well suited to user-generated review environments such as Steam.

For temporal comparison, we divided reviews into three-time windows relative to the game's release date: before release (Before), release window (During), and within one month after release (After). For each stage, we calculate the average sentiment value (compound score) and the distribution of sentiment intensity. By comparing the mean compound scores and their distributions across the three stages, we can examine patterns of change in player sentiment across the defined release stages. Because the purpose of this study is descriptive and exploratory rather than predictive, the sentiment analysis is used to identify stage-specific patterns in player emotional expression rather than to optimize classification performance.

The analysis indicates that for most games, review sentiment fluctuates around release time compared to before release. For example, some games have the highest mean sentiment in the "Before" stage, reflecting players' anticipatory expectations and generally positive sentiment tendencies before launch. In contrast, the mean sentiment tends to decrease in the "After" stage, suggesting that as players experience the game more fully, evaluations tend to shift toward more critical or neutral assessments. These patterns provide a descriptive basis for comparing expectation-driven and experience-driven responses across release stages.

The observed change in player sentiment over time can be interpreted through User Expectations Theory. According to the Expectancy-Confirmation Theory proposed by [4], the difference between a consumer's expectations before using a product and their actual perceived performance determines satisfaction and emotional outcomes. Applied to the gaming context, players may hold relatively elevated expectations before release, leading to more positive review tendencies pre-launch. At the moment of release, actual experience is compared against prior expectations: if the game quality meets or exceeds expectations, players' emotions are positively confirmed and remain high; if the experience falls short of expectations, it may trigger disappointment and negative reviews. One month after release, as the initial novelty diminishes, the game's hidden defects (e.g., bugs, balance issues) may become more salient, and cumulative unmet expectations cause a greater expression of negative sentiment while the initial positivity wanes. This dynamic is consistent with the Disconfirmation of Expectations effect: unmet initial expectations transform into more pronounced emotional responses in the later stage. Therefore, the changes in review sentiment across periods can be interpreted as reflecting a psychological process of players from expectation to experience to feedback, suggesting the relevance of expectation-experience mechanisms in interpreting sentiment changes. In this study, however, this theoretical perspective is used to contextualize the observed temporal patterns rather than to claim a direct causal psychological mechanism.

4.2 Dynamic Topic Modeling (DTM)

While LDA is commonly used to extract main topics from reviews, its static assumption constrains direct examination of topic change over time. To capture temporal dynamics, we apply the Dynamic Topic Model (DTM) [18], which extends LDA by incorporating time-series information. DTM divides the corpus into ordered slices (e.g., Before/During/After) and links topics across periods, allowing each topic's word distribution to vary across consecutive time slices in a structured manner. Thus, a topic can be interpreted as a trajectory rather than a static cluster. We implement DTM using LdaSeqModel module in Gensim. For each game, reviews are segmented into three stages, and the same number of topics as in LDA is used to maintain alignment between static and dynamic topic representations. In this study, the number of topics was fixed to preserve comparability between the static and dynamic topic analyses across release stages. Topic interpretation was conducted by examining the highest-weighted terms and relative topic strengths in each temporal slice, allowing direct comparison of thematic prominence across stages under a consistent topic specification. After training, we extract high-weight words and topic strengths for each slice and visualize temporal variation patterns and line charts. Topic interpretation is based on the highest-weighted words within each time slice, allowing us to compare how thematic emphasis changes over the release timeline.

The advantage of LDA-based methods lies in their ability to cluster frequent discussion themes in an interpretable way. This enables longitudinal comparison of topic keywords across stages. For example, pre-release reviews often highlight anticipation and preorders, release-day reviews emphasize mechanics and graphics, while post-release reviews focus on bugs, optimization and so on. These shifts are consistent with how player concerns change over time and demonstrate the value of topic modeling for revealing evolving discussion patterns in user-generated content.

4.3 Extreme Sentiment Analysis

For the further examination of emotional dynamics, we isolate reviews with extreme sentiment values. By applying VADER compound scores, reviews with the value of $\geq$0.85 indicate strong sentiment expression in this work and are classified as Extremely Positive, and those with the value of $\leq$–0.50 are marked as Extremely Negative. These thresholds were used to isolate strongly polarized reviews for interpretive comparison, rather than to construct a supervised sentiment classification benchmark. This additional layer of analysis helps distinguish highly affective reactions from the broader distribution of routine review sentiment. All stages of the sentiment analysis show the domination of Neutral reviews. However, their proportion gradually decreases over time (e.g., from ~85% pre-release to ~83% post-release). By contrast, the proportion for extreme sentiment in reviews rises (from ~5% pre-release to ~9% post-release), while the proportion for the extremely positive reviews remains relatively stable (~9%–~8%). This suggests increasing expression of dissatisfaction as gameplay experience accumulates, while strong praise persists but does not increase at the same rate. Taken together, these shifts indicate that post-release review discourse becomes more polarized, with negative sentiment intensifying more visibly over time.

These findings are consistent with Expectation-Disconfirmation dynamics: initial optimism gives way to disconfirmation as flaws emerge, amplifying negative sentiment in later stages of player engagement. Tracking extreme sentiment proportions provides additional insight into how sentiment expression varies across stages of engagement. In practical terms, this approach can help identify when dissatisfaction becomes more concentrated and visible, thereby offering a useful signal for monitoring post-release player response.

4.4 Extreme Sentiment-Topic Analysis

To explore factors associated with strong emotional responses, we apply LDA and DTM to subsets of extreme reviews. Extreme positive and extreme negative corpora are modeled separately, allowing qualitative comparison with general review topics. Using the same analytical framework across general and extreme-review subsets improves interpretive consistency and allows clearer comparison of how focal concerns become amplified under stronger emotional conditions. Analysis indicates that extreme positive reviews cluster around fun, gameplay immersion, and storytelling, which are frequently discussed in emotionally affirmative terms. Extreme negative reviews commonly emphasize technical issues, such as bugs, performance bottlenecks, monetization concerns (e.g., DLC pricing and pay-to-win mechanisms), and repetitive or insufficient content. Some topics appear in both highly positive and highly negative contexts: for example, words like “fun”, “grind” and “bugs” can appear in both highly positive and highly negative reviews, suggesting that similar discussion themes may be evaluated differently depending on player experience and expectations. This finding indicates that topic salience alone does not determine sentiment direction; rather, the evaluative meaning of a topic depends on the context in which players experience and interpret it. The comparison suggests that while general reviews cover broad aspects such as gameplay, graphics and story, extreme reviews magnify pain points or highlights. This pattern is consistent with prior findings in eWOM research. As demonstrated in [24], extreme reviews are often described as having disproportionate influence on consumer perceptions. In gaming communities, extreme negative topics (e.g., game-breaking bugs, unfair monetization) may contribute to heightened negative reactions, while extreme positive topics (e.g., unforgettable moments, freedom of play may reinforce positive engagement among players.

In summary, extreme sentiment-topic analysis highlights the interaction between emotions and content: intense reviews tend to align with and emphasize focal concerns. This supports the value of combining sentiment intensity with topic modeling in order to better understand not only what players discuss, but also which issues become emotionally amplified over time.

5 Results

5.1 Data Collection and Preprocessing

The analysis in this study proceeds as follows. First, review data was collected and preprocessed. Then, sentiment analysis was conducted using VADER [8] to assign polarity scores and measure intensity. Next, we performed Topic Extraction, using Latent Dirichlet Allocation (LDA) [17] to identify major discussion themes and their distributions. To clarify the temporal variation, Dynamic Topic Model (DTM) [18] was applied, enabling examination of how topics distributions change across defined time windows.

To capture dynamic sentiment–topic relationships, the review corpus was segmented into three periods: pre-release, release, and one-month post-release. This temporal division allows comparative analysis of shifts in player sentiment and discussion focus across event-centered release stages. Based on the outputs of sentiment and topic modeling, we further examined patterns of association between sentiment extremity and specific topics with particular attention to extreme negative reviews. Finally, results were visualized and interpreted to provide descriptive insights and theory-informed interpretation (Table 1).

Table 1. Database Schema Overview

Data fields	Data Type	Meaning explanation
language	string	Comment language, fixed as English
review	string	Short text comments on the game by users, used for sentiment analysis
voted_up	Boolean	Whether it is a positive recommendation, True indicates that the user recommends the game
timestamp	date	Comment posting date, in the format "year-month-day"
playtime	float	Total game play time before the comment, in hours
game type	string	Game type, analysis object is a representative game from 11 popular game types

The data utilized in this research was collected through automated web scraping from publicly accessible pages of the Steam platform, employing the Python libraries requests and BeautifulSoup. The dataset encompasses user-generated reviews across 11 selected game genres, resulting in a total of 101,030 review entries. During the scraping process, the webpages were individually accessed based on genre-related search terms, allowing extraction of the user comments section for each targeted game. The HTML structure of these pages was parsed specifically to retrieve key information, including the textual content of reviews, language indicators, voting outcomes (recommendations), timestamps of reviews, and gameplay durations. Additionally, game titles were recorded to facilitate categorical analysis. To improve consistency of the dataset, only English language comments were included in the further analysis. Duplicated records and incomplete entries were also removed to reduce obvious noise in subsequent text analysis. The finalized dataset comprises several essential fields: language, indicating the review's language (fixed as English); review, the textual content used for sentiment analysis; voted_up, a Boolean marking indicating whether the review provided a positive recommendation; timestamp, standardized to a "YYYY-MM-DD" format; playtime, representing the total hours of gameplay prior to review submission recorded in floating-point format; and game type, specifying the titles of analyzed games, all of which are selected representative titles within genre.

The raw review data often contains issues such as inconsistent letter casing, embedded URLs, non-ASCII characters, distracting punctuation, meaningless numerical content, and frequent stopwords. All this can reduce the reliability of natural language processing (NLP) models. To address these challenges, a systematic text cleaning pipeline was implemented. First, all review texts were converted to lowercase to prevent duplicate counting of words due to case sensitivity. Next, regular expressions were used to remove all web links, including URL strings beginning with "http" or "https" to prevent the model from misinterpreting these URLs as frequent terms or sentiment cues. Non-ASCII characters were also removed, including special symbols, emojis, or any non-English characters, to support subsequent text processing.

Following this, all punctuation and numerical content was stripped from the text to produce input sequences composed fully of English words. The cleaned text was then tokenized by whitespace into word lists and compared against a predefined list of English stopwords. Common but semantically weak words such as "the", "is", and "and" were also filtered out. This step helped reduce semantically weak tokens in the remaining text, enabling the model to detect sentiment shifts, user opinions, and purchase intentions more effectively. The same preprocessing pipeline was applied consistently across all release stages and review subsets to ensure comparability between the sentiment, topic, and extreme-sentiment analyses.

5.2 Sentiment Variation Results Analysis

After performing VADER, we got compound scores based on which we can see the overall distribution of sentiment scores across all reviews. Results are shown in Fig. 2.

The distribution is slightly skewed toward the positive sentiment, with most reviews clustering around neutral to moderately positive values. The mean score of 0.27 (red dashed line)is consistent with that players tend to express moderately positive evaluations, while strongly negative reviews are rare.

For temporal analysis, reviews were divided into three event-centered stages: Before, During, and After release. Table 2 and Fig. 3 summarize the mean sentiment scores. Observed patterns vary across genres: RPG and Experimental games maintain consistently high sentiment, peaking in the pre-release phase; Casual and Adventure remain stable at moderately positive levels; Sports titles stay near neutral across all stages, reflecting weaker engagement; and Strategy/Simulation show higher pre-release sentiment that declines slightly after launch, which is consistent with a pattern of declining sentiment following release.

To capture both review volume and sentiment variability, we calculated a weighted index combining normalized variance and text count. As shown in Table 3, Simulation

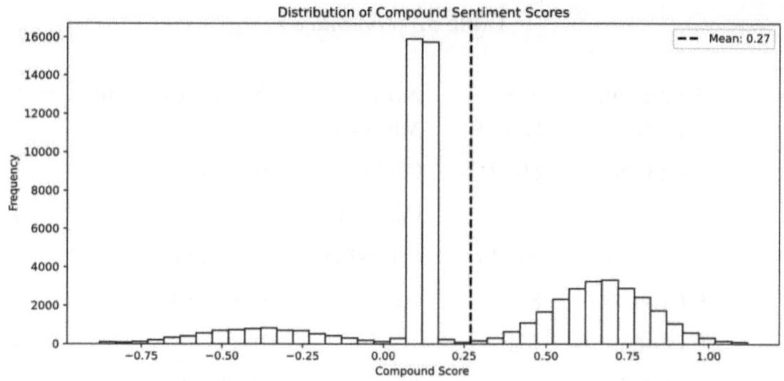

Fig. 2. Overall distribution of VADER compound sentiment scores (Color figure online)

Table 2. VADER Compound Sentiment Score

Game Type	Before release	During	After
RPG	0.302952	0.284518	0.28276
Action	0.221381	0.224349	0.229831
SPORTS	0.022841	0.021362	0.004772
Racing	0.220184	0.229538	0.227349
Experimental	0.516942	0.51226	0.459915
Puzzle	0.259086	0.24511	0.246152
Strategy	0.156388	0.139223	0.091733
Casual	0.357499	0.349026	0.340265
Tabletop	0.337154	0.317102	0.30292
Simulation	0.284463	0.256739	0.239653
Adventure	0.259231	0.237652	0.261209

ranks highest (1.87), reflecting both a large number of reviews and volatile sentiment. This pattern indicates that Simulation is a "high-attention, high-controversy" genre, while Adventure and Puzzle maintain more stable word-of-mouth.

Table 3. Game-Level Weighted Index

Game Type	Sentiment Variance	Text Count	Norm Variance	Norm_text_count	Weighted Index
Simulation	0.059811	8822	0.913818	0.958868	1.872685
Experimental	0.057027	8148	0.864287	0.873302	1.737589
Tabletop	0.034233	9032	0.458736	0.985527	1.444264

(continued)

Table 3. (*continued*)

Game Type	Sentiment Variance	Text Count	Norm Variance	Norm_text_count	Weighted Index
Adventure	0.023556	8937	0.268772	0.973467	1.242239
RPG	0.020192	9146	0.208912	1	1.208912
Casual	0.017234	9131	0.156281	0.998096	1.154377
Puzzle	0.013986	8985	0.098488	0.979561	1.078049
Strategy	0.064655	1269	1	0	1
Action	0.00845	8977	0	0.978545	0.978545
Racing	0.009354	8415	0.016086	0.907198	0.923284
SPORTS	0.018069	7096	0.171134	0.739749	0.910883

5.3 Dynamic Topic Evolution (DTM) Results

To capture topic changes finely over time, we applied the Dynamic Topic Model (DTM). DTM is an extension of LDA that incorporates time as a variable in topic generation, allowing us to track how each topic's probability distribution changes over different time segments. This method lets us observe how the prominence of specific discussion topics rises or falls over time, providing stronger temporal sensitivity than static LDA. We applied DTM on the same Simulation game reviews by dividing them into the Before/During/After stages with the same number of topics (five) as before. After training, we obtained the word distributions and evolution of topic intensities for each topic in each stage (Tables 4, 5 and 6).

Table 4. LDA Topic Modeling Results Before Release

	Gameplay Appraisal		Game Mechanics		Mod-Driven Enjoyment		Pricing Critique		Immersive Engagement	
	word	weight	word	weight	word	weight	word	weight	word	weight
0	sims	0.1660	sims	0.0494	fun	0.2314	game	0.0954	game	0.0886
1	game	0.0257	game	0.0491	game	0.1910	ea	0.0293	hours	0.0457
2	games	0.0249	building	0.0216	love	0.1133	dlc	0.0283	life	0.0335
3	playing	0.0140	life	0.0195	play	0.0414	free	0.0213	amazing	0.0248
4	life	0.0125	create	0.0173	sims	0.0348	packs	0.0181	sim	0.0237
5	bad	0.0116	build	0.0163	mods	0.0196	play	0.0178	played	0.0229
6	ive	0.0107	love	0.0141	playing	0.0183	sims	0.0171	ive	0.0212
7	love	0.0096	gameplay	0.0127	recommend	0.0148	money	0.0170	time	0.0195
8	bugs	0.0093	characters	0.0125	super	0.0133	dlcs	0.0151	cool	0.0187
9	play	0.0090	houses	0.0119	time	0.0112	dont	0.0149	sims	0.0175

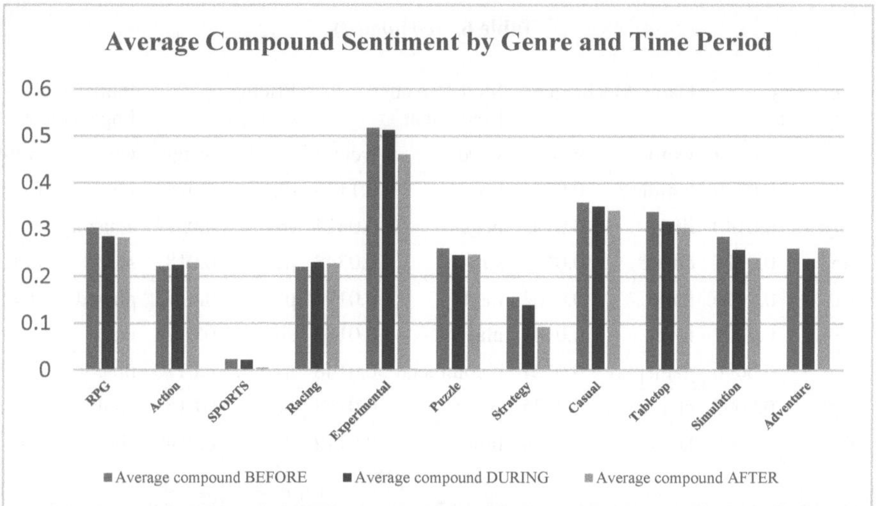

Fig. 3. Average VADER compound scores for each game in Before, During, and After stages

Table 5. LDA Topic Modeling Results at Release

	Gameplay Appraisal		Game Mechanics		Mod-Driven Enjoyment		Pricing Critique		Immersive Engagement	
	word	weight	word	weight	word	weight	word	weight	word	weight
0	sims	0.1669	sims	0.0496	fun	0.2320	game	0.0957	game	0.0890
1	game	0.0258	game	0.0492	game	0.1914	ea	0.0294	hours	0.0458
2	games	0.0250	building	0.0216	love	0.1135	dlc	0.0284	life	0.0337
3	playing	0.0140	life	0.0195	play	0.0414	free	0.0214	amazing	0.0249
4	life	0.0126	create	0.0173	sims	0.0348	packs	0.0182	sim	0.0238
5	bad	0.0116	build	0.0164	mods	0.0197	play	0.0178	played	0.0230
6	ive	0.0107	love	0.0141	playing	0.0183	sims	0.0171	ive	0.0212
7	love	0.0096	gameplay	0.0127	recommend	0.0148	money	0.0170	time	0.0195
8	bugs	0.0093	characters	0.0125	super	0.0133	dlcs	0.0151	cool	0.0188
9	play	0.0090	houses	0.0119	nice	0.0112	dont	0.0149	sims	0.0175

Table 6. LDA Topic Modeling Results for the First Month After Release

	Gameplay Appraisal		Game Mechanics		Mod-Driven Enjoyment		Pricing Critique		Immersive Engagement	
	word	weight	word	weight	word	weight	word	weight	word	weight
0	sims	0.1660	sims	0.0494	fun	0.2314	game	0.0954	game	0.0886
1	game	0.0257	game	0.0491	game	0.1910	ea	0.0293	hours	0.0457

(continued)

Table 6. *(continued)*

	Gameplay Appraisal		Game Mechanics		Mod-Driven Enjoyment		Pricing Critique		Immersive Engagement	
	word	weight	word	weight	word	weight	word	weight	word	weight
2	games	0.0249	building	0.0216	love	0.1133	dlc	0.0283	life	0.0335
3	playing	0.0140	life	0.0195	play	0.0414	free	0.0213	amazing	0.0248
4	life	0.0125	create	0.0173	sims	0.0348	packs	0.0181	sim	0.0237
5	bad	0.0116	build	0.0163	mods	0.0196	play	0.0178	played	0.0229
6	ive	0.0107	love	0.0141	playing	0.0183	sims	0.0171	ive	0.0212
7	love	0.0096	gameplay	0.0127	recommend	0.0148	money	0.0170	time	0.0195
8	bugs	0.0093	characters	0.0125	super	0.0133	dlcs	0.0151	cool	0.0187
9	play	0.0090	houses	0.0119	time	0.0112	dont	0.0149	sims	0.0175

The DTM results are visualized using line charts to illustrate how topic weights vary across the defined release stages. Overall, the analysis shows that different discussion themes exhibit distinct temporal patterns. Topic 2 (Mod-Driven Enjoyment), characterized by high-weight words such as "fun", "game", "love" and "play" carries the largest weight across all three stages and remains the dominant topic throughout the observation period. Its relative weight increases during the release (average weight approximately 0.077), suggesting heightened attention to enjoyable gameplay experiences at launch. Topic 3 (Pricing Critique), which includes terms such as "EA", "DLC", "packs" and "money" is more prominent prior to release, indicating early discussion of monetization strategies such as pricing and paid content policies. The relative weight of this topic declines in the post-release stage, reflecting reduced emphasis on pricing-related discussions over time. Topic 4 (Immersive Engagement) exhibits a comparatively low overall weight, with a modest increase around the release followed by stabilization, indicating that certain niche or secondary aspects attract temporary attention at launch but do not sustain long-term prominence. Topic 1 (Game Mechanics), represented by words such as "sims", "life", "building" and "create" shows increased weight during the release stage, consistent with players actively exploring game systems and sharing early impressions. In contrast, Topic 0 (Gameplay Appraisal), associated with terms such as "bad", "bugs", and "play" displays a gradual decline in weight from pre-release to post-release, indicating a decreasing emphasis on negative gameplay evaluations in later stages (Fig. 4).

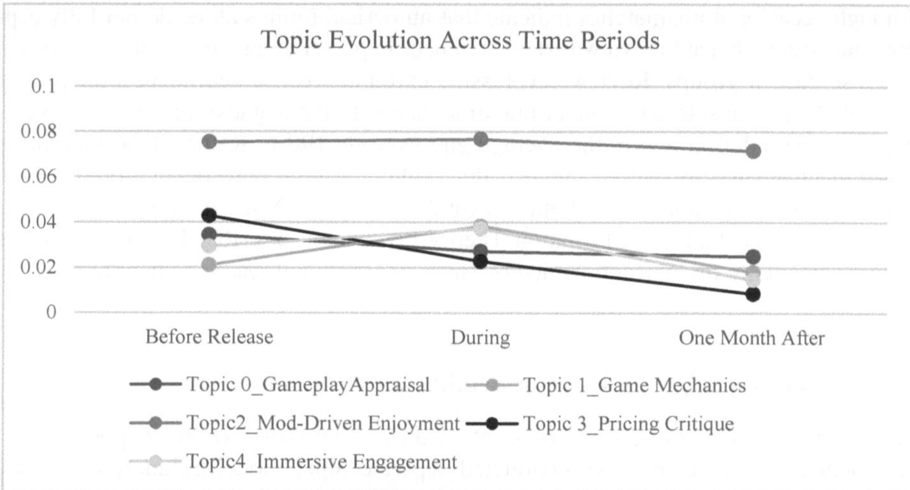

Fig. 4. Topic Evolution Over Time

Across the release stages, several types of discussion topics show contrasting temporal patterns. Topics related to positive gameplay experiences tend to be more visible around the release period, whereas discussions focused on technical issues appear less prominent in later stages. Monetization-related topics display a front-loaded pattern, with greater attention before and shortly after release, followed by a decline over time. This suggests that player concerns about pricing and perceived value are most salient around launch. These observations are broadly consistent with insights from the eWOM literature [24], which note that highly salient topics can shape how sentiment circulates within online communities. Early in the release process, positive themes such as enjoyable gameplay or engaging content are more likely to dominate discussion and contribute to favorable word-of-mouth. By contrast, when negative themes gain attention, they may cause a shift toward more critical sentiment expression. From a managerial perspective, these patterns underscore the importance of paying close attention to dominant discussion themes around release and maintaining ongoing responsiveness to technical feedback after launch, to limit the escalation of negative sentiment within the player community.

5.4 Distribution of Extreme Sentiments and Behavioral Characteristics

Reviews were categorized into three sentiment groups based on VADER compound scores: Extreme Positive ($\geq$ 0.85), Extreme Negative ($\leq$ -0.50), and Neutral. These thresholds are used as operational cutoffs to isolate highly polarized expressions rather than as theoretically derived boundaries. Across all stages, neutral reviews constitute the majority (approximately 82–85%) but show a modest decline over time. In contrast, the proportion of extreme negative reviews increases from 5.4% before release to 8.7% after release, while extreme positive reviews remain relatively stable at around 9%. Steam's recommendation labels largely correspond to these sentiment categories, although occasional mismatches indicate that numerical ratings alone do not fully capture contextual nuance in review text. Differences in player engagement are also evident across sentiment groups. Reviews expressing extreme positive sentiment are typically associated with substantially longer playtime than extreme negative reviews; for example, in the Simulation genre, the average gap exceeds 190 h. Rather than implying a causal mechanism, this pattern suggests that highly engaged players are more likely to express polarized evaluations, whether favorable or critical. This interpretation is consistent with Expectancy-Confirmation Theory [4], which describes how higher levels of involvement are often accompanied by stronger emotional reactions in online review contexts.

5.5 Structural Analysis of Extreme Sentiments Themes

To further examine how discussion content differs between extremely positive and extremely negative reviews we conducted separate topic modeling analyses for the two sentiment groups. Using the same LDA and DTM procedures described earlier reviews classified as extremely positive and extremely negative were analyzed independently while retaining the temporal dimension across the Before During and After release stages. For each extreme sentiment subset, the number of topics was set to five to capture salient discussion themes while preserving interpretability.

The analysis identifies five recurrent and polarized themes within extreme sentiment reviews. Topic 0 (Content Modularity) centers on expansions downloadable content and mods where some players emphasize richness flexibility and replay value while others criticize content gaps or reliance on paid add-ons. Topic 1 (Gameplay Appraisal) covers evaluations of core gameplay with positive reviews highlighting enjoyment and engagement and negative reviews emphasizing grind bugs or repetitive mechanics. Topic 2 (DLC Valuation) reflects dissatisfaction with monetization practices, particularly concerns about pricing perceived pay to win elements or limited value for money. Topic 3 (Pricing Critique) overlaps with these concerns but is marked by stronger language and broader frustration often combining criticism of value with dissatisfaction toward repetitive gameplay. In contrast Topic 4 (Immersive Engagement) captures strongly positive expressions where players describe extended playtime emotional attachment and sustained enthusiasm for the game experience.

Together, these results suggest that similar game attributes such as content scope gameplay design pricing and immersion are frequently referenced in both highly positive and highly negative reviews. Rather than reflecting distinct issue categories extreme reviews tend to amplify opposing evaluations of the same core elements highlighting the polarized nature of sentiment expression among highly engaged players.

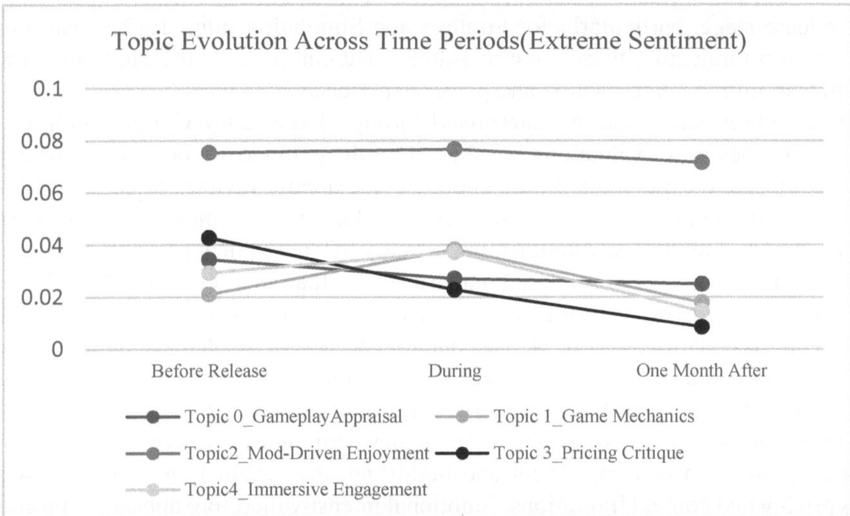

Fig. 5. Topic Evolution Across Time Periods for Extreme Sentiment Reviews

As shown in Fig. 5 Topic 1 (Gameplay Appraisal) reaches its highest average weight during the release stage at approximately 0.054. This pattern suggests that the launch period is characterized by heightened emotional expression with a concentration of both highly positive and highly negative evaluations. Topic 3 (Pricing Critique) shows a clear decline in relative weight from the pre-release stage at 0.0256 to lower levels afterward indicating reduced emphasis on pricing related criticism over time. Topic 2 (DLC Valuation) displays relatively stable weights across all three stages suggesting that issues related to pricing and monetization remain a recurring point of attention throughout the release cycle. Topic 4 (Immersive Engagement) maintains a comparatively low overall weight but exhibits a modest increase in the post-release stage. This pattern indicates that while strongly positive expressions represent a smaller share of reviews, a subset of players continue to express appreciation and sustained engagement over time.

6 Discussion

This study shows that player sentiment and discussion focus vary across release stages and across game genres. Because the study is intended as a descriptive and exploratory analysis, robustness is pursued through standardized preprocessing, consistent temporal segmentation, and aligned analytical settings across stages rather than through predictive benchmarking. In addition, the evaluation is strengthened through multiple complementary descriptive outputs, including mean stage-wise sentiment comparisons, sentiment-distribution analysis, extreme-sentiment proportion tracking, and temporal topic interpretation. Taken together, these analyses provide convergent evidence on how sentiment intensity and discussion focus evolve around release-related stages, thereby improving the robustness of the conclusions within the scope of an exploratory design. Sentiment expression tends to be more positive around the release period and more critical in the post-release stage, particularly for Strategy and Simulation titles. Rather than implying a uniform trajectory these patterns suggest that emotional expression in reviews is sensitive to timing genre context and player experience.

These observations can be interpreted through Expectancy Confirmation Theory which describes how evaluations are shaped by the comparison between prior expectations and actual experience. In the gaming context early reviews often reflect anticipation and first impressions while later reviews place greater emphasis on experienced shortcomings or unmet expectations. Importantly this theoretical perspective is used to contextualize the observed sentiment patterns rather than to infer a causal mechanism.

Topic modeling results further indicate that review content evolves across stages. Pre-release discussions focus more on anticipation and pricing related issues while release stage reviews emphasize gameplay mechanics and immediate experience. In later stages technical performance and monetization concerns receive relatively greater attention. Extreme sentiment reviews amplify these themes with highly positive evaluations highlighting immersion and enjoyment and highly negative evaluations concentrating on bugs pricing and content limitations. Emotional intensity therefore appears to be closely tied to the topics under discussion rather than evenly distributed across review content.

Finally, the association between sentiment extremity and playtime suggests that highly engaged players are more likely to express polarized evaluations. This relationship does not imply that playtime causes sentiment intensity but indicates that behavioral engagement provides useful context for interpreting review content. Together these findings highlight the value of combining sentiment topic and behavioral information when examining digital word of mouth in gaming communities. From an EBIS perspective, these temporal signals can be operationalized in several functional modules. In release management, they can support the identification of expectation gaps, launch-related friction, and patch-priority issues. In customer support, recurring negative themes can inform ticket triage, FAQ updates, and escalation priorities. In dynamic marketing, shifts in sentiment and topic prominence can guide message adaptation, campaign timing, and post-launch communication strategies aligned with changing user concerns.

7 Conclusions

This study proposes an event-centered analytical framework for examining user reviews in the gaming domain by integrating sentiment analysis, topic modeling, and behavioral engagement measures across game release stages. By distinguishing between pre-release, release, and post-release periods, the analysis demonstrates that both sentiment expression and discussion themes systematically vary around key moments in a game's lifecycle.

The study contributes to research on user-generated content (UGC) and electronic word-of-mouth (eWOM) by showing that review sentiment is not static; rather, it shifts depending on temporal context, topical focus, and user engagement intensity. While the study does not introduce new modeling techniques, its contribution lies in combining established analytical methods to provide a structured descriptive account of short-term sentiment dynamics and topic evolution in gaming reviews. Viewed through an EBIS lens, this framework may also serve as a decision-support logic for monitoring user feedback across event-centered service environments beyond the Steam ecosystem.

From a practical perspective, the findings suggest that temporal monitoring of review sentiment and topic prominence can support more targeted post-launch management. In particular, pre-release expectation-related discourse may help identify sources of anticipatory tension, while release-stage feedback can reveal immediate reactions to gameplay quality and usability. In the post-release period, increases in extreme negative reviews and the prominence of technical-performance or monetization-related topics may serve as early indicators of deteriorating community sentiment. These insights may help developers, publishers, and platform managers prioritize communication, patching, and community-response strategies in a more timely and interpretable manner.

Several limitations should be noted. First, the analysis relies exclusively on English-language reviews from the Steam platform, which restricts cultural and cross-platform generalizability. Relatedly, the transferability of the findings to other digital marketplaces should be interpreted with caution, because platform-specific affordances, community norms, review visibility mechanisms, and genre composition may shape both sentiment expression and topic salience. Thus, the general lifecycle logic may be portable to other review-based environments, whereas the magnitude of sentiment shifts and the prominence of specific topics are likely to remain context-dependent. Second, sentiment classification and topic modeling are based on heuristic approaches that may not fully capture nuanced emotional expression or contextual meanings. In addition, the study is designed as a descriptive and exploratory analysis rather than a predictive benchmarking exercise. Therefore, the findings should be interpreted as evidence of temporal patterns in review sentiment and topic prominence rather than as externally validated model-performance results. The results may also be sensitive to analytical design choices, including the selection of sentiment thresholds for extreme reviews, the fixed number of topics used in LDA and DTM, and the preprocessing decisions applied to short review texts. Although these choices were made to preserve interpretability and comparability across stages, alternative parameter settings could yield somewhat different thematic structures or sentiment distributions. Third, the temporal scope is limited to short-term dynamics around the release window, leaving longer-term sentiment evolution unexplored. Moreover, the release-stage segmentation represents an event-centered analytical simplification, and player response dynamics may not always align neatly with the predefined stage boundaries. Finally, this study focuses only on textual reviews and does not incorporate multimodal content such as images, videos, or broader social media interactions. Future research could address these limitations by extending the temporal horizon, incorporating multilingual and cross-platform datasets, testing alternative parameter settings, and integrating multimodal and network-based approaches to further advance the understanding of digital word-of-mouth dynamics in the gaming ecosystem.

Acknowledgments. This work was supported by the Soonchunhyang University Research Fund. This work was supported by the Ministry of Education of the Republic of Korea and the National Research Foundation of Korea (NRF-2024S1A5A2A01020049).

References

1. Newzoo: The global games market will generate $187.7 billion in 2024. Newzoo Industry Report, Newzoo (2024)
2. Dean, D.: Steam just reached 50,000 total games listed. PCGamesN (2023)
3. Liu, B.: Sentiment analysis and opinion mining. Synth. Lect. Hum. Lang. Technol. **5**(1), 1–167 (2012)
4. Oliver, R.L.: A cognitive model of the antecedents and consequences of satisfaction decisions. J. Mark. Res. **17**(4), 460–469 (1980)
5. Andreev, G., Saxena, D., Verma, J.K.: Impact of review sentiment and magnitude on customers' recommendations for video games. In: Proceedings of the International Conference on Computational Performance Evaluation (ComPE), pp. 992–995. IEEE (2021)
6. Pagano, D., Maalej, W.: User feedback in the App Store: an empirical study. In: Proceedings of the 21st IEEE International Requirements Engineering Conference (RE), pp. 125–134. IEEE (2013)
7. Khalid, H., Shihab, E., Nagappan, M., Hassan, A.E.: What do mobile app users complain about? IEEE Softw. **32**(3), 70–77 (2015)
8. Hutto, C.J., Gilbert, E.: VADER: a parsimonious rule-based model for sentiment analysis of social media text. In: Proceedings of the 8th International AAAI Conference on Weblogs and Social Media (ICWSM), pp. 216–225 (2014)
9. Chakraborty, S., Mobin, I., Roy, A., Khan, M.H.: Rating generation of video games using sentiment analysis and contextual polarity from microblog data. In: Proceedings of the International Conference on Computational Techniques, Electronics and Mechanical Systems (CTEMS), pp. 90–95. IEEE (2018)
10. Zuo, Z.: Sentiment analysis of steam review datasets using Naïve Bayes and decision tree classifiers. Master's thesis, University of Illinois at Urbana–Champaign (2018)
11. Tan, J.Y., Chow, A.S.K., Tan, C.W.: A comparative study of machine learning algorithms for sentiment analysis of game reviews. In: Proceedings of the International Conference on Digital Transformation and Applications (ICDXA), pp. 63–68. IEM (2021)
12. Fadhlurrahman, J.A.M., Herawati, N.A., Aulya, H.R.W., Puspasari, I., Utama, N.P.: Sentiment analysis of game reviews on Steam using BERT, BiLSTM, and CRF. In: Proceedings of the International Conference on Electrical Engineering and Informatics (ICEEI). IEEE (2023)
13. Coronado-Blázquez, J.: A NLP approach to "review bombing" in Metacritic PC videogames. arXiv:2405.06306 (2024)
14. Park, G., Kwak, M.: The life cycle of online smartphone reviews: investigating dynamic change in customer opinion using sentiment analysis. ICIC Express Lett. Part B **11**(5), 509–516 (2020)
15. Lu, C., Li, X., Nummenmaa, T., Zhang, Z., Peltonen, J.: Patches and player community perceptions: analysis of No Man's Sky Steam reviews. In: Proceedings of the Digital Games Research Association (DiGRA) Conference (2020)
16. Yu, Y., Nguyen, B.H., Yu, F., Huynh, V.N.: Esports game updates and player perception: data analysis of PUBG Steam reviews. In: Proceedings of the 13th International Conference on Knowledge and Systems Engineering (KSE), pp. 1–6. IEEE (2021)
17. Blei, D.M., Ng, A.Y., Jordan, M.I.: Latent Dirichlet allocation. J. Mach. Learn. Res. **3**, 993–1022 (2003)
18. Blei, D.M., Lafferty, J.D.: Dynamic topic models. In: Proceedings of 23rd International Conference on Machine Learning (ICML), pp. 113–120. ACM (2006)
19. Li, C., Li, S., Yang, J., Wang, J., Lv, Y.: Topic evolution and sentiment comparison of user reviews on an online medical platform in response to COVID-19. Front. Public Health **11**, 1088119 (2023)

20. Guzsvinecz, T., Szűcs, J.: Length and sentiment analysis of reviews about top-level video game genres on the Steam platform. Comput. Hum. Behav. **149**, 107955 (2023)
21. Kaplan, A.M., Haenlein, M.: Users of the world, unite! The challenges and opportunities of social media. Bus. Horiz. **53**(1), 59–68 (2010)
22. King, R.A., Racherla, P., Bush, V.D.: What we know and don't know about online word-of-mouth: a review and synthesis of the literature. J. Interact. Mark. **28**(3), 167–183 (2014)
23. Lengel, R.H., Daft, R.L.: An exploratory analysis of the relationship between media richness and managerial information processing. Technical report TRDG08ONR (1984)
24. Chevalier, J.A., Mayzlin, D.: The effect of word of mouth on sales: online book reviews. J. Mark. Res. **43**(3), 345–354 (2006)

Network

Optimization of Energy Consumption in Battery-Operated Real-Time Systems

Swathi Konduru[1], Ashikahmed Bhuiyan[2], and Md Amiruzzaman[2(✉)]

[1] Nano Analytics, Billerica, PA, USA
Swathi.konduru@nano-analytics.com
[2] West Chester University of Pennsylvania, West Chester, PA, USA
{ABhuiyan,MAmiruzzaman}@wcupa.edu

Abstract. Real-time applications emphasize worst-case scenarios due to their precise timing demands. However, many critical applications of embedded systems have other requirements, such as energy consumption. The results of this study can inform the e-commerce infrastructure, including payment gateways, online transactions, and data-driven logistics. This would be especially beneficial in terms of energy savings and improving operational costs for embedded systems in e-business. This study presents a model for work scheduling that minimizes energy usage by implementing a suitable scheduling algorithm for dynamic power management (DPM) and dynamic voltage scaling (DVS) and evaluating the effectiveness of power management approaches. Applying DVS leads to an 84.03% reduction in energy consumption, while using DPM reduces the total energy consumed by devices by 66.76%. Combining DPM and DVS yields similar energy savings to DVS alone (83.22%) but with the potential for more significant energy savings due to external device involvement. While this combination can lead to longer execution times, a significant reduction in energy consumption makes it a worthwhile trade-off for energy-efficient computing.

1 Introduction

In embedded systems, energy consumption is crucial to consider. Real-time energy systems are increasingly consuming electricity, and optimizing their use will yield significant savings and environmental benefits, as evidenced by recent statistics [17]. The demand for data center services has grown steadily in recent years, with a projected growth rate of 4% to 5% annually, according to a report from the International Energy Agency IEA. A corresponding increase in energy consumption is expected, with data centers projected to account for 3.2% of global electricity consumption by 2025 [9].

Optimized energy consumption is essential for the efficient and reliable operation of battery-operated real-time systems, ensuring they operate as long as possible. It is particularly relevant for applications in which the system is located

Published by Springer Nature Switzerland AG 2027
J. Kim et al. (Eds.): EBISION 2025, IFIP AICT 786, pp. 307–322, 2027.
https://doi.org/10.1007/978-3-032-26616-3_18

in a distant or hard-to-reach location, and, in some cases, replacing batteries regularly may be infeasible or costly. According to a study by the Department of Energy, wireless sensor networks consume up to 40% of energy for data transmission. The energy consumption of remote wireless network equipment can be reduced by optimizing protocols and techniques and improving performance in these devices [14]. By reducing the need to replace batteries and the energy costs associated with charging batteries, energy consumption can also lead to cost savings. In addition, energy savings can contribute to mitigating concerns about the environmental impact associated with battery storage.

Dynamic Power Management (DPM) and Dynamic Voltage and Frequency Scaling (DVFS) are known for energy optimization. During task execution, the DPM policy reduces processor power consumption by utilizing idle intervals. Suppose that the idle interval equals (or is greater than) a certain threshold, that is, the break-even time [4,8]. In that case, the processor is switched to a low-power sleep mode, thus reducing its power consumption. DVFS is to adjust the voltage and frequency of the processor dynamically based on the current workload. When the workload is high, the voltage and frequency are increased to provide the necessary processing power. When the workload is low, the voltage and frequency are decreased to save energy. This approach [2,3,6]enables the processor to operate at the minimum possible voltage and frequency while meeting performance requirements.

Although DVFS, DPM, and Least Slack Time (LST) scheduling have been individually studied in prior work, their coordinated use within a unified energy-aware scheduling framework remains an important area of investigation, particularly in the context of enterprise-scale computing environments. This work analyzes how these complementary techniques can be integrated to improve energy efficiency while preserving real-time scheduling guarantees. By examining their combined behavior within a structured optimization framework, the study provides insights into practical strategies for reducing energy consumption in systems that support continuous business-critical workloads. This combination can substantially reduce energy consumption but maintains the required performance level (and timing requirement). The DPM will adjust the system's power consumption based on workload, and the DVFS will adapt processor voltage and frequency to match this workload. The system can achieve even more significant energy savings by using this combination. For example, DPM can be used to put the system into a low power state during periods of low workload, while DVFS reduces the voltage and frequency of the processor to reduce the power consumption further. In a period of high workload, DPM can bring the system from a low power state, and DVFS increases processor voltage and frequency to provide sufficient processing power. The combination of DPM and DVFS has been widely adopted in a wide range of devices, including cell phones, computers, and servers. It's shown to deliver substantial power savings while maintaining the required level of performance [7].

This work focuses on three case studies that use DPM, DVS, and their integration, along with the Least Slack Time (LST) scheduling algorithm, to optimize energy consumption in battery-operated real-time embedded systems. Specifically, we have made the following contributions:

- We have analyzed DVS, DPM, and the integration of DVS and DPM techniques to evaluate their performance in optimizing energy consumption in battery-operated real-time systems using Python simulation.
- We explored different scheduling algorithms and chose the least Slack Time algorithm compatible with all three case studies. The challenge was to find one algorithm that would work with all three case studies because it is not ideal to compare the performance of these case studies if we were to use different scheduling algorithms for each case study.

1.1 Energy Efficiency in E-Business Computing Infrastructures

Energy optimization plays a critical role in ensuring the efficiency, reliability, and sustainability of modern commercial computing infrastructures. Many e-business platforms rely on large-scale distributed systems, data centers, and edge devices—such as retail point-of-sale terminals, payment gateways, and IoT sensors—that operate under strict real-time constraints. Reducing the energy footprint of these components can significantly lower operational costs, improve service availability, and support corporate sustainability initiatives [9]. In such environments, energy-efficient scheduling mechanisms such as Dynamic Voltage Scaling (DVS) and Dynamic Power Management (DPM) are essential for maintaining system performance while minimizing unnecessary energy consumption. These techniques are particularly important for infrastructures that continuously process financial transactions, customer interactions, and logistics operations.

Furthermore, as e-business ecosystems increasingly adopt edge computing, mobile commerce, and distributed service architectures, the energy behavior of embedded and edge devices directly influences system responsiveness, reliability, and overall cost-effectiveness. Consequently, the development of energy-aware scheduling and optimization strategies is not only technically important but also strategically valuable for ensuring business continuity and efficient resource management in digital enterprises. The optimization framework proposed in this work aims to contribute toward this goal by improving energy-aware task scheduling while maintaining the performance requirements of EBIS platforms that operate under high computational demand.

2 Literature Review

Some of the existing works in optimizing energy consumption are reviewed in this section. In [16], Zhou Tang et al. proposed an energy-efficient DVFS-enabled workflow task scheduling algorithm (DEWTS) that is based on Dynamic Voltage and Frequency Scaling (DVFS) to reduce the total power consumption. DEWTS is used in processors that are DVFS-enabled and applies to most data centers' scheduling systems. The proposed approach is shown to have reduced power consumption by up to 46.5% compared to other state-of-the-art models.

In [15], Tajana Simunic et al. proposed a system combining DVS and DPM techniques, thus enabling more power savings. DVS algorithm was proposed based on change point detection that is used to detect the change in arrival or decoding rates and the frequency setting policy, which uses the change point detection to set the frequency and voltage of the processor. This approach was tested on MPEG video and MP3 audio algorithms on a portable "SmartBadge" device. Then, this approach is combined with the DPM algorithm, resulting in a factor of three energy savings.

In [1], Ijaz Ali et al. proposed a dynamic power-aware scheduling scheme for mixed-criticality (MC) tasks on unicore processors. To reduce the overall energy, the energy level in high-criticality mode was reduced first to tackle the difficulty in minimizing power trade-off in high-criticality mode. When there is an idle period between high-critical job execution, the processor will be switched to low-critical mode. In terms of energy reduction in mixed-criticality, the proposed scheme is shown to be effective and superior to static methods. In [10], Ridha Mehalaine et al. proposed a flexible scheduling scheme to minimize energy consumption the using Dynamic Voltage Scaling (DVS) technique on a multiprocessor system with uncertain data. The proposed approach also reuses the time savings that show the difference between the worst-case execution time (WCET) and the actual execution time (AET). Simulations have been performed using MATLAB to evaluate the model and confirm its reliability for reducing energy consumption in period-independent tasks.

In [13], Sheik et al. proposed some changes to existing models by incorporating the change in execution time and energy consumption brought about by the number of cache partitions assigned to a task for a three-dimensional energy optimization problem that includes minimizing the energy consumption at the core, cache and system level. According to the results, optimizing cache energy plays a significant role in reducing overall energy consumption. Some of the limitations of these existing works are that these approaches are specified to a particular device or processor or tasks which limits their applicability to other scenarios or applications. The complexity and the lack of readability limit the practicality of these approaches. Additionally, numerous approaches and methods are involved in energy optimization, making it challenging to select a suitable approach that suits the specific application.

An extensive study has been performed in MC systems aiming to ensure better schedulability, fault tolerance, and energy optimization. Reghenzani et al. [12] extend traditional mixed-criticality scheduling theory to incorporate fault-tolerance mechanisms addressing transient faults while ensuring both timing and failure-rate requirements. By introducing generalized dropping relationships to capture task dependencies and certification constraints better, the approach enhances schedulability compared to classical MC models.

Zhang et al. [18] studied energy-aware real-time scheduling for mixed-criticality systems under a non-preemptive dynamic-priority model. By developing nonpreemptive EDF-based schedulability analyses and introducing an NP-EDFVD–driven energy-aware algorithm, the work provides a structured approach to energy minimization while preserving mixed-criticality correctness. The work by Reghenzani et al. [11] investigates energy-aware real-time scheduling for

DAG tasks by integrating a Dynamic Power Management (DPM)– based approach to reduce both)–based approach to reduce worst-case and average-case energy consumption. The work extends traditional worst-case analysis with probabilistic task behavior, focusing solely on DPM strategies to achieve improved energy efficiency. The work by Zhang et al. [19] investigated energy-aware mixed-criticality scheduling under an imprecise MC model, where low-criticality tasks continue executing at degraded quality rather than being dropped in high-criticality mode. Focusing solely on DVFS-based energy control, it introduces an EA-IMC scheduling strategy that selects energy-efficient speeds in low-criticality mode and maximum speeds in high-criticality mode to minimize overall energy consumption. This work by Bhuiyan et al. [5] studied energy-aware real-time scheduling of DAG tasks by incorporating a Dynamic Voltage and Frequency Scaling (DVFS)–driven strategy to reduce both worst-case and average-case energy consumption. The approach integrates probabilistic task information into precise scheduling to guide energy optimization while ensuring full timing correctness in all execution scenarios.

3 Task Definition

The tasks are periodic in nature, in which the deadline line of the task is equal to its period, and the first instance of the periodic task is released at time 0. The tasks are defined by task name, deadline, Worst Case Execution Time (WCET), Actual Execution Time (AET), which is less than WCET, and priority assigned to it.

3.1 Task Scheduling Algorithm

A task scheduling algorithm based on the Least Slack Time (LST) policy and task priority as the tiebreaker. It starts by setting the current time [11]. The algorithm updates the slack time for each task, which is defined as the amount of time a task has remaining before its deadline, sorts the tasks based on the slack time and priority, selects the task with the least slack time as the next task to be scheduled, adds the task along with its start and end times to the new list, updates the current time with the end time of the scheduled task. The process continues until all tasks have been scheduled. If tasks must be executed in a particular order, the assigned priority will handle scheduling. For simplicity purposes, this priority case is not considered.

Algorithm 1. Least Slack Time

procedure TASK_SCHEDULING(*taskslist*)
    current time = 0
    schedule tasks = [ ]   ▷ initialising a list for scheduled tasks
    while *taskslist not empty* **do**
        slack time = *deadline* − (*current time* + *WCET*)   ▷ slack time for all the tasks in the list
        Sort the tasks list in ascending based on slack time
        next task = *tasklist*[0]   ▷ task with least slack time is the next task
        schedule tasks.append(*next task*)
        current time+ = *AET*[*nexttask*]
        taskslist.drop(*next task*)

4 Methodology

This section will explore three detailed case studies highlighting different approaches to optimizing energy consumption. Subsection 4.1 examines DVS as a technique for energy optimization. Subsection 4.2 delves into DPM and its application for reducing energy consumption. Finally, Subsect. 4.3 integrates the principles of DPM and DVS to provide a comprehensive strategy for maximizing energy efficiency.

The proposed model makes several simplifying assumptions to enable tractable analysis and simulation. First, task execution times are assumed to be known or estimated with reasonable accuracy. Second, network latency and communication overhead are considered negligible relative to computation time. Third, device energy models are simplified to capture the dominant energy-consumption factors. While these assumptions allow clear evaluation of scheduling strategies, real-world deployments may involve additional variability. Future work will incorporate more detailed system models and dynamic workload characteristics to further validate the proposed approach.

In these energy optimization approaches, the temperature is treated as an outlier and therefore excluded from the present analysis. Our primary objective here is to validate the effectiveness of DVS and DPM techniques under controlled conditions. We also recognize that comparisons against state-of-the-art techniques and standardized benchmarks would further strengthen the evaluation. While such comprehensive benchmarking is not included in the current work, it remains an important direction for future research.

4.1 Case Study 1: Dynamic Voltage Scaling (DVS) for Energy Optimization

The power of a CMOS circuit can be divided into static power, which is independent of the frequency and dynamic power, which is affected by frequency and voltage change.

4.1.1 DVS Energy Model The energy model for Dynamic Voltage Scaling aiming to reduce energy consumption is defined here.

- **Dynamic power**
  It is calculated by the following formula [20]:

$$(P_{dyn} = aC_L V^2 f)$$

  where a is the switching probability, C_L is the load capacitance, V is the voltage, and f is the frequency. In the processor, scaling and C_L are not affected by frequency. When the frequency is scaled by a factor of s, as an effect, voltage is scaled by s; the current is scaled by a factor of s^2, and the dynamic power is scaled by s^3 which is given by, $P_{dyn}(s) = (1)^{-3} * P_{dyn}(1)$, where P_{dyn} (1) is the dynamic power when there is no scaling factor applied to the system (s=1).
- **Static power**
  Static power, P_{static}, is defined as the sum of leakage power and power consumption of components that are not scalable. While leakage power changes linearly with the voltage, power consumed by non-scalable components is not affected by the voltage. In this analysis, static power is considered to be constant, and no external device is considered scalable for the simplicity of the model.
- **Optimal Scaling Factor**
  The amount of energy the CPU uses changes depending on the frequency and voltage. Reducing the voltage doesn't always lead to lower energy consumption because it also increases the time it takes to complete a task. This results in the CPU using more energy while active and when the device is in standby. The rest of this section determines the maximum scaling factor for a DVS system that results in minimum energy consumption without considering any deadlines. This is referred to as the optimal scaling factor.
  For a task, consider an arbitrary value for WCET and AET, where AET $\leq$ WCET. when the frequency is scaled by a factor of s, the execution time is also extended by the same factor.
  The static CPU energy consumption is given by [20]

$$(E_{static}(s) = P_{static}(s) * (s * AET) = s * P_{static}(1) * AET = s * E_{static}(1))$$

  The dynamic CPU energy consumption is given by [20]

$$(E_{dyn}(s) = P_{dyn}(s) * (s * AET) = s^{-2} * P_{dyn}(1) * AET = s^{-2} * E_{dyn}(1))$$

  Total energy consumption, which is the sum of static and dynamic power, is given by

$$E_{cpu}(s) = E_{dyn}(s) + E_{static}(s) = (s - 2 * P_{dyn}(1) + s * P_{static}) * AET$$

  Consider $Q_{dyn} = s^{-2} * P_{dyn}(1), Q_{static} = s * P_{static}, and\ Q_{cpu} = Q_{dyn} + Q_{static}$. Then $E_{cpu} = Q_{cpu} * AET$. The optimal scaling factor is achieved by minimizing energy consumption, which involves minimizing Q_{cpu}. Which results in $s_{opt} = (2 * P_{dyn}(1)/P_{static})^{1/3}$ [20].

For the above plot, dynamic power is considered to be 125 W, and static power is considered to be 75 W. The dynamic power consumption, $P_{dyn}(1)$, is related to the amount of switching activity, a, which can vary from task to task. Therefore, the optimal scaling factor is specific to each task. We must consider static processor utilization if all the tasks are known. This refers to the amount of processor time the task occupies when executed periodically. It is calculated as the ratio of the total execution time of the task throughout the task [20].
Static processor utilization for n periodic tasks with P as the period is given by $\mu = \Sigma_{k=1}^{n} WCET^{k}/p^{[k]}$
The actual scaling factor is considered as the minimum of static power utilization and optimal scaling factor (Fig. 1).
$s_{\text{act}} = \min(\mu, s_{\text{oPt}})$

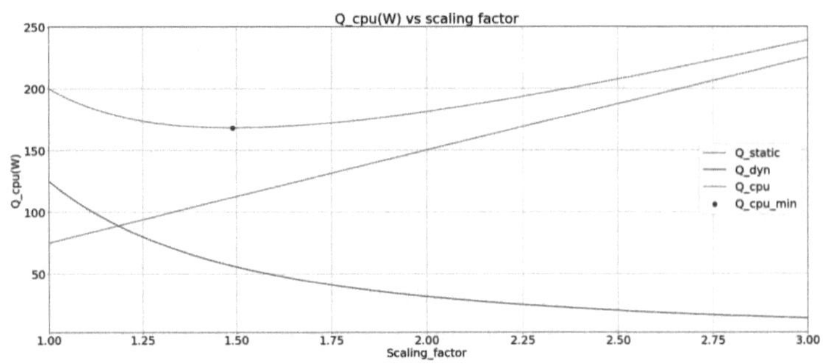

Fig. 1. $Q_{CPU}(W)$ vs Scaling factor

Table 1. Task specification.

Tasks	Deadline	WCET	Priority
Task 1	100	40	1
Task 2	50	45	2
Task 3	100	30	3
Task 4	70	20	4

4.1.2 Results

The frequency values are expressed as a proportion of the highest frequency and the energy values are expressed as a proportion of the energy used in the non-DVS scheduling profile. From Fig. 2, applying DVS increases the time it takes to complete tasks as the processor runs at a lower frequency. However, this leads to a reduction in overall energy consumption by 84.03%.

Table 2. Task execution order based on Least Slack Time scheduling algorithm

Tasks	Deadline	WCET	Priority
Task 2	50	45	2
Task 4	70	20	4
Task 1	100	40	1
Task 3	110	30	3

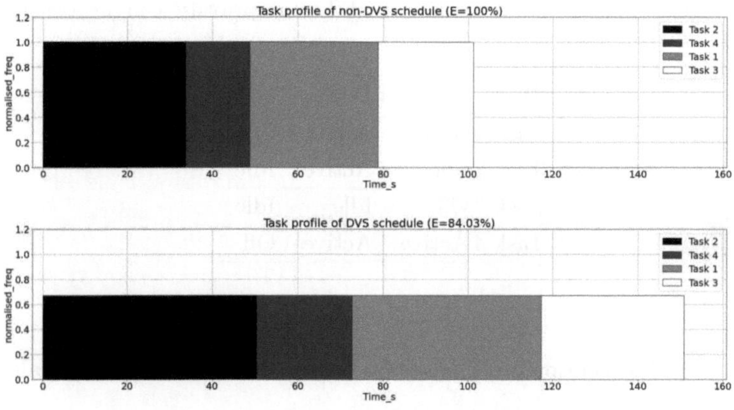

Fig. 2. DVS Task profiles for the task set in Table 2

4.2 Case Study 2: Dynamic Power Management for Energy Consumption Optimization

If there are a lot of external devices or sensors connected to the system, then DPM is implemented to reduce energy consumption by switching the states of inactive devices.

4.2.1 Device Energy Model

The devices are assumed to have three modes of operation: active, standby (idle), and off. Let D_j be the number of devices required by the task j. The device consumes some power depending on the state of the device; P_j^{act} for active power consumption, P_j^{idle} for standby (idle) power consumption and P_j^{off}=0 for off state. This model does not consider Transition energy consumption to reduce the complexity, and the device is assumed to remain in the same state until the task is executed.

- Active energy
  Assume that the device (D_j is in active state and consumes an active energy E_j^{act}, which is constant but in reality, it would not be constant. Active energy is given by $E_j^{act} = P_j^{act} * AET_j$ [20]

- Idle energy
  Assume that the device D_j is in idle state and consumes an active energy E_j^{idle} which is constant. Idle energy is given by $E_j^{idle} = P_j^{idle} * AET_j$ [20]
  If the processor's frequency is scaled by a factor s, then the execution time is also scaled by the same factor, which increases the device's energy consumption.

Table 3. Task specification:deadline, WCET and priority can be considered from Table 1

Tasks	Device 1	Device 2	Device 3
Task 1	Active	Active	Active
Task 2	Idle	Active	Idle
Task 3	Off	Idle	Idle
Task 4	Active	Active	Off

Table 4. Task execution order based on Least Slack Time scheduling algorithm

Tasks	Device 1	Device 2	Device 3
Task 2	Idle	Active	Idle
Task 4	Active	Active	Off
Task 1	Active	Active	Active
Task 3	Off	Idle	Idle

4.2.2 Results

See Fig. 3.
The energy values are expressed as a proportion of the energy used in the non-DPS scheduling profile. The total energy consumed by the devices is reduced to 66.76%. In this example, the processor is considered to be running at max frequency as DVS is not applied, as an effect the execution time is not scaled.

4.3 Case Study 3: Integration of DPM and DVS to Optimize Energy Consumption

DPM is implemented first for the combination of DVS and DPM, then DVS is implemented along with the device power. DPM implementation is similar to case study 2 (see Sect. 4.2).

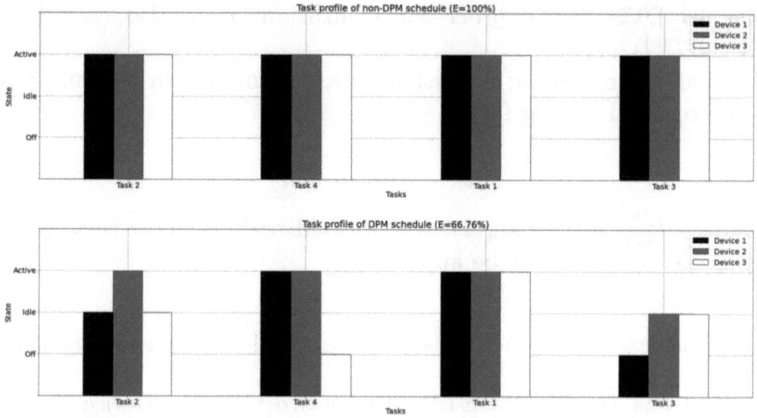

Fig. 3. DPM Task profiles for the task set in Table 4

Table 5. Task specification:deadline, WCET, and priority is considered from Table 1, and state of devices is considered from Table 3

Tasks	Deadline	WCET	Priority	Device 1	Device 2	Device 3
Task 1	100	40	1	Active	Active	Active
Task 2	50	45	2	Idle	Active	Idle
Task 3	100	30	3	Off	Idle	Idle
Task 4	70	20	4	Active	Active	Off

4.3.1 Modification of DVS Model See Table 5.
Consider a system with CPU and a set of devices/sensors. The total energy consumption now includes the energy consumed by the device ($E_{dev}(s)$) along with energy consumed by CPU ($E_{CPU}(s)$. As different tasks trigger different sets of devices, the optimal scaling factor for each task is different. Also, the device is assumed to stay active throughout the execution of a task, so it can be added to static power. The total energy of the system for a task k is given by

$$E(s) = (P_{\text{dyn}}(s) + P_{\text{static}}) \cdot s \cdot AET + P_{\text{dev}}^{[k]} \cdot s \cdot AET$$

$$E(s) = (s^{-2} \cdot P_{\text{dyn}}(1) + s \cdot (P_{\text{static}} + P_{\text{dev}}^{[k]})) \cdot AET$$

Similar to DVS in case study1,

The optimal scaling factor is achieved by minimizing energy consumption, which involves minimizing Q_{cpu}. Which results in

$$s_{opt} = \left[\frac{2 \cdot P_{dyn}}{P_{static} + \left(P_{dev}^{[k]} \right)} \right]^{\frac{1}{3}}$$

Similar to DVS, static processor utilization, μ is also considered $\mu = \Sigma_{(k=1)}^{n}(WCET^{[k]})/p[k]$

The actual scaling factor is considered as the minimum of static power utilization and optimal scaling factor.

$$s_{\text{act}} = \min(\mu, s_{opt})$$

If $P_{static} + P_{dev}^{[k]} \geq 2 * P_{dyn}(1)$, the optimal scaling factor is $S_{opt} \leq 1$ which implies that DVS should not be applied.

Table 6. Task execution order based on Least Slack Time scheduling algorithm

Tasks	Deadline	WCET	Priority	Device 1	Device 2	Device 3
Task 1	100	40	1	Active	Active	Active
Task 2	50	45	2	Idle	Active	Idle
Task 3	100	30	3	Off	Idle	Idle
Task 4	70	20	4	Active	Active	Off

4.3.2 Results

Consider the order of tasks from Table 6 and DPM is applied for each task as it is task dependent (Fig. 4).

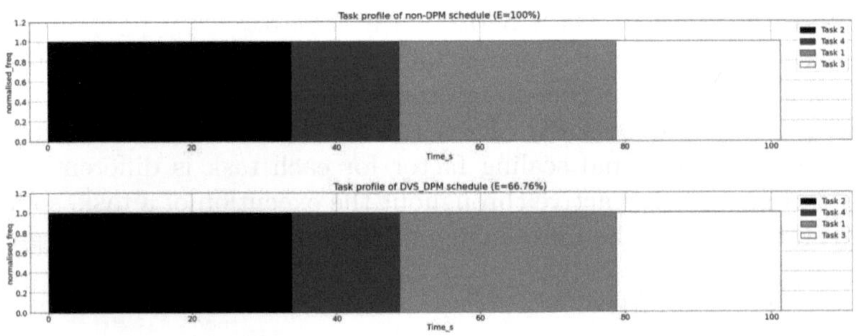

Fig. 4. DPM Task profiles for the task set in Table 6

As shown in the graph above, the energy savings percentage is 83.22%, the same as for DVS alone. However, because this system includes external devices, this method will achieve greater energy savings in absolute terms than DVS (mention section number). The reduced energy savings are due to the external devices remaining in their respective states throughout the task execution.

4.3.3 Experimental Assumptions, Limitations and Future Work

The experimental evaluation in this study uses synthetic task sets to model workloads in an Energy-Based Information System (EBIS). These workloads are designed to capture representative computational patterns, including periodic task arrivals, varying execution times, and energy-consumption characteristics. While this setup enables controlled evaluation of the proposed scheduling strategy, it does not fully capture the diversity and complexity of real enterprise workloads or business-level performance indicators such as service-level compliance, operational cost, or long-term energy efficiency.

In a typical Energy-Based Information System (EBIS), application services generate computational tasks that must be scheduled across available computing resources while considering both performance and energy consumption. The proposed scheduler can be integrated as an intermediate scheduling layer between the workload management component and the underlying computing infrastructure. Specifically, incoming tasks from the EBIS service layer are forwarded to the scheduling module, which evaluates task characteristics such as execution time and energy requirements. Based on these parameters, the scheduler determines an energy-efficient execution order and assigns tasks to appropriate processing units or devices. The resulting scheduling decisions are then executed by the system's resource management layer. This integration enables the EBIS platform to incorporate energy-aware scheduling without requiring significant modifications to the existing application or infrastructure layers. We leave the following two directions as potential future research. First, a detailed architectural implementation and deployment within a real EBIS stack remain part of our planned future work. Second, incorporating realistic EBIS workloads, heterogeneous device configurations, and business-oriented KPIs would provide a more comprehensive evaluation. Such an extended empirical study remains an important direction for future work.

5 Challenges

- As most of the systems are not programmed to operate in full voltage region. Usage of DVS is very limited in the lower regions of the voltage spectrum and there are very few applications that can take advantage of scaling at low voltage levels.
- In digital circuits, Propagation delay is inversely proportional to supply voltage. Most mathematical models do not consider leakage current.
- DVS can cause stability issues such as system crashes and hardware failures if not implemented correctly.
- DVS can affect the temperature of the system, and the thermal management system needs to be designed appropriately to handle the temperature changes.
- Due to the policy limitations in DPM, sometimes the estimation of idling periods might not be accurate which results in under or over-estimation of the idle periods.

- A potential loss in energy saving might occur if there is an underestimation of idling periods. Similarly, an overestimation can result in both performance delay and energy loss.
- The appropriate combination of DVS and DPM techniques presents various issues because aggressive DVS schemes result in short device idle times, limiting the effectiveness of DPM solutions; similarly, solutions with DPM as the focus may result in excessive CPU power usage. As a result, at the system level, there is a trade-off spectrum between DVS and DPM

6 Conclusion

This research aims to propose an optimal model for a work schedule that minimizes energy usage, develop a suitable scheduling algorithm for DPM and DVS, and assess the effectiveness of power management approaches. This objective strategy is easily adaptable to different needs. The findings of our study demonstrate that DVS and DPM can significantly reduce the energy consumption of computing devices. Applying DVS results in an 84.03% reduction in overall energy consumption, but it increases task completion time due to the lower processor frequency.

On the other hand, using DPM reduces the total energy consumption of devices by 66.76% without affecting execution time, assuming the processor is operating at its maximum frequency. Furthermore, the combination of DVS and DPM yields energy savings comparable to those of DVS alone (83.22%), with the potential for even greater savings due to the involvement of external devices. Although using a combination of DVS and DPM can increase execution time, the significant reduction in energy consumption makes it a worthwhile trade-off for energy-efficient computing.

In the context of e-business information systems, the findings of this research are particularly relevant, as energy-efficient computation directly contributes to sustainable and cost-effective data processing in online business platforms. Cloud-based e-business applications rely heavily on continuous data transactions, resource allocation, and backend computation—all of which can benefit from power-optimized scheduling models. The integration of DPM and DVS can enhance the operational efficiency of e-business infrastructures by reducing operational energy costs while maintaining the required performance levels. Thus, the proposed approach not only aligns with technical optimization goals but also supports the broader sustainability and green computing initiatives that modern e-business systems increasingly adopt.

Future Work. First, we plan to implement a more advanced scheduling algorithm to break down the task into multiple subtasks, thereby increasing efficiency. Second, we aim to use a more advanced Device model, considering the transition times and their respective powers. The device transition can also take break-even time as a parameter, which can help avoid unnecessary state transitions. Additionally, we will implement a different scheduling algorithm in which devices are active for only a fraction of the task execution time, rather than remaining active throughout the task. A different type of combination can be implemented for more energy saving, including Hybrid DPM, Fine-Grained Power Management, and Application-Specific Power Management. Finally, the work presented here is limited to simulation, so future efforts should focus on real-world validation and correlation.

References

1. Ali, I., Jo, Y.-I., Lee, S., Lee, W.Y., Kim, K.H.: Reducing dynamic power consumption in mixed-critical real-time systems. Appl. Sci. **10**(20), 7256 (2020)
2. Benini, L., Bogliolo, A., De Micheli, G.: A survey of design techniques for system-level dynamic power management. IEEE Trans. Very Large Scale Integr. (VLSI) Syst. **8**(3), 299–316 (2000)
3. Bhuiyan, A., Guo, Z., Saifullah, A., Guan, N., Xiong, H.: Energy-efficient real-time scheduling of DAG tasks. ACM Trans. Embed. Comput. Syst. (TECS) **17**(5), 1–25 (2018)
4. Bhuiyan, A., Pivezhandi, M., Guo, Z., Li, J., Modekurthy, V.P., Saifullah, A.: Precise scheduling of DAG tasks with dynamic power management. In: 35th Euromicro Conference on Real-Time Systems (ECRTS 2023). Schloss Dagstuhl-Leibniz-Zentrum für Informatik (2023)
5. Bhuiyan, A., Reghenzani, F., Fornaciari, W., Guo, Z.: Optimizing energy in non-preemptive mixed-criticality scheduling by exploiting probabilistic information. IEEE Trans. Comput. Aided Des. Integr. Circ. Syst. **39**(11), 3906–3917 (2020)
6. Bhuiyan, A., Sruti, S., Guo, Z., Yang, K.: Precise scheduling of mixed-criticality tasks by varying processor speed. In: Proceedings of the 27th International Conference on Real-Time Networks and Systems, pp. 123–132 (2019)
7. Chen, G., Huang, K., Knoll, A.: Energy optimization for real-time multiprocessor system-on-chip with optimal DVFS and DPM combination. ACM Trans. Embed. Comput. Syst. (TECS) **13**(3s), 1–21 (2014)
8. Cheng, H., Goddard, S.: Online energy-aware i/o device scheduling for hard real-time systems. In: Proceedings of the Design Automation & Test in Europe Conference, vol. 1, pp. 6–pp. IEEE (2006)
9. iea.org. https://www.iea.org/reports/data-centres-and-data-transmission-networks. iea.org
10. Mehalaine, R., Boutekkouk, F.: Energy consumption reduction in real time multi-processor embedded systems with uncertain data. In: Silhavy, R. (ed.) CSOC 2020. AISC, vol. 1225, pp. 46–55. Springer, Cham (2020). https://doi.org/10.1007/978-3-030-51971-1_4
11. Reghenzani, F., Bhuiyan, A., Fornaciari, W., Guo, Z.: A multi-level DPM approach for real-time DAG tasks in heterogeneous processors. In: 2021 IEEE Real-Time Systems Symposium (RTSS), pp. 14–26. IEEE (2021)
12. Reghenzani, F., Guo, Z., Santinelli, L., Fornaciari, W.: A mixed-criticality approach to fault tolerance: integrating schedulability and failure requirements. In: 2022 IEEE 28th Real-Time and Embedded Technology and Applications Symposium (RTAS), pp. 27–39. IEEE (2022)
13. Sheikh, S.Z., Pasha, M.A.: An improved model for system-level energy minimization on real-time systems. In: 2019 IEEE 27th International Symposium on Modeling, Analysis, and Simulation of Computer and Telecommunication Systems (MASCOTS), pp. 276–282. IEEE (2019)

14. Shipleyenergy. https://www.shipleyenergy.com/resources/efficiency/the-importance-of-unplugging-unused-appliances/. shipleyenergy.com
15. Simunic, T., Benini, L., Acquaviva, A., Glynn, P., De Micheli, G.: Dynamic voltage scaling and power management for portable systems. In: Proceedings of the 38th annual Design Automation Conference, pp. 524–529 (2001)
16. Tang, Z., Qi, L., Cheng, Z., Li, K., Khan, S.U., Li, K.: An energy-efficient task scheduling algorithm in DVFS-enabled cloud environment. J. Grid Comput. **14**, 55–74 (2016)
17. Thirunavukkarasu, M., Sawle, Y., Lala, H.: A comprehensive review on optimization of hybrid renewable energy systems using various optimization techniques. Renew. Sustain. Energy Rev. **176**, 113192 (2023)
18. Zhang, Y.-W.: Energy-aware nonpreemptive scheduling of mixed-criticality real-time task systems. IEEE Trans. Comput. Aided Des. Integr. Circuits Syst. **41**(9), 2891–2900 (2021)
19. Zhang, Y.-W.: Dvfs-based energy-aware scheduling of imprecise mixed-criticality real-time tasks. J. Syst. Architect. **137**, 102849 (2023)
20. Zhuo, J., Chakrabarti, C.: Energy-efficient dynamic task scheduling algorithms for DVS systems. ACM Trans. Embed. Comput. Syst. (TECS) **7**(2), 1–25 (2008)

A Context-Aware Framework for Adaptive Service Orchestration in Digital Tourism Ecosystems

Mario Casillo[1], Muhammad Khan[2], Marco Lombardi[1], Michele Pellegrino[1], Domenico Santaniello[1](✉), and Pietro Giuseppe Strollo[1]

[1] University of Salerno, Fisciano, SA, Italy
{mcasillo,malombardi,mipellegrino,dsantaniello, pstrollo}@unisa.it

[2] University of the West of England, Bristol, UK
muhammad40.Khan@uwe.ac.uk

Abstract. Digital transformation is reshaping how tourism services are designed, delivered, and experienced. As users increasingly interact across heterogeneous digital platforms, the ability to dynamically adapt service delivery to contextual and situational factors becomes essential. This paper presents a context-aware framework for adaptive service orchestration that enables interoperability, personalization, and explainability within digital tourism ecosystems.

The proposed framework integrates four key components: (i) a context modeling layer that captures and represents user, environmental, and temporal dimensions through a Context Dimension Tree (CDT); (ii) a reasoning and adaptation layer that combines symbolic and probabilistic inference to determine the most relevant services under varying contexts; (iii) a semantic orchestration layer that ensures dynamic and interoperable service composition using shared ontologies and RDF/OWL vocabularies; and (iv) a presentation layer that enhances transparency and engagement through narrative-based explainability.

An experimental validation involving 72 participants in real tourism settings demonstrated significant improvements in contextual relevance, user satisfaction, and perceived transparency compared to static and non-contextual baselines. Results confirmed that adaptive orchestration, guided by feedback learning, effectively personalizes service delivery while maintaining semantic consistency across providers.

This study contributes to advancing context-aware and adaptive information systems, highlighting the potential of semantic orchestration as a foundation for human-centred, interoperable, and sustainable digital tourism ecosystems.

Keywords: Context-Aware Systems · Adaptive Service Orchestration · Semantic Interoperability · Digital Tourism Ecosystems · Explainable Personalization

Published by Springer Nature Switzerland AG 2027
J. Kim et al. (Eds.): EBISION 2025, IFIP AICT 786, pp. 323–337, 2027.
https://doi.org/10.1007/978-3-032-26616-3_19

1 Introduction

Digital transformation has profoundly reshaped how organizations conceive and deliver services. Within tourism—one of the most dynamic and data-intensive domains—users continuously interact with heterogeneous digital systems such as booking platforms, cultural-heritage portals, mobility services, and smart-city infrastructures [1, 2]. As the boundaries between physical and digital environments blur, service providers face the challenge of ensuring that information and recommendations remain contextually relevant, adaptive, and interoperable across devices and organizational boundaries [38].

Despite the abundance of digital resources, most e-tourism solutions still rely on static service-delivery models [40]. They typically offer limited personalization and disregard the situational context that strongly influences user intent and decision-making [3]. For example, the relevance of a cultural itinerary depends not only on user preferences but also on weather, time, and companionship. Traditional recommender systems based on collaborative or content-based filtering [4] rarely capture such dependencies, and existing platforms often operate in isolation, preventing semantic interoperability and coordinated service delivery [5].

To move beyond these limitations, recent research advocates for adaptive and context-aware information systems that can interpret environmental, temporal, and behavioural signals to orchestrate personalized services dynamically [6, 7]. Tourism represents an ideal testing ground: it combines data heterogeneity, rapidly changing contexts, and a strong dependence on environmental and social variables [8]. However, current approaches remain largely domain-specific and seldom integrate semantic interoperability, contextual reasoning, and feedback-based adaptation within a unified framework [9].

This paper addresses that gap by introducing a context-aware framework for adaptive service orchestration tailored to digital tourism ecosystems. The framework unifies (i) ontology-based context modeling, (ii) hybrid symbolic–probabilistic reasoning, (iii) semantic orchestration of heterogeneous services, and (iv) feedback-driven adaptation. Through these components, the system continuously learns how contextual factors affect user satisfaction and reconfigures active services accordingly.

The framework was experimentally validated through a real-world deployment involving 72 participants in tourism scenarios. Results demonstrated measurable improvements in contextual relevance, personalization, and perceived transparency over static baselines, confirming the viability of adaptive orchestration as a mechanism for human-centred and interoperable digital ecosystems.

The remainder of this paper is organized as follows.

Section 2 reviews related work on context-aware systems, semantic interoperability, and adaptive orchestration. Section 3 describes the proposed framework and methodological design. Section 4 presents the experimental setup and results. Section 5 discusses theoretical and practical implications for e-Business Information Systems, and Sect. 6 concludes with directions for future research.

The novelty of this work lies in the integration of hierarchical context modeling, hybrid symbolic–probabilistic reasoning, semantic service orchestration, and reinforcement-based adaptation within a single explainable framework. While previous approaches typically address these aspects separately, the proposed architecture unifies them into a continuous adaptive loop capable of coordinating heterogeneous tourism services in real time.

2 Related Work

Research on context-aware systems and adaptive digital ecosystems has evolved substantially over the past two decades. However, the integration of contextual reasoning, semantic interoperability, and adaptive orchestration in a unified service framework remains limited. This section reviews the main research streams relevant to the proposed study: context-aware computing and recommendation, semantic interoperability and knowledge modeling, and adaptive service orchestration.

2.1 Context-Aware Computing and Adaptive Recommendation

The notion of context—defined as any information that characterizes the situation of an entity [8]—has been central to ubiquitous and personalized computing since Dey's seminal work [9]. Context-aware systems aim to sense and interpret environmental and behavioural signals to adapt their functionality dynamically [10]. Within the tourism domain, this capability has been applied to personalized itinerary planning, smart-mobility routing, and event recommendation [11, 12].

Traditional recommender systems rely on collaborative filtering or content-based techniques [4], but these models often fail to capture situational dependencies such as time, location, or user activity. To address this, Context-Aware Recommender Systems (CARS) incorporate contextual dimensions as part of the recommendation process, using either pre-filtering, post-filtering, or contextual modeling [13]. Recent studies have explored hybrid reasoning techniques that combine probabilistic learning with symbolic or ontology-based representations [14, 15], enabling recommendations that are both adaptive and explainable [22, 39].

Nevertheless, most existing CARS approaches focus on item-level recommendation (e.g., points of interest or products) rather than service-level composition or orchestration. They typically lack mechanisms for integrating multiple heterogeneous service providers or for managing interoperability across platforms [16]. This limitation highlights the need for models capable of reasoning over composite, semantically described services and orchestrating them dynamically based on evolving contexts.

2.2 Semantic Interoperability and Knowledge Representation

Semantic technologies provide a foundation for overcoming heterogeneity in distributed service environments. Ontologies, expressed through RDF and OWL standards, enable shared conceptualization and reasoning across systems [17, 32]. In digital tourism, ontological models such as schema.org, FOAF, and CIDOC-CRM have been employed to represent cultural assets, events, and visitor profiles [18]. These formal representations allow systems to infer relations between entities and to compose services across organizational and technical boundaries [19].

Semantic interoperability is a core requirement for adaptive ecosystems, where data and services must interact seamlessly regardless of their origin or format [20, 21]. Recent contributions have proposed semantic middleware and linked-data architectures to enable cross-domain interoperability in smart tourism and cultural heritage applications [22]. However, most of these solutions remain static: they define relationships at design time rather than adjusting them dynamically in response to contextual changes or user feedback.

2.3 Adaptive Service Orchestration

Service orchestration refers to the automated coordination and execution of multiple services to achieve complex goals [24]. In adaptive settings, orchestration must respond not only to technical dependencies but also to environmental and user-driven factors. Studies on adaptive service computing [25] and service ecosystems [26] emphasize the importance of feedback-driven reasoning, where service configurations evolve according to changing contexts or performance metrics.

Recent works have introduced hybrid orchestration frameworks that integrate machine learning with rule-based reasoning to enhance flexibility [27]. Others have explored context-aware orchestration in cloud and IoT environments, where services are bound dynamically through semantic matchmaking [28, 29]. Within tourism, adaptive orchestration remains underexplored: most systems focus on individual personalization rather than on dynamic coordination of services across providers [30]. Moreover, explainability—essential for user trust and accountability—has rarely been incorporated into orchestration mechanisms [31].

2.4 Research Gap and Contribution

The reviewed literature demonstrates significant advances in context modeling, recommendation, and semantic interoperability, yet a unified, explainable, and adaptive orchestration framework is still lacking. Current systems either provide context-aware recommendations without cross-service coordination, or orchestrate services without adaptive reasoning.

The present study addresses this gap by proposing an ontology-driven, context-aware framework for adaptive service orchestration. The framework combines hierarchical context representation, hybrid reasoning (symbolic and probabilistic), semantic service integration, and feedback-based learning. It thus contributes to the ongoing effort to design interoperable, explainable, and human-centred digital ecosystems, particularly in the complex and dynamic domain of tourism.

3 Proposed Framework

The proposed framework integrates context modeling, adaptive reasoning, and semantic service orchestration to support personalized, interoperable, and explainable service delivery in digital tourism ecosystems. The framework relies on several modeling assumptions. First, contextual dimensions are assumed to be observable and measurable through available sensors or external data sources. Second, the influence of contextual factors on service relevance is assumed to be probabilistically independent for computational tractability in the likelihood estimation process. Third, user feedback signals are assumed to provide a reliable approximation of contextual satisfaction, enabling reinforcement-based adaptation. These assumptions allow the system to balance modeling expressiveness with computational efficiency in real-time service orchestration scenarios. Its methodological foundation is inspired by three design principles:

1) Contextual intelligence, enabling the system to sense and interpret user and environmental conditions;
2) Adaptive orchestration, ensuring that services are dynamically coordinated according to changing contexts; and
3) Semantic interoperability, allowing distributed providers to share data and functionality through common ontological representations.

These principles are implemented within a multi-layered architecture that combines context acquisition, reasoning, semantic orchestration, and user interaction into a unified adaptive loop (Fig. 1).

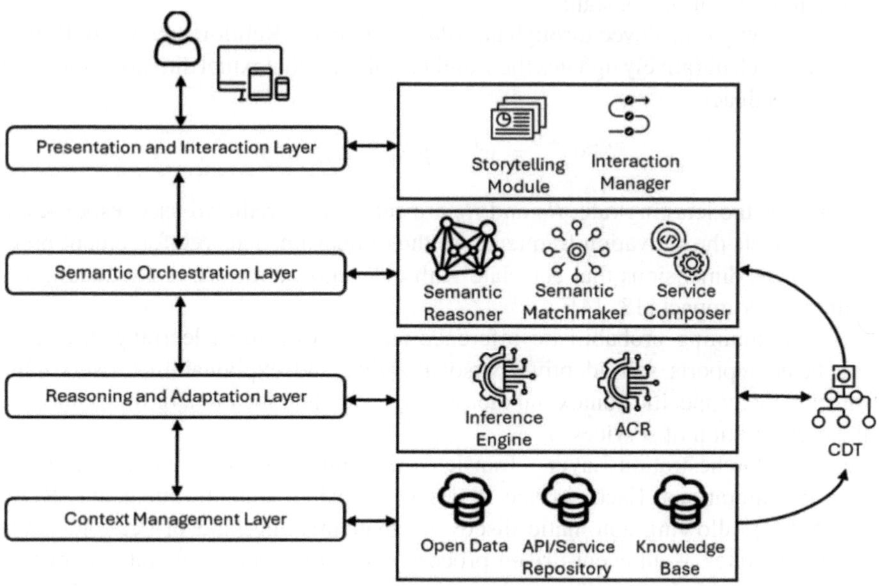

Fig. 1. Conceptual architecture of the proposed adaptive service orchestration framework.

3.1 Conceptual Design and Architecture

The framework follows a modular structure with four interoperable layers:

1. Context Management Layer – captures, preprocesses, and represents contextual information (e.g., location, time, weather, device type, user profile). Context is formalized

as a vector of dimension–value pairs:

$$C = \{(d_1, v_1), (d_2, v_2), \ldots, (d_n, v_n)\}$$

where d_i represents a contextual dimension and v_i its current value. Contextual knowledge is organized through a Context Dimension Tree (CDT) [8], an ontological structure that models hierarchical relationships among dimensions and supports reasoning under uncertainty through generalization and specialization. Metadata are expressed in RDF/OWL, aligning with existing vocabularies such as schema.org, FOAF, and CIDOC-CRM to ensure interoperability [17, 18].

2. Reasoning and Adaptation Layer – acts as the cognitive core of the framework. It integrates symbolic reasoning with probabilistic inference to determine the contextual relevance of candidate services. The probability that a service s fits the observed context C is computed as:

$$P(s \mid C) = \alpha \prod_k P(v\_k \mid s)$$

where $P(v_k \mid s)$ is the likelihood that contextual feature v_k supports service s, and α is a normalization constant.

Adaptivity is achieved through an Adaptive Context Reinforcement (ACR) mechanism, which iteratively updates the weight w_i of each contextual dimension according to user feedback:

$$w_i^{t+1} = w_i^t + \eta(R_u - \widehat{R_u})f(d_i)$$

where η is the learning rate, R_u and $\widehat{R_u}$ are actual and predicted user responses, and $f(d_i)$ reflects the activation frequency of the dimension. This reinforcement process strengthens dimensions that correlate with user satisfaction while attenuating those with weaker impact [13, 14].

By combining probabilistic inference and reinforcement learning, the reasoning layer supports self-adaptive personalization and explainability: users can be informed why specific contextual factors (e.g., weather, location, or time) influenced the orchestration of services.

3. Semantic Orchestration Layer – translates reasoning outcomes into actionable service configurations. Each service is described using semantic metadata (RDF or JSON-LD), allowing automatic discovery, matchmaking, and invocation. Orchestration operates as an event-driven process: when the contextual state changes, the system dynamically reconfigures the active service composition. Three orchestration modes are supported:

- Consumer orchestration (user-facing services such as itinerary generation);
- Business orchestration (B2B integration between tourism operators);
- Data orchestration (integration of heterogeneous open data sources).

The orchestration engine relies on SPARQL-based reasoning and semantic matchmaking to ensure that selected services comply with inferred contextual constraints [19, 20]. This approach guarantees both modularity and interoperability across independent providers, enabling the creation of composite, adaptive experiences.

4. Presentation and Interaction Layer – manages user experience and transparency. Instead of providing opaque lists of recommended services, the framework employs a storytelling-based interface that narratively connects recommended services to contextual cues. For instance, a visitor may receive a message such as "Since it's raining, we suggest visiting the Contemporary Art Museum nearby".

   This approach enhances user engagement, fosters trust, and transforms algorithmic decisions into human-understandable explanations [21]. The interface adapts presentation mode (text, image, or voice) to device type and situational context, operationalizing the framework's explainability principle.

3.2 Implementation and Technological Stack

A prototype of the framework was implemented as a mobile application backed by a modular microservice infrastructure. The system integrates:

- Python and Node.js for reasoning and orchestration services;
- RDFLib, OWL API, and GraphDB for semantic representation and querying;
- PostgreSQL for structured data storage;
- TensorFlow Lite for probabilistic computations and incremental learning; and
- RESTful APIs for inter-service communication.

This architecture supports scalability and interoperability, allowing new contextual dimensions or service providers to be integrated with minimal configuration. The microservice design adheres to current best practices in e-Business Information Systems [25, 26].

3.3 Methodological Summary

The methodological contribution of the framework lies in its ability to unify:

1. Context modeling – hierarchical and ontology-based representation of situational data;
2. Hybrid reasoning – symbolic inference combined with probabilistic adaptation;
3. Semantic orchestration – event-driven service coordination across platforms; and
4. Explainable interaction – narrative-based presentation of adaptive outcomes.

Together, these components establish a continuous adaptation loop: context is sensed → interpreted → used to orchestrate services → validated through feedback → and reintegrated into the reasoning process. This adaptive cycle enables information systems to evolve in real time with their operational environment, supporting the design of human-centred, interoperable, and transparent digital ecosystems (Table 1).

Table 1. Summary of main symbols and variables used in the framework

Symbol	Description
C	Context vector representing the current situational state
d_i	Contextual dimension (e.g., location, time, weather)

(continued)

Table 1. (*continued*)

Symbol	Description
v_i	Observed value associated with contextual dimension (d_i)
s	Candidate service considered for orchestration
$P(s \mid C)$	Probability that service (s) is relevant given context (C)
w_i	Weight associated with contextual dimension (d_i)
η	Learning rate of the Adaptive Context Reinforcement (ACR) mechanism
R_u	Actual feedback or satisfaction score provided by the user
$\widehat{R_u}$	Predicted user response estimated by the system
$f(d_i)$	Activation frequency of contextual dimension (d_i) during interaction cycles

4 Experimental Evaluation

The experimental evaluation aimed to validate the effectiveness, adaptability, and user acceptance of the proposed context-aware framework for adaptive service orchestration.

The study was conducted in Salerno (Southern Italy), a medium-sized coastal city with a strong cultural heritage and a steady flow of both domestic and international visitors. Salerno was selected as the experimental setting because it represents a medium-sized tourism ecosystem with diverse cultural, mobility, and hospitality services available through open APIs. This environment provides sufficient contextual variability while maintaining manageable experimental conditions.

The three-day interaction period was chosen to allow the adaptive reinforcement mechanism to observe repeated user interactions under varying contextual conditions. Shorter sessions would not provide sufficient feedback cycles for the ACR mechanism to converge, while longer deployments would introduce external variability unrelated to the framework evaluation. The three-day period therefore represents a balanced experimental window for observing adaptive behaviour in realistic tourism scenarios.

The experimental deployment integrated local open data and APIs from cultural institutions, public transport services, and hospitality providers, ensuring ecological validity and realistic contextual diversity.

A prototype mobile application implemented the full framework stack, including context sensing, hybrid reasoning, semantic orchestration, and storytelling-based presentation.

4.1 Experimental Setup

The experiment involved 72 participants aged 21–60, including tourists, local residents, and students. The sample size was determined to ensure sufficient statistical power for detecting medium effect sizes (Cohen's d $\approx$ 0.5) in pairwise comparisons between experimental conditions, with a confidence level of 95% and a target power of 0.8. This resulted in a minimum required sample of 24 participants per group, which was satisfied by the three-group experimental design. Participants were randomly assigned to one of three experimental configurations:

- Baseline A – Popularity-Based Recommendation, using static rankings without contextual adaptation;
- Baseline B – Static Context-Aware Model, integrating CDT-based reasoning but without adaptive feedback;
- Proposed Framework – Adaptive Orchestration Model, implementing full hybrid reasoning, reinforcement learning, and semantic orchestration.

Each participant interacted with the system for three consecutive days, receiving recommendations for cultural sites, restaurants, and events based on contextual variables such as location, time, and weather. Implicit (clickstream, dwell time) and explicit (ratings, feedback) signals were collected to assess system adaptation over time.

The experimental workflow consisted of four sequential phases: context acquisition, recommendation generation, user interaction logging, and adaptive learning. During the context acquisition phase, contextual variables such as location, time, weather conditions, and user profile attributes were collected through the mobile application sensors and external APIs. These data were preprocessed and mapped to the Context Dimension Tree structure before being used by the reasoning engine.

Model configuration followed a hybrid reasoning strategy. Symbolic reasoning operated through SPARQL queries over RDF-based contextual knowledge, while probabilistic inference estimated contextual relevance scores for candidate services using the likelihood formulation described in Sect. 3. Reinforcement-based adaptation was implemented through the Adaptive Context Reinforcement (ACR) mechanism with a learning rate η set to 0.05, empirically chosen to ensure stable convergence.

Data preparation involved filtering incomplete interaction logs and normalizing contextual dimensions to ensure consistent comparison across participants. The evaluation workflow then computed ranking metrics (Precision@5 and nDCG@5) for each interaction cycle and aggregated results across users and experimental conditions.

4.2 Evaluation Metrics

The quantitative evaluation focused on four categories of indicators:

- Accuracy and Relevance: measured by Precision@5 and nDCG@5, representing how well the top-5 recommended services matched user selections.
- Adaptivity: measured using Contextual Relevance Gain (CRG), defined as the improvement in relevance after successive adaptation cycles.
- User Experience and Trust: assessed through post-session surveys on a five-point Likert scale.
- Performance Efficiency: average response time (milliseconds) for generating contextual recommendations.

The system's learning behaviour was analysed through logs capturing changes in context-dimension weights w_i during the ACR process, allowing observation of convergence and stability patterns.

4.3 Results and Analysis

Table 2 summarizes the main quantitative results averaged across participants.

Table 2. Results and Analysis

Metric	Baseline A	Baseline B	Proposed Framework
Precision@5	0.61	0.74	**0.86**
nDCG@5	0.65	0.78	**0.90**
CRG (%)	–	+8.2	**+18.4**
Response Time (ms)	212	233	249

CRG is not applicable to Baseline A because the model does not perform contextual adaptation or feedback-based learning.

The proposed framework consistently outperformed both baselines in relevance and ranking quality. Statistical significance was assessed using a one-way ANOVA followed by post-hoc Tukey tests for pairwise comparisons between the three experimental configurations. Improvements in Precision@5 and nDCG@5 were found to be statistically significant ($p < 0.01$), confirming the robustness of the observed performance gains. Although response time increased slightly (+17 ms), this overhead was negligible relative to the personalization gains achieved.

Analysis of adaptation logs showed that context-dimension weights converged after approximately five interaction cycles per user, indicating stable learning. Dimensions such as location, time, and weather exhibited the strongest reinforcement, confirming their dominant role in contextual decision-making for tourism activities. Conversely, lower-impact dimensions (e.g., device type) naturally decayed in relevance, demonstrating the self-regulating nature of the Adaptive Context Reinforcement mechanism. This improvement is consistent with, and in some cases exceeds, gains reported in recent context-aware orchestration studies, such as Wang et al. [16], who reported relevance improvements in the range of 12–15% for adaptive service ecosystems.

4.4 Qualitative Feedback

Survey responses revealed that 84% of participants perceived the recommendations as contextually appropriate, while 81% agreed that the storytelling-based interface enhanced understanding and trust. Participants appreciated contextual explanations such as "Because it's raining, we suggest indoor cultural activities", describing them as intuitive and human-like. This aligns with recent findings in explainable recommendation research [21, 22], showing that narrative transparency increases perceived fairness and user engagement [23].

In open comments, users emphasized that the system "felt aware" of their situation, adapting not only to their preferences but also to circumstances (e.g., weather or schedule). Several respondents reported discovering less crowded or previously unknown attractions, illustrating how adaptive orchestration can also contribute to sustainable tourism management by distributing visitor flows more evenly.

4.5 System-Level Evaluation

The semantic orchestration component was stress-tested by integrating live APIs from museums, transportation providers, and local event registries. The system successfully reconfigured service compositions in real time when context changes occurred—such as switching from outdoor to indoor activities during rain. These results confirmed that semantic reasoning combined with adaptive orchestration provides robust interoperability even across heterogeneous data and service providers.

From a scalability perspective, the framework maintained stable latency (< 250 ms) under concurrent requests, validating the efficiency of the microservice architecture and SPARQL-based orchestration logic. These findings indicate that the approach can be generalized to larger tourism networks and smart-city infrastructures.

4.6 Discussion of Findings

The experimental results collectively validate the three research hypotheses. Adaptive orchestration substantially increased contextual relevance and personalization accuracy, while semantic interoperability enhanced cross-provider integration without sacrificing performance. The storytelling-based interaction further improved user trust, confirming that explainability and adaptivity are mutually reinforcing in digital ecosystems.

Overall, the experiment demonstrated that the proposed framework effectively operationalizes context-aware adaptive intelligence within real-world service environments. By embedding reasoning, learning, and semantic coordination, the system moves beyond static personalization toward dynamic, transparent, and interoperable digital tourism ecosystems.

5 Discussion and Implications

The experimental results confirm that adaptive and context-aware orchestration can substantially enhance the effectiveness, interoperability, and transparency of digital tourism services. Beyond quantitative improvements, the findings highlight that contextual reasoning, semantic interoperability, and user-centred adaptation are complementary foundations for next-generation information systems.

From a theoretical perspective, the proposed framework advances the understanding of adaptive service ecosystems by operationalizing context as a multidimensional, machine-interpretable construct. Compared with existing context-aware recommender and orchestration frameworks, the proposed approach introduces two key advances. First, while many context-aware recommender systems focus on item-level recommendation (e.g., points of interest), the proposed model performs orchestration at the service level, dynamically coordinating heterogeneous providers. Second, the framework integrates semantic interoperability, hybrid reasoning, and reinforcement-based learning within a unified architecture. This combination distinguishes it from earlier approaches that typically rely on either rule-based reasoning or machine learning alone. As a result, the system supports both adaptive personalization and cross-provider interoperability, which remain largely separate concerns in existing literature. Conceptually, this work aligns with the principles of Adaptive Service Computing proposed by Dustdar et al. [24], which emphasize continuous feedback loops and dynamic service reconfiguration as core properties of modern digital ecosystems. Similarly, the framework extends models of Contextual Personalization described by Felfernig et al. [35] by embedding semantic reasoning and narrative explainability directly into the orchestration layer, thereby bridging theoretical constructs with operational system design. Through the integration of symbolic and probabilistic reasoning, the system demonstrates how hybrid intelligence can simultaneously support personalization and explainability—two essential properties of trustworthy information systems. The introduction of the Adaptive Context Reinforcement (ACR) mechanism offers a feedback-driven method for refining contextual relevance without requiring large training datasets, enabling lightweight and continuous adaptation.

In practical terms, the framework illustrates how dynamic coordination among tourism stakeholders—hotels, museums, transport agencies, and event organizers—can be achieved through a shared semantic infrastructure. By continuously learning from user feedback and environmental signals, the system reduces manual configuration efforts, facilitates cross-provider integration, and fosters semantic interoperability across organizations. Adaptive orchestration also promotes sustainable tourism management: by suggesting alternative attractions based on crowding, weather, or environmental constraints, it helps distribute visitor flows and mitigate overtourism pressures. The storytelling-based interface enhances transparency and trust, encouraging user engagement and adoption. From a Human–Computer Interaction and Explainable AI perspective, the narrative-based design is grounded in established theories of cognitive fit and mental model formation, which suggest that users better understand and trust system behavior when explanations are presented in familiar, story-like structures rather than abstract technical terms [29, 31]. This theoretical grounding supports the use of storytelling as a mechanism for enhancing transparency and perceived fairness in adaptive digital services.

Within the broader landscape of e-Business Information Systems, this research supports the transition toward context-driven digital ecosystems that reason autonomously about their operating environment. The combination of semantic orchestration and adaptive feedback establishes a model of continuous co-evolution between users and services, where value creation stems from mutual adaptation rather than one-way personalization. Such systems demonstrate how digital ecosystems can evolve toward human-centred, explainable, and sustainable paradigms of service delivery [33, 34].

Nevertheless, some limitations remain. The prototype was evaluated in a single urban context, and further validation across diverse tourism scenarios is required to generalize findings. Future developments will integrate multi-agent reasoning, contextual privacy controls, and knowledge-graph enrichment to extend scalability and compliance with data-protection standards [35, 36]. Additional research will also explore the use of large-language-model-based reasoning to improve semantic interpretation and narrative generation [37, 38].

Overall, the discussion confirms that adaptive service orchestration is not merely a technical mechanism but a conceptual foundation for the design of responsive, explainable, and human-centred digital ecosystems. By aligning technological adaptivity with interpretability, the framework contributes to shaping a new generation of context-aware, interoperable, and sustainable information systems.

To address privacy and data protection concerns, future extensions of the framework will incorporate privacy-by-design principles, including context anonymization, on-device processing for sensitive dimensions, and user-controlled consent management. Given that the framework processes contextual and behavioural information, ethical and privacy considerations are essential for responsible deployment. In the experimental study, all participants provided informed consent prior to data collection. Interaction logs were anonymized and stored without personally identifiable information, ensuring compliance with standard research ethics guidelines.

From an architectural perspective, the framework supports privacy-by-design principles. Sensitive contextual dimensions can be processed locally on the user device, while anonymized contextual summaries are transmitted to orchestration services. Future implementations will integrate explicit consent management, context anonymization mechanisms, and differential privacy techniques to further strengthen compliance with data protection regulations such as the GDPR. These mechanisms aim to ensure compliance with data protection regulations while preserving the system's ability to perform meaningful contextual adaptation.

6 Conclusions

This paper presented a context-aware framework for adaptive service orchestration designed to enhance personalization, interoperability, and transparency in digital tourism ecosystems. The framework integrates hierarchical context modeling, hybrid reasoning, semantic service orchestration, and feedback-based adaptation within a unified architecture. Through the combination of symbolic and probabilistic inference, the system learns from user feedback to refine contextual relevance and dynamically reconfigure service compositions in real time.

An experimental evaluation involving 72 participants demonstrated that adaptive orchestration significantly improves contextual relevance and user satisfaction compared to static and non-contextual approaches. The framework also proved capable of maintaining semantic consistency and efficient interoperability among heterogeneous tourism service providers, validating its potential applicability in real-world environments.

The main contribution of this research lies in showing that adaptive service orchestration can serve as a foundation for next-generation information systems that are context-aware, explainable, and human-centred. Beyond the tourism domain, the proposed principles can be generalized to other sectors—such as healthcare, mobility, and smart cities—where context and adaptability are essential for effective digital service delivery.

Future work will focus on extending the framework's reasoning capabilities by incorporating multi-agent and large-language-model-based components to improve semantic understanding and narrative explainability. Additional studies will explore cross-domain validation, integration with knowledge graphs, and the development of contextual privacy mechanisms ensuring ethical and transparent personalization.

Ultimately, this research contributes to advancing the design of adaptive, interoperable, and trustworthy digital ecosystems, providing a methodological foundation for information systems that continuously evolve with their users and environments.

Future validation campaigns will extend the experimental deployment across multiple cities and tourism domains to assess cross-regional generalizability and to evaluate the robustness of semantic orchestration under heterogeneous regulatory, cultural, and infrastructural conditions.

References

1. Buhalis, D., Amaranggana, A.: Smart tourism destinations enhancing tourism experience through personalization and contextual services. Tour. Manage. Perspect. **35**, 100773 (2020)
2. Casillo, M., Colace, F., Gaeta, R., Lorusso, A., Pellegrino, M.: Artificial intelligence in archaeological site conservation: trends, challenges, and future directions. J. Comput. Appl. Archaeol. **8**(1), 224–241 (2025)
3. Fuchs, M., Höpken, W., Lexhagen, M.: Big data analytics for knowledge generation in tourism destinations—a case from Sweden. Tour. Manage. **82**, 104204 (2021)
4. Adomavicius, G., Tuzhilin, A.: Context-aware recommender systems. In: Recommender Systems Handbook, 2nd edn., pp. 191–226. Springer, New York (2022)
5. Gretzel, U., Koo, C., Sigala, M.: Digital transformation in tourism: rethinking value co-creation. Tour. Manage. **90**, 104480 (2022)
6. Tarik, M., Said, A., Ricci, F.: Contextual recommendation through hybrid reasoning: a review. Knowl.-Based Syst. **263**, 110238 (2023)
7. Verbert, K., Manouselis, N., Drachsler, H., Duval, E.: Context-aware recommender systems for learning: a survey and future challenges. ACM Comput. Surv. **55**(4), 84 (2023)
8. Dey, A.K.: Understanding and using context. Pers. Ubiquit. Comput. **25**(1), 5–23 (2021)
9. Hong, J.Y., Suh, E.H., Kim, S.J.: Context modeling for adaptive service systems. Expert Syst. Appl. **193**, 116448 (2022)
10. Li, X., Zhou, M., Pan, Y.: Hybrid reasoning for explainable context-aware recommendations. Knowl.-Based Syst. **273**, 110617 (2023)
11. Chen, C., Rojas, J., Cardoso, J.: Semantic web services and ontological reasoning for dynamic service composition. Inf. Syst. Front. **25**(3), 691–706 (2023)
12. Benatallah, B., Casati, F., Dustdar, S.: Principles of service orchestration and coordination. IEEE Internet Comput. **26**(2), 33–42 (2022)
13. Hussein, T., Linder, C., Tuma, K.: Reinforcement-based adaptation in recommender systems. ACM Trans. Interact. Intell. Syst. **12**(1), 1–22 (2022)
14. Jannach, D., Lerche, L., Zanker, M.: Recommender systems: beyond accuracy. User Model. User-Adap. Inter. **33**(2), 205–235 (2023)
15. Papazoglou, M.P., van den Heuvel, W.J.: Service-oriented design and composition: a decade later. SOCA **17**(1), 15–30 (2023)
16. Wang, J., Xu, Y., Benatallah, B.: Context-aware and explainable orchestration in adaptive service ecosystems. Inf. Syst. Front. **26**(1), 175–194 (2024)
17. Berners-Lee, T., Hendler, J., Lassila, O.: The semantic web revisited. Sci. Am. **328**(6), 34–43 (2021)
18. Hyvönen, E., Mäkelä, E.: Semantic portals for cultural heritage. J. Comput. Cult. Herit. **16**(2), 22–41 (2023)
19. Zhang, P., Zhang, Z., Zhao, L.: Event-driven service orchestration in context-aware environments. Futur. Gener. Comput. Syst. **141**, 360–372 (2023)
20. Kaldeli, E., Chrysanthis, P.K., Papazoglou, M.P.: Semantic interoperability in adaptive business ecosystems. J. Web Semant. **80**, 100732 (2024)
21. Nunes, I., Jannach, D.: A survey on explainable recommender systems. ACM Comput. Surv. **55**(5), 95 (2023)

22. Gaeta, A., Loia, V., Lorusso, A., Orciuoli, F., Pascuzzo, A.: Towards a LLM-based intelligent system for detecting propaganda within textual content. Comput. Electr. Eng. (2025)
23. Tintarev, N., Ricci, F.: Explainable recommendations for trust and transparency. User Model. User-Adap. Inter. **33**(4), 521–547 (2023)
24. Dustdar, S., Sheng, Q.Z., Rosenberg, F.: Principles of adaptive service computing. IEEE Trans. Serv. Comput. **17**(1), 110–125 (2024)
25. Sousa, R., Pereira, A., Ferreira, A.: Microservices and orchestration patterns for scalable information systems. Inf. Syst. **116**, 102287 (2024)
26. Leoni, M., Poels, G.: Towards adaptive business ecosystems: service orchestration and semantic integration. Enterp. Inf. Syst. **18**(3), 408–427 (2024)
27. Huang, L., Kaldeli, E., Dustdar, S.: Self-adaptive service composition using hybrid reasoning. IEEE Access **11**, 86524–86539 (2023)
28. Alonso, G., Casati, F.: Web services orchestration and choreography. Found. Trends Web Sci. **17**(2), 73–118 (2022)
29. Holzinger, A., Saranti, A., Molnar, C.: Explainable AI and trust in decision support systems. Information Fusion **94**, 74–90 (2023)
30. Xiang, Z., Fesenmaier, D.R.: Design of context-driven digital ecosystems. Tour. Rev. **78**(2), 412–430 (2023)
31. Gavalas, D., Kasapakis, V., Konstantopoulos, C.: Mobile context-aware tourism applications and their impact on user experience. Comput. Hum. Behav. **137**, 107405 (2023)
32. Grimaldi, M., Guadagno, F.M., Marano, L.: A GIS-BIM approach for the evaluation of urban transformations: a methodological proposal. WSEAS Trans. Environ. Dev. **18**, 817–826 (2022)
33. Bizer, C., Heath, T., Berners-Lee, T.: Linked data: evolving the web into a global data space. Commun. ACM **64**(10), 97–104 (2021)
34. Kang, J., Lee, D., Choi, J.: A hybrid orchestration model for smart city tourism platforms. IEEE Internet Things J. **10**(4), 3051–3064 (2024)
35. Felfernig, A., Friedrich, G., Jannach, D.: Contextual personalization through semantic reasoning. Decis. Support. Syst. **171**, 113915 (2024)
36. Bousquet, F., Moya, M., Heintz, M.: Contextual interoperability in adaptive ecosystems. J. Syst. Softw. **208**, 111417 (2024)
37. Thomas, C., Karanasios, S., Gheriss, F.: From service composition to adaptive orchestration: trends and challenges. IEEE Softw. **41**(3), 45–56 (2024)
38. Casillo, M., Colace, F., Lorusso, A., Santaniello, D., Valentino, C.: Integrating physical and virtual experiences in cultural tourism: an adaptive multimodal recommender system. IEEE Access **13**, 28353–28368 (2025)
39. Chen, M., Xu, L., Liu, L.: Sustainable digital ecosystems: balancing adaptation, transparency, and interoperability. Inf. Manage. **62**(4), 103609 (2025)
40. Cecere, L., Grimaldi, M., Lorusso, A., Marra, A., Stoia, F.: Immersive urban planning: evaluating park safety perception with digital twins and metaverse simulation. Sustainability **17**, 7608 (2025)

Security and Privacy in Wi-Fi Networks: From Legacy Protocols to Next-Gen Defenses

Aditya Jha[1(✉)], S. Hariharasitaraman[1], Radheshyam Singh[2], Gaurav Choudhary[3], and Nicola Dragoni[3]

[1] School of Computing Science and Artificial Intelligence, VIT Bhopal University, Sehore , Madhya Pradesh, India
aditya955559@gmail.com

[2] FORCE Technology, Hørsholm, Denmark
rds@forcetechnology.com

[3] DTU Compute, Technical University of Denmark, Lyngby, Denmark
{gauch,ndra}@dtu.dk

Abstract. Wi-Fi has become the backbone of wireless connectivity across homes, enterprises, and industrial systems, but its ubiquity makes it a constant target for security threats. This paper reviews the evolution of Wi-Fi security protocols from WEP and WPA to WPA2 and WPA3, highlighting vulnerabilities like KRACK, FragAttacks, Dragonblood, and Evil Twin attacks. It further explores privacy issues including MAC address tracking, device fingerprinting, and flaws in randomization mechanisms. Special attention is given to Industrial IoT (IIoT) environments, where resource-constrained devices and legacy protocols heighten risk. We evaluate defense strategies including WPA3 features, intrusion detection systems (WIDS), machine learning-based anomaly detection, and formal verification. Through synthesis of real-world exploits, protocol analysis, and academic work, the paper identifies persistent challenges and research gaps, while outlining future directions for building secure, resilient, and privacy-preserving Wi-Fi systems aligned with next-generation standards.

Keywords: Wi-Fi Security · WPA3 · KRACK · FragAttacks · Intrusion Detection · MAC Randomization · IIoT · Wireless Privacy · WPA2 · Machine Learning · IEEE 802.11 · WEP · WPA · Formal Verification · Evil Twin Attack · Wireless Encryption · Device Fingerprinting · IDS · Protocol Vulnerability · Network Defense

1 Introduction

Wi-Fi, based on the IEEE 802.11 standard, has become the primary wireless access medium, supporting over 20 billion devices as of 2024. With ongoing advancements like Wi-Fi 6 (802.11ax) and the upcoming Wi-Fi 7 (802.11be),

Published by Springer Nature Switzerland AG 2027
J. Kim et al. (Eds.): EBISION 2025, IFIP AICT 786, pp. 338–355, 2027.
https://doi.org/10.1007/978-3-032-26616-3_20

its role in smart homes, industry, healthcare, and public services continues to expand. Wireless networks are becoming increasingly critical for digital services and e-business infrastructures [20]. However, this ubiquity makes Wi-Fi a persistent target for attackers. Its open transmission medium and legacy protocol support introduce multiple vulnerabilities, even as security standards have evolved from WEP to WPA2 and WPA3 [5,7].

Practical attacks such as KRACK, FragAttacks, and Kr00k have exposed weaknesses in protocol design and implementation, impacting millions of devices globally and prompting standardization bodies like IEEE and the Wi-Fi Alliance to revise their security postures [1,3–5,7]. Beyond these, advanced threats like Evil Twin attacks, rogue APs, and side-channel exploits pose serious risks, especially in open or semi-secure environments like airports and public hotspots [16].

Privacy concerns have also intensified. Despite MAC address randomization and Protected Management Frames (PMF), devices remain traceable through timing signatures, static elements in probe frames, and side-channel metadata [6,15]. This allows adversaries to fingerprint and track users, even when privacy features are enabled.

The rise of Industrial IoT (IIoT) adds another dimension to Wi-Fi security. Low-power devices often lack robust encryption or timely updates, making them vulnerable to persistent threats. Weak authentication and poor configurations in industrial environments can lead to data breaches and system disruptions [13,14].

In light of these concerns, this paper presents a comprehensive review of the Wi-Fi security landscape, focusing on:

- Evolution of Wi-Fi protocols and their comparative strengths,
- Documented vulnerabilities and real-world attacks,
- Modern privacy threats and device tracking methods,
- Security challenges in IoT and IIoT environments,
- Emerging defenses including protocol enhancements, intrusion detection, formal verification, and ML-based solutions [9,11,12].

Drawing on current research, specifications, and practical findings, this review offers a holistic, forward-looking perspective to help guide future wireless security development.

2 Evolution of Wi-Fi Security Protocols

The security of Wi-Fi networks has evolved significantly since the inception of the IEEE 802.11 standard in 1997. Each generation of security protocols—WEP, WPA, WPA2, and WPA3—has aimed to address vulnerabilities discovered in previous iterations, while balancing performance, usability, and backward compatibility [7]. This section outlines the historical progression and core technical features of each protocol, highlighting their respective strengths and weaknesses.

As shown in Fig. 1, the evolution from WEP to WPA3 highlights a progressive enhancement in cryptographic design, protocol robustness, and resistance to modern attack vectors [5].

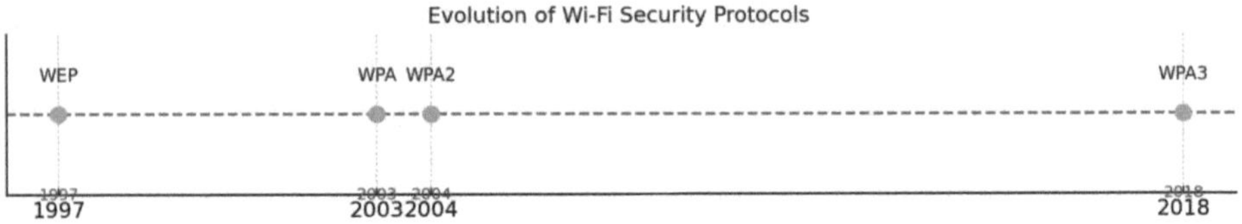

Fig. 1. Timeline of Wi-Fi security protocol evolution from WEP (1997) to WPA3 (2018).

Wired Equivalent Privacy (WEP): WEP was the original security protocol introduced with IEEE 802.11 to provide confidentiality comparable to wired networks. It utilized the RC4 stream cipher for encryption and a 24-bit Initialization Vector (IV) combined with a shared secret key [7]. Despite its widespread early adoption, WEP suffered from critical flaws. The limited IV space resulted in frequent key reuse, and statistical attacks could recover the key with minimal packet capture. The Fluhrer–Mantin–Shamir (FMS) attack and its variants demonstrated that WEP keys could be cracked within minutes using tools such as Aircrack-ng. Due to these vulnerabilities, the IEEE deprecated WEP in 2004.

Wi-Fi Protected Access (WPA): To address WEP's shortcomings, the Wi-Fi Alliance introduced WPA in 2003 as an interim solution [5]. WPA retained the RC4 cipher but introduced the Temporal Key Integrity Protocol (TKIP), which included per-packet key mixing, a message integrity check (MIC), and a replay protection mechanism [8]. While WPA improved security, it was still based on legacy cryptography. Subsequent attacks, such as the Beck–Tews and Ohigashi–Morii attacks, exploited weaknesses in TKIP's design, enabling packet injection and decryption under specific conditions. Consequently, TKIP has been officially deprecated by IEEE and should not be used in modern deployments.

Wi-Fi Protected Access II (WPA2): WPA2, standardized as IEEE 802.11i in 2004, marked a major advancement in wireless security [7]. It replaced RC4/TKIP with the Advanced Encryption Standard (AES) using the Counter Mode with Cipher Block Chaining Message Authentication Code Protocol (CCMP). WPA2 supports both personal (Pre-Shared Key) and enterprise (802.1X) modes, offering scalable security for a wide range of use cases. WPA2 was considered secure for over a decade, but multiple implementation-level vulnerabilities were later discovered. The most notable was the Key Reinstallation Attack (KRACK), which exploited weaknesses in the four-way handshake to reinstall encryption keys, allowing an adversary to decrypt traffic [1]. Despite the robustness of AES-CCMP, WPA2's reliance on correct implementation and configuration exposed it to real-world attacks.

Wi-Fi Protected Access III (WPA3): Introduced in 2018, WPA3 addresses WPA2's shortcomings with stronger security features [5]. It replaces PSK with Simultaneous Authentication of Equals (SAE), offering forward secrecy and resistance to offline dictionary attacks [2]. WPA3 mandates Protected Management Frames (PMF) to prevent deauthentication attacks, supports Opportunistic Wireless Encryption (OWE) for open networks [18], and offers a 192-bit security suite for high-assurance environments. Despite these advances, early WPA3 implementations were vulnerable to side-channel attacks like Dragonblood, which exploited weaknesses in SAE for password recovery or downgrade [2]. While patches have mitigated these risks, ongoing refinement by the Wi-Fi Alliance remains essential [5].

Table 1. Compact Summary of Wi-Fi Security Protocol Features

Protocol	Cipher	Handshake	Key Takeaways
WEP	RC4	None	Deprecated due to weak IV reuse, vulnerable to FMS attacks
WPA	RC4 (TKIP)	4-Way TKIP	Interim fix with per-packet keys, but legacy cipher vulnerabilities persist
WPA2	AES-CCMP	4-Way AES	Long-standing standard with strong encryption, but susceptible to KRACK if misconfigured
WPA3	AES-GCMP, 192-bit	SAE (Dragonfly)	Strong resistance to offline attacks, mandatory PMF, and support for forward secrecy

Table 1 presents a high-level comparison of the four major Wi-Fi security protocols.

In addition to the tabular overview, a visual comparison of security features is illustrated in Fig. 2, offering an intuitive understanding of the relative strengths of each protocol.

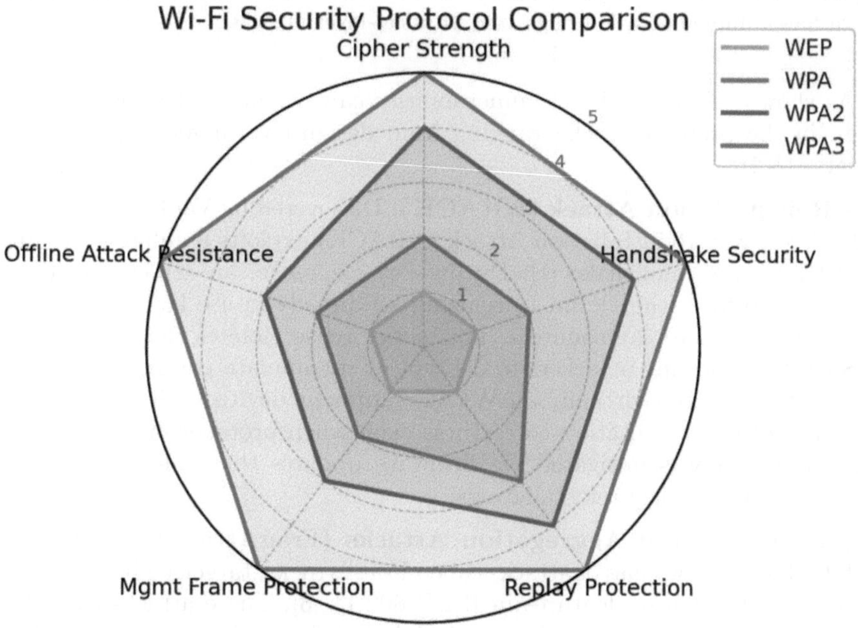

Fig. 2. Radar chart comparing Wi-Fi security protocols across key features including cipher strength, handshake security, replay protection, management frame protection, and offline attack resistance.

The evolution of Wi-Fi security protocols reflects the dynamic threat landscape and the continuous efforts of standardization bodies to adapt. While WPA3 addresses many legacy vulnerabilities, secure implementation, timely updates, and adherence to best practices remain critical to maintaining wireless network integrity [3,4].

3 Vulnerabilities and Real-World Attacks

Despite ongoing advancements in Wi-Fi security protocols, practical attacks have continued to surface due to both protocol design flaws and insecure implementations. This section reviews the major vulnerabilities that have affected Wi-Fi networks, highlighting how attackers have exploited cryptographic weaknesses, implementation oversights, and client behavior to compromise data confidentiality, integrity, and availability [1–4].

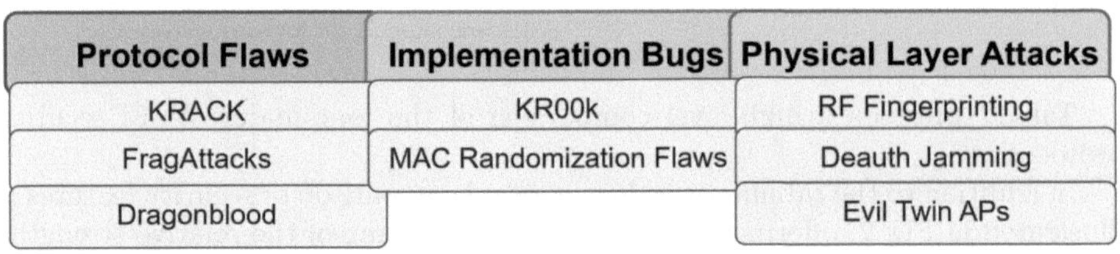

Fig. 3. Layered classification of major Wi-Fi security vulnerabilities across protocol design flaws, implementation bugs, and physical-layer attacks.

As shown in Fig. 3, Wi-Fi vulnerabilities can be categorized based on their origin in the protocol stack—ranging from design-level flaws to physical-layer threats [15,16].

Key Reinstallation Attack (KRACK): Discovered by Vanhoef and Piessens in 2017, the Key Reinstallation Attack (KRACK) exploits a vulnerability in the WPA2 four-way handshake [1]. During key exchange, an attacker can replay message 3 to force the victim to reinstall an already-in-use key, resetting associated nonce and replay counters. This nonce reuse violates the assumptions of AES-CCMP, allowing attackers to decrypt or manipulate packets.

KRACK affected virtually all WPA2-compliant devices and highlighted the criticality of implementation correctness even when protocols are cryptographically sound. It was mitigated via firmware updates that enforce nonce reuse checks and restrict key reinstallations.

Fragmentation and Aggregation Attacks (FragAttacks): In 2021, Vanhoef disclosed a new class of attacks called FragAttacks, targeting frame fragmentation and aggregation features in IEEE 802.11 [3]. These attacks exploit how receivers handle mixed encrypted and plaintext fragments or aggregate frames with overlapping data.

FragAttacks can enable:

- Injection of plaintext frames into encrypted streams,
- Bypassing of firewall rules via crafted frame structures,
- Remote code execution on vulnerable devices.

The vulnerabilities stemmed from protocol ambiguities and were present in both WPA2 and WPA3 implementations. Mitigation required both firmware updates and improved device-side input validation.

KR00k: KR00k is a vulnerability disclosed in 2020 that affected Wi-Fi chips from Broadcom and Cypress [4]. When a device disconnected from an access point, some chipsets would erroneously transmit remaining buffered data encrypted with an all-zero key.

This allowed attackers to force disassociation (e.g., using deauthentication frames) and capture sensitive data sent post-disconnection. KR00k was resolved through firmware patches but highlighted the risks posed by low-level chipset behavior.

Dragonblood Attacks on WPA3: Though WPA3 was designed to address WPA2's limitations, early implementations of its Simultaneous Authentication of Equals (SAE) handshake were found to be susceptible to side-channel and downgrade attacks.

Dragonblood, a set of attacks published in 2019, demonstrated [2]:

- Timing side-channels in SAE's password element derivation,
- Downgrade attacks that forced WPA3-capable devices into WPA2 mode,
- Resource exhaustion via invalid curve attacks.

Vendors responded with patched firmware and improved SAE implementations. Dragonblood emphasized the need for side-channel resistance and robust transition mode handling in WPA3.

Rogue Access Points and Evil Twin Attacks: Rogue access point (AP) attacks, especially Evil Twin scenarios, involve adversaries setting up fake APs that mimic legitimate networks [16]. Unsuspecting clients may auto-connect or be tricked into joining the rogue AP, enabling man-in-the-middle (MitM) attacks.

Attackers can:

- Intercept and manipulate traffic,
- Phish for credentials using fake captive portals,
- Force device associations using deauthentication and signal jamming.

These attacks are particularly effective in open or poorly secured public networks. Even WPA2-protected clients are vulnerable if the SSID is shared and no server certificate verification is enforced.

Side-Channel and Implementation Attacks: Several additional classes of vulnerabilities exploit side-channels or implementation-specific weaknesses:

- Timing attacks: Exploiting time variations in key handling (e.g., Dragonblood) [2].

- All-zero key bugs: As seen in KR00k and similar chipset flaws [4].
- Incorrect randomization: Leading to MAC address leaks and device fingerprinting [6,15].

Such vulnerabilities underline the importance of robust, side-channel-hardened implementations and regular audits.

Denial-of-Service (DoS) Attacks: Wi-Fi networks remain susceptible to a variety of DoS attacks, including:

- Deauthentication flooding: Exploiting unprotected management frames (in pre-WPA3 networks),
- Beacon spamming and channel jamming Overloading the wireless medium with interference or fake networks [16].

WPA3's enforcement of Protected Management Frames (PMF) mitigates some of these issues [5,18], but jamming and physical-layer DoS remain difficult to counter in practice.

Table 2 summarizes the major vulnerabilities and their respective targets and mitigations.

These vulnerabilities demonstrate that Wi-Fi security must be approached holistically. Protocol design, implementation rigor, and proactive monitoring are all essential to defending against evolving attack techniques.

4 Privacy Threats and MAC Address Tracking

While Wi-Fi security protocols primarily aim to protect data confidentiality and integrity, privacy remains an under-addressed yet critical concern. Modern Wi-Fi-enabled devices frequently emit signals—including probe requests, authentication frames, and association attempts—that may unintentionally leak identifying information. These emissions can be exploited by adversaries to track, fingerprint, or re-identify users across locations and time [6,15].

Table 2. Compact Summary of Major Wi-Fi Vulnerabilities

Vulnerability	Target Protocol	Key Impact and Mitigation
KRACK	WPA2	Allows decryption and packet injection via key reuse; mitigated by firmware updates enforcing nonce validation
FragAttacks	WPA2/WPA3	Exploits frame aggregation/fragmentation for injection or remote code execution; patched via frame validation
KR00k	WPA2	Leaks encrypted frames using an all-zero key post-disassociation; resolved via chipset firmware patch
Dragonblood	WPA3	Side-channel and downgrade attacks on SAE; mitigated by implementation hardening and transition mode fixes
Evil Twin APs	All	Enables MitM, phishing via rogue AP impersonation; prevented through PMF, WIDS, and user awareness
Deauth/DoS Attacks	WEP/WPA/WPA2	Causes service disruption through jamming and spoofed management frames; mitigated using PMF and RF monitoring

4.1 MAC Address Leakage and Tracking

Wi-Fi devices use a unique 48-bit MAC address at the data link layer, which has historically been broadcast in probe and association requests, allowing easy tracking across networks and locations [15]. Passive attackers can use inexpensive tools like a Raspberry Pi to capture these broadcasts and compile movement histories without user consent. This method has been applied in public spaces such as airports and malls for surveillance and targeted marketing [6].

4.2 MAC Address Randomization and its Limitations

MAC address randomization, adopted by platforms like Android, iOS, and Windows, replaces a device's real MAC with a temporary pseudonym during network scans to improve privacy [6]. However, its effectiveness is limited—many devices fail to randomize consistently across all scan types, and persistent randomized MACs reduce anonymity. Additionally, constant frame fields (e.g., supported rates, IEs) enable fingerprinting, while authentication may reveal the original MAC. Research confirms that devices can still be tracked using temporal patterns and signal-level characteristics despite randomization efforts [6,15].

As illustrated in Fig. 4, even with MAC address randomization, adversaries can capture broadcasted frames and perform fingerprinting to track users across locations and time.

4.3 Device Fingerprinting via Frame Characteristics

Even with MAC randomization, devices can be fingerprinted through unique combinations of probe request features such as supported channels, information element (IE) order, vendor fields, and timing behaviors [10]. These patterns often reveal device models or OS versions and can link multiple randomized MACs to the same user. Moreover, flaws in randomization—like fixed global addresses or shared identifiers—further weaken privacy protections [6].

4.4 Physical Layer Tracking and RF Fingerprinting

Advanced adversaries can exploit hardware-level imperfections such as Carrier Frequency Offset (CFO), phase noise, and transient signal behaviors to fingerprint a device based on its unique radio signature [15]. These radio frequency (RF) fingerprints can remain consistent across MAC changes and are especially concerning in high-surveillance environments.

Although RF fingerprinting requires more sophisticated equipment and signal processing, it demonstrates that anonymization at the software layer may not suffice to ensure wireless privacy.

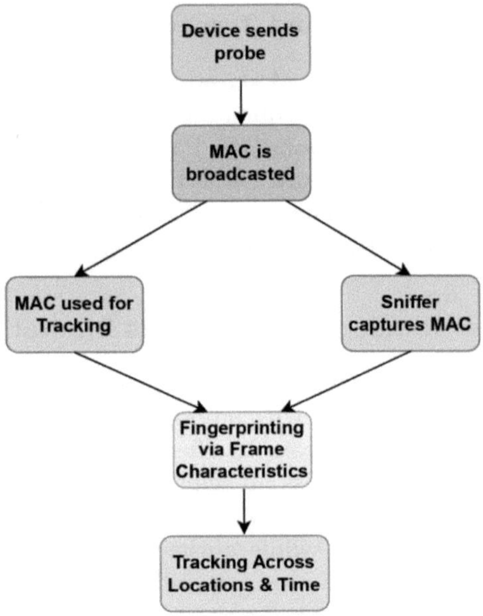

Fig. 4. Flow of MAC address-based tracking. Devices broadcast MACs in probe requests, enabling sniffers to capture them and use frame characteristics for user fingerprinting and tracking.

4.5 Hotspot 2.0 and Privacy Trade-Offs

Hotspot 2.0 (also known as Passpoint), designed to enable seamless Wi-Fi roaming, introduces new privacy risks. Devices pre-configured to auto-connect to known networks may disclose identifying information during the discovery and negotiation process. An attacker advertising a rogue Hotspot 2.0-compatible SSID could trick devices into revealing credentials or service set identifiers (SSIDs) associated with enterprise networks [19].

Without strict mutual authentication and certificate validation, these automated processes may expose users to tracking and impersonation attacks.

4.6 Real-World Implications

Wi-Fi tracking poses serious risks, enabling passive surveillance, behavioral profiling, and user de-anonymization—often without consent. It can be exploited for location analytics, security breaches in sensitive areas, or even stalking through repeated MAC address detection. These threats are especially pronounced in environments where devices constantly emit Wi-Fi signals due to background services or installed apps [15].

4.7 Mitigation Strategies

Effective Wi-Fi privacy protection demands a multi-layered approach, including short-lived randomized MACs, frame obfuscation through randomized non-essential elements, and user control over probe emissions. Regulatory policies must also enforce ethical tracking standards and consent practices [6,19]. While ongoing research aims to balance connectivity with privacy, evolving tracking techniques continue to challenge the resilience of current mitigation strategies.

5 Wi-Fi in Industrial and IoT Environments

Wi-Fi plays a critical role in Industrial IoT (IIoT) by enabling wireless connectivity across factories, utilities, and smart infrastructure for monitoring and automation [13]. However, its integration introduces security challenges that traditional frameworks often fail to address, especially in resource-constrained environments [14]. As illustrated in Fig. 5, IIoT Wi-Fi topologies support cloud-to-device communication but are vulnerable to threats like rogue access points and unauthorized traffic injection [16].

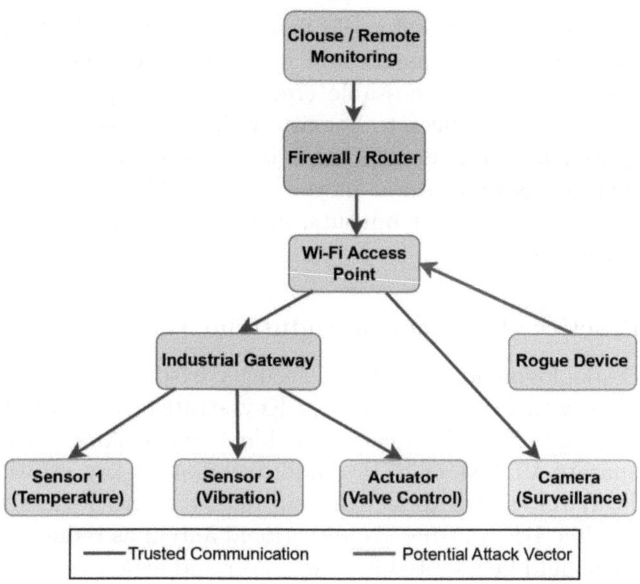

Fig. 5. Typical IIoT Wi-Fi network topology showing secure communications among industrial components and a potential attack path from a rogue device.

5.1 Adoption of Wi-Fi in IIoT

Wi-Fi's broad availability, affordability, and IP compatibility make it a practical option for IIoT applications [13]. It enables mobility, flexible infrastructure, and supports use cases such as real-time monitoring in smart factories, remote diagnostics, smart meter connectivity, and wireless data offloading in logistics. However, its adoption in industrial settings also introduces new attack vectors and operational challenges due to the constrained nature of embedded devices.

5.2 Security Challenges in IIoT Deployments

IIoT devices typically operate with limited processing power, memory, and battery life, restricting their ability to perform strong encryption, manage certificates, or support timely firmware updates. These constraints also hinder real-time intrusion detection. As a result, many IIoT nodes still use outdated protocols like WPA2-PSK or insecure defaults such as open networks and hardcoded credentials, making them vulnerable to attacks like KRACK, Evil Twin, and FragAttacks [1,3,16].

5.3 Case Studies of IIoT Vulnerabilities

Studies have exposed several real-world flaws in industrial Wi-Fi networks [14], including unprotected access points still using outdated encryption, weak key management with shared or guessable credentials, and poor network segmentation that allows IIoT devices to coexist with enterprise systems. Additionally, misconfigured networks enable rogue device insertion, increasing the risk of unauthorized access and lateral movement [16]. Once inside, attackers can disrupt operations, alter sensor outputs, exfiltrate data, or escalate privileges within the infrastructure.

5.4 Best Practices for Securing Industrial Wi-Fi

Securing IIoT deployments requires a security-by-design approach that balances protection with device limitations. Key strategies include using WPA3-Enterprise with 802.1X authentication to block rogue APs [5], isolating IIoT devices on separate VLANs or SSIDs, and automating key rotation via protocols like DPP. Wireless IDS tools can help detect rogue devices and jamming attempts [17], while RF controls like directional antennas reduce signal leakage. These methods should be adapted for low-power and legacy devices using hybrid models that blend strong perimeter controls with lightweight protections.

5.5 Future Outlook and Standardization

As Wi-Fi 6E and Wi-Fi 7 improve latency, efficiency, and scalability for dense IIoT deployments, security must advance accordingly. Adopting standards like IEC 62443 and NIST guidelines is essential to establish strong baseline protections [19]. Growing interest in zero trust models—where every device requires continuous, contextual authentication—further emphasizes the need for dynamic, policy-driven Wi-Fi security [19]. Achieving this requires collaboration among manufacturers, architects, protocol designers, and cybersecurity teams to ensure future IIoT infrastructures remain resilient and trustworthy.

6 Countermeasures and Intrusion Detection Systems

The continuous discovery of vulnerabilities in Wi-Fi protocols and implementations highlights the need for a layered security approach that goes beyond encryption. This section surveys prominent countermeasures designed to detect, prevent, or mitigate wireless attacks, spanning from protocol-level enhancements to advanced anomaly detection systems [5,17].

6.1 Protocol-Level Enhancements

Several enhancements have been introduced to strengthen Wi-Fi security against known attacks. WPA3 includes Simultaneous Authentication of Equals (SAE) to resist offline dictionary attacks and Opportunistic Wireless Encryption (OWE) for encrypting open traffic, while Protected Management Frames (PMF) are now mandatory to prevent deauthentication-based disruptions [2,5,18]. Post-KRACK and FragAttacks, vendors implemented nonce reuse checks, improved reassembly handling, and stricter packet parsing [1,3]. Additionally, measures were taken to harden WPA3 transition mode, ensuring devices are not easily downgraded to WPA2 [2]. These improvements enhance baseline security but rely on timely and consistent adoption across diverse devices and platforms.

6.2 Wireless Intrusion Detection Systems (WIDS)

WIDS plays a vital role in wireless security by monitoring radio traffic to detect rogue APs, Evil Twin impersonations, deauthentication floods, and MAC spoofing. Tools like Kismet, AirDefense, and Cisco WIPS use distributed sensors for real-time anomaly detection, particularly in enterprise and industrial environments with centralized control [16,17]. However, WIDS can suffer from high false positives, limited stealth detection, and challenges in analyzing encrypted traffic. Its effectiveness increases when combined with broader monitoring systems and threat intelligence platforms, enabling more contextual and reliable wireless intrusion defense.

6.3 Machine Learning-Based Detection

Machine learning (ML) is increasingly adopted to overcome the rigidity of rule-based intrusion detection systems [9,17]. ML models can detect wireless anomalies by learning from traffic patterns and identifying irregularities in packet timing, MAC behavior, and malformed frames. Thang et al. demonstrated a multi-stage model using unsupervised clustering and outlier detection to accurately identify attacks like slow deauthentication floods and MAC spoofing [22]. Despite promising results, ML-based WIDS face challenges such as the need for high-quality training data, regular model updates, and computational optimization for low-power environments. Explainability and trust in ML decisions also remain active research areas in cybersecurity applications.

6.4 Formal Verification of Protocols

Formal methods provide a rigorous approach to verifying the correctness and security of Wi-Fi protocols. Tools like Tamarin Prover and ProVerif have modeled the WPA2 4-way handshake, WPA3-SAE, and fragmentation logic to uncover vulnerabilities such as nonce reuse and offline dictionary attack potential [2,11,12,21]. These analyses have led to important protocol patches and highlighted flaws that typical testing may miss. Though computationally intensive, formal verification is invaluable for identifying logic errors, state inconsistencies, and subtle security flaws, making it a best practice in secure protocol development [21].

6.5 Best Practices for Holistic Defense

Effective Wi-Fi security demands a layered approach combining preventive controls like WPA3, strong passwords, and secure onboarding [5]; detective measures such as WIDS/WIPS and centralized logging [17]; and reactive responses like automated rogue AP isolation. Analytical tools using machine learning help predict evolving threats [9], while formal verification ensures protocol integrity [11,12]. No single control suffices—true resilience depends on redundancy, continuous monitoring, and proactive defense.

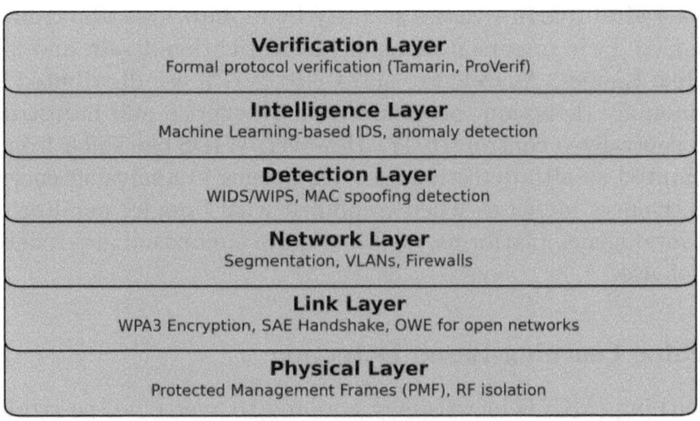

Fig. 6. Layered architecture for Wi-Fi security integrating physical-layer protections, cryptographic safeguards, intrusion detection, machine learning intelligence, and formal verification.

As illustrated in Fig. 6, a layered security architecture integrates various defenses across the Wi-Fi protocol stack, from physical isolation to formal protocol verification, providing holistic protection against evolving threats.

7 Research Gaps and Future Directions

Despite progress in protocol design, intrusion detection, and privacy mechanisms, Wi-Fi security still faces numerous unresolved challenges. With new use cases, adversarial methods, and evolving IEEE standards, continuous research is essential.

As shown in Fig. 7, future progress depends on advancing protocol resilience, ML integration, zero trust adoption, and device-level authentication.

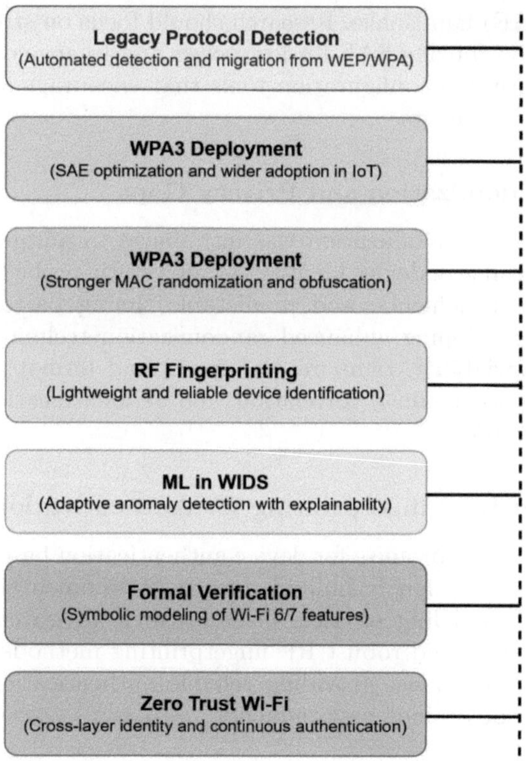

Fig. 7. Future research roadmap for Wi-Fi security highlighting open challenges and priority areas such as WPA3 optimization, MAC obfuscation, ML in WIDS, formal verification, and Zero Trust frameworks.

7.1 Legacy Protocols and Insecure Deployments

Despite the availability of WPA3, many networks still operate with outdated protocols like WEP or poorly configured WPA2, exposing them to preventable attacks. These issues often stem from compatibility needs, limited awareness, or upgrade challenges in large or resource-constrained systems. Research should develop automated tools to detect insecure configurations, enforce security baselines, and enable scalable migration strategies for enterprise and IIoT environments.

7.2 Limited Adoption and Weaknesses in WPA3

Although WPA3 offers significant security improvements over its predecessors, its adoption remains limited due to device compatibility challenges, vulnerabilities in transition modes, and early weaknesses in the Simultaneous Authentication of Equals (SAE) handshake. Research should focus on strengthening downgrade resistance, optimizing SAE for low-power and legacy-constrained devices, and developing intuitive configuration tools that encourage secure deployment across diverse environments.

7.3 MAC Randomization and Privacy Gaps

While MAC address randomization was introduced to mitigate tracking, most implementations still leak device identity through static probe behaviors, vendor-specific information elements, and predictable timing patterns. Future work should focus on developing enhanced randomization techniques that incorporate frame-level variability, temporal dynamics, and formal privacy models to strengthen resistance against correlation and re-identification attacks across diverse threat scenarios.

7.4 Underused RF Fingerprinting for Authentication

RF fingerprinting holds promise for device authentication based on unique radio emissions, but its adoption is limited due to environmental interference and the complexity of modeling physical layer features. Research should focus on developing lightweight and robust RF fingerprinting methods that are resilient to environmental variations, providing reliable authentication, particularly in IoT and resource-constrained environments.

7.5 WIDS in Noisy and Dynamic Environments

Conventional Wireless Intrusion Detection Systems (WIDS) face limitations in dynamic, mobile, or device-diverse environments, often producing high false positives or failing to detect novel threats. Advancing WIDS with adaptive machine learning models capable of real-time analysis, improved explainability, and reduced false alarm rates can significantly enhance threat detection in complex wireless ecosystems.

7.6 Unverified IEEE 802.11 Extensions

Recent IEEE 802.11 extensions such as Target Wake Time (TWT), Fast Initial Link Setup (FILS), and Wi-Fi Aware introduce new protocol logic, yet many of these features have not undergone formal security verification, leaving potential vulnerabilities undiscovered. Expanding formal modeling efforts to include modular and scalable analysis of these emerging amendments can support early-stage validation and improve the overall resilience of future Wi-Fi standards.

7.7 Security in Wi-Fi 6/6E/7 Evolution

Wi-Fi 6, 6E, and 7 introduce features like OFDMA, MU-MIMO, and higher modulation rates that enhance performance but also add protocol complexity and potential vulnerabilities. These upgrades may increase fingerprinting risk, complicate handshakes, and expose downgrade paths. Targeted security evaluations of these innovations are needed to uncover emerging threats and ensure that new capabilities do not compromise overall system resilience or compatibility.

7.8 Cross-Layer and Zero Trust Design

As Wi-Fi networks increasingly interface with cloud services and multi-device systems, traditional link-layer security alone is no longer sufficient. A shift toward cross-layer integration is needed to handle identity, access control, and data integrity holistically. Future Wi-Fi architectures should natively support cross-layer identity management, encrypted telemetry, and policy enforcement mechanisms consistent with enterprise-grade zero trust frameworks.

8 Conclusion

Wi-Fi has become central to modern communication across personal, enterprise, and industrial domains. Although the progression from WEP to WPA3 has strengthened wireless security, vulnerabilities such as KRACK, FragAttacks, and Dragonblood persist due to protocol complexity, legacy support, and evolving threats. This review highlighted ongoing challenges, including MAC tracking, device fingerprinting, and side-channel attacks, with particular concern in Industrial IoT (IIoT) deployments where low-power devices and outdated configurations amplify risk. We surveyed defense strategies including WPA3, WIDS, machine learning-based detection, and formal protocol verification. However, critical gaps remain in privacy preservation, real-time detection, and secure protocol rollout—especially as Wi-Fi 6, 6E, and 7 introduce new technical layers. Ensuring resilient Wi-Fi infrastructure demands a layered approach combining strong protocols, adaptive monitoring, and privacy-centric engineering. As wireless networks become foundational to digital infrastructure, continuous research and collaboration are essential for securing next-generation connectivity.

References

1. Vanhoef, M., Piessens, F.: Key Reinstallation attacks: forcing nonce reuse in WPA2. in: Proceedings of the 2017 ACM SIGSAC Conference on Computer and Communications Security (CCS), pp. 1313–1328 (2017)
2. Vanhoef, M., Ronen, E.: Dragonblood: analyzing the dragonfly handshake of WPA3 and EAP-PWD. In: Proceedings of the 2019 IEEE Symposium on Security and Privacy (S&P), pp. 517–533 (2019)
3. Vanhoef, M.: Fragment and forge: breaking WPA3, WPA2, and WEP using fragmentation and aggregation attacks. In: Proceedings of USENIX Security Symposium (2021). https://www.fragattacks.com
4. ESET Research, "Kr00k: Serious Vulnerability Affected Encryption of Over a Billion Wi-Fi Devices," ESET Whitepaper (2020). https://www.welivesecurity.com/2020/02/26/kr00k-serious-vulnerability-affected-encryption-over-billion-wi-fi-devices
5. Wi-Fi Alliance, "Wi-Fi Certified WPA3: Next Generation of Wi-Fi Security," Wi-Fi Alliance Whitepaper (2018). https://www.wi-fi.org/discover-wi-fi/security
6. Martin, J., Ye, D., Juels, A.: A study of MAC address randomization in mobile devices and when it fails. In: Proceedings of ACM WiSec, pp. 45–56 (2017)
7. IEEE Std 802.11i-2004, "IEEE Standard for Information technology—Telecommunications and information exchange between systems—Local and metropolitan area networks—Specific requirements—Part 11: Wireless LAN Medium Access Control (MAC) and Physical Layer (PHY) Specifications—Amendment 6: Medium Access Control (MAC) Security Enhancements (2004)
8. Aboba, B.: IEEE 802.11i and TKIP, Microsoft Research (2004). https://technet.microsoft.com/library/bb726942.aspx
9. Javaid, A., Niyaz, Q., Sun, W., Alam, M.: A deep learning approach for network intrusion detection system. In: Proceedings of IEEE Green Computing and Communications (GreenCom), pp. 21–26 (2016)
10. Pang, R., Allman, M., Bennett, M., Lee, J., Paxson, V., Tierney, B.: A first look at modern enterprise traffic. In: Proceedings of ACM SIGCOMM Internet Measurement Conference (IMC), pp. 1–14 (2005)
11. Kohbrok, K., Basin, D.J.: A formal analysis of 802.11's WPA2: countermeasures for KRACK. In: Proceedings of IEEE European Symposium on Security and Privacy (EuroS&P), pp. 316–331 (2019)
12. Blanchet, B.: Modeling and verifying security protocols with the applied Pi calculus and ProVerif. Found. Trends Priv. Secur. **1**(1–2), 1–135 (2016)
13. Wan, J., Yan, H., Suo, H., Li, F.: Advances in cyber-physical systems research. In: Proceedings of IEEE ICSP, pp. 1–6 (2011)
14. Humayed, A., Lin, J., Li, F., Luo, B.: Cyber-physical systems security–a survey. IEEE Internet Things J. **4**(6), 1802–1831 (2017)
15. Cunche, M.: I know your MAC address: targeted tracking of individual using Wi-Fi. J. Comput. Virol. Hacking Tech. **10**(4), 219–227 (2014)
16. Bellardo, J., Savage, S.: 802.11 denial-of-service attacks: real vulnerabilities and practical solutions. In: Proceedings of USENIX Security Symposium, pp. 15–28 (2003)
17. Mehboob, H., Javaid, A., Ali, Z.: Intelligent intrusion detection system for IoT networks using fuzzy logic and machine learning. In: Proceedings of IEEE ICIOT, pp. 10–16 (2020)

18. Harkins, D.: Opportunistic Wireless Encryption (OWE). IETF RFC 8110 (2017). https://tools.ietf.org/html/rfc8110
19. NIST, "Zero Trust Architecture," NIST Special Publication 800-207 (2020). https://doi.org/10.6028/NIST.SP.800-207
20. Lutu, A., Bagnulo, M., Crowcroft, J.: On the use of Wi-Fi in the wild: the case for secure wireless connectivity in public spaces. In: Proceedings of ACM HotNets, pp. 17–23 (2019)
21. Hariharasitaraman, S., Balakannan, S.P.: A dynamic data security mechanism based on position aware Merkle tree for health rehabilitation services over cloud. J. Ambient Intell. Humanized Comput. **1**, 1–15 (2019)
22. Thang, V.V., Pashchenko, F.F.: Multistage system-based machine learning techniques for intrusion detection in WiFi network. J. Comput. Netw. Commun. **2019**(1), 4708201 (2019)

Author Index

Published by Springer Nature Switzerland AG 2027
J. Kim et al. (Eds.): EBISION 2025, IFIP AICT 786, pp. 357–358, 2027.
https://doi.org/10.1007/978-3-032-26616-3

MIX
Papier aus verantwortungsvollen Quellen
Paper from responsible sources
FSC® C105338

If you have any concerns about our products,
you can contact us on
ProductSafety@springernature.com

In case Publisher is established outside the EU,
the EU authorized representative is:
Springer Nature Customer Service Center GmbH
Europaplatz 3, 69115 Heidelberg, Germany

Printed by Libri Plureos GmbH
in Hamburg, Germany

